Scottish Border Country

Kelso Abbey.

SCOTTISH BORDER COUNTRY

ANDREW & JOHN LANG

SENATE

Scottish Border Country

First published in 1913 as *Highways and Byways
in the Border* by Macmillan & Co., London

This edition published in 1999 by Senate,
an imprint of Tiger Books International plc,
26A York Street, Twickenham,
Middlesex TW1 3LJ, United Kingdom

Cover design © Tiger Books International 1999

1 3 5 7 9 10 8 6 4 2

ISBN 1 85958 543 4

Printed and bound in the UK by
Cox & Wyman, Reading, England

PREFACE

At the time of his death, my brother had proceeded but a little way in this task which he and I began together, and I must frankly own my inability to cope with it on the lines which he would doubtless have followed. It is probable, for example, that his unrivalled knowledge of "the memories, legends, ballads, and nature of the Border" would have led him to show various important events in a light different from that in which my less intimate acquaintance with the past has enabled me to speak of them; whilst, as regards the Ballad literature of the Border, I cannot pretend to that expert knowledge which he possessed. I do not think, therefore, it is fitting that I should attempt to carry out his intention to deal more fully with those of the Ballads which are most closely connected with places treated of in this volume.

To him, more perhaps than to any other Borderer, every burn and stream, every glen and hill of that pleasant land was

> ". . . full of ballad notes,
> Borne out of long ago."

It is many a year since he wrote those verses wherein he spoke of

> " Old songs that sung themselves to me,
> Sweet through a boy's day-dream."

But it was not alone in a boy's day-dream that they sounded. To the end, they echoed and re-echoed in his heart, and no voice ever spoke to him so eloquently as that of Tweed,— by whose banks, indeed, in a spot greatly loved, had it been permitted he would fain have slept his long sleep.

JOHN LANG.

CONTENTS

CHAPTER I

PAGE

BERWICK, TWEED, WHITADDER 1

CHAPTER II

BLACKADDER, NORHAM, FLODDEN, COLDSTREAM, WARK, AND THE
EDEN 32

CHAPTER III

KELSO, ROXBURGH, TEVIOT, KALE, AND OXNAM 71

CHAPTER IV

JEDBURGH, AND THE JED 90

CHAPTER V

JED (*continued*), FERNIHIRST, RAID OF THE REDESWIRE, OTTER-
BURNE 130

CHAPTER VI

ALE, RULE WATER, TEVIOT, HAWICK 169

CHAPTER VII

TWEED, ST. BOSWELLS, DRYBURGH, NEWSTEAD, AND THE LEADER 204

ix

CHAPTER VIII

PAGE

ST. BOSWELLS GREEN, MELROSE, DARNICK, ABBOTSFORD, AND THE ELLWAND 220

CHAPTER IX

GALASHIELS AND THE GALA, LINDEAN 237

CHAPTER X

SELKIRK 249

CHAPTER XI

THE ETTRICK, CARTERHAUGH, OAKWOOD, TUSHIELAW, THIRLE-STANE, ETTRICK KIRK 273

CHAPTER XII

YARROW 292

CHAPTER XIII

UPPER TWEED, YAIR, FAIRNILEE, ASHIESTEEL, ELIBANK, INNER-LEITHEN, TRAQUAIR 319

CHAPTER XIV

PEEBLES, NEIDPATH, MANOR, LYNE, DRUMMELZIER DAWYCK . 336

CHAPTER XV

BROUGHTON, TWEEDSMUIR, TALLA, GAMESHOPE, TWEED'S WELL. 355

CHAPTER XVI

LIDDESDALE, HERMITAGE, CASTLETON 378

CHAPTER XVII

KERSHOPEFOOT, CARLISLE CASTLE, SOLWAY MOSS 392

CHAPTER XVIII

BEWCASTLE, LIDDEL MOAT, NETHERBY, KIRK ANDREWS, GIL-NOCKIE, LANGHOLM 410

INDEX 429

LIST OF ILLUSTRATIONS

	PAGE
KELSO ABBEY . . . . *Frontispiece*	
HALIDON HILL AND THE TWO BRIDGES, BERWICK	3
OLD BRIDGE AT BERWICK	6
BUTTRESSES WITH CANOPIED NICHES AT EDROM	14
AT CHIRNSIDE	15
DOORWAY IN GRAVEYARD AT EDROM	16
NORHAM CASTLE	46
LADYKIRK	47
FORD CASTLE FROM THE ROAD	49
LOOKING UP THE TILL FROM TWIZEL BRIDGE	50
THE RIDGE ON WHICH THE SCOTTISH ARMY WAS ENTRENCHED BEFORE THE BATTLE OF FLODDEN	51
TWIZEL BRIDGE	52
THE SLOPES AT BRANXTON ON WHICH THE BATTLE OF FLODDEN WAS FOUGHT	53
SYBIL GREY'S WELL AT FLODDEN	55
BRIDGE OVER THE LEET, COLDSTREAM	57
THE CHEVIOTS FROM COLDSTREAM FERRY	60
FLOORS CASTLE FROM KELSO	72

  PAGE

KELSO   73

KELSO ABBEY   75

KELSO. TEVIOT IN FOREGROUND   76

MEETING OF TWEED AND TEVIOT NEAR KELSO   77

RUINS OF ROXBURGH CASTLE   79

JEDBURGH FROM THE PARK   91

JEDBURGH ABBEY   103

QUEEN MARY'S HOUSE, JEDBURGH   105

FERNIHIRST CASTLE   131

CATCLEUCH RESERVOIR LOOKING SOUTH   142

BRIDGE OVER JED WATER AT OLD SOUDEN KIRK.   THE CHEVIOTS
    BEHIND.   148

OTTERBURNE   162

OTTERBURNE   163

SOUDEN KIRK   166

JOHN LEYDEN'S BIRTHPLACE, DENHOLM   179

CAVERS   185

HAWICK   186

THE TOWER INN, HAWICK   187

HORNSHOLE BRIDGE   188

ST. MARY'S, HAWICK   189

VALE OF THE BORTHWICK WATER LOOKING TOWARDS HAWICK .   191

A GLIMPSE OF HARDEN   192

GOLDIELANDS TOWER AND THE TEVIOT   193

BRANKSOME.   194

BRANKSOME.   196

LOOKING DOWN TEVIOTDALE FROM CAERLANRIG   197

TEVIOTHEAD KIRK   202

PAGE

TOMB OF SIR WALTER SCOTT, DRYBURGH 207

SMAILHOLME TOWER 210

THE EILDONS FROM BEMERSYDE HILLS 211

EARLSTON 218

THE RIVER AT DRYBURGH ABBEY 221

EILDON HILLS AND GORGE OF THE TWEED FROM LESSUDDEN . 223

MELROSE FROM NEWSTEAD 224

MELROSE CROSS 225

EAST WINDOW, MELROSE ABBEY 226

DARNICK TOWER 228

ABBOTSFORD 230

THE RHYMER'S GLEN 232

GALASHIELS, THE EILDONS IN THE DISTANCE 238

THE TWEED FROM THE FERRY, ABBOTSFORD 241

TORWOODLEE 243

ABBOTSFORD FROM THE LEFT BANK OF THE TWEED. THE
    EILDON HILLS BEHIND 244

WHERE TWEED AND ETTRICK MEET 245

SELKIRK FROM THE HEATHERLIE 250

THE ETTRICK FROM THE OUTSKIRTS OF SELKIRK 260

SELKIRK 264

THE ETTRICK AT BOWHILL 274

OAKWOOD TOWER 277

KIRKHOPE TOWER 279

LOOKING UP ETTRICKDALE FROM HYNDHOPE 280

ETTRICK WATER AT THE DELORAINES 281

THE BRIDGE AT TUSHIELAW 283

ETTRICK VALE FROM HYNDHOPE 284

PAGE

BUCCLEUCH 285

A GLIMPSE OF CLEARBURN LOCH 286

ETTRICK KIRK 288

MILL GANG AT ETTRICK 290

HYNDHOPE BURN 291

ST. MARY'S LOCH AND THE LOCH OF THE LOWES 293

ST. MARY'S LOCH 295

SITE OF ST. MARY'S CHURCH 296

THE DOUGLAS BURN AND BLACKHOUSE TOWER 297

COCKBURNE'S GRAVE 299

COPPERCLEUCH POST-OFFICE AND A GLIMPSE UP MEGGETDALE . 301

TIBBIE SHIEL'S 302

DRYHOPE TOWER 304

THE GORDON ARMS 306

LOOKING UP THE VALE OF YARROW—THE GORDON ARMS IN THE
     DISTANCE 307

DEUCHAR BRIDGE 310

THE DOWIE DENS 311

NEWARK 315

YAIR BRIDGE 317

FAIRNILEE 320

CADDONFOOT LOOKING TOWARDS YAIR 321

THE INN AT CLOVENFORDS 322

THOMAS PURDIE'S GRAVE, MELROSE ABBEY 323

THE TWEED AT ASHIESTEEL 325

THE TWEED BETWEEN ASHIESTEEL AND THORNILEE 326

TOWER OF ELIBANK 328

INNERLEITHEN 329

PAGE

A ROAD BESIDE THE TWEED, NEAR CADDONFOOT 331

THE CLOSED GATES AT TRAQUAIR HOUSE 332

TRAQUAIR HOUSE 333

WHERE THE QUAIR ENTERS THE TWEED ABOVE INNERLEITHEN . 335

ON THE ROAD TO PEEBLES 336

NEIDPATH CASTLE 341

PEEBLES FROM NEIDPATH 343

THE " BLACK DWARF'S " COTTAGE IN THE MANOR VALLEY . . 344

LOOKING UP THE MANOR VALLEY 346

BRIDGE OVER THE LYNE WATER 348

LOOKING UP TALLA FROM TWEEDSMUIR POST-OFFICE 360

BRIDGE OVER TWEED AT TWEEDSMUIR 361

TWEEDSMUIR 363

TALLA RESERVOIR FROM TALLA LINN 366

A SKETCH ON THE GAMESHOPE BURN 368

THE DEVIL'S BEEF TUB 376

HERMITAGE CASTLE 384

MEETING OF THE HERMITAGE AND LIDDEL 386

MILLHOLME OR MILNHOLM CROSS 389

ON THE LIDDEL AT MANGERTON 390

CARLISLE CASTLE 393

CARLISLE AND THE RIVER EDEN 394

CARLISLE FROM THE CASTLE RAMPARTS 395

A BYWAY IN CARLISLE 396

THE MARKET CROSS, CARLISLE 397

DICK'S TREE. THE BLACKSMITH'S SHOP WHERE KINMONT WILLIE'S
    FETTERS WERE TAKEN OFF 399

THE REPUTED GRAVE OF KINMONT WILLIE IN SARK GRAVEYARD 400

PAGE

SARK BRIDGE AND TOLL-BAR 402

THE BLACKSMITH'S SHOP, GRETNA GREEN 403

SOLWAY MOSS 404

ANCIENT CROSS, ARTHURET 405

GORGE ON THE LIDDEL 406

STUDY IN CARLISLE CATHEDRAL 407

BRAMPTON 408

BEWCASTLE CHURCH AND CASTLE 410

BEWCASTLE CROSS 411

NAWORTH CASTLE 412

BEWCASTLE CROSS 414

KIRK ANDREWS TOWER, NETHERBY 417

THE ARMSTRONG TOWER ON THE ESK 419

GILNOCKIE BRIDGE 420

ON THE ESK AT HOLLOWS 422

LANGHOLM 424

HIGHWAYS AND BYWAYS

IN

THE BORDER

CHAPTER I

BERWICK, TWEED, WHITADDER

THE "Border" is a magical word, and on either side of
a line that constantly varied in the course of English and
Scottish victories and defeats, all is enchanted ground, the
home of memories of forays and fairies, of raids and recoveries,
of loves and battles long ago. In the most ancient times of
which record remains, the English sway, on the east, might
extend to and include Edinburgh; and Forth, or even Tay,
might be the southern boundary of the kingdom of the Scots.
On the west, Strathclyde, originally Cymric or Welsh, might
extend over Cumberland; and later Scottish kings might hold
a contested superiority over that province. Between east and
west, in the Forest of Ettrick, the place-names prove ownership
in the past by men of English speech, of Cymric speech, and
of Gaelic speech. From a single point of view you may see
Penchrise (Welsh) Glengaber (Gaelic) and Skelfhill (English).
Once the Border, hereabouts, ran slantwise, from Peel Fell in
the Cheviots, across the Slitrig, a water which joins Teviot at

E

B

Hawick, thence across Teviot to Commonside Hill above Branksome tower, to the Rankle burn, near Buccleuch, an affluent of Ettrick. Thence, across Ettrick and Yarrow, over Minchmuir, where Montrose rode after the disaster at Philiphaugh, across Tweed, past the camp of Rink, to Torwoodlee, goes that ancient Border, marked by the ancient dyke called the Catrail, in which Sir Walter Scott once had a bad fall during his "grand rides among the hills," when he beat out the music of *Marmion* to the accompaniment of his horse's hooves. The Catrail was a Border, once, and is a puzzle, owing to its ditch between two ramparts. There are many hill forts, mounds even now strong and steep in some places, on the line of the Catrail. The learned derive the word from Welsh *cad*, Gaelic *Cath*, "a battle," and some think that the work defended the Border of the Christian Cymric folk of Strathclyde from the pagan English of Northumbria. In that case, Sir Herbert Maxwell has expressed the pious hope that "the Britons were better Christians than they were military engineers." Is it inconceivable that the word Catrail is a mere old English nickname for a ditch which they did not understand, *the cat's trail*, like Catslack, the wild cat's gap, and other local cat-names?

I am no philologist !

Once when taking a short cut across a hill round which the road runs from Branksome to Skelfhill, I came upon what looked like the deeply cut banks of an extinct burn. There was no water, and the dyke was not continued above or below. Walking on I met an old gentleman sketching a group of hill forts, artificial mounds, and asked him what this inexplicable deep cutting might be. "It is the Catrail," he said : I had often heard of it, and now I had seen it. The old man went on to show that the Border is still a haunted place. "Man, a queer thing happened to me on Friday nicht. I was sleeping at Tushielaw Inn, (on the Upper Ettrick) I had steikit the door and the windows : I woke in the middle o' the nicht, —there was a body in the bed wi' me!" (I made a flippant remark. He took no notice of it.) "I got up and lit the candle, and looked. There was naebody in the bed. I fell asleep, and wakened again. The body was there, it *yammered*. I canna comprehend it." Nor can I, but a pair of amateur psychical researchers hastened to sleep a night at Tushielaw. *They* were undisturbed; and the experience of the old antiquary was "for this occasion only."

"My work seeks digressions," says Herodotus, and mine has already wandered far north of the old Border line of Tweed on the east, and Esk on the western marches, far into what

Halidon Hill and the Two Bridges, Berwick.

was once the great Forest of Ettrick, and now is mainly pasture land, *pastorum loca vasta*. In the old days of the Catrail and the hill forts this territory, "where victual never grew," must have been more thickly populated than it has been in historic times.

We may best penetrate it by following the ancient natural tracks, by the sides of Tweed and its tributaries. We cross the picturesque bridge of Tweed at Berwick to the town which first became part of the kingdom of Scotland, when Malcolm II, at Carham fight, won Lothian from Northumbria. That was in 1018, nine centuries agone. Thenceforward Berwick was one of the four most important places of Scottish

trade; the Scots held it while they might, the English took it
when they could; the place changed hands several times, to
the infinite distress of a people inured to siege and sack.
They must have endured much when Malcolm mastered it;
and again, in 1172, when Richard de Lacy and Humphrey de
Bohun, at war with William the Lion, burned the town.
William, after he inadvertently, in a morning mist, charged the
whole English army at Alnwick, and was captured, surrendered
Berwick to England, by the Treaty of Falaise, when he did
homage for his whole kingdom. The English strongly fortified
the place, though the fragments of the girdling wall near the
railway station, are, I presume, less ancient than the end of
the twelfth century. William bought all back again from the
crusading Richard of the Lion Heart: the two kings were
" well matched for a pair of lions," but William the Lion was
old by this time.

In 1216, Alexander II attacked England at Norham Castle,
but King John, though seldom victorious, was man enough to
drive Alexander off, and brute enough to sack Berwick with
great cruelty, setting a lighted torch to the thatch of the house
in which he had lain; and " making a jolly fire," as a general of
Henry VIII later described his own conduct at Edinburgh.
Fifty years later the woman-hating friar who wrote *The Chronicle
of Lanercost* describes Berwick as the Alexandria of the period;
the Tweed, flowing still and shallow, taking the place of the
majestic river of Egypt. One is reminded of the Peebles man
who, after returning from a career in India, was seen walking
sadly on Peebles Bridge. " I'm a leear," he said, " an unco
leear. In India I telled them a' that Tweed at Peebles was
wider than the Ganges !" And he had believed it.

However, Berwick *was* the Scottish Alexandria, and paid
into the coffers of the last of her " Kings of Peace," Alexander
III, an almost incredible amount of customs dues. After three
peaceful reigns, Scotland was a wealthy country, and Berwick
was her chief emporium. But then came the death of the

Maid of Norway, the usurpation by Edward I, the endless wars
for Independence : and Berwick became one of the cockpits
of the long strife, while Scotland, like St. Francis, was the
mate of Poverty.

While Edward was in France, his "toom tabard," King
John, (Balliol) renounced his allegiance.   Edward came home
and, in the last days of March 1296, crossed Tweed and be-
leaguered Berwick, in which were many trading merchants of
Flanders.   The townsfolk burned several of his ships, and sang
songs of which the meaning was coarse, and the language,
though libellous, was rather obscure.   Edward was not cruel,
as a rule, but, irritated by the check, the insults, and the
reported murder by the Scots of English merchants, he gave
orders for a charge.   The ditch and stockade were carried, and
a general massacre followed, of which horrible tales are told by
a late rhyming chronicler.   Hemingburgh, on the English side,
says that the women were to some extent protected.   The
Scots avenged themselves in the same fashion at Corbridge,
that old Roman station, but the glory and wealth of Berwick
were gone, the place retaining only its military importance.
To Berwick Edward II fled after Bannockburn, as rapidly as
Sir John Cope sought the same refuge after Prestonpans.

Berwick is, for historically minded tourists, (not a large proportion of the whole), a place of many memories.   In July, 1318,
Bruce took the castle after a long blockade ; an English attempt
to recover it was defeated mainly through the skill of Crab, a
Flemish military engineer.   Guns were not yet in use :
"crakkis of war," (guns) were first heard in Scotland, near
Berwick, in 1327.   In 1333, after a terrible defeat of the Scots
on the slopes of Halidon Hill, a short distance north of
Berwick, the place surrendered to Edward III, and became
the chief magazine of the English in their Scottish wars.

By 1461, the Scots recovered it, but in 1481, the nobles of
James III mutinied at Lauder bridge, hanged his favourites,
and made no attempt to drive Crook-backed Richard from his

siege of Berwick. Since then the town has been in English hands, and was to them, for Scottish wars, a Calais or a Gibraltar. The present bridge of fifteen arches, the most beautiful surviving relic here of old days, was built under James VI and I. They say that the centre of the railway station covers the site of the hall of the castle of Edward I, in which that prince righteously awarded the crown of Scotland to John Balliol. The town long used the castle as a quarry,

Old Bridge at Berwick.

then came the railway, and destroyed all but a few low walls, mere hummocks, and the Bell Tower.

Naturally the ancient churches perished after the Blessed Reformation : indeed the castle was used as a quarry for a new church of the period of the Civil War.

Immediately above Berwick, and for some distance, Tweed flows between flat banks, diffusely and tamely : the pools are locally styled "dubs," and deserve the title. The anti-Scottish satirist, Churchill, says,

> " Waft me, some Muse, to Tweed's inspiring stream
> Where, slowly winding, the dull waters creep
> And seem themselves to own the power of sleep."

"In fact," replies a patriotic Scot, "'the glittering and resolute streams of Tweed,' as an old Cromwellian trooper and angler, Richard Franck, styles them, are only dull and sleepy in the dubs where England provides their flat southern bank."

Not flat, however, are the banks on either side of Whitadder, Tweed's first tributary, which joins that river two or three miles above Berwick. From its source in the Lammermuirs, almost to its mouth, a distance of between thirty and forty miles, the Whitadder is quite an ideal trouting stream, "sore fished" indeed, and below Chirnside, injured, one fears, by discharge from Paper Mills there, yet full of rippling streams and boulder-strewn pools that make one itch to throw a fly over them. But most of the water is open to the public, and on days when local angling competitions are held it is no uncommon sight to see three, or maybe four, competitors racing for one stream or pool, the second splashing in and whipping the water in front of the first, regardless of unwritten sporting law; a real case of "deil tak the hindmost." "Free-fishing" no doubt, from some points of view, is a thing to be desired, but to him who can remember old times, when the anglers he met in the course of a day's fishing might easily be counted on the fingers of one hand, the change now is sad. Yet men, they say, do still in the open stretches of Whitadder catch "a pretty dish" now and again. They must be *very* early birds, one would suppose—and perhaps they fish with the lure that the early bird is known to pick up.

On both sides of Whitadder are to be seen places of much interest. First, Edrington Castle, on the left bank a few miles from the river's mouth, once a place of great strength, now crushed by the doom that has wrecked so many of the old strongholds in this part of the country—it was for ages used as a convenient quarry. Then, on the right bank, higher up, on an eminence overhanging the stream, stands Hutton Hall, a picturesque old keep of the fifteenth century, with additions of later date. The original tower was probably built by the Lord Home, who obtained the lands in 1467 by his marriage with the daughter of George Ker of Samuelton. Nearly opposite Hutton, about a mile away, are the ruins of an old castle at Edington. It is remarkable the number of names in this district, all beginning with "Ed":—Edrington, Edington, Ednam, Eden, Edrom, Edinshall, all probably taking their origin from Edwin, king of Northumbria, 616–633. Or does the derivation go still further back, to Odin?

Higher up, we come to Allanton and the junction of Whitadder with its tributary, Blackadder. Near this lies Allanbank, haunt for many generations of that apparition so famous in Scotland, "Pearlin Jean." Jean, or rather Jeanne, it is said, was a beautiful young French lady, in Paris or elsewhere loved and left by a wicked Baronet of Allanbank, Sir Robert Stuart. The tale is some hundreds of years old, but "Pearlin Jean" and her pathetic story still retain their hold on the imagination of Border folk. The legend goes that when the false lover, after a violent scene, deserted his bride that should have been, the poor lady accidentally met her death, but not before she had vowed that she would "be in Scotland before him." And sure enough, the first thing that greeted the horrified gaze of the baronet as he crossed the threshold of his home, bringing another bride than her he had loved and left, was the dim form of Jeanne, all decked, as had ever been her wont, in the rich lace that she loved, and from which the apparition derived the name of Pearlin Jean, "pearlin" being the Scottish term for lace. Tradition says nothing as to the end of the false lover, but the ghost was still known—so say the country people—to have haunted the house until it was pulled down sometime early in last century. Sir Thomas Dick Lauder in his "Scottish Rivers" tells how an old woman then anxiously enquired: "Where will Pearlin Jean gang noo when the house is dismolished?"

That is the tale of "Pearlin Jean" as it is generally told. There is another story, however, less known but much more probable.

When the reckless extravagance of succeeding generations ended as it always must end; when cards and dice and the facile aid of wine and women had sent bit after bit of the broad lands of an old family into alien keeping, and not tardily the day had come when the last acre slipped through heedless fingers, and even the household furniture—all that remained to the last Baronet of Allanbank—was brought to the hammer, there was one room in the old house into which, ere the gloaming fell, the country folk peered with awe greater even than their curiosity. It was a room in which for near on two generations the dust had been left to lie undisturbed on table and chair and mantel-shelf, a room whose little diamond-shaped window panes the storms of more than fifty winters had dimmed, and on whose hearth still lay the ashes of a fire quenched half a century back. Here it was that Pearlin Jean had passed those few not unhappy months of her life, while yet a false lover was not openly untrue to her. But into this chamber, since Jean quitted it for the last time no servant would venture by day or by night, unaccompanied, lest in it might be seen the wraith of that unfortunate and much wronged lady.

It is a story common enough, unhappily, that of Jeanne. She was the daughter of a Flemish Jew, very beautiful, very young, very light-hearted and loving, and unsuspecting of evil, of a disposition invincibly generous and self-sacrificing. In an evil hour the Fates threw across her path Sir Robert Stuart of Allanbank, then visiting the Hague during his travels on the Continent. Sir Robert was a man now no longer in his first youth, self-indulgent, callous of the feelings and rights of others where they ran athwart his own wants or desires, one

to whom the seamy side of life had long been as an open book.
His crop of wild oats, indeed, was ere now of rankest growth,
and already on the face of the sower were lines that told of
the toil of sowing. But he was a handsome man, with a
fluent, honeyed tongue, and it did not take him long to steal
the heart from one who, like the poor little Jeanne, suspected
no evil.

To the Merse and to Allanbank there came word that the
laird was returning to his home. The house was to be put in
order, great preparations to be made. No doubt, folk thought,
all pointed to a wedding in the near future ; the wild young
baronet was about to settle down at last—and not before it
was time, if what folk said regarding his last visit to Allanbank
might be trusted. But the local newsmongers were wrong, in
this instance at least of the home-coming and what might be
expected to follow. When Sir Robert's great coach lumbered
up to the door of Allanbank, there stepped down, not the
baronet alone, but a very beautiful young woman, a vision all
in lace and ribbons, whom the wondering servants were in-
structed to regard in future as their mistress. And though
neighbours—with a few male exceptions—of course kept
severely aloof, steadily ignoring the scandalous household of
Allanbank, yet after a time, in spite of the fact that no plain
gold band graced the third finger of Jeanne's left hand, servants,
and the country folk generally, came to have a great liking, and
even an affection, for the kindly little foreign lass with the
merry grey eyes and the sunny hair, and the quaintly tripping
tongue. And for a time Jeanne was happy, singing gaily
enough from morning to night some one or other of her
numberless sweet old French *chansons*. She had the man she
adored ; what mattered neighbours ? And so the summer
slid by.

But before the autumn there came a change. The merry
lass was no longer so merry, songs came less often from
her lips, tears that she could not hide more and more often

brimmed over from her eyes; and day by day her lover
seemed to become more short in the temper and less con-
siderate of her feelings, more inclined to be absent from home.
In a word, he was bored, and he was not the man to conceal
it. Then when April was come, and the touch of Spring
flushed every bare twig in copse or wooded bank down by the
pools where trout lay feeding, when thrush and blackbird,
perched high on topmost bough, poured out their hearts in a
glory of song that rose and fell on the still evening air, a little
daughter lay in Jeanne's arms, and happiness again for a brief
space was hers. But not for long. The ardour born anew in
her man's self-engrossed heart soon died down. To him now
it seemed merely that a squalling infant had been added to
his already almost insufferable burden of a peevish woman.

More and more, Jeanne was left to her own society and to the
not inadequate solace of her little child. Then " business "
took Stuart to Edinburgh. Months passed, and he did not
return ; nor did Jeanne once hear of him. But there came at
last for her a day black and terrible, when the very foundations of her little world crumbled and became as the dust that
drives before the wind. From Edinburgh came a mounted
messenger, bearing a letter, written by his man of business,
which told the unhappy girl that Sir Robert Stuart was about
to be married to one in his own rank of life ; that due pro-
vision should be made for the child, and sufficient allowance
settled on herself, provided that she returned to her own
country and refrained from causing further scandal or trouble.
She made no outcry, poor lass ; none witnessed her bitter
grief that night. But in the morning, she and the child were
gone, and on her untouched bed lay the lace and the jewels she
once had liked to wear because in early days it had pleased
her to hear the man she loved say that she looked well in
them.

Time went by, and Stuart, unheeding of public opinion,
brought his bride to Allanbank. Of Jeanne he had had

no word; she had disappeared—opportunely enough, he thought. Probably she had long ago gone back to her own land, and by this time the countryside had perhaps found some other nine days' wonder to cackle over. So he returned, driving up to the house in great state—as once before he had driven up.

Surely an ill-omened home-coming, this, for the new bride! As the horses dashed up the avenue, past little groups of gaping country people uncertain whether to cheer or to keep silence, suddenly there darted from a clump of shrubbery the flying figure of a woman carrying in her arms a little child, and ere the postilions could pull up, or any bystander stop her, she was down among the feet of the plunging horses, and an iron heel had trodden out the life of the woman. It was the trampled body of that Jeanne whom he had lightly loved for a time and then tossed aside when weary of his toy, that met the horrified gaze of the white-lipped, silent man who got hurriedly down from inside that coach, leaving his terrified bride to shrink unheeded in her corner. And perhaps now he would have given much to undo the past and to make atonement for the wrong he had done. At least, he may have thought, there was the child to look after; and his heart—what there was of it—went out with some show of tenderness towards the helpless infant. But here was the beginning of strife, for Jeanne's baby did by no means appeal to the new-made bride. Nor was that lady best pleased to find in her withdrawing room a fine portrait in oils of her unlawful predecessor.

And so there was little peace in that house; and as little comfort as peace, for it came to pass that no servant would remain there. From the day of her death Pearlin Jean "walked", they said, and none dared enter the room which once she had called her own. That, of all places, was where she was most certain to be seen. For one day, when the master entered the room alone, they that were near heard his

voice pleading, and when he came out it was with a face drawn
and grey, and his eyes, they said, gazed into vacancy like those
of one that sees not. So the place got ever an increasingly bad
name, and the ghost of the poor unhappy Jeanne could get no
rest, but went to and fro continually. And long after that day
had arrived when her betrayer, too, slept with his fathers, the
notoriety of the affair waxed so great that seven learned ministers,
tradition says, united vainly in efforts to lay the unquiet spirit
of Pearlin Jean. So long as the old house stood, there, they
will tell you, might her ghost be seen, pathetically constant to
the place of her sorrow. And there may not be wanting, even
now, those who put faith in the possibility of her slender
figure being seen as it glides through the trees where the old
house of Allanbank once stood.

Some miles above Allanton, on the left bank of Whitadder,
stands Blanerne, home of a very ancient Scottish family. And
farther back from the river are the crumbling fragments of
Billie Castle—"Bylie," in twelfth century charters,—and of
Bunkle, or, more properly, Bonkyll, Castle. All these have
met the fate assigned to them by the old local rhyming
prophecy :

> " Bunkle, Billie, and Blanerne,
>   Three castles strang as airn,
>   Built whan Davy was a bairn ;
>   They'll a' gang doun
>   Wi' Scotland's crown,
>   And ilka ane sall be a cairn."

A cairn each has been, without doubt, or rather a quarry,
from which material for neighbouring farm buildings has been
ruthlessly torn. Of Blanerne, I believe the Keep still exists,
as well as some other remains, to tell of what has been ; but
Billie Castle is now little more than a green mound at foot of
which runs a more or less swampy burn, with here and there a
fragment of massive wall still standing ; whilst Bunkle is a mere
rubble of loose stones. All these were destroyed in Hertford's

raid in 1544, when so much of the Border was "birnd and
owaiertrown."

More ruthless than Hertford's, however, was the work at
Bunkle of our own people in 1820.   They pulled down an

Buttresses with Canopied Niches at Edrom.

eleventh century church in order to build the present edifice.
Only a fragment of the original building remains, but many of
its carved stones may be seen in the walls of the existing

church. Possibly the old structure was in a bad state of repair. One does not know for certain; but at date of its demolition the building appears to have been entire. Our ancestors of a hundred years ago were not to be "lippened to" where ecclesiastical remains were concerned. They had what amounted to a passion for pulling down anything that was old, and where they did not pull down, they generally covered with hideous plaster any inside wall or ornamental work, which to them perhaps might savour of " papistry." Parish ministers, even late in the eighteenth and early in the nineteenth centuries, appear to have taken no interest in those beautiful Norman remains, numerous fragments of which even now exist in Berwickshire; of all those ministers who compiled the old Statistical Account of this county, but one or two make any mention of such things. One fears, indeed, that to some of those reverend gentlemen, or to others like them of later date, we are indebted for the destruction of priceless relics of the past. At Duns, for instance, as late as 1874

At Chirnside.

the original chancel of an old Norman church was pulled down by order of the incumbent, "to improve the church-yard." Then, as already mentioned, there is Bunkle, an instance of very early Norman work, pulled down in 1820. At Chirnside, the tower of its Norman church was sacrificed in 1750, though great part of the old church walls remain ; in the south side is a Norman doorway six feet ten inches in height to the lintel and two feet ten and three-quarter inches wide. Of Edrom church, a very beautiful Norman doorway, said to be " the finest of its style in Scotland," has been preserved, entirely owing, apparently, to the fact that it had been made the entrance to a burial vault. At Legerwood, near Earlstoun, where stands the chancel of a Norman church, the arch is still entire but is defaced with plaster. Berwickshire, however, is not the only part of the Border where such things have been done. Higher up Tweed, at Stobo in Peeblesshire, there is an interesting old church of Norman structure, with sixteenth and seventeenth century alterations; roof and interior fittings are modern, and the building is still used as the Parish Church. Sixteenth and seventeenth century alterations have now at least age to commend them, but it is

Doorway in Graveyard at Edrom.

difficult to see what plea can be advanced for some of those of comparatively recent date. According to "Ecclesiastical Architecture of Scotland," the most serious injury inflicted on the building was the entire destruction of the Norman chancel arch, in order to insert a modern pointed one, at the restoration of the church in 1868.

Over in Teviotdale, too, the same passion for altering, or for sweeping away relics of old times, ran its course. In 1762, the Town Council of Hawick gave orders for the destruction of the Town's Cross. So Popish a thing as a Cross could not be tolerated by those worthy and "unco" pious persons. The treasurer's accounts of the time show that tenpence per day was paid to two men for the work of taking down the Cross, and the carved stones seem to have been sold afterwards for eleven shillings and sixpence. No doubt the worthy bailies congratulated themselves on having not only rid the town of an emblem of Popery, but on having made quite a handsome monetary profit over the transaction.

But to return to Whitadder. In his "Scottish Rivers," Sir Thomas Dick Lauder writes of Billy Castle as the scene of a grisly tale connected with the Homes. He tells how, to the best of his reckoning about a century prior to the date at which he wrote, an old lady of that family resided here in a somewhat friendless condition, but with a considerable household of servants, chief of whom was a butler who had been in her service for many years, and in whose integrity she had entire confidence. This old lady, it seems, was in the habit of personally collecting rents from her tenants, and as there were then no country banks in which to deposit the money, it was her custom to count it in presence of the butler, prior to locking the guineas away in a strong cupboard in her bedroom. The door of this room was secured by an ingenious arrangement, whereby a heavy brass bolt, or cylinder, was allowed to fall by its own weight into an opening made exactly to fit it. To an eye in the head of the cylinder was attached a cord which worked through a pulley fastened to the ceiling, and thence by a series of running blocks passed to the bedside. Thus the old lady, without troubling to get out of bed, could bolt or unbolt her door at will, and so long as the cylinder was down, no one could possibly enter the room. Now, the butler had for years witnessed this counting and stowing away of the rent monies, and temptation had never yet assailed him. He might, indeed, plume himself on his honesty, and say with Verges: "I thank God I am as honest as any man living that is an old

C

man and no honester than I." But alas! there came a night
when the guineas chinked too seductively, and the devil
whispered in the butler's ear. Perhaps some small financial
embarrassment of his own was troubling the man. Anyhow,
it came to his mind that if he could quietly fill up the hole
into which the bolt of his mistress's bedroom door dropped,
he might help himself to as much money as he needed. The
time of year was the cherry season. What so easy as to fill
up the bolt hole with cherry stones? The "geans" grew
thick in Scotland, and they were black ripe now. "At midnight," says Sir Thomas, "he stole into his mistress's chamber,
cut her throat from ear to ear, broke open her cabinet, and
possessed himself of her money; and although he might have
walked down stairs and out at the door without exciting
either alarm or suspicion, he opened the window and let himself down nearly two stories high, broke his leg, and lay thus
among the shrubbery till morning, without ever attempting to
crawl away. He was seized, tried, condemned, and
executed."

It is grisly enough, but hardly so grisly as the real story of
what happened. The scene of the murder, however, was not
Billy Castle—which, indeed, had then been dismantled and
in ruins for two hundred years—but Linthill House, a fine old
mansion standing on a "brae" overhanging Eye-water, five or
six miles from Billy. Linthill is now inhabited by families of
work-people, but it is still in good preservation, and at date of
Sir Thomas Dick Lauder's story (1752), must have been a very
fine specimen of the old Scottish château.

The old lady's room was entered as Sir Thomas describes,
but the butler did not immediately cut her throat. She was
awakened by the sound of the stealthy rifling of the cupboard,
or strong iron-bound box, in which her valuables were kept,
and with that pluck which is characteristic of the old-time
Scottish lady, she jumped up to grapple with the robber.
Then he cut her throat, and leaving her for dead on the bed,

proceeded with his rifling. A slight noise, nowever, disturbed him, and, looking round, a terrifying sight met his gaze; the woman whom he had believed to be dead was on her feet, blindly groping her bloody way along the wall to the bell. Before he could seize her and complete his work, she had pulled the rope with all the strength left to her, and had alarmed the other servants. Thus the murderer had no opportunity to leave by way of the stairs. He jumped from the window—no great feat for an active man with his wits about him. But the butler was flurried; perhaps, also, he was stout, as is not uncommon with pampered servants. In any case, he missed his footing, came down badly, and broke his leg. He did not, however, lie where he fell, inert and helpless. With painful effort the man dragged himself to a field near by, where, amongst sweet-scented flowering beans, he lay concealed for some days. On the fourth day, as he lay groaning beside a tiny spring of water which still flows near the middle of the field, he chanced to be seen by some children, who gave information. The wretched man was taken, tried, and executed—the last instance in Scotland of a criminal being hung in chains. The blood of a murdered person, they say, refuses to be washed clean from any wood-work into which it may have soaked—witness that ghastly dark patch that disfigures a floor in Holyrood. Here at Linthill at least there is no doubt of the fact that those marks remain; in spite of very visible attempts to remove the stains from the wood-work by planing them out, the prints of the poor lady's bloody hands still cling to the oak wainscoting of the gloomy old room where the deed was committed. About house and grounds there hangs now an air of dejection and decay, though Eye ripples cheerily just beyond the garden foot and the surrounding landscape is bright with pleasant woods and smiling fields.

Surely if ever ghost walked, it should be here at Linthill; that midnight bell should clang, a window be thrown open, the thud be heard of a heavy body falling on the ground.

C 2

But it is not mistress or man that haunts that house. It is of other things they tell who have been there; of an upper chamber, to which nightly comes the shuffling tramp of men bearing from a vehicle which is heard to drive up to the house door, a heavy weight, which they deposit on the floor. More shuffling, a room door quietly closed, the sound of retreating steps, then silence. "Hout!" say the womenfolk of those who now inhabit part of the old house, "it'll no be naething." But they look behind them with a glance not too assured, and the voice that says it is "naething" is not over-steady in tone.

A little higher up the river than Blanerne we come to Broomhouse, where also once stood a castle. In a field on this estate is a spot, still called "Bawtie's Grave," where the body of Sir Anthony Darcy—"Le Sieur de la Beauté"— Warden of the Marches in 1517, is said to lie buried. Darcy, or de la Bastie (or de la Beauté), as he was generally called, was a Frenchman, a man possessed of great personal beauty and attraction; but the fact that he had been appointed Warden of the Marches and Captain of Dunbar Castle in room of Lord Home, who had been treacherously put to death in Edinburgh, rendered him very obnoxious to the inhabitants of that part of Berwickshire in which the Homes held sway. It was through Darcy that Lord Home and his brother had been decoyed to Edinburgh, said the kin and supporters of the Home family. Vengeance must be taken.

Nor was time wasted over it. An occasion soon arose when Darcy in his capacity of Warden had to visit Langton Tower, (no great distance from Duns), in order to settle some family feud of the Cockburns, relatives by marriage of the Homes. Here, out-side the tower, Sir David Home, with a party of horsemen, came up, and speedily picked a quarrel with the Sieur. Swords were out in a minute, and Home's band was too strong for Darcy and his men. Several of the French attendants of the Sieur fell, and as the rest of his party were mostly Borderers, and therefore not very eager to fight for him, the Warden found himself compelled to ride for it. He headed in the direction of Dunbar. But the ground over which he had to gallop was swampy, and de la Beauté's heavy horse sank fetlock-deep at every stride, finally "bogging" in a morass some distance to the east of Duns. Darcy is said to have continued his flight on foot, but the chase did not last long ; Home and his followers bore down upon him—a well-mounted "little foot-page," they say, the first man up.

> " The leddies o' France may wail and mourn,
> May wail and mourn fu' sair,
> For the Bonny Bawtie's lang broun locks
> They'll never see waving mair."

They were on him at once ; his head was fiercely hewn off, carried in triumph to Home Castle, and there fastened to the end of a spear on the battlements, to gaze blind-eyed over the wide Merse, the land he had tried to govern. Pitscottie says that Sir David Home of Wedderburn cut off Darcy's long flowing locks, and plaiting them into a wreath, knit them as a trophy to his saddle bow.

Perhaps the Sieur in the end got no more than his deserts, or at least no more than he may frequently have dealt out to others. He came of a stock famed in France for cruelty and oppression ; and the peasants round Allevard, in the Savoie,—where stand the fragments of what was once his ancestral home—still tell of that dreadful night when Messire Satan himself was seen to take his stand on the loftiest battlement of the castle. And they relate how then the walls rocked and swayed and with hideous crash toppled to the ground. Perhaps it was this very catastrophe which sent the "Bonny Bawtie" to Scotland.

A cairn once marked the spot where the Sieur's body found a resting place. But, unfortunately, such a ready-made quarry of stones attracted the notice of a person who contracted to repair the district roads. It is many years ago now, and there was no one to say him nay. He carted away the interesting land-mark and broke up the cairn into road metal.

Home Castle still dominates this part of the Border, but no longer is it the building of " Bawtie's " day. That was pulled down in the time of the Protector, by Cromwell's soldiers under Colonel Fenwick. Thomas Cockburn, Governor in 1650 when Fenwick summoned the castle to surrender, was valiant only on paper; a few rounds from the English guns caused his valour to ooze from his fingers' ends, and sent up the white flag. That was the end of the old castle. Fenwick dismantled it and pulled down the walls; the present building, imposing as it seems, standing grim and erect on its rocky height, is but a dummy fortress, built in the early eighteenth century on the old foundations, from the old material, by the Earl of Marchmont. The original building dated from the thirteenth century, and a stormy life it had, like many Border strongholds alternately in Scottish and in English hands. In 1547, after a gallant defence by the widow of the fourth Lord Home, it was taken by the English under Somerset; two years later it was recaptured by that lady's son, the fifth Lord Home.

"Too old at forty," is the cry raised in these days— presumably by those who have not yet attained to that patriarchal age—but when a state of war was the chronic condition of the Border-land, men of vastly greater age than forty were not seldom able to show the way to warriors young enough to be their grandsons. At this taking of Home Castle in the closing days of December 1548, it was a man over sixty, one of the name of Home, who was the first to mount the wall. The attack was made at night, on the side where the castle was both naturally and artificially strongest, and where consequently least vigilant guard might probably be kept. As Home, ahead of his comrades, began to slide his body cautiously over the parapet, the suspicions of a sentry pacing at some little distance were roused, and he challenged and

turned out the guard. This man had not actually *seen* anything, the night was too dark for that, but he had, as it were,
smelt danger, with that strange extra sense that sometimes in
such circumstances raises man more nearly to the level of his
superior in certain things—the wild animal. However, in this
case the sentry got no credit, but only ridicule, from his
comrades, for examination showed that there was no cause
whatever for his having brought the guard out into the cold,
looking for mares' nests over the ramparts. Home and his
party had dropped hurriedly back, and during the time that
the Englishmen were glancing carelessly over the wall, they lay
securely hidden close at its base. As soon, however, as the
English soldiers had returned to the snug warmth of their
guard-room, and the mortified sentry was once more pacing up
and down, Home was again the first of the Scots to clamber
up and to fall upon the astonished Englishman, whom
this time he slew, a fate which overtook most of the castle's
garrison. "Treachery helped the assailants," said the English.
"Home Castle was taken by night, and treason, by the Scots,"
is the entry in King Edward's Journal.

Again, in 1569, it was battered by the heavy siege guns of
the Earl of Sussex and once more for a time was held by
England; finally in 1650 came its last experience of war. It
was at Home Castle that Mary of Gueldres, Queen of James
II of Scotland, lay whilst her husband besieged Roxburgh in
1460. One hundred and six years later, Mary Queen of Scots
was there on her way to Craigmillar from Jedburgh.

In days when the bale-fire's red glare on the sky by night,
or its heavy column of smoke by day, was the only means of
warning the country of coming invasion from the south, Home
Castle, with its wide outlook, was the ideal centre of a system
of beacon signals on the Scottish border. The position was
matchless for such purpose ; nothing could escape the watchful
eyes of those perched on the lofty battlements of this
"Sentinel of the Merse," no flaming signal from the fords over

Tweed fail to be seen. In an instant, at need, fires would be flashing their messages over all the land, warning not only the whole Border, but Dunbar, Haddington, Edinburgh, and even the distant shores of Fife. "A baile is warnyng of ther cumyng quhat power whatever thai be of. Twa bailes togedder at anis thai cumyng in deide. Four balis, ilk ane besyde vther and all at anys as four candills, sal be suthfast knawlege that thai ar of gret power and menys." So ran part of the instructions issued in the fifteenth century. But almost in our own day—at least in the days of the grandfathers of some now living—Home Castle flashed its warning and set half Scotland flying to arms. Britain then lived under the lively apprehension of a French invasion. With an immense army, fully equipped, Napoleon lay at Boulogne waiting a favourable opportunity to embark. Little wonder, therefore, that men were uneasy in their minds, and that ere they turned in to bed of a night country folk cast anxious glances towards some commanding "Law" or Fell, where they knew that a beacon lay ready to be fired by those who kept watch. In the dull blackness of the night of 31st January, 1804, the long-looked-for summons came. All over the Border, on hill after hill where of old those dreaded warnings had been wont to flash, a tiny spark was seen, then a long tongue of flame leaping skyward. The French were coming in earnest at last!

Just as ready as it had been in the fiercest days of Border warfare was now the response to the sudden call to arms. Over a country almost roadless, rural members of the various Yeomanry corps galloped through the mirk night, reckless of everything save only that each might reach his assembly point in time to fall in with his comrades. Scarce a man failed to report himself as ready for service—in all the Border I believe there were but two or three. And though it turned out that the alarm fires had been lit through an error of judgment on the part of one of the watchers, there is no doubt that to the bulk of the men who turned out so full of courage and enthusiasm that night, the feeling at first, if mixed with relief, was one of disappointment that they had had no chance of trying a fall with " Boney " and his veterans. The man who was the first to fire his beacon on that 31st of January was a watcher at Home Castle. Peering anxiously through the gloom, he imagined that he saw a light flare up in the direction of Berwick. It was in reality only a fire lit by Northumbrian charcoal-burners that he saw, and its locality was many points to the south of Berwick, but as the blaze sprang higher, and the flames waxed, the excited watcher lost his head, and, forgetting to verify the position, feverishly set a light to his own beacon and sent the summons to arms flying over the Border. Had it not chanced that the watcher by the beacon on St. Abb's Head was a man of cool temperament, all Scotland had been buzzing that night like a hornets' nest. This man, however, reasoned with himself that news of an invasion, if it came at all, must necessarily come from a coastal, and not from an inland station, and therefore he very wisely did not repeat the signal.

The spirit shown on the occasion of this false alarm, and the promptitude with which yeomanry and volunteers turned out, are things of which Borderers are justly proud. Many of the yeomanry rode from forty to fifty miles that night in order to be in time; and even greater distances were covered. Sir Walter Scott himself was in Cumberland when word of the firing of the beacons came to him, but within twenty-four hours he and his horse had reached Dalkeith, where his regiment was assembled, a distance of one hundred miles from his starting point. In one or two instances, where members of a corps chanced to be from home, in Edinburgh on private business, mother or wife sent off with the troop when it marched, the horse, uniform, and arms of husband or son, so that nothing might prevent them from joining their regiment at Dalkeith. The substance of the message then sent to her son by the widowed mother of the writer's grandfather, will be found in Sir Walter's Notes to *The Antiquary*. If in our day

like cause should unhappily arise, if the dread shadow of
invasion should ever again fall on our land, no doubt the
response would be as eager as it was in 1804; the same spirit
is there that burned in our forefathers.   But of what value
now-a-days are half-trained men if they come to be pitted
against the disciplined troops of a Continental Power?   Of no
more avail than that herd of wild bulls that the Spaniards in
1670 tried to drive down on Morgan's Buccaneers at Panama.

Many a tale is still told of the events of that stirring night of
31st January, 1804.   One of the Selkirk volunteers, a man
named Chisholm, had been married that day; but there was
no hesitation on his part.   "Weel, Peggy, my woman," he
said in parting with his day-old bride, "if I'm killed, ye'll hear
tell o't.   And if I'm no killed, I'll come back as sune as I
can."   A particularly "canny" Scot was another volunteer,
whose mother anxiously demanded ere he marched if he had
any money with him in case of need.   "Na, na!" he said,
"they may kill me if they like, but they'll get nae siller off *me*."

A few cases of the white feather there were, of course;
in so large a body of undisciplined men there could hardly
fail to be some who had no stomach for the fight, but instances
of cowardice were surprisingly few.   One or two there were
who hid under beds; and one youth, as he joined the ranks,
was heard to blubber, "Oh, mother, mother, I wish I'd been
born a woman."   But of those who should have mustered at
Kelso, only two out of five hundred failed to answer to their
names, and possibly they may have had legitimate cause for their
absence.   Many of the members of foot regiments were long
distances away when the alarm was given.   Of the Duns
volunteers, for instance, two members were fifteen miles
distant when the beacons blazed up.   Yet they made all
speed into the town, got their arms and accoutrements,
marched all through the night, and fell in alongside their
comrades at Haddington next forenoon.   Many—all the men
of Lessudden, for example—marched without uniforms.   An

unpleasant experience had been theirs had they fallen, in civilian dress, into the hands of the enemy.

To return to Whitadder.—Some miles above Broomhouse we come to Cockburn Law, a conical hill of about 1100 feet in height, round three sides of which the river bends sharply. On the northern slope of the hill is the site, and what little remains to be traced, of Edinshall, a circular tower dating probably from the seventh century. According to the old Statistical Account of the Parish, the walls of this tower,— Edwin's Hall,—measured in diameter 85 feet 10 inches, and in thickness 15 feet 10 inches, enclosing in their depths many cells or chambers. Their height must once have been very considerable, for even at date of the Statistical Account—the end of the eighteenth century—they stood about eight feet high, and were surrounded on all sides by a scattered mass of fallen stones. The ground around shows traces of having been fortified, but the tower itself probably was never a place of strength. The stones of which the building was constructed were large, and close fitting, but not bound together with mortar, which indeed was not in use in Scotland so early as the date of the building of Edinshall,—hence the tower was a quarry too convenient to be respected by agriculturists of a hundred years ago. Most of the material of the ancient building has been taken to construct drains, or to build "dry stane dykes." The "rude hand of ignorance" has indeed been heavy on the antiquities of Scotland.

Where the stream bends sharply to the left as one fishes up those glorious pools and boulder-strewn rapids, there stands a cottage not far removed from Edinshall, which on the Ordnance Survey maps bears the very un-Scottish name of Elba. It has, however, not even a remote connection with the place of exile of an Emperor. The learned would have us believe that the name is derived from the Gaelic "Eil," a hill, and "both," a dwelling. It may be so; but it seems much more likely that "Elba" is merely the Ordnance Survey people's spelling of the word "elbow," as it is pronounced in Scotland ; the river here makes an extremely sharp bend, or elbow. Near Elba is an old copper mine which was worked to advantage by an English company midway in the eighteenth century. Abandoned after a time, it was reopened in 1825, but was soon again closed. Copper was not there in sufficient quantity to pay ; probably it had been worked out before. Four or five miles from here we come to Abbey St. Bathans, a name which conjures up visions of peaceful old ruins nestling among whispering elms by clear and swift flowing waters. There is now, however, little of interest to be found. St. Bathans was originally a convent of Cistercian Nuns, with the title of a Priory, and was founded towards the end of the twelfth century by Ada, daughter of William the Lion. As late as 1833, the then recently written Statistical Account of the Parish says that the north and east walls of the church "still bear marks of antiquity," and that in the north wall is "an arched door which communicated with the residence of the Nuns" ; but, says the Account, this door "is now built up." "Adjoining the church, and between it and the Whitadder, remains of the Priory were visible a few years ago." Where are they now? Built into some wall or farm building, no doubt, or broken up, perhaps, to repair roads or field drains. And where is the font, with its leaden pipe, that stood "in the wall near the altar"? Perhaps—if it still exists, unbroken,—it may now be used as a trough for feeding pigs, as has been the fate of many another such vessel. It is hard to forgive the dull, brutish ignorance that wilfully wrecked so much of the beauty and interest that the past bequeathed to us.

It is not easy to say who was the saint from whom Abbey St. Bathans inherited its name. Probably it was Bothan, Prior of Old Mailros in the seventh century, a holy man of great fame in the Border. There is a well or spring not far distant from the church of St. Bathans, whose miraculous powers of healing all sickness or disease were doubtless derived

from the good Father. These powers have now long decayed,
but as late as 1833—possibly even later—some curious beliefs
regarding the well were held in the neighbourhood, and its
waters, it was well known, would "neither fog nor freeze" in
the coldest weather.

Shortly after leaving Abbey St. Bathans, as we gradually
near the Lammermuirs, the land on both sides of Whitadder
begins more to partake of the hill-farm variety, where grouse
and blackgame swarm thick on the stooked corn in late
autumn. From the south side, a little above Ellemford, there
enters a considerable stream, the water of Dye, said to be of
good repute as regards its trout. One of these high, round-
backed hills here is probably the scene of some great battle of
old times. "Manslaughter Law" is the satisfying name of the
hill. There is a tumulus still remaining on the north side of
it, and near at hand weapons have been dug up, says the
Statistical Account. One wonders what their fate may have
been. They, at any rate, would surely be preserved? It is by
no means so sure. One sword, at least, that was found many
years ago on the west side of Manslaughter Law, met with the
fate one might expect from the kind of people who used to
quarry into beautiful old abbeys in order to get material to
build a pig-stye. It was taken to the village smithy, and there
"improved" out of existence—made into horseshoes perhaps,
or a "grape for howkin' tatties." Had it been a helmet that
was then unearthed, no doubt a use would have been found
for it such as that which the Elizabethan poet sadly suggests
for the helmet of the worn out old man-at-arms:

> " His helmet now shall make a hive for bees."

Eastward from the spot where this sword was found is a barrow
which, says the Statistical Account, "probably covers more
arms"; and on a hill by Waich Water, a tributary of the Dye,
are the Twin-Law Cairns, which are supposed to mark the resting place of twin brothers who fell here,—perhaps in pre-historic

times. Tradition says that these two were commanders of rival
armies, Scottish and Saxon, and that, neither at the time being
aware of their relationship, they undertook to fight it out, as
champions of the rival hosts. When both lay dead, some old
man, who had known the brothers in their childhood, gazing on
them, with grief discovered the relationship of the slain men;
and to commemorate the tragedy, the soldiers of both hosts
formed lines from Waich Water to the hill's summit, and passed
up stones wherewith they built these cairns.

At Byrecleuch Ridge, towards the head of Dye Water, is
another enormous and very remarkable cairn called the
Mutiny Stones. This great mass of piled up stone measures
two hundred and forty feet in length; where broadest, seventy-
five feet; and its greatest height is eighteen feet. What does it
commemorate? A great fight, say some, that took place in
1402 between the Earl of Dunbar and Hepburn of Hailes, in
which the latter was killed. A prehistoric place of sepulture,
hazards Sir Herbert Maxwell. But it was not here that
Hepburn fell; that was elsewhere in the Merse. And they
were little likely in the fifteenth century to have taken such
titanic pains to hand his memory down to posterity. The pre-
historic place of sepulture sounds the more probable theory.
But why "Mutiny Stones"? There must surely be some
local tradition more satisfying than that of the Hepburn-
Dunbar fight.

The upper part of Whitadder must once have been well
fitted to check hostile raids from the south whose object was
to strike the fat Lothians through the passes over the
Lammermuirs. In the few miles of wild hill country that
sweep from its source on Clint's Dod down to its junction with
Dye Water, there formerly stood no fewer than six castles,
Chambers tells us,—John's Cleuch, Gamelshiel, (the lady of
which was killed by a wolf as she walked near her home one
evening in the gloaming) Penshiel, Redpath, Harehead, and
Cranshaws. Except in the case of Cranshaws, there are now

few traces left standing of these strongholds. Cranshaws, a
building of the sixteenth century, is in good preservation ;
of Gamelshiel there remains a bit of wall, of Penshiel a fragment
of vaulting ; of the others no stone.   Cranshaws of old, it is
said, was long the haunt of one of those Brownies, or familiar
spirits, that were wont in the good old days of our forefathers
mysterious ly to do by night, when the household slept, all
manner of domestic or farm work for those who humoured
them and treated them well in the matter of food, or other
indulgence affected by their kind.   There was nothing a
Brownie would not do for the family he favoured, provided
that he was kept in good humour ; otherwise, or if he were
laughed at or his work lightly spoken of, it were better for that
family that it had never been born ; their sleep was disturbed
o' nights, malevolent ill-luck dogged them by day, until he was
propitiated.   But leave out for him each night a jug of milk
and a barley bannock,—they were not luxurious in their
tastes, those Brownies,—and at dawn you would find

> " .   .   .   . how the drudging goblin sweat
> To earn his cream bowl duly set ;
> When in one night, ere glimpse of morn,
> His shadowy flail hath threshed the corn
> That ten day-lab'rers could not end ;
> Then lies him down, the Lubber-fiend,
> And stretched out all the chimney's length,
> Basks at the fire his hairy strength ;
> And crop-full out of doors he flings
> Ere the first cock his matin rings."

They tell that this particular Brownie at Cranshaws, being
offended at some reflection made on his work, the following
night took up an entire crop that he had thrashed, carried it to
the Raven Craig, two miles down the river, and threw it over
the cliff.   Belief in the Brownie died hard in the Border.   I am
not sure that in remote "up the water" districts he did not
survive almost till the advent of motor cars and bicycles.

CHAPTER II

But a step over the moor from Waich Water, across by
Twin-Law Cairns and down by the Harecleuch Hill we come to
the head-waters of the most considerable of Whitadder's
tributaries—Blackadder, "vulgarly so pronounced," says the old
Statistical Account. Its real name is "Blackwater," according
to that authority, because it rises out of peaty swamps that
impart to its waters a look of sullen gloom. I am unable to
say what now may be its reputation as a trout stream, but long
years ago it abounded with "a particular species of trout, much
larger than the common burn trout, and remarkably fat."
The Statistical Account mentions a notable peculiarity of
Blackadder, on the accuracy of which one would be inclined
to throw doubt. It says that though every other stream in the
country which eventually mingles its waters with Tweed,
swarms with salmon in the season, yet into Blackwater they do
not go ; or if they enter at all, it is found that they die before
they can ascend many miles. The swampy source of the
stream "is commonly ascribed as the reason why the fish
cannot frequent the river," says the Account. Drainage, one
would be inclined to think, has long ago removed that fatal
nature from the water, if it ever existed. Trout thrive on it,
at all events, red-fleshed beauties, "similar," says the clerical

writer of the Statistical Account of the Parish of Fogo—a man and a fisher, surely—" to those of Eden Water, which joins Tweed three miles below Kelso. The Eden rises also in a marshy district, which may be the cause of this similarity of the fish." But most Border streams take their rise in more or less marshy districts, though they may not flow direct from a swamp.

Was it in the Eden that Thomson, author of " The Seasons," learned to fish ? Or was it in Jed ? He was born at Ednam,—Edenham,—a village on the Eden, and he may have loved to revisit it in later years, and to catch the lusty speckled trout for which the stream has always been famous. Probably, however, he learned to throw a fly on Jed, for he passed his boyhood at Southdean—to which parish his father had been transferred as Minister long ere the son was fit to wield a rod—and he himself got his early education at Jedburgh. In Jed or in Eden, then, and perhaps in Teviot and Ale—he was much at Ancrum—he learned the art; and not unskilled in it indeed must he have been. Where in all literature can one find a description of trout-fishing so perfect as the following ?

> " Just in the dubious point, where with the pool
> Is mix'd the trembling stream, or where it boils
> Around the stone, or from the hollow'd bank
> Reverted plays in undulating flow,
> There throw, nice judging, the delusive fly ;
> And, as you lead it round in artful curve,
> With eye attentive mark the springing game.
> Strait as above the surface of the flood
> They wanton rise, or, urged by hunger, leap,
> There fix, with gentle twitch, the barbed hook ;
> Some lightly tossing to the grassy bank
> And to the shelving shore slow dragging some
> With various hand proportion'd to their force.
> If yet too young, and easily deceived,
> A worthless prey scarce bends your pliant rod,
> Him, piteous of his youth, and the short space
> He has enjoy'd the vital light of heaven,
> Soft disengage, and back into the stream

D

> The speckled captive throw ; but, should you lure
> From his dark haunt, beneath the tangled roots
> Of pendent trees, the monarch of the brook,
> Behoves you then to ply your finest art.
> Long time he, following cautious, scans the fly,
> And oft attempts to seize it, but as oft
> The dimpled water speaks his jealous fear.
> At last, while haply o'er the shaded sun
> Passes a cloud, he desperate takes the death
> With sullen plunge : at once he darts along,
> Deep struck, and runs out all the lengthen'd line,
> Then seeks the farthest ooze, the sheltering weed,
> The cavern'd bank, his old secure abode,
> And flies aloft, and flounces round the pool,
> Indignant of the guile.   With yielding hand
> That feels him still, yet to his furious course
> Gives way, you, now retiring, following now,
> Across the stream, exhaust his idle rage,
> Till floating broad upon his breathless side,
> And to his fate abandon'd, to the shore
> You gaily drag your unresisting prize."

Many a long day of Spring and Summer must the man who
could paint so perfect a picture have passed, rod in hand and
creel on back, by the hurrying streams and quiet pools of
some Border Water, many a time have listened to the summer
breeze whispering in the leafy banks, and heard, as in a dream,
the low murmur of Jed or Ale. And what sport must they
have had in the old days when Thomson fished—and even in
the days when Stoddart fished—when farmers were ignorant,
or careless, of the science of drainage, and rivers ran for days,
nay, for weeks after rain, clear and brown, dimpled with rising
trout. What sport indeed of all kinds must there have been
here in the south of Scotland in very ancient days when the
country was mostly forest or swamp, and wild animals, now
long extinct, roamed free over hill and dale. It has been
mentioned a page or two back how the lady of Gamelshiel
Tower was killed by a wolf. Here, at the head waters of
Blackadder—as the crow flies not a dozen miles from Gamel-

shiel — we are in the midst of a district once infested by
wolves. Westruther, through which parish Blackadder runs,
was originally "Wolfstruther," the "swamp of the wolves."
And all over the surrounding country, place names speak of
the beasts of the field. An MS. account of Berwickshire tells
how Westruther was "a place of old which had great woods,
with wild beasts, fra quhilk the dwellings and hills were
designed, as Wolfstruther, Raecleuch, Hindside, Hartlaw and
Harelaw."

> " There's hart and hynd, and dae and rae,
> And of a' wilde bestis grete plentie,"

as we read in the "Sang of the Outlaw Murray."

The last-mentioned name, Harelaw, calls up visions of another
chase than that of the hare. Sir Thomas Dick Lauder in his
"Scottish Rivers," (written sometime about 1848), mentions that
one of the most curious facts connected with Harelaw Moor
was that a man, who, Sir Thomas says, died "not long ago,"
recollected having seen Sir John Cope and his dragoons in
full flight across it from the battle of Prestonpans, breathlessly
demanding from all the country people they met information
as to the shortest road to Coldstream.

> " Says the Berwickers unto Sir John,
> ' O what's become o' all your men ?'
> ' In faith,' says he, ' I dinna ken ;
> I left them a' this morning.' "

He must have been a very aged man, but if "not long ago"
meant any time, as late, say, as the Twenties of last century,
no doubt it would be possible that as a boy of eight or ten, he
might have seen the panic-stricken dragoons spurring over the
moor. Such a sight would remain vivid in the memory of
even a very old man. Childhood's incidents outlive all others.

Above Harelaw Moor, on a feeder of the Blackadder, is
Wedderlie, formerly an old Border keep of the usual pattern,
but towards the close of the seventeenth century embodied
with a fine building in the Scottish style of that day. It is

said to have belonged originally to that family, the Edgars, the graves of two members of which are commemorated by the Twin-Law Cairns. The family name lives still in that of the neighbouring Edgar-burn, near to which streamlet is Gibb's Cross, said to be the scene of a martyrdom for sake of the Reformed Faith ; and hard by is Evelaw Tower—a house apparently without a history—still in tolerable preservation. At Wedderlie, of old time, says Sir Thomas Dick Lauder, there stood a very ancient chapel, of which some traces of a vault remain, or remained at a recent date. Local tradition had it that at time of the Reformation the monks hid in this vault all their church plate and other precious possessions, meaning at the first convenient opportunity to remove them to a place of greater safety. The convenient opportunity, it was thought in more modern times, had never come, for in a cave hard by the vault there was one day discovered a great quantity of coins—all of which, by the way, speedily and mysteriously disappeared. It is said, however, that they were not of dates that could in any degree connect this *cache* with the Reformation, and it is suggested in Sir Thomas's book that they were concealed there by the inhabitants of Wedderlie during the Religious wars of the seventeenth century. Those "in the know" may all have been killed, of course; the secret of the hiding place was not likely to be within the ken of more than one or two.

These finds of coins of all dates are by no means rare in the Scottish border counties. One would fain know something of those who hid them, and of the events which were passing at the time when they were buried. Were they the spoil of some reiver, ravished from a roof-tree blackened and left desolate south from Cheviot and Tweed ; spoil for convenience sake thus put away by one to whom the chance of a more convenient season to recover it was ended by a bloody death? Or were they, sometimes, store of coins hastily secreted by quiet country folk fleeing in terror from the violence of English

ended Lords Sussex and Hunsdon in a despatch written by them to the Queen from "Barwick" on 23rd April, 1570.

The lost Pay-chest of Montrose's army at Philiphaugh has given rise to many a story of treasure hunted for or recovered. Sir Walter Scott tells how on the day of the battle the Earl of Traquair and one of his followers, a blacksmith, carrying with them a large sum of money, the pay of the troops, were on their way across the hills to join Montrose at Selkirk. When as far away as Minchmuir, they heard the sound of heavy firing, to which Lord Traquair attached little importance, believing it to be merely Montrose exercising his men, but which, from the long continued and irregular nature of the firing, the blacksmith made certain was an engagement. By the time they reached Broadmeadows, there was no question as to whose conjecture was the correct one. By ones and twos, like the first heavy drops, forerunners of a deluge to follow from some ink-black cloud, came men flying for their lives, on horses pushed beyond the utmost limits of their speed ; then more fugitives, and more, and hard on their heels, Leslie's troopers thundering. Lord Traquair and the blacksmith turned and fled with the throng. But the money was in Lord Traquair's saddle-bags, and the weight was great ; he was like to be captured, for his horse thus handicapped could not face the hill and the heavy ground. Whether the blacksmith offered to sacrifice himself to save his master, or the master ordered the servant to dismount, one does not know, but the outcome was that Lord Traquair fled over the moor on the blacksmith's comparatively fresh horse, and the blacksmith, on a spent animal, was left to make the best of his way with the silver. Leaving the press of fugitives, he fled up Yarrow at the top speed of his tired horse, but finding himself closely pursued, to save himself and to lighten the animal's load, he flung away the bags of money. He *said* afterwards that he threw them into a well or pond near Tinnis, a little above Hangingshaw, and many a well and many a pond has since been vainly dragged for the lost treasure. No man has yet recovered it. Probably that blacksmith knew a thing or two, and he was not likely to give away the show. Whether or no, however, it is certain that many silver coins having dates of about the time of the battle were in Sir Walter's day ploughed up on the river haughs of Tinnis. And at a much later date, a quantity of coins and some silver plate were unearthed nearer Philiphaugh, on the actual scene of the fight. These coins were claimed by the Exchequer. A dozen wine bottles, also, of old pattern, were found buried here, but what had been the liquor contained in them it was not possible to say; the bouquet had entirely perished, and even the colour.

There is a pool in Yarrow, near Harehead, into which tradition says that Montrose flung his treasure chest, telling the Devil to keep it till he should return to claim it. Up to the present the Foul Fiend has not released his care, for when—as is said,—the pool was run dry, or nearly dry, a good many years ago, only a Lochabar-axe was found in it. A somewhat more probable story of the chest is that the bearer, as he hurried past, flung it into a cottage, near Foulshiels, and then rode for his life. Some of Leslie's men got it there, and looted it.

Whose is the portrait that is contained in the little locket which was found, years ago, on the field of Philiphaugh? On the one side is the representation of a heart pierced by darts, and the motto "I dye for Loyalty"; on the other, a long straight sword is engraved. Inside is a portrait, and opposite the portrait, the words "I mourne for Monarchie."

Sometimes coins have been found, too, as at Blackcastle Rings, on Blackadder, at its junction with the Faungrist Burn. Here, on the northern bank of the river, is what must once have been a strongly fortified camp; opposite, on the southern side, and running along the river's bank for fully half a mile, after which it branches to the south, is a well marked line of entrenchment. Eighty years ago, or thereabouts, an old silver chain was unearthed in the camp; and in the trench, a little distance away, when turf was being removed, they came upon quite a number of gold and silver coins of the reign of Edward III. It was somewhere in this neighbourhood, (though probably nearer Duns,) that Lord Percy the English Warden, at the head of seven thousand men, lay encamped in the year 1372, when (as is mentioned by Redpath), his host was dispersed, or at least was said to have been compelled to retire across the Tweed, on foot and without their baggage, owing to a simple stratagem of the Scots. To scare away from their poor little crops the deer and wild cattle that were wont when night fell to ravage the ill-cultivated patches, the country folk of that district were accustomed to sound at frequent intervals a primitive kind of drum. To the ends of long poles were fixed what may best be termed huge rattles, made of dried skins tightly stretched over semi-circular ribs of wood. Inside each skin were put a few round pebbles. Obviously, when shaken vigorously, these rattles would give out a noise quite terrifying to any four-footed animal, especially when heard in the stillness of night. Accordingly, one pitchy night, in the hour before dawn when sleep lay heavy on the invading force, a certain number of the Scots, bearing with them those unwarlike instruments, stole quietly through the tangled growth to the heights on either side of the English camp.

Then broke out a din truly infernal. Picketed horses, mad with terror, strained back on their head-ropes, and breaking loose, stampeded through the camp, trampling over the recumbent forms of men wearied and even yet but half-awake, many of the younger among them more than ready to share the panic of their horses. If the tale be not exaggerated, daylight showed an army deprived of its transport animals, its horsemen compelled to foot it, their steeds the prey of the wily Scots ; a baggageless force compelled to fall back in disorder across Tweed.

In this part of Berwickshire you may still faintly trace here and there the outline of a ditch and earthen rampart called

Herrits Dyke, which, local tradition says, once ran from Berwick inland to near Legerwood on Leader Water,—a work not dis-similar to the Catrail, (which cuts across something like fifty miles of the Border, from Peel Fell in the Cheviots to Torwoodlee on Gala), but without the double wall of Catrail. There are various sections of defensive works of this nature in the Border—if they *were* defensive, for instance, on the hill less than half a mile from the old castle of Holydean, near St. Boswells, in Roxburghshire, there is a particularly well-marked ditch and double rampart running for some distance across the moor. It can scarcely be a continuation of Herrits Dyke, for its construction is different, and its course must run almost at a right angle to Herrits, which is, indeed, many miles away from Holydean. This ditch points almost directly towards Torwoodlee, but it is out of the accepted Catrail track, unless the latter, instead of stopping at Torwoodlee, (as one has been taught), turned sharply and swept down the vale of Gala, and once more crossed Tweed. It is curious, if these works are defensive, that no ancient weapons have ever been found in or near them.

Down the water a few miles from Blackcastle Rings stands the little town of Greenlaw, a settlement which dates from very early times, but not on its present site. Originally the village stood about a mile and a half to the south east, on the isolated green "law" or hill from which it takes its name. The history of the present town goes no farther back than the end of the seventeenth century, a date about contemporaneous with that of its Market Cross, which stands now on the west side of the place. This cross is said to have been erected by Sir Patrick Home of Polwarth (afterwards created Earl of March-mont) in the year 1696. In 1829 it was pulled down, to make room for something else—in the maddening fashion that possessed our ancestors of the period—and, in the usual manner, it was chucked aside as " auld world trash." In 1881, however, the cross, or at least the greater part of it, minus the top, which originally bore a lion-rampant, was discovered in the basement of the old church tower, and was then re-erected where it now stands.

Still farther down the river is the Roman camp at Chesters. But even as long ago as 1798, the writer of the Statistical Account of the Parish of Fogo complained that the old camp was " very much defaced," and that the stones had mostly been " removed to make room for the plough." The rage for agricultural improvement was in 1798 but in extreme infancy; and as no Society for the preservation of ancient monuments came into existence for many a long year afterwards, and interest in such things was confined to the very few, it is safe to infer that not a great deal of this camp now exists.

From Chesters to Marchmont is but a step. Marchmont House dates from about 1754, and was built by the third Earl of Marchmont, near the site of Redbraes, the residence of his grandfather, that Sir Patrick Home of Polwarth who erected the cross in Greenlaw. The village and church of Polwarth are at no great distance. The original church was consecrated in the tenth century, and was restored in 1378, from which date it stood till 1703, when Sir Patrick Home (then Earl of Marchmont) rebuilt it. In the family vault of this church, Sir Patrick lay in hiding for several weeks in 1684, when the search for him was hot and discovery would have cost him his head. The secret of his whereabouts was known to three persons—to his wife, his daughter Grisell (whose name as Lady Grisell Baillie, lives still in the affectionate remembrance of the Scottish Border), and to Jamie Winter, a faithful retainer. Grisell Home, then a girl of eighteen, during all the time of his concealment contrived, with very great risk and difficulty, to convey food to her father in his gruesome lodging. Each night, she slipped stealthily from the house, and—sorest trial of all to the nerves of an imaginative Scot,—made her cautious way in the darkness across the " bogle "-haunted churchyard to her father's lair. Many a shift were she and her

mother put to in order to get food sufficient for their prisoner
without rousing suspicion among the servants, and more than
once the situation was all but given away by the innocent but
embarrassing comments of young and irresponsible members of
the family. Sometimes the servants cannot have been present at
meals, one would think ; or else they smelt a rat, and were discreetly blind. One day at dinner, Grisell had with careful cunning
succeeded in smuggling an entire sheep's head off the dish on
to her own lap, thence presently to be borne surreptiously from
the room, when her young brother, with the maddening
candour and persistency of childhood, called the company's
attention to his sister's prodigious appetite, which not only
enabled her to gobble up in next to no time so much good
meat, but even rendered her able to make the very bones
vanish.

But the scent at length began to grow hot ; they had nearly
run the fox to his earth. Suspicion hovered over the
neighbourhood of the church, and no longer could the vault be
deemed even a moderately safe hiding place. A new den was
necessary ; and a new den was found, one perhaps even more
cramped than the old quarters, if a trifle less insanitary. A
large deal box was made by the faithful Jamie Winter, and
was secretly conveyed into a cellar at Redbraes, of which Lady
Home kept the key. But to get the "muckle kist" snugly
into its resting place, it was necessary to scrape away the
earthen floor of the cellar under the flooring boards, so that
the box might be entirely hidden when the boards were re-laid.
This work could not be done with pick and shovel, lest the
noise should betray what was going on. Grisell, therefore, and
Jamie Winter literally with their own hands carried out the
arduous job ; the earth was *scraped* away, and poor Grisell
Home's nails had almost entirely disappeared ere the work
was finished and the hiding place made ready for her
father. It was scarcely an ideal place of concealment ; water
oozed in so quickly that one night when Sir Patrick was about

to descend into his narrow lodging, it was found that the bedding on which he was used to lie was afloat. And, with its other drawbacks, it had not even the advantage, as a hiding place, of being above suspicion. Had it not been, indeed, for the presence of mind of a kinsman and namesake, Home of Halyburton, a party of dragoons had certainly captured Sir Patrick one day. But Halyburton's liquor was good, and after their thirty mile march from Edinburgh, the temptation to wet their whistle could not be resisted. It did not take long, but it was long enough; a groom on a fast, powerful horse slipped away over the moor to Redbraes, bearing with him no word of writing, but a letter addressed to Lady Home, of which the contents were nothing but a feather,—a hint sufficiently well understood. Ere the dragoons arrived at Redbraes, Sir Patrick was clear away and well on the road to the coast and Holland, and safety.

As we travel down Blackadder towards its junction with the Whitadder, about equi-distant between the two rivers we come to the only town of any importance in the district— Duns, or Dunse as it used, not very appropriately, to be spelled from 1740 to 1882, in which latter year the ancient spelling was revived. The original hamlet or settlement stood on the Dun or Law which adjoins the present town. But Hertford wiped that pretty well out of existence in 1545, as he wiped out many another stronghold and township in the south of Scotland. What was left of the place soon fell into utter decay and ruin, and a new settlement on the present site, then guarded on three sides by a more or less impassable swamp, sprung up in 1588. Duns is one of several places which claim the honour of having been the birthplace of the learned Duns Scotus (1265–1338), but even though she be unable quite to substantiate this claim, her record of worthy sons is no short one. And was not that woman, famed in the seventeenth century, she who was possessed of an evil spirit which caused her, an illiterate person, to talk fluently in the Latin tongue, a native of Duns! The Privy Council Record, under date 13th July, 1630, contains an order for bringing before it Margaret Lumsden, "the possessed woman in Duns," along with her father-in-law and her brother, that order might be taken in the case, "as the importance and nature of such a great cause requires." A fast for her benefit was even proposed by sundry clergymen; interest in her case was acute and widespread. Twenty-nine years later, an account of the circumstances was written by the Earl of Lauderdale, and was published in Baxter's "Certainty of the World of Spirits." Lord Lauderdale was a schoolboy in 1630, but he was accustomed to hear the case very fully discussed by his father and the minister of Duns, the latter of whom, at least, firmly believed that the woman was possessed by an evil spirit. The Earl wrote as follows to Baxter: "I will not trouble you with many circumstances; one only I shall tell you, which I think will evince a real possession. The report being spread in the country, a knight of the name of Forbes, who lived in the north of Scotland, being come to Edinburgh, meeting there with a minister of the north, and both of them desirous to see the woman, the northern minister invited the knight to my father's house (which was within ten or twelve miles of the woman), whither they came, and next morning went to see the woman. They found her a poor ignorant creature, and seeing nothing extraordinary, the minister says in Latin to the knight: '*Nondum audivimus spiritum loquentem.*' Presently a voice comes out of the woman's mouth: '*Audis loquentem, audis loquentem.*' This put the minister into some amazement (which I think made him not mind his own Latin); he took off his hat, and said: '*Misereatur Deus peccatoris!*' The voice presently out of the woman's mouth said: '*Dic peccatricis, dic peccatricis*'; whereupon both of them came out of the house fully satisfied, took horse immediately, and returned to my father's house at Thirlestane Castle, in Lauderdale, where they related this passage. This I do exactly remember. Many more particulars

might be got in that part of the country; but this Latin
criticism, in a most illiterate ignorant woman, where there was
no pretence to dispossessing, is enough, I think." It was, of
course, an infallible sign of demoniac possession that the
victim, mostly an illiterate person, should break out into Latin
or Greek, Hebrew or what not. That was how the devil
usually betrayed himself; he could by no means control his
weakness for talking—generally very badly—in foreign tongues.

The wonders of Duns in the seventeenth century by no
means ceased, however, with this demon-possessed Margaret

Norham Castle.

Lumsden. In 1639, when Leslie camped on Duns Law with
the Covenanting army and its superfluity of ministers, there
occurred a remarkable land-slide which the excited imaginations
of those witnessing its effects could not fail to interpret as an
assured sign that Providence meant to fight on their side. A
bank on the slope of the hill near to the camp slid down,—it had
probably become water-logged as the result of heavy rain,—
disclosing "innumerable stones, round, for the most part, in
shape, and perfectly spherical, . . . like ball of all sizes, from
a pistol to fixed pieces, such as sakers or robenets, or battering
pieces upwards." Men looked on them with awe, and bore

about with them specimens in their pockets, gravely showing
them to excited throngs. "Nor wanted there a few who
interpreted this stone magazine at Duns Hill as a miracle, as if
God had sent this by ane hid providence for the use of the
Covenanters."

Ladykirk.

We return now to Tweed, where on a steep slope stand the
mighty ruins of Norham Castle, guarding the ford; we all
know the scene, castle and ford in the gloaming, from Turner's
beautiful plate in *Liber Studiorum*. Bishop Flambard of
Durham built the castle to bridle the wild Scots, in 1121; some
twenty years later it was taken, under David; but the eastern
side shows the remains of the warlike prelate's work. "The

Norman Keep still frowns across the Merse," and few of the castles of the age of chivalry display more of their ancient strength than Norham. Yet it yielded promptly to James IV. in the first week of the campaign which closed in the terrible defeat of Flodden Edge. In this castle, in the Lent of 1200, William the Lion kept his fast on fourteen kinds of fish, including salmon; he certainly "spelled his fasts with an *e*." While Berwick yielded to the Scots in the dark days of Edward II., good Sir Thomas de Grey, of that ancient Northumbrian house, held Norham stoutly, with pretty circumstances of chivalry, as his son tells in *Scalacronica*.

Over against Norham is Ladykirk, with its ancient church, dedicated, tradition says, by James IV. to the Virgin Mary, in gratitude for his narrow escape from death here when fording the swollen Tweed. A field to the east of the village shows some remains of military works, ramparts for guns probably, from which to fire on Norham. In a line between this spot and the castle there was found in the river a stone cannon-ball, fifty-seven inches in girth, probably one fired from " Mons Meg " when she was here in 1497.

Following the right bank of Tweed we reach Carham burn, where Malcolm II. won Lothian in battle; from Carham to the sea the right bank is English. The next important tributary on the English side, as we ascend the stream is Till, formed by Bowmont and Breamish Waters, which rise in the " Cheeviots," as the Scots pronounce the name.

> " Tweed says to Til'
> ' What gars ye rin sae still ?'
> Says Till to Tweed,
> ' Though ye run wi' speed,
> And I rin slaw,
> Whaur ye droon ae man,
>   I droon twa.' "

The ominous rhyme sounds with the slow lap of the green-grey waters of Till among her alders, and appears to hint at the burden of the ruinous fight of Flodden. On August 22nd, James IV., "a fey man," kept his plighted word to France, which Henry VIII. was invading, and led the whole force of

Ford Castle from the Road.

Highlands and Lowlands across the Border. He made his quarters at Ford Castle, where he did not, as legend says, dally with Lady Heron, still less did his young son, the Archbishop of St. Andrews, fleet the time carelessly with her daughter.

E

James cleared his position by capturing Wark (now scarcely visible in ruin), Chillingham, and Eital castles. Surrey with the English levies, including the Stanleys, sent a challenge from Alnwick. On September 3rd, the Scots are said to have wrecked Ford Castle, now a substantial and comfortable home, still containing the king's rooms. James crossed the Till by

Looking up the Till from Twizel Bridge.

a bridge at Ford, as the tourist also does, if he wishes to see the field of the famous battle. We climb to the crest of Flodden Edge; look south to the wooded hills beyond the Till, and northwards note three declivities like steps in a gigantic staircase.

The Scots were well provisioned, and should easily have

held the hill-crest against Surrey's way-worn and half-starved mutinous men. They pitched their camp on the wide level of Wooler haugh, six miles to the right of Flodden ; and on this plain Surrey challenged James to meet him, "a fair field and no favour." For once chivalry gave place to common sense in James's mind : "he would take and keep his ground at his own pleasure." But he neglected his scouting, though he had hundreds of Border riders under Home, who should never have lost touch of Surrey. That wily "auld decrepit carl in a chariot" as Pitscottie calls him, disappeared ; James probably thought that he was retiring to Berwick. Really, he was

The Ridge on which the Scottish Army was entrenched before the Battle of Flodden.

throwing himself, unseen, on James's line of communication with the north : he camped at Barmoor wood, and then re-crossed Till by Twizel bridge. Scott, in *Marmion* and else-where, blames the king for failing to see this manœuvre and discuss Surrey before his men could deploy after crossing by Twizel bridge and at Millford. But Twizel bridge you cannot see from Flodden Edge ; Sir Walter had forgotten the lie of the ground. Unseen, the English crossed and formed, advancing from the north towards the second of the three great steps in the declivity, called Branxton hill. In the early evening, *Angli se ostentant*, the English come into view. In

E 2

place of holding his ground, which he is said to have entrenched, James yielded to his impetuous temper, fired his
camp, and his men throwing off their boots, for the ground was
wet and slippery, rushed down to the Branxton plateau. "The
haggis, Cott pless her, could charge down a hill," like Dundee's
men at Killiecrankie, but the expected impetus must have
been lost before James's Highlanders under Lennox and
Argyll, his right wing, could come to sword-strokes. James's

Twizel Bridge.

right, in addition to the clans, had a force led by d'Aussi and
Bothwell, with whom may have been the ancestors of John
Knox, as the Reformer told the wild Earl, Queen Mary's lover.
The main body, the centre, under the flower of Scottish
noblesse, were with the king; who "always fought before he
had given his orders," says Ayala, the ambassador of Spain.
His left was led by Crawford and Errol; his extreme left by
Huntly with the gay Gordons; and Home with his Border
spears, mounted men.

The English front appears to have been "refused" so that Edward Howard was nearest to Home, and, slanting back·wards to the right of James, were the forces of Edmund Howard, the Admiral, the Constable, Dacre, Surrey with the rear, and the large body of Cheshire and Lancashire, led by Stanley.   The Admiral sent a galloper to bring Surrey forward ; and Home and Huntly charged Edward Howard, while Dacre's Tyneside men ran, as he advanced to support Howard.   The Borderers, fond of raiding each other, could never be trusted

The slopes at Branxton on which the Battle of Flodden was fought.

to fight each other in serious war ; they were much inter-married.   Brian Tunstal fell, Dacre stopped Huntly ; Home's men vanished like ghosts, no man knew whither ; for they appeared on the field next morning.   Probably they were plundering, but " Down wi' the Earl o' Home," says the old song of the Souters of Selkirk.   In the centre of the vanguard the Admiral and the Percys clashed with Crawford and Errol. Both leaders fell, and James threw the weight of his centre against Surrey.   To slay that general with his own hand was the king's idea of the duty of a leader.   But the English guns

mowed down his ranks, and the Scots could not work their
French artillery. The king pressed in with Herries and
Maxwell at his side; the ranks of England reeled, but the
Admiral and Dacre charged James's men in flank. "Stanley
broke Lennox and Argyll" on the king's right; the noble
leaders fell, and the nimble Highlanders rapidly made a
strategic movement in the direction of safety. Stanley did
not pursue them, but fell on James's right, which now had the
enemy on each flank and in front.

> "The stubborn spearmen still made good
> Their dark impenetrable wood"

under a rain of arrows, against the charging knights, and the
terrible bill-strokes of the English infantry.

The king was not content to remain within the hedge of
spears. Running out in advance, he fought his way to
"within a lance's length" of Surrey, so Surrey wrote; his
body was pierced with arrows, his left arm was half severed by
a bill-stroke, his neck was gashed, and he fell. James was
not a king to let his followers turn his bridle-rein; he fought
on foot, like a Paladin, and died with honour. His nobles
advanced; the spears defended the dead, and the bodies of
thirteen of his peers and of two Bishops who, like Archbishop
Turpin at Roncesvaux, died in harness, lay round him. An
episcopal ring with a great sapphire, found at Flodden, is in
the Gold Room at the British Museum.

Such was the great sorrow of Scotland; there is perhaps not
a family of gentle blood in the Lowlands which did not leave a
corpse on Branxton slope, where

> "Groom fought like noble, Squire like Knight,
> As fearlessly and well."

As matter of plain history, this honourable defeat was to my
country what, as matter of legend, the rear-guard action of
Roncesvaux has been to France. It was too late in literary
times for an epic like the *Chanson de Roland ;* the burden of

the song was left for the author of *Marmion*. But Flodden, till my own boyhood, left its mark on Scottish memories. When any national trouble befell us, people said, "There has been nothing like it since Flodden." My friend the late Lord

Sybil Grey's Well at Flodden.

Napier and Ettrick told me that when his father took him to Flodden in his boyhood, tears stood in the eyes of the senior.

This is the difference between us of the north, and you of the south. Along the Border line, my heart, so to speak, bleeds at Halidon and Homildon hills, where our men made a frontal attack, out-flanked on either hand by lines of English archers, and left heaps as high as a lance's length, of corpses on corpses, (as at Dupplin); but an Englishman passes Bannockburn "more than usual calm," and no more rejoices on the scene of the victories of his ancestors, than he is conscious of their defeats. Pinkie is nothing to him, and a bitter regret to us! Dunbar to him means nothing; to us it means the lost chance which should have been a certainty, of annihilating Cromwell's force. Our preachers ruined our opportunity, bidding Leslie go down, in accordance with some Biblical text, from his safe and commanding position, after they had purged our army of the Royalist swords.

Surrey "had his bellyful" at Flodden. In Edinburgh

> " The old men girt on their old swords,
>   And went to man the wall,"

which was hastily erected. But the English general had enough, and withdrew southwards. I visited Flodden Edge on my return from the west of Ireland, where I found the living belief in Fairies. I picked up a trifle of the faith at Flodden. The guide, a most intelligent elderly man, named Reidpath, told me this yarn: "A woman came to my brother," (I knew that he meant a woman of the Faery), "and told him to dig in such a place. He would find a stone, below it a stone pillar; and another stone, and beneath it a treasure. My brother and my father dug, found the stone, and the pillar, and the stone below—but no treasure!" Probably you will not find even this last trace of the fairy belief on the Border, but, from notes of my grandfather, it was not quite dead in his day.

Here we leave Till to those who choose to fish it up towards the Cheviots, and move up the right bank of Tweed towards its junction with Teviot.

Before reaching that point, however, there are one or two places to notice on both sides of the river—Coldstream, for example, where Leet water enters Tweed; Eden water, a few miles higher up; and, on the English side, Wark Castle.

Regarding the Leet, in order to find oneself filled with envy and with longing unutterable, it is only necessary to read Stoddart's account of the fishing to be had in his day in that curious little stream. "Of all streams that I am acquainted with," says Stoddart, "the Leet, which discharges itself into the Tweed above Coldstream, was wont, considering its size,

Bridge over the Leet, Coldstream.

to contain the largest trout. During the summer season it is a mere ditch, in many places not above four or five span in width, and, where broadest, still capable of being leapt across. The run of water is, comparatively speaking, insignificant, not exceeding on the average a cubic foot. This, however, as it proceeds, is every now and then expanded over a considerable surface, and forms a pool of some depth; in fact, the whole stream, from head to foot, pursuing, as it does, a winding course for upwards of twelve miles, is a continued chain of pools, fringed, during the summer, on both sides, with rushes and water-flags, and choked up in many parts with pickerel weed and other aquatic plants. The channel of Leet contains shell-marl, and its banks, being hollowed out beneath, afford, independent of occasional vines and tree roots, excellent shelter for trout. Not many years ago the whole course of it was infested with pike, but the visit of some otters, irrespective of the angler's art, has completely cleared them out, and thus allowed the trout, which were formerly scarce, to become more numerous. On the first occasion of my fishing Leet, which happened to be early in April 1841, before the sedge and rushes had assumed the ascendency, I captured, with the fly, twenty-six trout, weighing in all upwards of twenty-nine pounds. Of these, five at least were two-pounders, and there were few, if any, small-sized fish." On another occasion, in June 1846, Stoddart caught in the same water, in four hours, three dozen and five fish, the biggest of which weighed 3 lbs., and a dozen of the others 1 lb. apiece. This stream, in its characteristics so unlike the usual Scottish burn, is not open to the public, but it may be assumed that no such fishing is now obtainable there, any more than it is to be got elsewhere in Scotland. Once they establish themselves and make unchecked headway, pike are very hard to extirpate; it is not in every stream that one finds otters so accommodating, and so careful of the interests of anglers, as they appear to have been in Leet in Stoddart's day.

Coldstream, where Leet joins Tweed, was of old chiefly known for its ford, the first of any consequence above Berwick. It was here that the invading army of Edward the First crossed the river into Scotland in 1296; here, indeed, it was that most armies, English or Scottish, plunged into country hostile to them once they had quitted their own bank of the river; it was here that all Scottish travellers, from royalty to peasant, must halt when southward bound, and await the falling of the waters should Tweed chance to be in flood. Consequently, at

a very early date a settlement sprang up, and in it many an
historical personage has temporarily sojourned. Sir Thomas
Dick Lauder says that as late as his own day an old thatched
two storied building in the village was pointed out as the house
in which "many persons of distinction, including kings and
queens of Scotland, are enumerated by tradition as having
resided . . . . occasionally several days at a time," waiting till
the river was fordable. It was not till 1766, when Smeaton
completed his fine bridge, that any other crossing of the
stream than by the ford was possible. In pre-Reformation
times, there was in Coldstream a rich Priory of Cistercian
Nuns, not a stone of which, however, now remains. But in
its little burial ground, between the river and what used to be
the garden of the Priory, in 1834 there was dug up a great
quantity of human bones, and a stone coffin. The bones were
supposed to be probably those of various Scottish persons of
rank who fell but a short five or six miles away on the fatal
field of Flodden. Tradition tells that the Abbess of that day,
anxious to give Christian burial to her slain countrymen, caused
the bodies of many Scots of rank and birth to be borne from
the field of battle to the Priory, and there laid them to rest
in consecrated ground.

Till about 1865 there stood in the village another interesting
old house, and on the building which now occupies its site
may be read the following inscription : "Headquarters of the
Coldstream Guards, 1659 ; rebuilt, 1865." Here it was that
General Monk formed that famous regiment, than which there
is but one in the British army whose history goes further back,
none which in achievements can surpass it. In one of his
works on England at the period of the Restoration of Charles
the Second, M. Guizot, the French historian, records that
Monk "spent about three weeks at Coldstream, which was a
favourable spot for the purpose, as the Tweed was there fordable ; but he seems to have found it a dismal place to quarter
in. On his first arrival, he could get no provisions for his own

dinner, and was obliged to content himself with a quid of
tobacco. His chaplains, less easily satisfied, roamed about till
they obtained a meal at the house of the Earl of Home, near
by." This place, to which the fine instinct of those preachers
guided them, was no doubt The Hirsel, which is at no great
distance from Coldstream.

There is yet another thing for which this little town was
famed in former days. In the time of our grandsires, and
indeed, down to as late a date as 1856, when clandestine

The Cheviots from Coldstream Ferry.

weddings were prohibited by Act of Parliament, it was a common
sight to see a post-chaise come racing over Coldstream Bridge,
or, in days before a bridge existed, splashing through the water
from the English side, bearing in it some fond couple (like Mr.
Alfred Jingle and the Spinster Aunt), flying on love's wings
from stony-hearted parent or guardian. Coldstream was almost
as famous a place for run-away marriages as was Gretna Green
itself. At the former place, the ceremony was usually performed
in the toll-house at the Scottish end of the bridge, where
"priests" were always in readiness to tie up the run-away

couples, and to issue to them thereafter a Certificate of Marriage, such as the following, which is a copy of one issued in 1836 : " This is to certify that John Chambers, Husbandman, from the Broomhouse, in the Parish of Chatton, with Mary Walker from Kelso, in the Parish of Kelso, in Roxboroughshire, was married by me this Day. As witness to my hand, William Alexander, Coldstream, 15th Dec., 1836.

Witnesses' names $\begin{cases} \text{Miss Dalgleish,} \\ \text{Miss Archer.''} \end{cases}$

But though for convenience' sake, and probably for speed of dispatch, the toll-house was chiefly patronised, those who had command of money and were not unduly pressed for time could arrange to have their nuptials celebrated in less public fashion than would probably be the case at the bridge-end.   It is I believe an undoubted fact that in 1819 Lord Brougham was married in the chief inn of the village.

Those irregular marriages were in the eighteenth century a great source of trouble and annoyance to the Kirk Session of Kelso.   A good many of them at one time were celebrated by a certain Mr. Blair, whom the Privy Council had ejected from the incumbency of Coldstream in 1689 because he had refused to pray for the King and Queen, (William and Mary), and would neither read the proclamation of the Estates nor observe the national thanksgiving.   Mr. Blair, however, after the loss of his incumbency continued to live in the village, and, it was alleged, was, in the matter of these marriages sometimes over accommodating and goodnatured regarding dates ; in his certificates he did not always rigidly adhere to the true day of month or year in cases where it might be represented to him that a fictitious date would be less compromising to the contracting parties.   Mr. Blair was "sharply rebukit" by the Session.   The reverend gentleman was not in Coldstream later than 1728, and he died at Preston, in Northumberland, in 1736, at the age of eighty-five. The following is the epitaph composed on him :

> " Here lies the Reverend Thomas Blair,
>   A man of worth and merit,
> Who preached for fifty years and mair,
>   According to the spirit.
>
> He preached off book to shun offence,
>   And what was still more rare,
> He never spoke one word of sense—
>   So preachéd Tammy Blair."

In examining Scottish Border records of those times, nothing strikes one more than the power of the Kirk Sessions ; it is indeed hard to imagine a country more priest-ridden than Scotland in the eighteenth century. The "Sabbath" was then as easy to break as a hedge-sparrow's egg, and there were a thousand—to modern eyes not very heinous—ways of breaking it. What in the way of punishment may have been meted out to the unfortunate who fell asleep under the infliction of a long, dull, prosy sermon in a stuffy, ill-ventilated church on a warm summer's day, one hardly cares to conjecture, so rigidly enforced was the duty of listening to sermons ; whilst to be abroad " in time of sermon " was sin so heinous that Elders were, so to speak, specially retained to prowl around and nose out offenders. Walking on the Sabbath day—"vaguing," they called it,—was looked on with horror, and called for stern reprimand. In 1710, it was observed that sundry persons in Kelso were "guiltie of profaning the Sabbath by walking abroad in the fields after sermons," and the Session called on the parish minister to " give them a general reproof out of the pulpit the next Lord's Day, and to dehort them from so doing in time coming, with certification that the Session will take strict notice of any one guiltie of it." For less than " vaguing," however, a man might be brought before the Session. In 1710, Alexander Graemslaw of Maxwellheugh was " dilated for bringing in cabbage to his house the last Lord's Day between sermons," and was "cited to the next Session." ("Dilate" is probably less painful than it sounds). He was only "rebuked" about the cabbages : but then they fell on him and demanded an explanation of his not having been at church. Altogether they made things unpleasantly warm for Alexander. In 1708, Alexander Handiside and his son, and a woman named Jean Ker were had up for "walking to and fro on the Sabbath." At first they "compeared not" on being cited, but on a second citation Handiside "compeared," and vainly advanced the plea that his walking to and fro was occasioned by the fact that he had been attending a child who had broken a leg or an arm. He "was exhorted to be a better observer of the Sabbath." A Scot, apparently, might not upon the Scottish Sabbath draw from a pit his ox or his ass which had fallen in. This same year, "those who searched the town" discovered two small boys "playing on the Sabbath day in time of sermon." The Session dealt sternly with the hardened ruffians. Amongst other cases that one reads of there is that of Katherine Thomson. One's sympathies rather go with Katherine, who when reproved by a sleuth-hound Elder for "sitting idly at her door in time of sermon," abused her reprover. But the Session made it warm for a woman who thus not only, as they said, "profaned the Sabbath," but was guilty of "indescreet carriage to the Elder." One trembles to think how easy it was to slip into sin in those days.

But over and above this Juggernaut power of the Session, there was another weapon much used by eighteenth century ministers, whereby they kept a heavy hand on the bowed backs of their congregations. It was their habit, where the conduct, real or fancied, of any member of their flock offended them, to speak *at* the culprit during service on Sundays, and to speak at him in no uncertain voice. The practice is probably now dead, even in remote country parishes, but fifty years ago it was still a favourite weapon in the hands of old-fashioned ministers, and in the eighteenth century it seems to have been in almost universal use. The Reverend Mr. Ramsay, minister of Kelso from 1707 till his death in 1749, was a dexterous and unsparing wielder of this ecclesiastical flail. It chanced once that there "sat under" him—as we say in Scotland—a Highlander, a man who had deserted from the ranks of the rebel army in the '15, and had afterwards managed to get appointed to a post in the Excise at Kelso. This man's seat in church was in the front pew of the gallery, immediately facing Mr. Ramsay, and his every movement, therefore, was likely to catch the minister's eye. Now, the exciseman had a habit which greatly annoyed Mr. Ramsay. As soon as the sermon commenced, the Highlander produced a pencil, with which he proceeded to make marks on a slip of paper. He may, perhaps, have been making calculations not unconnected with his duties as exciseman,—a scandalous proceeding when he should have been all ears for the Word as expounded by the minister ; or, again, on the other hand he may really have been devoutly attentive to the sermon, and engaged in making notes on it,—a thing perhaps not over and above likely in an ex-Highland rebel. In any case he annoyed Mr. Ramsay, and one day the irritation became acute. Pausing in his discourse in order to give emphasis to his words, and looking straight at the exciseman, he cried : "My brethren, I tell ye, except ye be born again, it is as impossible for you to enter the Kingdom of Heaven as it is for a Hielander no to be a thief! Man wi' the keel-o-vine," he thundered, "do ye hear *that*?" (For the benefit of non-Scottish readers it may be necessary to explain that a "keel-o-vine" is a pencil).

A few miles above Coldstream, after a course of about four and twenty miles, the beautiful little Eden Water joins Tweed. Its capabilities as a trout stream are spoken of elsewhere in this volume, and the little river is now mentioned only to record a tragedy of unusual nature which occurred in it in the earlier half of the nineteenth century. Two young ladies, sisters of the then proprietor of Newton Don, a beautiful estate on the right bank of Eden, had come from Edinburgh to pass the summer and autumn at their brother's house. With them was a friend, a Miss Ramsay. It chanced that one afternoon these three young ladies were walking along the banks of the river, on the side opposite to Newton Don. They had strolled farther than at starting had been their intention, and time had slipped past unnoticed, and while they still had some distance to go on their return way, they were surprised by the sound of the house bell ringing for dinner. Now, a little below the spot where they then were, it was possible to cross the river by stepping stones, an easy, and to every appearance a perfectly safe way by which anybody beyond the age of childhood might gain the other side, without much risk even of wetting a shoe. The three girls, accordingly, started to go over by these stones. The water was low and clear, the weather fine; there had been no thunderstorm that might have been capable of bringing down from the hills a sudden spate; the crossing could have been made a million times in such circumstances without peril greater than is to be met with in stepping across a moorland drain. Yet now the one thing happened that made it dangerous.

At some little distance up stream there stood a mill, the water power of which was so arranged, that if the sluice of the mill should for any reason be suddenly closed, that body of water which normally flowed down the mill dam after turning the wheel, was discharged into the river some way above the stepping stones. In the narrow channel of the Eden at this point, this sudden influx of water was quite sufficient to raise the stream's level to a height most dangerous to anyone who at the time might be in the act of crossing by these stones. Unhappily, at the exact moment when the three poor girls were stepping cautiously and with none too certain foot from stone to stone, and had reached to about mid-channel, the miller, ignorant of their situation and unable from where he stood to command a view to any distance down stream, closed his sluice. Down Eden's bed surged a wave crested like some inrushing sea that sweeps far up a shingly beach. In an instant the three girls,

evacuations, burnings, restorations, slaughters," that has not
been amply borne out by its history, many of them again
and again.   David took it in 1135, but restored it to England
in the following year.   Twice afterwards, the same monarch
vainly attempted to take it by storm, but finally, after the fall of
Norham, he reduced it by means of a long blockade.   After
this it remained in Scottish possession till 1157, when England
again seized, and at great expense rebuilt, the castle.   In 1216
it was destroyed by fire ; in 1318, reduced by King Robert the
Bruce ; in 1385, taken by storm by the Scots.   Then in 1419,
William Halliburton of Fast Castle surprised the English and
took the castle, putting all the garrison to the sword.   But the
same fate was dealt out to the Scots themselves a few months
later ; Sir Robert Ogle and his men gained access to the
building by way of a sewer from the kitchen, which opened on
the bank of Tweed.   Creeping up this unsavoury passage,
they in their turn surprised and slew the Scotsmen.   Again in
1460, after the widow of James II. had dismantled Roxburgh
and razed it almost to the foundations, the Scots forded
Tweed and retook Wark.   But they did not hold it long.
More valuable now to the English than ever it had been before,
owing to the loss of Roxburgh, it was partially repaired by
them, only, however, to be again pulled down by the Scots
before the battle of Flodden ; after which Surrey for the last
time restored and strengthened it.   After the accession of
James VI. to the throne of England, Wark, like other Border
strongholds, began to fall into decay ; the need for them was
gone.   Buchanan, the historian, has left a description of Wark
as it was in 1523, when he was with the Scottish army at
Coldstream, which then besieged it.   " In the innermost area,"
he says, " was a tower of great strength and height ; this was
encircled by two walls, the outer including the larger space,
into which the inhabitants of the country used to fly with their
cattle, corn, and flocks in time of war ; the inner of much
smaller extent, but fortified more strongly by ditches and

towers. It had a strong garrison, good store of artillery and ammunition, and other things necessary for defence."

On this occasion the Scottish commander sent against the castle a picked force of Scottish and French troops, supported by heavy siege artillery, all under the command of Ker of Fernihurst. "The French," says Sir Walter Scott, "carried the outer enclosure at the first assault, but were dislodged by the garrison setting fire to the corn and straw laid up in it. The besiegers soon recovered their ground, and by their cannon effected a breach in the inner wall. The French with great intrepidity mounted the breach, sustaining great loss from the shot of that part of the garrison who possessed the keep; and being warmly received by the forces that defended the inner vallum, were obliged to retire after great slaughter. The attack was to have been renewed on the succeeding day, but a fall of rain in the night, which swelled the Tweed and threatened to cut off the retreat of the assailants to the main army, and the approach of the Earl of Surrey, who before lay at Alnwick with a large force, obliged the Duke [of Albany] to relinquish his design and return into Scotland."

Wark, it is said, once belonged to the Earl of Salisbury, and the tale is told how, in the time of King David Bruce, a gallant deed was done by Sir William Montague, Lord Salisbury's governor of the castle. King David, returning from a successful foray into England, passed close to Wark, making for the ford over Tweed at Coldstream, and his rear-guard, heavily laden with plunder, was seen from the castle walls by Montague's garrison. The rear was straggling. Such an opportunity was not to be wasted. The Governor, with forty mounted men, made a sudden dash, slew a great number of the Scots, cut off one hundred and sixty horses laden with booty, and brought them safely into the castle. David instantly assaulted the place, but without success; and he thereupon determined to take it by siege. There was but one way whereby the place might be saved; a message must be conveyed to King Edward III.,

who was then on his way north with a great army. The risk
was great; failure meant death, and the castle was closely
invested. Sir William himself took the risk. In a night dark
and windy, with rain falling in torrents, the Governor dashed
out on a swift horse and cut his way through the Scottish lines
before almost the alarm had been raised; and so rapidly did
Edward advance on hearing of the plight of the garrison, that
the rear of the Scottish force was barely over the ford before
the English van had reached the southern bank of Tweed. It
is of this occasion that the more or less mythical tale of King
Edward and the Countess of Salisbury's Garter is told. In the
great Hall of Wark Castle the story finds a dubious resting
place.

The countless war-like events that have taken place in and
around Wark give to the place an interest which is perhaps
hardly appreciated by the majority of us, and that interest is
largely added to when one thinks of the many characters noted
in history who from time to time sojourned within its walls.
King Stephen lay here with a large army in 1137; Henry III
remained in the castle for some time with his queen in 1255;
in 1296 Edward I paid it a visit; Edward II mustered here his
army in 1314 before his crushing defeat at Bannockburn, and,
as already stated, Edward III, after he had driven off the Scottish
marauding force, was entertained here for a time by the Countess
of Salisbury.

Wark, one thinks, would be an ideal place in which to
conduct excavations,—though, indeed, a little in that line has
already been undertaken. In the volume for 1863–68 of the
"Proceedings of the Berwickshire Naturalists' Club," it is
recorded that a good many years ago Mr. Richard Hodgson
had traced a wide sewer to the north of the castle, opening on
to the river bank. This sewer is said to be so wide that it
might easily have been used for the passage of men or material.
Probably it was by this hidden way that Sir Robert Ogle in 1419
forced his way into the interior. But if the opening was so wide,

CHAPTER III

KELSO, ROXBURGH, TEVIOT, KALE, AND OXNAM

COMING now to Kelso,—with Melrose the most pleasing of the towns on Tweed,—we pass the meeting of the waters of Tweed and its largest affluent, Teviot. Kelso has a fine airy square, good streets, and an air of quiet gentility, neighboured as it is by Floors, the palatial seat of the Duke of Roxburghe, and by the trees of Springwood Park, the residence of Sir George Douglas.

We are now in the region of the clan of Ker of Cessford, from which the ducal family descends: while the Lothian branch descends from the Kers of Fernihurst. The name, Ker, is said to mean "left handed," and like the left-handed men of the tribe of Benjamin, the Kers were a turbulent and grasping clan, often at deadly feud with their neighbours and rivals, the Scotts of Buccleugh. These, with the Douglases, for long predominant, were the clans that held the Marches, and freely raided the English Borderers, while they fought like fiends among themselves.

It is in the early sixteenth century that the chiefs of the two branches of Ker, or Kerr, and of the Scotts, become more and more prominent in history, both as warriors and politicians. From these Houses the Wardens of the Border were often chosen, and were not to be trusted to keep order; being more disposed to use sword and axe. Within a century the chiefs

throve to Earl's estate, and finally "warstled up the brae" to
Dukedoms. Meanwhile the Douglases, for long the most
powerful House in Scotland, the rivals of the Crown, were
crushed by James II, and of the Douglases, Sir George, of
Springwood Park, is descended from the House of Cavers,
(on Teviot, below Hawick), scions sprung from Archibald,
natural son of the Earl of Douglas who fell at Otterburne (1388)

Floors Castle from Kelso.

and is immortal in the ballad. The whole land is full of scenes
made famous by the adventures of these ancient clans; they
may be tracked by blood from Hermitage Castle to the dowie
dens of Yarrow and the Peel Tower on the Douglas burn.

Sir Herbert Maxwell, in " The Story of the Tweed " (p. 139)
not unnaturally laments the " sadly suburban " name of
Springwood Park, standing where it ought not, in place of the

ancient name of Maxwell, originally "Maccus whele," "the pool of Maccus," on Tweed.   Maccus was a descendant of the primeval Maccus, who, before the Norman Conquest, signed himself, or was described, as *Maccus Archipirata*, "the leading

Kelso.

pirate."   To a later Maccus David I gave the salmon fishing at Kelso; the pool, called "Maccus whele" became Maxwell, and the lairds "de Maxwell."   The Maxwells moved to the western Border to Caerlaverock and into Galloway; and of all

this history only the name, " Max wheel," of a salmon cast
below the pretty bridge of Kelso, is left.

The name Kelso is of Cymric origin : *calch myaydd*, "Chalkhill."
To be sure, as the man said of the derivation of *jour* from *dies*,
the name is *diablement changé en route*. The ruins of Kelso
Abbey are the chief local remains of the Ages of Faith.   When
David I, not yet king, brought French Benedictines to Scotland,
he settled them in Ettrick Forest.   Here they raised the *schele
chirche* : the Monastery, on a steep hill above Ettrick, (now
Selkirk), and here they " felt the breeze down Ettrick break "
with its chill showers, and wept as they remembered pleasant
Picardy ; the climate of Selkirk being peculiarly bitter.   David,
when king, moved his Benedictines to the far more comfortable
region of Kelso, or " Calkow," where they began to build in
1128.   The style of their church is late Norman, and the tower
was used in war as a keep in the fierce wars of Henry VIII.
The place was gutted and the town burned by Dacre, in 1523 ;
and suffered again from Norfolk, in 1542, and Hertford in 1545.
Henry VIII chivalrously destroyed this part of the Border
from the cottage to the castles of the Kers and the pleasant
holy places of the Church, during the childhood of his
kinswoman, Mary Stuart, Queen of Scots.   His aim was always
to annex Scotland ; and, of course, to introduce the Gospel.
In 1545, after overcoming the garrison of the church tower,
Hertford's men wrecked the whole place, leaving little more
than we see to-day ; though that little is much compared with
what the Reformers have left of St. Andrews and Lindores.

Kelso saw more than enough of very ugly fighting in those
days ; not even her monks stood aloof when blows fell fast
and their cloisters were threatened.   In 1545, twelve monks
and ninety laymen gallantly held the Abbey against the English,
and when at length Hertford's guns created a practicable breach,
they retreated to the church tower.   Hill Burton says, in his
History of Scotland, that then "the assault was given to the
Spaniards, but, when they rushed in, they found the place

Kelso Abbey.

cleared. The nimble garrison had run to the strong square
tower of the church, and there again they held out. Night
came before they could be dislodged from this their last citadel,

so the besiegers had to "leave the assault till the morning,
setting a good watch all night about the house, which was not
so well kept but that a dozen of the Scots in the darkness of the
night escaped by ropes out at back windows and corners, with
no little danger of their lives. When the day came, and the
steeple eftsoons assaulted, it was immediately won, and as many
Scots slain as were within." So may Kelso Abbey be said to
have been finally wrecked; though, fifteen years later, the
Reformers did their own little bit of work in the same line.

Kelso. Teviot in foreground.

The Abbey buildings, however, or part of them, continued to
be used long after this date; from 1649 to 1771 the transept,
roughly ceiled over, served as the parish church, but it was
given up in the year last mentioned owing to a portion of the
roof falling in whilst service was being held. The kirk "skailed"
that day in something under record time; Thomas the
Rhymer's prediction that "the kirk should fall at the fullest"
was in the people's mind, and they stood not much upon the
order of their going.

Kelso was the most southern point reached by Montrose in

his efforts to join hands with Charles the First after his year of victories. The Border chiefs who had promised aid all deserted him ; the Gordons and Colkitto had left him, and he marched north to the junction of Ettrick and Tweed and the fatal day of Philiphaugh. In 1745, Kelso for two days saw Prince Charlie, in his feint against General Wade ; from Kelso he turned to Carlisle, his actual, and by no fault of his, hopeless line of invasion of England. The Prince's own strategy, as he wrote to his father, was " to have a stroke for't," as near the

Meeting of Tweed and Teviot near Kelso.

Border and as promptly as possible. He therefore wished to cross the Tweed near Kelso, and beat up the quarters of the senile Marshal Wade at Newcastle. If he discussed Wade to the same tune as he had settled Cope, English Jacobites might join him. Holding Newcastle, he could thereby admit French reinforcements, while, if defeated, he was near the sea, and had a better route of retreat than if he were defeated going by Carlisle and the western route, in the heart of England. His council of chiefs, unhappily, forced him to take the western route. Halting at Kelso, he sent the best of the Border cavaliers, Henry Ker of Graden, to make a feint on Wade ; he rode as far as Wooler, near Flodden. Next day the Prince marched up Teviot, and up Jed, to Jedburgh, with the flower of the fighting clans ; then up Rule water, another of the tributaries of Tweed, to Haggiehaugh on the Liddell, and so into England near Carlisle. Of old he would have picked up the Kers, Elliots, and Scotts ; Haggiehaugh, where he slept, is Larriston, the home of the Elliot chief, "the Lion of Liddesdale." But the tartans waved and the bagpipes shrilled in vain, and the Blue Bonnets did not go over the Border. One of the writers of this book possesses the armchair in which the Prince rested at Haggiehaugh.

It was at Kelso, one remembers, that Sir Walter Scott first met James Ballantyne, with whose fortunes his own were afterwards to become so inextricably blended. Scott was then but a growing boy ; his health had been giving trouble, and he was sent by his father to stay for six months with an aunt "who resided in a small house, situated very pleasantly in a large garden to the eastward of the churchyard of Kelso, which extended down to the Tweed." During the time of Scott's stay, Ballantyne and he were class-mates under Mr. Lancelot Whale, master of the Kelso Grammar School. The acquaintance then formed was never quite broken off, and all the world knows the story of its outcome.

We now follow Prince Charles into

> " Pleasant Teviotdale, a land
> Made blithe with plough and harrow,"

a rich, well-wooded grassy land, cultivated of old under the Benedictines of Kelso.

Little more than a mile from that town, by the road leading to St. Boswells up Tweed's southern bank, on a wooded ridge overhanging Teviot and separated from Tweed by but a narrow flat haugh, stands all that is left of Roxburgh Castle,—a few isolated portions of massive wall defended on the north and

east sides by a ditch. At the west end a very deep cutting
divides this ridge from the high ground farther to the west.

Ruins of Roxburgh Castle.

Ditch and cutting apparently were in former times flooded
with water run in from Teviot, for even as late as the end of
the eighteenth century remains of a weir or dam could still be

seen stretching across the river.   No trace of it now remains.
Those who razed the castle took care that the dam should be
broken beyond repair, and countless winter floods have long
since swept away the little that may have been left.   Close
to the castle probably stood the once important town of
Roxburgh, with its streets and churches, its convent and
schools, and its Mint, where many of our Scottish coins
were struck.   Where are those streets and churches now?
Not a trace of them is to be found.   The houses were
of wood, no doubt, and easily demolished, but the
churches, the convent, and the Mint, one would expect to
have been of build substantial enough to leave some indication
of where they had stood.   Roxburgh, more than any other
Border town, experienced the horrors of war.   Her castle was
one of four great Scottish strongholds—Edinburgh, Stirling,
Berwick, Roxburgh—and it mattered little whether it were
temporarily held by England or by Scotland, on the inhabitants of the town fell the brunt of those horrors.   Castle and
town were continually being besieged, continually changing
hands, sometimes by stratagem—as when on Shrove Tuesday,
1314, the Good Sir James Douglas, with sixty men, surprised
the garrison and took the castle from the English ;—sometimes
by siege and assault, as in 1460, when James II was killed by
the bursting of "the Lion," one of his own clumsy pieces of
ordnance, a gun similar to that ancient weapon, " Mons Meg,"
which is still to be seen in Edinburgh Castle.   To the Queen
of James II was due the complete destruction of Roxburgh as
a stronghold.   The castle had been for something like a hundred
years continuously in England's hands,—a rankling sore in
Scotland's body.   The knife must be used unflinchingly.
Under her orders, therefore, when the castle was captured
after James's death, the place was thrown down and made
entirely untenable ; and probably at this time also the dam
across Teviot was cut, thus permanently emptying fosse and
ditch.   Roxburgh ceased then almost entirely to be a place of

strength, and time and decay have wiped her out ; no man may say where stood any portion of a town which, in point of population, was once the fourth most important burgh in Scotland. Of the last siege, and the death of James, the historian Pitscottie writes : "The King commanded the souldeouris and men of weir to assault the castell, but the Inglischemen defendit so walieiantlie within, the seige appeirit so to indure langer nor was beleiffit, quhairthrow the King determinat to compell them that was within the house be lang tairrie to rander and gif it ower." Reinforcements at this time arrived, "which maid the King so blyth that he commanded to chairge all the gunnis to gif the castell ane new wollie. But quhill this prince, mair curieous nor becam him or the majestie of ane King, did stand neir hand by the gunneris quhan the artaillyerie was dischargeand, his thie bane was doung in twa with ane piece of ane misframit gun that brak in the schutting, be the quhilk he was strickin to the grund and dieit haistilie thereof, quhilk grettumlie discuragit all his nobill gentlemen and freindis that war standand aboot him." Near at hand on the farther bank of Tweed stands, or until lately stood, an old thorn tree which is said to mark the spot where the King fell.

The ancient Roxburgh has utterly disappeared ;

> " Fallen are thy towers, and where the palace stood
> In gloomy grandeur waves yon hanging wood ;
> Crushed are thy halls, save where the peasant sees
> One moss-clad ruin rise between the trees."

But there lingers yet one relic of the days when her Markets and Trysts were famed throughout the country. St. James's Fair, which was held at Roxburgh as long ago as the days of King David I, is still kept each August in the pleasant haugh by the ruins of the castle, between Teviot and Tweed. There, on a little eminence, the Town Clerk of Jedburgh each year reads this Proclamation :

G

" OYEZ,   OYEZ,   OYEZ.

Whereas the Fair of St. James is to be held this ——th day of August
19——, and is to continue for the space of eight days from and after this
proclamation.   Therefore, in name and authority of Our Sovereign King
George V, by the Grace of God of the United Kingdom of Great Britain
and Ireland, King, Defender of the Faith, and in name and authority
of the Honourable the Provost and Bailies of the Royal Borough of
Jedburgh, and in name and authority of a High and Potent Prince the
Duke of Roxburghe, and his Bailie of Kelso, I make due and lawful
proclamation that no person or persons shall presume to trouble or molest
the present Fair, or offer any injury one to another, or break the King's
peace,—Prohibiting all old Feuds and new Feuds, or the doing of anything to disquiet the said Fair, under the highest pains of law.   As also
that no person or persons make any private bargains prejudicial to the
customs and Proprietors of said Fair,—Certifying those who contravene
any part of said customs that they will be prosecuted and fined according
to law.

"GOD SAVE THE KING."

In these degenerate days, the Fair lasts but one day in place of
eight, and Feuds, new or old, are unknown.   But not so very
long ago the rivalry at this Fair of the neighbouring towns of
Kelso and Jedburgh was very bitter.   Roxburgh had ceased to
be, indeed, but the Fair survived, and it chanced that the
Provost and Bailies of Jedburgh—like Roxburgh, a Royal
burgh,—having under some old charter acquired a right to
"proclaim" the Fair and collect the market dues, duly came
in state each August in order to exercise this privilege at the
ancient stance.   Now, Kelso in the course of time became a
larger and more important town than Jedburgh; it is, moreover, in close proximity to the ground on which the Fair is held,
whereas Jedburgh was no better than a foreign land, miles
removed—ten, at least,—from Roxburgh.   Hence Kelso resented what it considered to be an outrage on the part of her
officious neighbour.   What was Jedburgh that she should oust
them from those market tolls and dues ! A beggarly interloper,
no less ! The outcome of such a frame of mind was generally
what might be expected amongst men whose forebears for many

hundreds of years had been fierce fighters. As the procession
of Jedburgh magistrates, all in their robes and escorted by a
compact body of townsmen, advanced towards the place of
proclamation, taunts of " Pride and Poverty ! "—" Pride and
Poverty ! " were hurled at their ears by the irritated men of
Kelso. " Doo Tairts an' Herrin' Pies ! " fiercely retorted
Jedburgh's inhabitants. It is difficult now-a-days to see where
came in the sting of the original taunt, or the appositeness of
the " Countercheck Quarrelsome." But in those old days they
were amply sufficient. Some man, more hasty, or less sober,
than his neighbour would follow up the taunt by a push or a
blow, and St. James's Fair was speedily as lively a spot as now
could be any Fair even in Ireland. Kelso and Jedburgh were
" busy at each other " ; and sometimes one prevailed, sometimes
the other. An attempt that Kelso once made to hold the Fair
on its own side of the river was utterly defeated ; Jedburgh
marched across the bridge and made things so warm that the
experiment of shifting the venue of St. James's Fair has never
been repeated.

No doubt, when Roxburgh ceased to be a Royal Burgh, its
rights naturally devolved on Jedburgh, the only other Royal
Burgh in the country. But Jedburgh tradition tells of a time when
the English, taking advantage of heavy floods which prevented
Kelso men from crossing the river, raided the Fair and carried
off rich plunder. Then Jedburgh, coming to the rescue, smote
the English and recaptured the booty, and for their gallant
conduct were awarded those privileges which they still exercise.

The Kelso taunt of " Pride and Poverty " may possibly have
originated from a custom to which the economical burgesses of
Jedburgh seem to have been addicted. In a letter written in
1790, Sir Walter Scott mentions that when he himself visited
the Fair in that year, he found that, there not being in possession of the men of Jedburgh enough riding boots to accommodate
all the riders in the procession, the magistrates had ruled that
only the outside men of each rank should wear boots, or, rather

each a boot on his *outer* leg. Thus, as the men rode in threes,
one pair of boots would be sufficient to maintain the dignity of
each rank,—a device worthy of Caleb Balderstone himself. It
is easy enough to assign an origin to " Pride and Poverty," but
the local custom which gave occasion for the bitter taunt of
" Doo tairts and Herrin' Pies " is baffling. There are many
such taunts in the Border, hurled by town at rival town.
" Selkirk craws," is the reproach flung at that burgh by its
neighbour, Galashiels ; and

> " Galashiels Herons, lockit in a box,
> Daurna show their faces, for Selkirk gamecocks,"

is, or was, the jibe that stung Gala lads to fury.

Before quitting the subject of Roxburgh, it may be of interest
to mention that in the churchyard of the present village of that
name there is a gravestone to the memory of the original
of Edie Ochiltree, the bluegown of Sir Walter's *Antiquary*.
Andrew Gemmels was his name. He died in 1793 at Roxburgh
Newtown, a farm on the banks of Tweed a few miles from
Roxburgh, at the great age of one hundred and six.

The first tributary received by Teviot on the right bank is
the Kale Water, running through the parish of Linton, which
was in King David's time an appanage of Kelso Abbey. The
church has been restored, but the walls are, like those of
Kelso, Norman work, and in the porch is an enigmatic piece
of sculptors' work ; apparently somebody is fighting a dragon
—Sir Herbert Maxwell suggests St. George, but St. Michael
was the more orthodox dragon slayer. About the object grew
an aetiological myth ; a Somerville of old times

> " Slew the Worm of Wormes glen
> And wan all Lintoun parochine."

The dragon-slaying story is found in most parts of the
world, from Troy to Dalry in the Glenkens. Here the Worm
twisted himself round the Mote, or tumulus (apparently the
basis of an old fort), and was killed by the local blacksmith.

In 1522–1533, Linton tower was among the scores of such
Border Keeps which the English destroyed. They could hold
their own against a Border raid; not in face of a regular
English army. Roxburghshire was not so deeply tainted by
Covenanting principles as Galloway, Lanarkshire, and the
south-west, Ayrshire and Renfrewshire. Covenanters needed
wild hills and wild wastes. They are said to have held conventicles in a deep glen of Kale; but, as a rule, they knew
enough to preach in places of wide outlook, where they could
detect the approach of parties of dragoons. In the bed of a
burn they would be at great disadvantage.

A tower more interesting than that of Linton, namely
Ormistoun, fell when Linton fell; but it must have been
rebuilt, for here, in Mary Stuart's day, dwelt the Black Laird
of Ormistoun, James, with Hob, his brother, two of Bothwell's
most cruel and desperate "Lambs." The Black Laird was
with Bothwell, Hay of Talla (on upper Tweed), and one of
Bothwell's own clan, Hepburn of Bowton, when they placed
the powder under Darnley's chamber in Kirk-o'-Field
(February 9–10, 1567), and so, in the feeling words of
Bothwell, "sent him fleeing through the air." After doing
another deed as treacherous as this murder, the Black Laird
was taken, tried, and hanged in 1573. Bothwell was Warden
of the Border, which he ruled from Hermitage Castle on the
Liddel water, and all these loose Border lairds rode and slew
at his bidding. They had probably, in that twilight of faith,
no religion in particular; Catholicism lingered in the shape of
oaths, Calvinism was not yet well settled in these regions.
But, probably in prison, the Black Laird "got religion." He
professed to be of the Elect, and confident of his salvation,
while he drew a dark enough picture of life among lairds of
his quality. On the day of his hanging he said, "With God I
hope this night to sup. . . . Of all men on the earth I have
been one of the proudest and most high-minded, and most
filthy of my body. But specially, I have shed innocent blood

of one Michael Hunter with my own hands. Alas, therefore, because the said Michael, having me lying on my back, having a pitchfork in his hand, might have slain me if he pleased, but did it not, which of all things grieves me most in conscience. Within these seven years I never saw two good men, nor one good deed, but all kinds of wickedness."

This wretch, once on his feet, must have butchered some poor hind who had spared him. In reading Pitcairn's *Criminal Trials,* and the Register of Privy Council for the period of the Reformation, we find private war, murder, and rapine to have been almost weekly occurrences, from the Upper Tweed to the Esk. The new Gospel Light made the darkness visible, and we see robberies and vendettas among the dwellers in the peel towers, of which the empty shells stand beside every burn in the pleasant lands then clouded with smoke from blazing barn and tower and cottage. The later Ormistouns had "particularly deadly feud" with the Kers of Cessford; the Kers annexed their lands, and the last Ormistoun was a public hangman; the ancestral Orm was a flourishing and pious gentleman of the twelfth century, a bene-factor of the early monks of Melrose. Meanwhile, the castle of Cessford, the ancestral hold of that line, is not far from a place called Morbattle in the Black Laird's day, and now, more pleasantly, Morebattle. The name has no connection either with festivity or feud, and "More" is not the Celtic *mor*, "great." "More" is "mere," a lake, and "botl" is Anglo-Saxon, "a dwelling." Cessford Castle had the name to be only second to Bothwell's castle of Dunbar, and Logan of Restalrig's eyrie on a jutting rock above the sea, Fastcastle. In the great English raid of 1523, "Dand Ker," Sir Andrew, the head of the clan, rather feebly surrendered the place, which was secure in walls fourteen feet thick.

An interesting find was made at Cessford in 1858. Whilst excavating, a few yards from the north wall of the castle, a workman unearthed a very fine old sword, and a dagger, both in fair preservation. The dagger measured about twenty-six inches, and bore on its blade the Scottish Thistle, surmounted by a crown. The sword was basket-hilted, richly carved and embossed in silver. It measured forty inches in length ; on one side of the blade was the Scottish Crown ; on the other, the date 1511.

It was a Ker of Cessford, tradition tells, who in 1622 tried to carry off the goods and gear of Hobbie Hall of Haughhead, father of the famous Covenanter, Henry Hall. Hobbie, apparently, was quite able to take care of himself, as is testified by a large stone which stands on a knoll amid trees, near Kale water, on which is carved :

> " Here Hoby Hall boldly maintained his right
> 'Gainst reef plain force armed w. lawless might
> For twenty pleughs harnessed in all their gear
> Could not this valiant noble heart make fear
> But w. his sword he cut the formost soam
> In two : hence drove both pleughs and pleughmen home."
>
>   1622.

The stone was repaired and restored in 1854 by Lady John Scott.

Higher up than Kale comes Oxnam (locally, Ousenam) Water, which joins Teviot hard by Crailing. Once a nice trout stream, there is not left at this day much to tempt the angler whose dreams are of giant fish, though doubtless many a " basket " can be caught of fingerlings. In none of the Border streams, unhappily, is any restriction made as regards the size of the fish that may be taken. Everything goes into the creel of the fisher with worm in "drummly" waters, and of the holiday sportsman ; moved by no compunctions, trammelled by no absurd qualms,—to them a fish is a fish ; and as the latter, at least, probably never even sees a big trout, he attaches vast importance to the capture of a "Triton of the minnows." The writer, who had one day fished a Border river with all the little skill at his command, and had succeeded neither with dry fly

nor with wet in capturing anything worthy to be kept, once
came upon a sportsman of this holiday breed, rigged out with
all the latest appliances which should inevitably lure the wiliest
of trout from his native element. He "had had a splendid
day," he said, in reply to enquiries. "What had he got them
with? Oh–h, Fly." But *what* fly, he would not say. It was
just " FLY." "Might he see the basket?" the baffled enquirer
asked. Proudly the lid was thrown back, and the contents
displayed—a basket half filled with parr, and with trout, not
one of which could have been six inches in length. Thus are
the streams depleted.

It is a pleasant valley, that of the Oxnam. Across it runs
the old Roman Road,—in days not very remote a favourite
camping place of gipsies,—and up the valley to the south lies
that noble sweep of blue hills, the Cheviots, smiling and friendly
enough in summer, but dour and forbidding when the north-
east blast of winter strikes their blurred and gloomy faces.

Did those "muggers" and "tinklers," who of old frequented
the Roman Road that runs south over Teviot and Jed and
Oxnam, and away over the Cheviots down into Rede valley
past Bremenium (High Rochester), did they ever come upon
buried treasure or hoarded coins, one wonders. It is not many
years since a well-known Professor, as he sat resting one day
by the side of the old Road a little farther south than Oxnam
valley, idly pushed his walking stick into a rabbit hole close to
where he was seated. A few scrapes with the point of the
stick, and something chinked and fell; then another, and
another. But this buried treasure consisted only of copper
coins, a vast number, none very rare; and no farther search
revealed anything of value. Yet there must be plenty along
that route, if one could but chance upon the proper spots.
And surely, wherever there befell one of those countless fights
or skirmishes that were for ever taking place in these Border
hills, both in the days of the Romans and since, there must lie
buried weapons. At Bloodylaws, up Oxnam, for instance. The

name is suggestive ; but what occurred there, one cannot say—
though there is the vague tradition of a mighty battle that left
Oxnam for three days running red with blood.   The country
people, if you enquire from them the name of that hill, pronounce it with bated breath ;—"Bluidylaws," they say in
lowered voice.   But I doubt that their tone is less the effect
of old unhappy tradition telling how some great slaughter took
place here, than the fact that "bluidy" is a word banned by
the polite.   This "three days red with blood," too, is an
expression curiously common in the account given by country
folk of any battle of which they may have local tradition.   You
will find it used in connection with at least half a dozen other
places in the Border-land besides Bloodylaws ; and in the ballad
of "The Lads of Wamphray" there occurs the line : "When
the Biddes-burn ran three days blood."   Wamphray is in
Annandale, and the fight alluded to was between the John-
stons and the Crichtons in 1593.   But the affair was a mere
skirmish ; "three days blood" is but a figure of speech in this
and probably in most other instances.   Still, on a spur of
Bloodylaws there exists a well-defined circular camp, and there
may be foundation for the local tradition of some grim slaughter.

CHAPTER IV

JEDBURGH, AND THE JED

Two or three miles up Teviot from the junction of Oxnam Water, we come to Jed, a beautiful stream, on whose banks dreams the pleasant county town where, close on ninety years ago, they cried that cry of which they do not now like to think—"Burke Sir Walter!"

In all the Border there stands no place more picturesquely situated than Jedburgh, nor in historical interest can any surpass it. And though its ancient castle, and the six strong towers that once defended the town, have long since vanished, there remain still the noble ruins of its magnificent abbey, and other relics of the past, less noticeable but hardly less interesting; whilst the surrounding countryside brims over with the beauty of river, wood, and hill.

History gives no very definite information as to the date at which first took place the building of a castle at Jedburgh, but it appears certain that as early as the year 950 A.D. there existed in these parts some great stronghold, if, at least, " Judanbyrig "—where, when he had suppressed an insurrection in Northumbria, King Edred of England confined the rebel Archbishop of York—may be identified with " Jedburgh." Probably, however, there was in this neighbourhood a castle of sorts long prior to the date above mentioned, for both " Geddewrdes," or " Jedworths," the old and the new, were known

settlements before the expiry of the earlier half of the ninth
century, and in those turbulent days no community was rash
enough to plant itself in hamlet or town except under the
protecting shield of castle or strong place of arms. In any
case, before the end of the eleventh century, there certainly
existed at Jedburgh a castle of formidable strength, which at
frequent intervals continued to be used by the Scottish kings
as a royal residence. Here, in 1165, died Malcolm the
Maiden. From Jedworth was issued many a Charter by

Jedburgh from the Park.

Malcolm's predecessor, David I, by William the Lion, by
Alexander II. Here, too, the queen of Alexander III bore
him a son in the year 1264; and here at a masque held after
Alexander's second marriage in 1285, appeared and vanished
the grizzly skeleton that danced a moment before the king,
threading its ghastly way through the ranks of dismayed guests;
frightened women shrank screaming from its path, men brave
to face known dangers yet fell back from this horror, hurriedly
crossing themselves. An evil omen, they said, a presage of
misfortune or of death to the highest in the land. And surely

the portent was borne out, for less than six months saw
Scotland mourning the violent death of her King.

Like its not distant neighbour, the more famed castle of
Roxburgh, Jedburgh castle as time went on became a stronghold continually changing hands ; to-day garrisoned by Scots,
to-morrow held by English, taken and retaken again and again,
too strong and of importance too great to be anything but a
continuous bone of contention between the two nations, yet
more often, and for longer periods, in English than in
Scottish keeping.   When in the summer of the year 1316, King
Robert the Bruce went to Ireland, Sir James Douglas was one
of the wardens left by him in charge of the Scottish Kingdom.
Jedburgh Castle, probably with a garrison far from strong, was
then in English keeping.   Douglas established himself at
Lintalee, little more than a mile up the river from Jedburgh,
where, by throwing across the neck of a promontory between
the river and a precipitous glen, fortifications which even
now are not quite destroyed, he converted a post of great
natural strength into a position almost unassailable.   Here, or
in the immediate neighbourhood, in 1317 he inflicted two
severe defeats on separate bodies of English troops, detach-
ments from a larger army under the Earl of Arundel.   As the
outcome of these victories, Jedburgh Castle was probably
regained by the Scots, for the English monks in Jedburgh
Abbey were expelled by their Scottish brethren in February,
1318, a step they would scarcely have dared to attempt had an
English garrison still been in the castle.   In 1320 town and
castle were bestowed by the Bruce on Sir James Douglas, and
five years later the grant was confirmed, with further additions
of land.   But in 1334 Edward Baliol, who two years earlier
had assumed the Crown of Scotland, handed over to King
Edward III, to remain for ever in the possession of England,
amongst other places, the town, castle, and forest of Jedworth.
These Edward now bestowed on Henry Percy, thus providing
ground for a very pretty quarrel between the Douglases and

Percies.   From now onward, practically for seventy-five years,
Jedburgh Castle remained in English hands.

Ultimately, its fate was as that of a land wilfully devastated
by its own people to hamper the march of an invading
army.   If the Scots could not permanently hold it, neither,
they resolved, should it any more harbour those vermin of
England.   Accordingly, when in 1409 the men of Teviotdale,
fierce progenitors of the more modern reiving Border Elliots
and Scotts, wiping out the English garrison, retook the castle,
they at once set about its final destruction.   Burnt, so far as it
would burn, cast down bit by bit to its very foundations, with
strenuous toil riven asunder stone from stone, ere their work was
ended little part of its massive walls remained to speak of
former glories.   Walter Bower, Abbot of Inchcolm, who was
a young man at the time of its destruction writes in the
"*Scotichronicon*" that: " Because the masonry was exceedingly
holding and solid, not without great toil was it broken down
and demolished."

Perched above the town on a commanding eminence that
on one side sloped steeply to the river, and on the other to a
deep glen or ravine, defended also, doubtless, on the side
farthest from the burgh by a deep fosse, the castle must once
have been of great strength—how strong as regards position
may best be judged from the bird's-eye view of it to be gained
if one climbs at the back of Jedburgh the exceedingly steep
direct road that runs to Lanton village.   From this point, too,
one sees to advantage the venerable Abbey nestling among
the surrounding houses, and can best appreciate the wisdom of
the old monks, who chose for their abode a site so pleasant.
A valley smiling in the mellow sunshine ; a place to which one
may drop down from the heights above where bellows and raves
a north-westerly gale, to find peace and quiet, undisturbed by
any blustering wind ; a valley rich in the fruits of the earth,
and wandering through it a trout stream more beautiful than
almost any of the many beautiful Border " Waters," a stream

that once was, and now should be, full of lusty yellow trout rising under the leafy elms in the long, warm, summer evenings. An ideal water for trout is Jed, and many a pretty dish must those old monks have taken from it, by fair means or foul ; pity that woollen-mills below, and netting, and the indiscriminate slaughter of fingerlings, above the town, should have so greatly damaged it as a sporting stream.

Possibly upper Jed is not now quite so bad as it was a few years ago, but what of the lower part of that beautiful river ? The same may be said of it that may be said of Teviot immediately below Hawick, or of Gala, and, alas ! of Tweed, below Galashiels. The waters are poisoned by dyes and by sewage, rendered foul by sewage fungus, reeking with all manner of uncleanness, an offence to nostril and to eye. Five and thirty years ago Ruskin wrote : "After seeing the stream of the Teviot as black as ink, a putrid carcase of a sheep lying in the dry channel of the Jed, under Jedburgh Abbey, the entire strength of the summer stream being taken away to supply a single mill, I know finally what value the British mind sets on the beauties of nature." What, indeed, are the 'beauties of nature' that they should interfere with the glories of com- merce ! Truly we are a Commercial Nation. Here is the condition of things that Ruskin found in the Borderland in the mid-seventies of last century, as described by him in a lecture delivered at Oxford in 1877.

"Two years ago," he said, "I went, for the first time since early youth to see Scott's country by the shores of Yarrow, Teviot, and Gala Waters." Then to his hearers he read aloud from " Marmion " that picture of the Border country which is familiar to everyone :

> " Oft in my mind such thoughts awake,
> By lone St. Mary's silent lake ;
> Thou know'st it well,—nor fen, nor sedge,
> Pollute the clear lake's crystal edge ;
> Abrupt and sheer, the mountains sink
> At once upon the level brink ;

And just a trace of silver sand
Marks where the water meets the land.
Far in the mirror, bright and blue,
Each hill's huge outline you may view ;
Shaggy with heath, but lonely bare,
Nor tree, nor bush, nor brake is there,
Save where, of land, yon slender line
Bears thwart the lake the scatter'd pine.
Yet even this nakedness has power,
And aids the feeling of the hour :
Nor thicket, dell, nor copse you spy,
Where living thing conceal'd might lie ;
Nor point, retiring, hides a dell,
Where swain, or woodman lone, might dwell ;
There's nothing left to fancy's guess,
You see that all is loneliness :
And silence aids—though the steep hills
Send to the lake a thousand rills ;
In summer tide, so soft they weep,
The sound but lulls the ear asleep ;
Your horse's hoof-tread sounds too rude,
So stilly is the solitude.

Nought living meets the eye or ear,
But well I ween the dead are near ;
For though, in feudal strife, a foe
Hath laid Our Lady's chapel low,
Yet still, beneath the hallow'd soil,
The peasant rests him from his toil,
And, dying, bids his bones be laid,
Where erst his simple fathers pray'd."

"What I saw myself, in that fair country," continued Ruskin, "of which the sight remains with me, I will next tell you. I saw the Teviot oozing, not flowing, between its wooded banks, a mere sluggish injection, among the poisonous pools of scum-covered ink. And in front of Jedburgh Abbey, where the foaming river used to dash round the sweet ruins as if the rod of Moses had freshly cleft the rock for it, bare and foul nakedness of its bed, the whole stream carried to work in the mills, the dry stones and crags of it festering unseemly in the

evening sun, and the carcase of a sheep, brought down in the
last flood, lying there in the midst of the children at their play,
literal and ghastly symbol, in the sweetest pastoral country in
the world, of the lost sheep of the house of Israel."

That is how these once fair scenes struck the outraged eye
of one who was a sincere lover of our beautiful Border land.
What might he say of these rivers now that five and thirty
years have passed? Compared to Teviot, ink is a fluid that
may claim to be *splendidior vitro*, and Jed below the town is in
little better case.

However, to return to Jedburgh. Of the old castle no trace
now remains; but early in the nineteenth century a small portion
of one wall yet stood, some outline of foundations yet met
the eye. Probably the fosse was filled up when the buildings
were razed—it was a convenient place to shoot rubbish ; indeed,
when about 1820 the site was being cut down preparatory to
the erection of a new "castle" (until recent years used as a
County Prison), charred oaken beams and blackened stones
were unearthed, relics certainly of the ancient building. A few
coins have also been found, and at various dates an iron lock,
a key of curious design, a rusty dagger, arrowheads, and
portions of a gold chain.

Jedburgh, deprived of her castle, was yet a strong place ; but
if her townsmen and the fierce men of Teviotdale imagined
that by harrying and destroying the nest that so long had
sheltered them, the English birds of prey would be permanently
scattered down the wind, they made a vast mistake. No more
than a year had passed ere the English returned under Sir
Robert Umphraville and burned the town about their ears ;
and in 1416 the same commander repeated the performance of
six years earlier. Again and again as the years rolled on
were fire and sword the fate of Jedworth. The town, with its
flanking towers, was strong, strong in natural position, and,
owing to the manner of building of its houses, difficult of access
except by one or other of its four ports ; but it had no walls or

defending fosse, and however brave its men, however skilled in the use of arms, their numbers were generally too meagre to cope with the formidable bands the English could bring against them. Time and again the place was sacked, and on each occasion her magnificent Abbey suffered grievously at the hands of the stormers.

Founded about the year 1118, the ancient Abbey occupies the site of a building more ancient still by probably two or three hundred years, a church built in the ninth century by Ecgred, Bishop of Lindisfarne, who died A.D. 845. Osbert was the first Abbot of Jedburgh (1152–1174); previous to his day the establishment ranked merely as a Priory. In the troublous times between 1297 and 1300, the Abbey suffered much. Sacked and partially destroyed, the lead stripped from its roof, the conventual buildings to such an extent gutted that the brethren, fleeing, were forced to seek refuge for a time in Abbeys and Monasteries south of the Border, it can have been but the massiveness of its walls that then preserved it from total destruction.

But compared to the treatment later meted out to Abbey and town by the Earl of Surrey, all former chastenings were as a comparatively mild scourging with whips; Surrey chastised with scorpions. In this matter, his little finger was thicker than the loins of those who had preceded him. In 1523, an English force—compared to the meagre number of defenders, a vast army—marched on the town. All that human power could do in defence of hearth and home was done that day by the men of Jedworth. When, since history began, has it ever been recorded of them that they shrank from battle?

> " And how can man die better
>   Than facing fearful odds,"

summed up their creed, then and ever. There were of them, now, but two thousand at the most, opposed to an army many times their number—one man as against four, or perhaps even

H

as one to five. Yet so stubborn was their resistance, so
fiercely they fought, that at the last it was only by the aid of
fire that this wasps' nest was laid waste. Driven back at length
by superior numbers, forced to retire to the towers and to the
Abbey, the attack could be pushed home no farther till Surrey
gave orders to set fire to the town. Even then, Jedworth held
out till far in the night, when the entire place was little more
than a smouldering heap of embers. "I assure your Grace,"
wrote the Earl to his King, "I fownd the Scottis at this tyme
the boldest men and the hottest that ever I sawe any nation,
and all the journey upon all parts of the armye kepte us with
soo contynual skyrmish that I never sawe the like." . . .
"Could 40,000 such men be assembled," he says in the same
letter, "it would bee a dreadful enterprise to withstand them."
If valour alone could have won the day, to the men of
Jedburgh had now been the victory. They fought like fiends
incarnate. The Devil himself, in truth, must have been
amongst them, for, says Surrey farther : "I dare not write the
wonders that my Lord Dacre and all hys company doo saye
they sawe that nyght six tyms of sperits and fereful syghts.
And universally all their company saye playnly the devyl was
that nyght among theym six tyms."

Thus was Jedburgh wiped out, "soo surely brent that no
garnysons nor none others shal bee lodged there unto the
tyme it bee newe buylded." And to rebuild equal to what it
had been, would surely be no light undertaking, for, says
Surrey, "the towne was much better than I went (weened) it
had been, for there was twoo tymys moo houses therein than
in Berwicke, and well buylded, with many honest and faire
houses therein sufficiente to have lodged a thousand horsemen in
garnyson, and six good towres therein, which towne and towres
be clenely destroyed, brent, and throwen downe." The
slaughter of Jedworth's defenders no doubt must also have
been great. But that the inhabitants were not indiscriminately
put to the sword is evidenced by the fact that some time during

the night, when Lord Dacre's picketed horses—terrified no doubt by the same Scottish devil that had troubled the hearts of the stormers in the town—suddenly stampeding, galloped wildly through Surrey's camp, over two hundred of them, bursting in amongst the still burning houses, were caught and carried off by the Scottish women who still clung to the place —"keening," probably, over their devastated hearths. In all, before this stampede ended, Surrey lost upwards of eight hundred horses; for when the maddened beasts came thundering through his camp, the English soldiers, imagining that they were being attacked by a fresh army of Scots, loosed off into the mob flights of arrows, and fired into the terrified animals with musketry. It is scarcely the method best suited to calm a maddened mob of horses; little wonder that many in their helpless terror plunged over the great "scaurs," or cliffs, that near the town overhang Jedwater, and were dashed to pieces.

In his letter of 27th September, to Henry VIII, Surrey thus describes the incident: "And he [Lord Dacre] being with me at souper, about viij a clok, the horses of his company brak lowse, and sodenly ran out of his feld, in such nombre, that it caused a marvellous alarome in our field; and our standing watche being set, the horses cam ronnyng along the campe, at whome were shot above one hundred shief of arrowes, and dyvers gonnys, thinking they had been Scotes that wold have saulted the camp; fynally, the horses were so madde that they ran like wilde dere into the feld, above xv c at the leest, in dyvers companys; and in one place above L felle downe a gret rok, and slew theymself, and above ij c ran into the towne being on fire, and by the women taken, and carried awaye right evill brent, and many were taken agayne. But, fynally, by that I can esteme by the nombre of theym that I sawe goe on foote the next daye, I think there is lost above viij c horses, and all with foly for lak of not lying within the campe."

H 2

So, for a time, Jedburgh perished. But the recuperative power of settlements in those days was great—like the eels, they were used to the process of skinning—and in no long time a rejuvenated township sprang from the ashes of the old burgh. When Surrey gave orders that the towers should be "throwen downe," possibly his commands were not obeyed to the letter. In a district where a plentiful supply of stone is not lacking, doubtless these defending towers would be massive buildings constructed of that material, run together—as was the custom in those days—with a semi-liquid mortar, or kind of cement, which, when it hardened, bound the entire mass into a solid block that clung stone to stone with extraordinary tenacity. Probably the towers may not have been so "clenely destroyed" as he supposed them to be. In any case, in twenty years' time the place was again formidable, its men as prone as had been their fathers to shout the old battle-cry of " Jethart's here," and fly at the throat of their hereditary foe.

Nor was the hereditary foe in any way reluctant to afford them opportunity. In 1544 Lord Evers stormed and captured the town ; and again the roar and crackle of flaming houses smote on the ears of Jedburgh's women. According to an Englishman's account of "The late Expedition in Scotland made by the King's Highness' Army under the Conduct of the Right Honourable the Earl of Hertford, the year of owr Lord God 1544," an account "Sent to the Right Honourable Lord Russell, Lord Privy Seal; from the King's Army there, by a Friend of his," the men of Jedburgh on this occasion did not behave with their wonted valour. But if this writer is to be trusted, nowhere during Hertford's entire campaign of 1544 did the Scots make a stand. It was a sort of triumphal English progress ; everywhere the Scots fled almost without striking a blow, everywhere they were cut down. Only occasionally, and almost as it were by accident, was an Englishman hurt, whilst the slaughter among the Scots was prodigious. They "used for their defence their light feet, and fled in so much haste that divers

English horses were tired in their pursuit : but overtaken there
was a great number, whereof many were 'slain, partly by the
fierceness of the Englishmen, partly by the guilty cowardice of
the Scots. . . . And yet in this skirmish, not one Englishman
taken, neither slain : thanks be to God." Everywhere it is the
same story—a pleasant picnic for Hertford and his men ; death
and destruction, and panic flight for the Scots. Men, women,
and children, it was all the same apparently in that campaign,
if one may judge by incidents such as this at Dunbar : " And
by reason that we took them in the mornynge, who, having
wautched all nyghte for our comynge and perceyvynge our
Army to dislodge and depart, thoughte themselves safe of us,
were newly gone to their beds ; and in theyr fyrste slepes closed
in with fyre, men, women, and children were suffocated and
burnt. . . . In these victories," comments this pious and
humane scribe, "who is to bee moste highest lauded but
God ? " But war is a rough game, and such happenings were
the natural outcome at that time of Henry's orders anent the
giving of quarter, and to the "putting man, woman and child
to fire and sword, without exception, when any resistance shall
be made against you."

Here, at Jedburgh, "upon the approachment of the men to
their entries, the Scots fled from their ordnance, leaving them
unshot, into the woods thereabout, with all other people in the
same town." Thereafter, having caught and slain something
over one hundred and sixty Scots, with " the loss of six Englishmen only," Abbey, and Grey Friars, the town, and "divers hostel
and fortified houses " were sacked and given to the flames,
" the goods of the same toune being first spoyled, which laded,
at their departing, five hundred horses." Again, in his notice
of the capture of Skraysburgh, "the greatest towne in all
Teviotdale," we are told that "it is a marvellous truth . . . .
not one Englishman was either hurt or wounded." A craven
band, those Scots, it would appear, fallen strangely from the
level at which Surrey had found them so few years before—

" the boldest men and the hottest that ever I sawe any nation"; far sunk, too, beneath the level of their immediate descendants, the men who turned the day in the fight of the Redeswire in 1575. And yet one remembers to have heard of a certain fight about this period, in the near neighbourhood of Jedburgh, at a place called Ancrum Moor, when Angus, Arran, and Scott of Buccleuch, with a force numerically very inferior. turned the tables on the "auld enemy" to a lusty tune. It may all be quite accurate, of course, this story told to Lord Russell, but it smacks somewhat of a tale told by one who himself was not a very bold fighting man. The warrior whose place is ever the forefront of the battle is not the man who belittles his enemies, nor is he usually one who regards with complacency the sufferings of helpless women and children. Accurate, or not, however, Hertford seems to have had a partiality for harrying this district and slaying its hapless people, for he returned the following year with a larger following—a mongrel gang, in which Turks and Russians were almost the only European nations unrepresented—and completed his work of destruction so far as it lay in his power. He could not utterly destroy the glorious Abbey, but the Brethren were scattered, never to return, and so far as it could be done, the building that for four hundred years had sheltered them was wrecked. Mute now the solemn chants that had been wont to echo through its dim lit aisles, gone for ever the day of matins and vespers ; in Jedburgh the sway of the Church was over. Black with the smoke of sacrilegious fires, stained by the flames that had licked its desecrated walls, still a rudely fitted fragment of the great Abbey for a little time continued to be used by worshippers ; for the rest, the building would appear to have been regarded chiefly as an excellent and useful outlook or watch tower.

It was the followers of the Reformed Faith that next held public worship there. Did no one of the old-time Abbots who lie asleep within its ancient walls turn in his grave, one wonders,

when in 1793 the south aisle was pulled down, and "a wall
built between the pillars to make the church more comfortable"? They had no room in their compositions for any
sentiment of reverence, little use for such a thing as respect
for historical buildings, those eighteenth century Scottish
ancestors of ours. Our old foes of England at least had the

Jedburgh Abbey.

excuse that what they did was done in the heat of conflict; it
was left to our own people in cold blood to lay sacrilegious
hands on a glorious relic of the past; like monkeys to deface
and tear to pieces something the beauty and value of which
they had not wit to recognise. All that could be done,
however, to atone for past misdeeds was done in 1875 by the
Marquess of Lothian. The "comfortable church" of 1793 has

been removed, and what remains of the Abbey is reverently
cared for.   Safe now from further desecration,

> " The shadows of the convent towers
> Slant down the snowy sward ; "

and in the peace of long-drawn summer twilights only the
distant cries of children, the scream of swift or song of thrush,
may now set the echoes flying through those ruined aisles.
The Presbyterian Manse that once stood in the Abbey
grounds—itself no doubt, like other houses in the town, built
wholly or in part of stone quarried from the Abbey ruins—has
long since been removed, and little now remains which may
break the tranquil sadness that broods over these relics of
past grandeur.

A few hundred yards from the Abbey, down a back street,
there stands a picturesque old house, robbed now of some of
its picturesqueness by the substitution of tiles for the old
thatched roof that once was there.   It is the house where, in a
room in the second story whose window overlooks a pleasant
garden and the once crystal Jed, Mary, Queen of Scots lay
many days, sick unto death,—a house surely that should now
be owned and cared for by the Burgh.   Local tradition (for
what it may be worth) has it that the Queen lodged first in
the house which is now the Spread Eagle Hotel, but that a
fire breaking out there, she was hastily removed to that which
now goes by the name of "Queen Mary's House."   It
stands in what must in her day have been a beautiful garden,
sloping to the river.   Hoary, moss-grown apple trees still
blossom there and bear fruit. "With its screen of dull trees
in front," says Dr. Robert Chambers, "the house has a somewhat lugubrious appearance, as if conscious of connection with
the most melancholy tale that ever occupied the page of
history."   In those long past days, however, its appearance
must have been far from lugubrious ; and indeed even now,
on a pleasant sunny evening of late spring when thick-clustered

apple and pear blossom drape the boughs, and thrushes sing,
and Jed ripples musically beneath the worn arches of that fine

Queen Mary's House, Jedburgh.

old bridge near at hand, (across which they say that the stones for building the Abbey were brought these many centuries agone), it is more of peace than of melancholy that the place speaks.

Yet there is sadness too, when one thinks of the—at least on *this* occasion—sorely maligned woman who lay there in grievous suffering in the darkening days of that October of 1566. "Would that I had died at Jedworth," she sighed in later years. She had been spared much, the Fates had been less unkind, if death had then been her part. And not least, she might have been spared the malignant slanders of the historian Buchanan, who, at any rate in this matter, showed himself a master of the art of suppressing the true and suggesting the false.

When, according to Buchanan, news was brought to Mary at Borthwick Castle of the wounding of Bothwell by "a poor thief, that was himself ready to die,"—how, one wonders, would the famous "Little Jock Elliot" have relished that description of himself?—" she flingeth away in haste like a mad woman, by great journeys in post, in the sharp time of winter." As a matter of fact, when the news of Bothwell's mishap reached the Queen, she was already on her way to Jedburgh, to hold there a Circuit Court ; and the time, of course, was not winter, but early October, not unusually one of the pleasantest times of the whole year in the south of Scotland.

Arrived at Jedburgh, says Buchanan, "though she heard sure news of his life, yet her affection, impatient of delay, could not temper herself, but needs she must bewray her outrageous lust, and in an inconvenient time of the year, despising all discommodities of the way and weather, and all danger of thieves, she betook herself headlong to her journey, with such a company as no man of any honest degree would have adventured his life and his goods among them." Buchanan's estimate of the Queen's escort on this occasion is not flattering to the Earl of Moray, (the "Good Regent," Mary's half-brother,) the Earl of Huntly, (Bothwell's brother-in-law,) and Mr. Secretary Lethington, who formed part of that escort. These, one would suppose, were scarcely the men most likely to have been selected to accompany her had it been " outrageous lust " that prompted her journey. And as to this " headlong " dash to the side of the wounded Bothwell, of which Buchanan makes so much, they would call now by an ugly name such statements as his if they chanced to be made on oath. Buchanan must have known very well that the Queen transacted business for a week in Jedburgh before she set out to visit her wounded Warden of the Marches,—a visit which, after all, was official, and which under any circumstances it had been ungracious in her to refrain from making. There was no justification for speaking of her visit as " headlong," there is no warrant for such words as " hot haste," and " rode madly," which have been employed by other writers in speaking of her journey. If she made " hot haste " there, (at the end of a week devoted to business,) she made equally hot haste back again that same day. When one has to ride fifty or sixty miles across trackless hills and boggy moors in the course of a day in mid-October, when the sun is above the horizon little more than ten hours, there is not much time for loitering by the way; the minutes are brief in which one may pause to admire the view.

Suppose that she left Jedburgh soon after sunrise, (that is to say, at that time of year in Scotland, a few minutes before 7 o'clock) going, as she certainly must have done, across Swinnie Moor into Rule Water, thence across Earlside Moor and over the Slitrig some miles above Hawick, then up and between the hills whose broad backs divide Slitrig from Allan Water, up by the Priesthaugh Burn and over the summit between Cauldcleuch Head and Greatmoor Hill, thence by the Braidlee Burn into Hermitage Water, and so, skirting the Deer Park, on to the Castle,—she would do well, in those days when draining of swamp lands was a thing unknown, and the way, therefore, not easy to pick, if she did the outward journey in anything under five hours. Hawick local tradition claims that the Queen on her way to Hermitage visited that town, and rested for a time in what is now known as the Tower Hotel; and, as corroborative evidence, a room in that inn is said to be known as "Queen Mary's Room." It may be that she did pay a flying visit to Hawick, but the chances are against her having made such a detour. It would have considerably added to the length of her journey, and there can have been small time to spare for resting.

In mid-October the sun sets a few minutes after 5 o'clock. Therefore, in returning, the Queen and her escort must have made a reasonably early start; for to find oneself, either on horseback or afoot, among peat bogs and broken, swampy ground after dark is a thing not to be courted. As it was, Mary and her horse were bogged in what has ever since been called the Queen's Mire, where years ago was found a lady's spur of ancient design—perhaps hers. The day had turned out wet and windy,—it is a way that October days have, after fine weather with a touch of frost,—and the Queen and her escort were soaked to the skin, bedraggled, and splashed to the eyes with black peaty mud from the squelching ground through which their horses had been floundering.

Even in these days, when the Border hills are thoroughly drained, you cannot ride everywhere across them in "hot haste" without having frequently to draw rein. What must they have been like in the sixteenth century, when, in addition to the rough, broken surface, and the steep braes, every hillock was a soaking mossy sponge, every hollow a possibly treacherous bog, when spots such as the "Queen's Mire" were on every hand, and every burn brimmed over with the clear brown water that the heart of the ardent trout fisher now vainly pants after? Going and coming, between Jedburgh and Hermitage, a party in Mary's day, travelling as she travelled, could not well have done the journey in less that nine hours. Truly it does not leave much time for the dalliance suggested by Buchanan,—

more especially as the Privy Seal Register of that date testifies that the Queen transacted a not inconsiderable amount of public business whilst at the castle. But, poor lady, she could do no right in the eyes of certain of her subjects. She was a Catholic ; and that was sufficient ; even her very tolerance of other people's religion was an offence, a trap set for the unwary. Every suggestion of evil with regard to her conduct was eagerly seized on and greedily swallowed by her enemies and ill-wishers. It is so fatally easy to take away character. Especially, for some reason, in the case of one high in rank are certain people prone to believe evil, strangely gratified if they may be the first to unfold to a neighbour some new scandal against their betters. Away to the winds with Christian charity ! All is fish that comes to *their* net ; to them every scandalous tale is true, and needs no enquiry, provided only it be told against one of exalted station.

Queen Mary rode that day in the wind and the wet a matter of fifty or sixty miles. She was used to long rides, no doubt,— there was indeed no other means for her to get about the country,—and she was never one who shrank from rough weather. But wet clothes, if worn for too long a time, have a way of finding out any weak spot there may chance to be in one's frame, and the exposure and the wetting dealt hardly this time with the Queen. She was never physically strong, and of late a world of anxiety, worry, and sorrow, caused by the conduct of her husband, had drained the strength she possessed. Moreover, ever since her confinement three months earlier, she had been subject to more or less severe attacks of illness, accompanied by much pain. In her normal condition, probably the fatigue and exposure might have affected her not at all ; now, it brought on a serious malady. By the morning of the 17th—the day following her long ride—she was in a high fever, and in great pain. As the disease progressed, she was seized with violent paroxysms, vomiting blood ; and day by day her condition gave rise to ever more grave fear. She herself, believing that

her end was at hand, took leave of the Earl of Moray and of
other noblemen, expressing at the same time great anxiety regarding the affairs of the kingdom and the guardianship of her
infant son after her death.   But never throughout the illness
did her courage falter.   Lack of courage, at least, is a thing of
which not even her bitterest enemies can accuse Mary Stuart.

On the evening of the ninth day of this severe illness, after a
particularly acute attack of convulsions, the Queen sank, and
her whole body became cold and rigid. "Every one present,
especially her domestic servants, thought that she was dead,
and they opened the windows.   The Earl of Moray began to
lay hands on the most precious articles, such as her silver plate
and jewels.   The mourning dresses were ordered, and arrangements were made for the funeral."[1]   John Leslie, Bishop of
Ross, writing from Jedburgh at the time, says that on the
Friday "her Majesty became deid and all her memberis cauld,
her Eene closit, Mouth fast, and Feit and Armis stiff and
cauld."

Buchanan's account is that, after leaving Hermitage, "she
returneth again to Jedworth, and with most earnest care and
diligence provideth and prepareth all things to remove Bothwel
thither.   When he was once brought thither, their company
and familiar haunt together was such as was smally agreeing
with both their honours.   There, whether it were by their
nightly and daily travels, dishonourable to themselves and
infamous among the people, or by some secret providence of
God, the Queen fell into such a sore and dangerous sickness
that scarcely there remained any hope of her life."   It would
be hard to conceive anything more poisonous than this, or
anything less in accord with the facts.   Buchanan's zeal outran
his love of the truth ; with both hands he flung mud at the
Queen.   In his eyes, any story against her was worthy of
credence—or at least he wished it to appear so.   As a matter of

[1] MS. in British Museum, by Claude Nau, Secretary to Queen Mary,
1575-1587.

fact, before Bothwell reached Jedburgh the Queen had been dangerously ill, and incapable of making any preparation to receive him had she wished to do so, for close on ten days, and the day after his coming she lay for several hours unconscious, and as one dead.   Writing on 24th October to the Archbishop of Glasgow, M. Le Croc, the French Ambassador, can only say that he hopes " in five or six days the Queen will be able to sign " a dispatch ; but on the following day her illness again took an unfavourable turn.

She left Jedburgh within fifteen days of the date of M. Le Croc's letter, not an excessive time in which to recover from an illness which admittedly had brought her to the point of death, and which must have left her in a condition of extreme weakness.   Yet, according to Buchanan, this time of convalescence was devoted to "their old pastime again, and that so openly, as they seemed to fear nothing more than lest their wickedness should be unknown."   His conscience must have been of an elastic nature, if, having any knowledge of the facts, he could so write ; and if he had no knowledge of the facts, one wonders how it is possible that a man of his position and ability should commit himself to statements so foul and uncharitable.   But at any cost, and by any means, he wanted to make out his case ; and he knew his audience.

Buchanan's bias against the unfortunate Queen was very great.   It even caused him to lend himself here to the task of bolstering up the case of that petulant, contemptible creature, Darnley.   In view of the latter's known degrading habits and evil practices, as well as of his general conduct towards the Queen, the following sentence from the historian's writings is almost grotesque : "When the King heard thereof," [Mary's illness] "he hasted in post to Jedburgh to visit the Queen, to comfort her in her weakness by all the gentle services that he could, to declare his affection and hearty desire to do her pleasure."   Of course Darnley did nothing of the sort.   When he did come, (twelve days after her illness began,) he came most reluctantly and tardily from his "halkand and huntand" in the west country. He "has had time enough if he had been willing ; this is a fault which I cannot excuse," wrote M. Le Croc on the 24th October.

According to Buchanan, Darnley, when he did reach Jedburgh, found no one ready to receive him, or " to do him any reverence at all " ; the Queen, he says, had "practised with " the Countess of Moray to feign sickness and keep her bed, as an excuse for not receiving him. " Being thus denied all duties of civil kindness, the next day with great grief of heart he returned to his old solitary corner." A pathetic story, if it were wholly true ; a heart-stirring picture, that of the " solitary corner." But all the King's horses and all the King's men could not have set Darnley back again in the place he had forfeited in the esteem of the Nobles, and in the esteem of the country at large. If the nobles were not pleased to welcome him, if he was forsaken of all friends, whose fault was that but Darnley's ? "The haughty spirit of Darnley, nursed up in flattery, and accustomed to command, could not bear the contempt into which he had now fallen, and the state of insignificance to which he saw himself reduced."[1]   Darnley was an undisciplined cub. It was the sulky petulance of a spoilt child, that delayed his visit to Jedburgh ; it was the offended dignity of an unlicked schoolboy that took him out of it again so hurriedly. The Queen's sufferings were as nought, weighed in the scale against a petty dignity offended by the lack of "reverence" with which he was received in Jedburgh. Truly, Queen Mary at her marriage had " placed her love on a very unworthy object, who requited it with ingratitude and treated her with neglect, with violence, and with brutality."[2]

Buchanan, the historian, Queen Mary's traducer, died in September, 1582. His contemporary, Sir James Melville of Halhill, in writing of him says he was "a man of notable endowments for his learning and knowledge in Latin poesy,

[1] Robertson's *History of Scotland*.   [2] Robertson.

much honoured in other countries, pleasant in conversation, rehearsing at all occasions moralities short and instructive, whereof he had abundance, inventing where he wanted. He was also religious, but was easily abused, and so facile that he was led by every company that he haunted, which made him factious in his old days, for he spoke and wrote as those who were about him informed him; for he was become careless, following in many things the vulgar opinion; for he was naturally popular, and extremely revengeful against any man who had offended him, which was his greatest fault." Truly these phrases : " he spoke and wrote as those who were about him informed him"; "inventing where he wanted"; "easily abused, and so facile that he was led by every company that he haunted"; "extremely revengeful against any who had offended him," seem to be not without application to much of what he wrote regarding Mary Stuart.

On 9th November Jedburgh saw its last of this most unfortunate among women. On that day the Queen and her Court set out for Craigmillar, travelling on horseback by way of Kelso, Home Castle, Berwick, and Dunbar. But the effects of that grievous sickness at Jedburgh long remained with her.

Many, in the days that are long dead, were the Burgh's royal visitors; but no figure more romantic in history has ever trod its streets than his who in 1745 passed one night there on his disastrous march southward. At no great distance from the house where Mary lay ill, stands a fine old building, occupied once by a being no less ill-fated than was the unfortunate Queen of Scots. In a "close" leading from the Castle gate you find the door of this house—on its weather-beaten stone lintel the date 1687. The sorely worn stone steps of a winding old staircase lead to rooms above, all panelled in oak. But as in the case of the "comfortable church" that once took away from the beauty and dignity of the grand old Abbey, so here the ruthless hand of modern "improvement" has been at work. The tenants of the building—there are several—pre-

I

sumably finding the sombre oak all too gloomy to meet their view of what is fitting in mural decoration, have remedied this defect by papering the panels, and in some instances by giving them what is call "a lick of paint." Sadly altered, therefore, is the interior of the building from what it was that night in November, 1745, when Bonnie Prince Charlie slept within its massive walls. But the outside, with its quaint double sun-dial set in the wall facing the Castle-gate, is no doubt now as it was then.

Of this visit, local tradition has not much to tell. There is the story that the advance guard of that section of the Prince's army which he himself led, marching from Kelso, reached Jedburgh on the Sunday when the entire community was at church, and it is said that a message was sent to the minister of the Abbey church requiring him to close the service and send his congregation home to prepare rations for the main body of the army. The order, if it were really given, was apparently not resented, for when the Prince himself marched in, the women of Jedburgh, at least, flocked into the street to kiss his hand. The regard and homage of the women he got here, as elsewhere, but of that of which he stood most in need, the swords of the men, he got none. As at Kelso, not a single recruit followed him. One, indeed, a neighbouring farmer, did ride in to join the Royal standard, but he was a day after the fair; the army had already marched. Did the sound that tradition says Jedburgh heard long ere the Prince's arrival, the sound as of an army on the march, the distant rumble of moving artillery, the tramp of innumerable feet, and the dull throb of drums pulsing on the still night air, scare Borderers away from his enterprise? Was it superstition, or was it a real lack of interest, or was it merely "canniness," that so effectually damped the ardour of recruits both at Kelso and at Jedburgh? Whatever the cause, no man followed him; only the blessings and good wishes of the women were his wherever he went.

After leaving Jedburgh, the Prince's army made over the

hills in two divisions, one following the old Whele-Causeway (over which the main Scottish army marched on Carlisle in 1388, what time Douglas's flying column made a dash into England down the Rede valley from Froissart's "Zedon"); the other marching by Note o' the Gate, the neighbouring pass that runs between Dog Knowe and Rushy Rig. These were then the only two practicable ways over the hills into Upper Liddesdale. "Note o' the Gate" is a puzzle. What does the name mean? "Note" may be merely the Cumberland "Knot" or "Knote," a knob or projection on a hillside. I understand the term is common enough in that part of the country, as in Helmside Knot, Hard Knot, etc. But even if this word, though differently spelled, does bear the same meaning both in Cumberland and in Liddesdale, I do not know that it gets us any nearer the "Gate." There is no rugged pass here, no Gate between precipitous mountains. One explanation—for what it may be worth—comes from a tradition that the name was given by Prince Charlie himself, through his misunderstanding a remark made by one of his officers. As they tramped over the moorland pass, the Prince overheard this officer say to another: "Take note of the gait," i.e., "Take note of the way." That night, when they were at Larriston, the Prince puzzled everyone by referring to something that had taken place back at "Note of the Gate." The story seems far fetched.

Many a tale survives of the doings and iniquities of the Prince's wild Highlanders as they straggled over these lonely Border moors. "Straggled," seems to be a more appropriate term than "marched," for, according to the testimony of eye-witnesses, the men appear to have kept no sort of military formation. Or at least what formation they did keep was of the loosest, and no check on plundering. It is a lonely countryside at best; human habitations were few and widely separated, but from the infrequent cottages, property of an easily portable nature took to itself wings as the army passed,

I 2

and sheep grazing on the hills melted from sight like snow before the softening breath of spring. Once they caught and killed some sheep in a " stell," and they cooked one of them in an iron pot that lay in the stell. Unfortunately, they did not take the precaution to cleanse the pot, and the resulting brew disagreed so sorely with one of the thieves that the spot is called the Hielandman's Grave to this day. Some others, that evening when they were encamped, forced a man to kill and cut up sheep for them, and for this work he was given a guinea. The pay did not benefit him much ; for a party of Highlanders, as the man went towards home, put a pistol to his head and made him refund. They tried the same game on a man named Armstrong, down on the Liddel at Whithaugh Mill. But Armstrong was too much for them ; one who shared the old reiver blood was not to be intimidated, and he knocked the pistol out of the hand of the threatening Highlander, secured it himself, and turned the tables most unpleasantly.

One unlooked-for result of the Prince's march through those desolate regions, was a very great increase in the number of illicit stills, and in the consumption of whisky that had paid no revenue to King George. So impressed were the Highlanders with the wild solitude of the glens on all sides of their line of march, and with the facilities presented by the amber-clear burns that tinkle through every cleuch, that when the rebels were returning from Derby, numbers of the men got no farther north than the hills of Liddesdale and the Border, but entered there on the congenial pastime of whisky-making.

Though the proportion of Borderers who followed Prince Charlie down into England, or throughout his campaign, was so very meagre, yet there lived among those solemn Border hills many faithful hearts, whose King he was to the end.

> " Follow thee ! Follow thee ! Wha wadna follow thee ?
> King o' our Highland hearts,
> Bonnie Prince Charlie."

They were not only Highland hearts that were true to him.   In her *Border Sketches*, Mrs. Oliver mentions a Hawick man, named Millar, who accompanied his master, Scott of Gorrenberry, all through the campaign of 1745–46, and who to the end of his days had an undying devotion to his Prince, and till the day of the latter's death, an imperishable faith that he would come to his own again.   Long after the '45, Miller became "minister's man" in one of the Hawick churches, and his grief, one Sunday morning in 1788, was overwhelming when the news was told to him that the Prince was dead. "E-eh! Doctor," he cried brokenly to his reverend informant, "I'll get nae good o' your sermon the day; I wish ye hadna told me till this afternoon.   If it had been the German Lairdie, now, there wad hae been little mane made for *him*. But there'll be mony a wae heart forby mine this day." Indeed, who even now can read of Bonnie Prince Charlie's end, and *not* have "a wae heart"?

Few of the Scottish Border towns in 1745 showed open hostility, or indeed anything but a luke-warm friendship, for the gallant young Pretender.   Dumfries, however, was an exception.   The inhabitants of that town, with men from Galloway, Nithsdale, and Annandale, full of zeal for King George and secure in the belief that the fighting men of the Prince's army were all safely over the March into England, hurried to intercept the rebel baggage train as it passed near Lockerbie, and carried off thirty-two carts to Dumfries.   The Highlanders, however, getting word of this affair before the army marched from Carlisle, detached a party to Dumfries to demand the return of the waggons or the payment of an indemnity, "the notice of which has put Dumfries in greater fear and confusion than they have since the rebellion broke out, and expect no mercy."   But the Prince's party was recalled before it had reclaimed the lost baggage-carts or exacted this alternative sum of £2,000, and Dumfries imagined that now all was well.   They had the waggons ; and for a little time they triumphed. So triumphant, indeed, were they, and so filled with confidence in their own warlike powers, that when false rumours reached them that the Highlanders had been utterly routed and cut to pieces at Lancaster, not only were there " great rejoicings in Dumfries by ringing of bells and illuminating their windows," but " a considerable party of our light horse were sent off immediately, after the Chevalier," and " about three hundred militia, composed of townspeople and the adjacent paroches . . . are to go to the water of Esk to stop their passing and to apprehend any small parcels of them flying." Dumfries was not so warlike a couple of weeks or so later, when Lord Elcho at the head of five hundred men of the Prince's advance guard marched in and demanded the immediate payment of £2,000 in money and the delivery of a thousand pairs of shoes, two hundred horses, and a hundred carts. Not all that the Prince demanded was paid before the northward march was resumed, but his visit cost the town something like £4,000—irrespective of what the Highlanders took. Whilst he remained in Dumfries, the Prince lodged in the Market Place, in a private house which is now the Commercial Inn. It is said that when his army marched up Nithsdale, halting for the night at the Duke of Queensberry's property, Drumlanrig, the Highlanders in the morning, to show their loyalty to King James, slashed with their swords portraits of King William and Queen Mary which had been presented to the Duke by Queen Anne,—an inconvenient method of declaring allegiance.

Though of minor interest, there are other houses in Jedburgh besides Queen Mary's and that in which Prince Charlie lodged, in which the townsfolk take some pride. There is the building in which Sir David Brewster was born in 1781 ; that where Burns lodged when he visited Jedburgh in 1787 ; that in Abbey Close in which Wordsworth and his sister had lodgings in 1803, when Sir (then Mr.) Walter Scott visited them and read to them part of the then unpublished " Lay of the Last

Minstrel"; there is the old Black Bull Inn,—no longer an inn,—and interesting only as the place where in 1726 Sir Gilbert Eliott of Stobs stabbed Colonel Stewart of Stewartfield with his sword one evening as they sat at supper. Claret was plentiful and good in Scotland in those days, and Colonel Stewart had not given his vote to Sir Gilbert, who was candidate for the county. Swords flew out on slender excuse in the eighteenth century. This particular sword was long kept in the family of Sir Gilbert Elliot's butler, and after passing through the hands of a resident in the village of Denholm, became the property of Mr. Forrest, the well-known gun-maker of Jedburgh, by whom it was finally deposited in the Marquess of Lothian's museum at Monteviot.

Jedburgh, of course, amongst other claims to distinction was famed for its witches—as what place was not, indeed, in times when harmless old women were adjudged innocent or guilty of the charge of witchcraft according as they sank or floated when thrown into deep water. If they sank—well and good, that meant that they were innocent, and they went to Heaven, having at any rate the satisfaction of knowing before-hand that, in such case, at least their memory would be cleared of the suspicion under which they had lain; if they floated—again well and good; that proved conclusively that the charge against them was a true one, and they were rescued from the water only to be burned alive. "Thou shalt not suffer a witch to live," was the text which our ancestors regarded as the Eleventh Commandment. We were not a whit better even at as late a date as the seventeenth century, than are those West African tribes of the present day whose medicine-men still "smell out" witches. Only, the West Africans practise the art now more or less in secret, and they are more humane in the death they inflict than were our ancestors; they do not burn.

Jedburgh's testing place for witches was a pool below the spot where now the Townfoot Bridge crosses the river. There is a story told of a notorious witch who was ducked here along with

a batch of her sinful associates. No doubt *they* all floated
right enough ; their reputation as witches of the most mis-
chievous description had long been almost too well established
to need such a test as that of the river. But this is what led
to their final overthrow. The chief witch of this "covine"
had a husband, the village pedagogue, a man of repute for
piety and for the rigour of his Sabbath keeping, and it was
notorious that in season and out of season this good man
would remonstrate with his wife—without doubt, people said,
endeavouring to wean the woman from her sinful habits.

Now, one must of course admit that such continued efforts to
save could not fail to be excessively irksome to any witch, and
must goad not only her, but also her accomplices, as well as her
Master, the Devil, to revenge. Hence, when the schoolmaster's
dead body was found one fine morning floating in the river,
the majority of the drowned man's neighbours had no hesitation
in believing that his wife and her partners in iniquity had
dragged him in the night from his hard-earned rest, and had
thrown him into the deepest pool in Jed. And this was the
more certain, because the deceased man had several times
confided to friends a pitiful tale of how he stood in terror of
his life, and how his wife and her "covine," had already more
than once hauled him through the roughest streams of Jed.
Sundry pious elders, moreover, affirmed that they had attended
with him a sederunt of their church rulers the previous evening
—when, perhaps, a trifle of something may have been taken in a
quiet way to keep out the cold—and that at a late hour afterwards they accompanied him to his own door, whence, they
admitted, they had come away in a hurry because of the wrathful
and threatening tones in which they heard this witch addressing
her husband. And this evidence was to some extent cor-
roborated by the neighbours, who told how they had been
awakened from sound sleep that night by the noise made by the
poor victim loudly singing the twenty-third Psalm as the horrid
troupe hurried him down the street towards the river—a rope

about his neck, said some.   Moreover, it was told, on evidence which people saw no reason to doubt, that at the time this poor man was being hurried to his death, a company of fairies was seen dancing on the top of the tower of Jedburgh Abbey, where after the drowning of the unfortunate schoolmaster by the witches, the whole company regaled themselves liberally with wine and ale.   Certainly, both wine and ale *were* found to be missing from a neighbouring cellar the following day ; and as the door of the cellar had been locked, obviously the loss could only be attributed to the schemes of fairies or witches. The one tale lent an air of truth to the others ; therefore people were not backward in crediting both.   He who accepted the story of the dancing fairies could have little difficulty in giving credence to that of the witches' "covine" dragging their unresisting prey through the streets.   And so another wretched victim or two went to her long home by a fiery death.   The schoolmaster was probably insane on some points, and trumped up the story of the witches having repeatedly ducked him. Our ancestors could swallow anything in the way of marvel. This story of the Jedburgh schoolmaster is told in "Historical Notices of the Superstitions of Teviotdale" ; and it is added therein that popular tradition says that "a son of Lord Torpichen, who had been taught the art of witchcraft by his nurse," was of the party of witches, and that it was he who first gave information regarding the murderers.

The Ettrick Shepherd must have known this story well. Perhaps it suggested some of the verses in "The Witch of Fife," in "The Queen's Wake."

> " Where have ye been, ye ill woman,
>   These three lang nichts frae hame ?
> What gars the sweit drap frae yer brow,
>   Like clots o' the saut sea faem ?
>
> " It fears me muckle ye have seen
>   What guid man never knew ;
> It fears me muckle ye have been
>   Where the grey cock never crew."

*   *   *   *   *

" Sit down, sit down, my leal auld man,
　　Sit down and listen to me ;
I'll gar the hair stand on yer crown
　　And the cauld sweit blind yer e'e.
　　　　*　　　　*　　　　*　　　　*

" The first leet night, when the new moon set,
　　When all was douf and mirk,
We saddled our naigs wi' the moon fern leaf,
　　And rode frae Kilmorran Kirk.

" Some horses were of the broom-cow framed,
　　And some of the green bay tree :
But mine was made of a hemlock-shaw,
　　And a stout stallion was he.

" We rode the tod doon on the hill,
　　The martin on the law ;
And we hunted the hoolit out o' breath,
　　And forcit him doon to fa'."

" What guid was that, ye ill woman ?
　　What guid was that to thee ?
Ye wad better have been in yer bed at hame
　　Wi' yer dear little bairns and me."

" And aye we rade and sae merrylie we rade,
　　Through the merkist gloffs o' the night ;
And we swam the flood, and we darnit the wood,
　　Till we cam to the Lommond height.

" And when we cam to the Lommond height,
　　Sae blythlie we lighted down ;
And we drank frae the horns that never grew
　　The beer that was never brewin.
　　　　*　　　　*　　　　*　　　　*

" And aye we danced on the green Lommond
　　Till the dawn on the ocean grew,
Nae wonder I was a weary wicht
　　When I cam hame to you.
　　　　*　　　　*　　　　*　　　　*

" And we flew ow'r hill, and we flew ow'r dale,
　　And we flew ow'r firth and sea,
Until we cam to merry Carlisle,
　　Where we lightit on the lea.

> " We gaed to the vault beyond the tow'r
>   Where we entered free as air,
> And we drank, and we drank of the Bishop's wine,
>   Until we could drink nae mair."

If, however, our forbears were drastic in their manner of dealing with witches and warlocks, and rigid in the infliction of capital punishment on criminals guilty of very minor offences, they were extraordinarily lax as regards the condition in which they kept their prisons. It is told that, sometime during the eighteenth century, the chief magistrate of Jedburgh was waited on by the burgh gaoler, who complained that the main door of the gaol had parted company with its hinges—which, in fact, had long been eaten through with rust. He had no means of securing his prisoners. What was he to do? It was a question calculated to puzzle any ordinary person. But the magistrate was a man of resource. " Get a harrow," said he. " And set it on end in the doorway, wi' its teeth turned inwards. If that winna keep them in,—'deed then they're no worth the keepin'." To as late a date as 1833, Selkirk also was not much better off than this, as regards its prison. The writer of the Statistical Account of the Parish at that date complains that prisoners " *have been frequently in the practice of coming out in the evening, and returning again before the jailor's visit in the morning.*"

If by chance there was ever a period of his life when the Poet Burns was *not* susceptible, it certainly was not at the time when he visited Jedburgh in 1787. Regarding that visit he has left in his diary some very characteristic notes. He was " waited on by the magistrates and presented with the freedom of the burgh," he records ; he meets and dines with " a polite soldier-like gentleman, a Captain Rutherfurd, who had been many years in the wilds of America, a prisoner among the Indians," and who apparently rather bored the poet. Captain Rutherfurd's adventures were assuredly such as could not fail to be well worth listening to, but what between Burns' respectful

admiration of an armchair that the old soldier possessed, which
had been the property of James Thomson, author of "The
Seasons," and his latest attack of love's sickness, host and guest
do not seem to have been quite in accord.   Perhaps the old
soldier prosed, and told his battles o'er again to too great an
extent—it is a failing not unknown in old gentlemen ; perhaps
the poet wanted to compose a sonnet to his new mistress's
eyebrows,—or whatever may have been Burns' equivalent.
(He had just met by the "sylvan banks" of Jed a young lady
possessed of charms that ravished his too tender heart).   Anyhow,
he left the district in a very despondent frame of mind, relieved
only by such consolation as might be gleaned from presenting
the lady with a copy of his latest portrait.   In his diary is the
following entry: "Took farewell of Jedburgh with some
melancholy, disagreeable sensations.   Jed, pure be thy crystal
streams and hallowed thy sylvan banks !   Sweet Isabella
Lindsay, may peace dwell in thy bosom uninterrupted, except
by the tumult throbbings of rapturous love !   That love enkind-
ling eye must beam on another, not on me ; that graceful form
must bless another's arms, not mine."   Burns' loves were
almost as many in number as the birds of the air, and scarcely
less trammelled.

As one proceeds up Jed from the ancient royal burgh,
probably the first thing that forces itself on the mind is that the
old coach road was not constructed for present-day traffic.   In
less than a couple of miles the river is crossed no fewer than
four times by bridges which are curiously old-fashioned, turning
blindly across the stream in some instances almost at right
angles to the road, and in the steepness of their ascent and
descent conveying to the occupant of a motor car a sensation
similar to that given to a bad sailor by a vessel at sea when she
is surmounting "the league-long rollers."   Nor are some of the
gradients on the road a few miles farther out such as entirely
commend themselves to motorists, two or three of them being
as abrupt as one in twelve, and one in thirteen.

Nevertheless the beauties of road and country are great, especially if it should chance that a visit is paid to the district when the tender flush of early Spring lies sweet on Jed's thick-wooded banks, and the trout have begun to think at last of rising again freely to the natural fly. Or better still, perhaps, when the green and gold, the russet and yellow, the crimson of Autumn combine with and melt into the crumbling red cliffs, —surely more generous tinted than ever were cliffs before. Above, a sky of tenderest blue, an air windless yet brisk, and just a leaf here and there fluttering leisurely into the amber clear water that goes wandering by ; and from the bushes the sweet thin pipe of a robin, or the crow of pheasant from some copse. That is the Indian Summer of Scotland, her pleasantest time of year,—if it were not for the shortening days, and the recollection that trout fishing is dead till another season.

It was a heavily wooded district this in former days, and one or two of the giants of old still survive,—the widespreading "Capon tree," for instance, that you pass on the road a mile from Jedburgh (but why " Capon " it passes the knowledge of man to decide) ; and the " King of the Woods," near Fernihirst, a beautiful and still vigorous oak, with a girth of 17 feet, four feet from the ground.

On the right, across the river, as you begin to quit the precincts of the town, there hangs the precipitous red " scaur " over which, that grim night in 1523, Surrey's horses came streaming, an equine cascade. Farther on, a mile or so, there perches Douglas's camp at Lintalee. But his " fair manor " is gone, and that great cave in the face of the cliff where he kept stock of provisions " till mak gud cher till hys men " ; a fall of rock swept away that, or most part of it, in 1866. It was to this cave, within Douglas's camp, that in 1317 a priest named Ellis brought a body of three hundred English soldiers, whilst Douglas was elsewhere, dealing with Sir Thomas Richmond and his men. But, (as the song says), Father Ellis " had better have left that beggar alone." Douglas returned

while yet the holy man and his unruly flock were feasting in
the cave. And "then"—it is needless to say,—"there began a
slaughter grim and great," and whatever else Father Ellis and
his men had feasted on, at least they got now a bellyful of
fighting. It was the last meal of which the most part of those
Englishmen partook. The cave is gone, but there still remain,
guarding the neck of the promontory—ruined indeed, and
partially filled up, but still prominent to the eye—the double
wall and fosse that Douglas threw across it six hundred years
ago.

Of caves, such as this Douglas cave at Lintalee, there is a
vast number scattered along the cliffy banks of Jed and Teviot,
and by some of their tributary waters or burns. At Mossburnfoot, on Jed, there is a cave, others are at Hundalee, and elsewhere. Near Cessford Castle, on a small affluent of the Kale
there is one, Habbie Ker's Cave, the same wicked Habbie—"a
bloodie man in his youth"—whose ghost to this day walks by
the old draw-well at the ruined castle of Holydene; on Kale
itself there are several of considerable size; in the cliff overhanging Oxnam, near Crailing, are others, and at Ancrum, on
the Ale; whilst at Sunlaws, near Roxburgh, in the red sandstone cliffs of Teviot, is a group of five caves, arranged in two
tiers, some of them of fair dimensions, the largest about twenty
six feet long, with a height of eight feet and a width of eight
and a half feet. Another in the upper tier has a length of
twenty-three feet, but at the mouth is no more than three feet
in height. In the lower tier, in one of the caves it is said in
the Statistical Account that horses were hid in 1745, to save
them from being taken for the use of the rebel army, when the
detachment under Prince Charlie's own command marched
from Kelso to Jedburgh. Many of the caves in different parts
of the country are so well concealed that a stranger might pass
very near to the mouth without suspecting their existence; some,
on the other hand, force themselves on the eye. But probably
in olden times thick undergrowth shut them from view. There

is no doubt that most of them at various times have been used as places of concealment; probably during the cruel old English wars they were much resorted to; certainly some of them were places of refuge in Covenanting times. Very efficient places of refuge no doubt they were, so long as the entrance was not discovered, but many of them would probably be easy enough to smoke out. It is mentioned in Patten's "Account of Somerset's Expedition into Scotland," how "a gentleman of my Lord Protector's . . . happened upon a cave in the grounde, the mouth whereof was so worne with fresh printe of steps, that he seemed to be certayne thear wear some folke within; and gone doune to trie, he was redily receyved with a hakebut or two. He left them not yet, till he had known wheyther thei wold be content to yield and come out, which they fondly refusing, he went to my Lord's grace, and upon utterance of the thynge, gat licence to deale with them as he coulde; and so returned to them with a skore or two of pioners. Three ventes had that cave, that we wear ware of, whereof he first stopt up one; another he fill'd full of strawe, and set it a fyer, whereat they within cast water apace; but it was so wel maynteyned without, that the fyer prevayled, and thei within fayn to get them belyke into anoother parler. Then devysed we (for I hapt to be with him) to stop the same up, whereby we should eyther smoother them, or fynd out their ventes, if thei hadde any mor: as this was done at another issue, about XII score of, we moughte see the fume of their smoke to come out: the which continued with so great a force, and so long a while, that we coulde not but thinke they must needs get them out, or smoother within: and forasmuch as we found not that they did the tone, we thought it for certain thei wear sure of the toother."

Who first made and used those caves, one wonders. The stone is soft, and easy to work, and I do not think it was beyond the skill and the tools of our very remote forbears to have patiently hollowed them out, in suitable places, from the solid face of the cliff. Tool marks may yet be plainly seen in some of them, marks not such as would be made by anything in the nature of a chisel, but such as are more suggestive of a pick, of sorts, an implement—single pointed—not unknown to even very primitive races.

Scattered all over the Jedburgh district are many ancient camps—hoary even in the day when Douglas fortified Lintalee ; many old castles and peel-towers, all, or nearly all, now in ruins, some indeed with very little left save tradition to indicate where once they stood ; and here and there are found vestiges of chapels or shrines, of which possibly there may remain hardly more in some instances than the green mounds which cover their fallen walls. The monks wandered far up this pleasant vale of Jed, carrying the Gospel of Peace through a land that knew of little save war, but the history of their resting places is even more vague than is now the outline of their chapel walls. At Old Jedward, however, five miles up stream from Jedburgh, you may still in some measure trace the line of foundations of that venerable little building which is said to have been built here away back in the ninth century. Of camps, the number is legion. That near Monklaw, the writer has not seen, but it is said to be Roman, and its measurements are something like one hundred and sixty yards each way. At Scraesburgh there is a circular camp, with a diameter of about one hundred and eighty feet, and with ramparts still nearly twenty feet in height,—surely that " Skraysburgh, the greatest towne in all Teviotdale," which, according to the English version, seems in 1544 to have fallen almost as fell Jericho of old, when the enemy shouted and blew their trumpets.

Of castles and peel-towers the most are utterly ruined, but Fernihirst (to which we come presently), still stands, and, over the hill towards Teviot, Lanton Tower, the latter now incor-porated with a comfortable modern dwelling. Lanton in the twelfth century was the property of Richard Inglis, who also owned the adjacent tower of Hunthill. Both these towers

were sacked and burned in 1513, after Flodden, by an
English flying column under Sir Roger Fenwicke, and its
existence at the present day Lanton Tower may owe to the
fact that when Evers swept the country-side in 1544, and
Hertford brought fire and sword in the following year, it
had possibly neither been repaired nor was inhabited. It was
over near Jedburgh, too, to have escaped the notice of Surrey
in 1523. Hunthill was burned again in 1549, and had Lanton
then been anything but dismantled, it could scarcely have
escaped the attentions of the party sent from Jedburgh by
the Earl of Rutland to attack d'Essé's rear-guard at Ancrum
ford. A force coming over the hill from Jedburgh and making
for Ancrum would necessarily pass within easy hail of Lanton.
In any case, however, there it stands, its solid walls of a
tenacity not shared by buildings put together with modern
mortar. Strange are the vicissitudes of places and of people.
Over this Forest of Jedworth, and here at Lanton, where of
old too often were heard the blast of trumpet, shouts and
oaths of fiercely striving men, the roar and crackle of burning houses, you will hear now no sound more startling than
the "toot–toot" of the Master's horn and the babble of fox-
hounds ; for at Lanton Tower are the kennels of the Jedforest
Hunt, and many a glorious run is had with this pack, sometimes in enclosed country, sometimes among the great round-
backed Border hills towards Carterfell, over country that will
tail off all but the best of men and horses.

CHAPTER V

JED (*continued*), FERNIHIRST, RAID OF THE REDESWIRE, OTTERBURNE

ACROSS Jed, on a high and leafy bank nearly opposite to Lintalee, stands the picturesque old stronghold of Fernihirst. The original castle was erected by Sir Thomas Ker probably about the year 1476, and the present building dates only from 1598. Its predecessor "stode marvelous strongly within a grete woode," as Dacre and Surrey found to their cost in 1523; yet they took it, after "long skirmyshing and moche difficultie," as Surrey reported. Brief and stormy was the existence of this original Fernihirst, stirring, and in some instances horrible, the deeds done within and around its walls. In 1548 the English held it, Shrewsbury, when he returned to the south in that year, having left there a garrison of something like eighty or ninety men. At this period Scotland, still dazed and stricken under the stunning blow of Pinkie in 1547, was in a deplorable, and apparently a very helpless, condition. Most of her strongholds were in English hands; her chief men for the greater part had come in and made submission to Somerset; the poorer sort in most parts of the Border were at the mercy of the hated invader. Here, at Fernihirst, the English garrison was under the command of one whose oppression and cruel lust were devilish, and whose treatment of unprotected country-folk was such as would justify almost any conceivable form of revenge

130

on the part of the men of Jedforest. M. de Beaugué, a French
officer who was then in Scotland, and who in his " *Histoire de
la Guerre d'Ecosse*" chronicles the campaigns of 1548, 1549,
says that during all the time this savage licentious devil remained
near Jedburgh " he never came across a young girl but he
outraged her, never an old woman but he put her to death
with cruel torture."   And, as the proverb has it : " Like

Fernihirst Castle (Sep. 27, 1911).

master, like man " ; where their captain forgot his manhood,
and disgraced the name of Englishman, how were the men
under his command likely to conduct themselves ?   The people
of the Forest of Jedworth thus had ghastly wrongs to wipe out ;
and when their chance came, they seized on it with avidity.

The cruelties inflicted on each other by both nations at
this period were detestable and revolting.   " Put men, women,
and children to fire and sword without exception, when any

K 2

resistance shall be made against you," wrote Henry VIII. to Lord Hertford in 1544, instructions which were most faithfully carried out. Here at Fernihirst our countrymen went, if possible, " one better," and their treatment of prisoners was of the most inhuman and savage nature. Yet if their wrongs were such as are depicted by de Beaugué, can one wonder that, like wild beasts, they tore and mangled?

Early in 1549 there came to Jedburgh a large body of French troops under the Sieur d'Essé, sent to recapture that town, which at the moment was held for the English by a force chiefly composed of Spanish mercenaries. The Spaniards made no great stand, and for the moment the Sieur and his little army were left with time on their hands. To the Sieur went Sir John Ker, then laird of Fernihirst, suggesting that the French general should aid him in recapturing the castle. French and Scots—a small body of the latter, the personal following of Sir John Ker—accordingly made a combined attack and quickly carried the outwork, the garrison retreating to the keep. Here, whilst a party laboured hard to effect a breach in the wall, French arquebusiers were so planted that no man of the garrison could show his face with impunity, or dared to attempt to interfere with the working party, who already in little over one hour had made a practicable breach, large enough at least to admit a man's body. About this time the main French force had come up, and the English garrison could not but see that their position was now desperate. Accordingly they showed a flag of truce, and the English commander, on receiving assurance that he would be allowed to return, came out through the hole in the wall and offered to give up the castle, provided that the lives of the garrison were spared. The Sieur d'Essé, however, would listen to no conditions; the surrender, he said, must be unconditional, and the Englishman therefore returned to his men.

Meantime, news of the attack on Fernihirst had flown abroad over the countryside, and men of Jedforest came hurrying to the scene, breathless with the lust of slaughter, panting with unquenchable thirst for a bloody vengeance. Letting their horses go, and, regardless of everything, rushing in, they burst open and swarmed through the doors of the lower court. And now the bowels of the English leader turned indeed to water, for well he knew what fate would be his were he once to fall into the hands of those frenzied men. Therefore once more hurriedly pressing through the breach, he surrendered himself to two French officers, MM. Dussac and de la Mothe-Rouge. Scarcely, however, had he done so, and even as they led him away, a prisoner, there rushed up a Scot, a dweller in the neighbouring forest of Jed, one who had only too terrible a reason to remember the face of this fiend who had outraged his wife and his young daughter. He said no word, but with a roar as of a wounded beast that charges, he smote with all his strength. And the head of a man went trundling and bumping loosely over the trampled grass, as the knees doubled under a headless trunk that sank almost leisurely to the ground. Then those Scots who most had foul reason to execrate the memory of this treacherous brute, joyfully plunged their hands into his blood as it gushed, and with shouts of exultation seizing his head, they placed it on a long pole and stuck it up by a stone cross that stood by the parting of three ways, that all might see and rejoice over their vengeance.

That was but the beginning of a scene long drawn and terrible in its ferocity. Prisoners were ruthlessly butchered, and when the Scots had murdered all whom they themselves had taken, their lust for blood was so far from slaked that they brought others from the Frenchmen—bartering even some of their arms in exchange—and slew these also with extreme barbarity. "I myself," writes M. de Beaugué, "sold them a prisoner for a small horse. They tied his hands and feet and head together, and placed him thus trussed in the middle of an open space, and ran upon him with their lances, armed as they were and on horseback . . . . until he was dead and his body hacked in a thousand pieces, which they divided among them and carried away on the iron points of their spears." "I cannot," naïvely adds the chronicler, "greatly praise the Scots for this practice. But the truth is the English tyrannised over the Borders in a most barbarous manner, and I think it was but fair to repay them, as the saying goes, in their own coin."

So Sir John Ker got back his strong castle. But it did not long remain undisturbed in the family possession. In 1570 there came into Scotland that English expedition under the Earl of Sussex and Lord Hunsdon which played such havoc in the Border, and once more the Merse and Teviotdale were burned and laid waste. "Apon Monday last," writes Lord Hunsdon from Berwick to Sir W. Cecil, under date 23rd April, 1570, "beyng the 17th of thys ynstant, we went owt of thys towne by 6 a cloke at nyght and rode to Warke, where we remayned tyll three or four yn the mornyng ; and then sett forward the hole army that was with us att that present, ynto Tyvydale bernyng on bothe hands at the lest two myle ; levyng neyther castell, towne, nor tower unburnt tyll we came to Jedworth. Many of the townes beyng Bukklews, and a proper tower of hys, called the Mose Howse, wythe three or four caves, wheryn the cuntrey folk had put such stufe as they had : and was very valyantly kept by serten of the cuntrey for two or three owars, but at last taken. . . . The next day we marchyd to Hawyke ; wher by the way we began with Farnhurst and Hunthylle, whose howsys we burnt, and all the howsys about them. We could nott blow up Farnhurst, but have so torne ytt with laborars, as ytt wer as goode ley flatt." The building must have been of remarkable solidity, for in spite of its being burnt, and left roofless and dismantled, "torne with laborars," in 1570, there can be little doubt that in less than two years it was again at least tenable, for in 1572 Lord Ruthven, after dispersing at Hawick the forces of Buccleuch and Fernihirst, (who supported the cause of the abdicated Queen,) on his return march to Jedburgh "tuik the housses of Pherniherst, and put men in them," and the place was held for some time after this by the King's troops. Possibly it was more thoroughly knocked about in 1593 than it had been at any other period of its existence. Sir Andrew Ker, then head of the house, when summoned to appear before James and his Privy Council at Jedburgh to answer for his part in aiding the schemes of the Earl of Bothwell, and for other acts, had failed to put in an appearance, and had consequently been outlawed and declared a rebel. It was also proposed to render him homeless, for on 16th October of that year Carey reports to Burghley that " the King has proclaimed to remain at Jedworth fifteen days, and summoned the barons, gentlemen and freeholders to attend him, minding this day or tomorrow to pull down the lairds of Fernihirst and Hunthill's houses, and all others who have succoured Bothwell." Probably the threat was carried into execution, to a greater or less extent. In any case, 1598 saw a renovated Fernihirst, much as it stands at the present day, when, according to " Castellated and Domestic Architecture of Scotland," it presents "a charming example of a Scottish mansion of the period." Built into the wall above the main doorway of the mansion, (as may be seen in Mr. Hugh Thomson's sketch,) are two panels, that to the left showing the armorial bearings of the Kers, and above, on a scroll, the words:

S. SOLI·DEO

"FORWARD IN Yᴱ NAME OF GOD"; at the foot, A.K. 1·5·9·8·. On the panel to the right is the word "FORWARD"; in the centre of the panel the arms of Sir Andrew's wife, Dame Ann

D. SOLI·DEO

Stewart, and beneath, A.S. 1·5·9·8·.

As late as 1767 the house seems to have been occasionally used by the Lord Lothian of that day, but it was even then showing signs of dilapidation. It was, however, occupied by farming tenants down to a recent date, as late, I believe, as 1889. About that year extensive repairs were carried out;

the ivy which—however picturesque it may have been—was slowly throttling the old walls, was removed, the panels were refaced, the roof made wind and weather proof, and the interior to a great extent restored.

At Smailcleuchfoot, a little higher up the river, and nearly opposite to Fernihirst Mill, almost, as one might say, within a stone's cast of the castle, stood once the house of a man greatly famed in Jedforest,—Auld Ringan Oliver.   No vestige of the house now remains, but the memory of Ringan and the story of the siege he stood within his cottage here still live in Border lore, and were sung of in James Telfer's "Border Ballads" close on a century ago.

> " The crystal Jed by Smailcleuchfoot
>   Flows on with murmuring din;
>   It seems to sing a dowie dirge
>   For him that dwelt therein."

Ringan's forebears, men of mark all of them in their day, dwelt here at Smailcleuchfoot for many a generation.   They were there, no doubt, when the Sieur d'Essé recaptured Fernihirst for Sir John Ker ; there when Dacre stormed it in 1523 ; there perhaps, helping Douglas, when Father Ellis and his Englishmen were caught feasting on the good fare at Lintalee in 1317.   With ancestors such as these, whose whole lives were passed in the midst of endless strife, men ever ready, and glorying in their readiness, to turn out against invading Southern bands, or to slip over Carterfell into Redesdale to plunder those same Southrons, how could Ringan fail to be, what he was, a born fighter !   With his enormous frame, immense personal strength, and dauntless courage, there was none in the Border so famed as he.   Endless were the tales told of him,—how he could take " a ten half-fou boll of barley in the wield of his arm and fling it across a horse's back with the utmost ease "; how in his youth he raided Newcastle Jail, and rescued two of his friends, who had been, as he thought, unjustly imprisoned therein.   The stories of him are endless.

Ringan lived in the stirring times of the Covenant, and with a disposition such as his, dourly religious, it is almost needless to say that he was prominent among the more militant section of the Covenanters of the seventeenth century. He was probably present at Drumclog, and he was certainly present at Bothwell Brig, in 1679, fighting as few fought that bloody day. His home was in caves and among rocks, beneath dripping peat-hags, and in holes in the ground, for many a day after this, but in 1680 he joined the outlawed Hall of Haughhead, and was in the tussle when that Champion of the Covenant was taken at Queensferry what time "those two bloody hounds the Curates of Borrowstonness and Carriden smelled out Mr. Cargill and his companion." Hall was killed, or at least died of his wounds before he could be brought to Edinburgh; but Ringan Oliver and "worthy Mr. Cargill" escaped the net of the fowler. Then, in 1689, he was with Mackay at Killicrankie; and the following day, though exhausted with the precipitate flight from the battlefield, he fought at Dunkeld his famous duel with the Highland champion, Rory Dhu Mhor, whom he slew after a most desperate and bloody fight. Bleeding from half a score of wounds, Ringan had been beaten to his knees, and the affair seemed a certain victory for the Highlander. But the latter was over-confident; he thought he had a beaten man at his mercy, and one instant's carelessness gave Ringan his chance. Before his adversary could recover, the point of the Borderer's sword was out between the Highlander's shoulders, and with a roar of astonishment and wrath he fell dead.

But perhaps it was for the siege he stood at Smailcleuchfoot when he was now an old man, that Ringan is best remembered. After a stormy youth and middle age, he had at length settled down in his ancestral home, where he was leading the quiet life of a farmer. As the story is told, it seems that Ringan's strict integrity and high sense of honour had gained for him the respect and friendship of his powerful neighbour at Fernihirst—probably either the first or the second Marquess of

Lothian.   Perhaps, too, there may have been something in the mutual belief and manner of thought of the two men that drew them together.   (There was a Ker of about that date, or a little earlier, who was a zealous Covenanter.)   In any case, the friendship was of such a nature that when Lord Lothian found himself, towards the close of his life, compelled to undertake what was then the long and trying journey to London, he left Ringan in charge of his private papers, and entrusted him with the key of a locked room in which valuable documents were kept, and into which he desired that no one should be permitted to enter whilst he himself was absent in the south.   As it chanced, after Lord Lothian had started on his journey, his heir, considering, as a matter of course perhaps, that the old lord's prohibition did not apply to him, sent to Ringan demanding the key of the room, into which he had, or said he had, occasion to go.   Ringan naturally, but perhaps not very deferentially or even politely, refused to give it up.   Thereupon arose hot words, and bitter enmity on the part at least of the younger man, who, with that rather irrational form of vanity not un-common in youth, imagined himself to be slighted.

And hence came serious consequences to the old Covenanter. For the Marquess died, and the man whom Ringan had offended succeeded to the title and estates.   He had always—so the story goes—nursed his wrath to keep it warm, and he might be depended on to pay off, with interest, all old scores against him whom he talked of as that "dour old Cameronian devil." So it happened one day, towards the time of harvest, when corn lay waiting for the sickle in the smiling haughs of Jed, the young lord and his friends, attended by servants in charge of several dogs, came on horseback across the river and began to ride up and down through Ringan's crop, ostensibly looking for hares.   The old man remonstrated in vain ; no heed was paid to him, and at length, goaded to fury as he saw the havoc being played among his good oates and bere, he snatched up an old musket (that perhaps had seen service at Bothwell Brig) and shot one of the dogs dead. That was enough; the old man had put himself now in the wrong. For the Marquess could plead that, after all, he had only been riding on his own land; and he and his friends could assert that the harm they had done, if any, had been infinitesimal. So the young lord rode off to Jedburgh, and had a summons issued by the Sheriff against Ringan.

It was one thing, however, to issue the summons, quite another to serve it, or afterwards to get Ringan to obey the call. If he persisted in ignoring the summons, there were not many to be found bold enough to go to Smailcleuchfoot for the purpose of haling him before the Court; old as he now was, Ringan's reputation for strength and courage, and for reckless daring, was still great enough to keep the wolves of the law at bay. "But," said the Sheriff, "the law cannot thus be flouted; if he does not come willingly, then he must be *made* to come." Which of course was quite the right thing to say, especially if he had at hand the force necessary to carry out his threat. But that was where the difficulty came in. Finally, the Sheriff had to go himself to arrest old Ringan, impressing on his way everybody whom he could find capable of helping, including the Marquess himself.

Ringan was warned of their coming, and advised to fly. "No!" said the old man. "I've dune no wrong. Let them touch me wha daur!" But he set about barricading his house, and when the Sheriff and his party came on the scene they found a building with doors fast and windows shuttered, and no one visible. At their knock, Ringan appeared at a small upper window, but entirely declined to be taken, or to open the door. Then commenced a vigorous assault by the Sheriff and his party. They attempted to break in the door and to rush the building. Ringan opened fire on them with his old musket, and drove them back.

And then for a time there occurred nothing more than a fruitless exchange of shots, as one or other of the Sheriff's

men left cover or Ringan showed himself at one of the
windows.   It appears, however, that there was in the house
with the old man a young girl, either his adopted daughter
or a domestic who looked after household affairs.   This girl
had been told to keep out of harm's way, to shelter in a " press "
or cupboard well out of any possible range of bullet ; but in
the heat of battle the old man did not notice that curiosity had
drawn her from the safety of this hiding place, and had brought
her right behind him at the moment that he fired a shot through
the window.   It was a good shot, for it clipped away a curl
from the Sheriff's wig, and perhaps in his satisfaction at going
so near to his mark the old man may have showed himself a
little too openly.   Anyhow, at that moment two or three
muskets replied, the heavy bullets coming with sullen " phut "
into the woodwork of the little window-frame.   But one flew
straighter than the others ; Ringan heard behind him a sound,
half gasp, half sob, and turned just in time to see the lass sink
on the floor, blood pouring from her throat.   The old man
tried to stanch the wound, but it needed hardly more than a
glance to tell that it was far beyond his simple skill, and that
she was past hope.

Then the lust of battle seized him, blind fury filled his
breast, and he thought only of revenge.   He forgot his age,
forgot that his fighting days should have been long over,
forgot everything but the mad desire to clutch the throats
of his foes and to choke the life out of them.   So, tearing down
the barricades of his door, he rushed out on his enemies like a
wild bull charging.   But alas for Ringan ! part of the discarded
barricade caught his foot as he burst over the threshold, and
down he came with a crash.   Before he could struggle even
to his knees, the enemy was on him, and he was down
again on his face, half a dozen men swarming over him.   Even
yet, however, old and hopelessly outnumbered as he was, the
fight for a time was not so very unequal, and he might in the
end have cast off the crowd that strove to hold and bind him.

An ill day it would have been for some of them had he succeeded. But a treacherous pedlar, who had joined the fray for
the sake of hire, watching his chance, came behind, and with
a blow from a hammer smashed Ringan's jaw and brought him
to the ground, stunned. The old man was taken then, bound
hand and foot, and carted off to Edinburgh. There, in the
foul air of the Tolbooth he lay for eight weary years, suffering
tortures great part of the time, not only from the broken jaw,
but from old wounds which had broken out afresh, and which
from the insanitary condition of the prison now refused to heal.
It was a broken, frail old man who came out from that long
imprisonment. And he never got back to his beloved Jed.
Ringan Oliver died in Edinburgh in 1736; his huge frame
sleeps in Greyfriars Churchyard.

As one travels up Jed by the old coach road—whose wind-
ings do not invariably desert even the abruptest elbow of the
stream—road and river finally part company at the bridge below
Camptown. Here the latter's course swings gradually to the
right, through leafy banks and under spreading trees, whilst the
former, following a straighter route, enters on a long, steady bit
of collar-work up the side of a pine-clad brae where, on one
hand, lies the old camp from which the adjacent little settlement
derives its name, and, on the other, Edgerston, sleeping in its
woods. Here once stood Edgerston Castle, which Hertford's
men took " by pollicie " in 1544 ;—someone sold the Rutherfurd
of that day. Castle and lands then belonged to the Rutherfurds,
one of the most ancient families in Scotland, and still the lands
are theirs.

A little way past Edgerston the road begins its long two mile
climb to an elevation of close on 1500 feet near the summit of
Catcleuch Shin. There, immediately after passing the Carter
Bar, it crosses the Border line, and drops steadily down into
Redesdale, past the new Catcleuch Reservoir that supplies
Newcastle with water, a work which has wiped out of existence
one of the pleasantest bits of fishing in the kingdom, where

trout were many and game, and of enviable size.   Perhaps the
trout are there still—for those who may take them—but the
capture of a dozen fish in still water cannot match the joy
experienced in fighting one good Rede trout in the strong
rushing stream where he has passed all his days.

Beyond the Catcleuch Reservoir, a road of easy gradients
sweeps down the delightful Rede valley, past innumerable old
camps, British and Roman ; past Rowchester, into whose little
school-house, that stands solitary in the angle of two ways, are
built numerous stones (carved and otherwise) handily quarried

Catcleuch Reservoir looking South.

from the adjacent old Roman station of Bremenium ; and high
up, on the roof of the building, from the same source are
various large round stone balls that may have formed part of
the ammunition for a Roman ballista.   It was this route that
the Roman legions followed over the Cheviots in their northward march from the mighty wall they had stretched across
England from sea to sea.   A few miles east from Catcleuch
Shin, their military road bursts suddenly into view of that
glorious sweep of country where the triple-peaked Eildons
dominate the scene, a landmark that no doubt led them first
to the site of their famous Newstead camp.

In early nineteenth century days, when His Majesty's mail coaches between Newcastle and Edinburgh came jangling over the crest of this bleak, unprotected bit of road at Catcleuch Shin, taking at a gallant trot the long, stiff gradient that faced them whether they were heading to the south or to the north, the trials of outside passengers in winter time must not seldom have been of a nature truly unenviable. Bitter sleet, driving before a westerly gale, lashed their faces and stole chill wet fingers inside their wraps and upturned collars ; drifting, blinding snow, swirling on the wings of a wild north-easter, blurred the guiding line of snow-posts, and even at times hid his leaders from the coachman's sight, so that his first warning of being off the road and on the moor, was a heavy lurch as the coach buried its side in some blind hollow ; frost, and a thermometer in the neighbourhood of zero, nipped from ears and nose and toes every vestige of feeling, and chilled to the very bone those whom duty or business forced to travel. It was truly a large assortment of evils that our ancestors had to choose from, in the winter, on that road over into England by the Carter Bar.

But if winter was bad, surely in the better time of year there were pleasures that atoned for all they had suffered. In the long twilight of a summer's evening, when moorland scents fill all the air and the crow of grouse echoes from the heathery knolls, what pleasure more satisfying could there be in life than to sit behind a free-going team of bays, listening lazily to the rhythm of the chiming hoofs, to the ring of steel bitts and the merry jingle of the splinter-bars? And as the coach breasted the summit, and began to make up time on the down gradient, the glorious view that broke on the eye of the north-bound passenger of itself would make amends for half the ills of life. Away to the west, stretched ever more dim in the fading sunset glow, the long-flung line of Cheviots—Carterfell, the Carlin's Tooth (where springs the infant Jed), Peel Fell, Hartshorn Pyke, all blending, far down, into the round green

hills of Liddesdale; then, more to the north-westward, set in
the wide expanse, the Windburgh Hill and Cauldcleuch Head;
farther off, away over the high land of upper Teviotdale,

> "The far grey riot of the Ettrick hills,"

and the dim shapes of the mighty "Laws" of Peeblesshire—
Broad Law, Dollar Law, Black Law. Then far below this vantage
point on Catcleuch Shin, in middle foreground Edgerston's
darkening woods; beyond, Ruberslaw, Minto Crags,—"where
falcons hang their giddy nest,"—and the Dunion; then, to the
right, Eildon's cloven peak, and, near-by, the Black Hill at Earlston, with the Lammermuirs in dimmest background; to the
right again, Smailholme Tower, erect and watchful; east of that,
the green Merse, wide-spread like a map, stretched almost to the
sea, and on the extreme right, far off, Cheviot himself, blocking
the view. What a truly magnificent sweep of country it is! A
sense of space, and room to breathe, such as one finds seldom
in this country.

Three hundred and thirty-eight years ago, however, there
were Scots and English assembled on that Catcleuch ridge one
summer's day, who had no eyes for the view;

> "The seventh of July, the suith to say,
>   At the Reidswire the tryst was set;
> Our Wardens they affixed the day,
>   And, as they promised, so they met.
> Alas! that day I'll ne'er forget!"

As was customary, the English and Scottish Wardens of the
Marches had met for the discussion and settlement of Border
claims and disputes, and for the redressing of wrongs. Sir
John Carmichael in this instance acted for Scotland, Sir John
Forster for England. The former was accompanied by the
young Scott of Buccleuch,—according to Sir Walter the same
who, twenty-one years later, was famous for the rescue of
Kinmont Willie from Carlisle Castle,—by sundry Armstrongs,

Elliots, Douglases, Turnbulls of Rule Water, and other wild
Borderers.

> " Of other clans I cannot tell
>   Because our warning was not wide."

But it was a turbulent band, one would think, and not easy of
control. Forster had at his back Fenwicks—"five hundred
Fenwicks in a flock," says the ballad,—Shaftoes, Collingwoods,
and other of the great English Border families, the men from
Hexham and thereabout, and many of the fiercest fighters of
Redesdale and Tynedale, the two latter said to be then the
most lawless people of the North of England. Indeed, their
reputation was so evil that the merchants of Newcastle passed
a by-law in the year 1564 that no apprentices should be taken
" proceeding from such leude and wicked progenitors." Thus
it may be seen that both nations were strongly represented,
and that on both sides there was superabundance of most
inflammable material waiting but for a spark to set it ablaze.
In most promising and peaceful fashion, however, the proceedings opened :

> " Yett was our meeting meek eneugh ;
>   Begun wi' merriment and mowes.
> *   *   *   *   *
> Some gaed to drink, and some stude still,
>   And some to cards and dice them sped."

And all went smoothly and well, till the case of one Robson, a
notorious Redesdale horse and cattle-thief, came up for discussion. The Scottish warden, following the usual Border
custom in such cases, demanded that the culprit, having been
guilty of theft on the northern side of the March, should be
given into Scottish custody till such time as reparation be made
to the parties robbed by the Redesdale man. Sir John Forster
demurred, giving as his reason for evading the usual practice
in such cases, that Robson had fled and could not be captured.
"Oh ! Play fair !" cried Carmichael contemptuously. Whereupon Forster not unnaturally lost his temper, and made a fierce
and insulting reply. Hot words leapt from angry lips, and

L

swords, which in those days were never long idle, began to flash
in the warm sunshine as they left the scabbards.   And then the
Tynedale men—"Fy, Tyndale, to it!"—eager to take time
by the forelock, and determined not to stand out of what fray
might be going, loosed off a flight of arrows among the Scots.
And all the fat was in the fire.   Like fiercest wolves, the two
sides flew at each other's throats, trampling over the heathery
ground, cursing, slashing, stabbing.

The Scots at first were getting rather the worst of the affray ;
Carmichael was down, and a prisoner ; others were disabled.
The English had the slope of the hill slightly in their favour
and made the most of their advantage, gradually forcing their
foes to fall back in tardy and sullen retreat.   Then came to the
hot headed Tynedale men the irresistible temptation to plunder.
It was customary at those Wardens' Meetings for pedlars or
small tradesmen to erect on the ground selected for the meeting,
tents, or, as we say in Scotland, "crames," sort of temporary
shop-counters sheltered by canvas, in or on which they displayed the wares they had for sale.   So it had been at this
Reidswire Meeting.   And as the Scots were forced back past
those "crames," the desire for loot proved too strong for some
of the English combatants.   By ones and twos, as opportunity
offered, they edged away from the fight, and, like marauding
wasps to crop of ripe plums, made for this booty that might be
had for the taking.   Fighting and plunder were equally congenial to the men of Tynedale.

At that very moment, however, in which a large number had
so withdrawn themselves, unfortunately for them reinforcements
arrived for the Scots.   "Jethart's here!" rang out over the
roar and stress of the fight, and into the "tulzie" plunged the
men of Jedburgh, hot off their ten mile march.

> " Bauld Rutherfurd, he was fou stout,
>   Wi' a' his nine sons him about ;
> He led the toun o' Jedburgh out,
>   All bravely fought that day."

The tables were badly turned on the English; now they in turn began to give way, and to be forced back up the hill down which till now they had been successfully pressing the Scots. Too late the Tynedale men tried to retrieve their error; the Scots got them on the run and gave no breathing space; speedily the run became a rout. Over the crest into Redesdale fled the discomfited English, dropping here a man, there a man, as they fled. " Sir George Hearoune of Schipsydehouse," (Sir George Heron Miles of Chipchase Castle,) fell early in the fight, and four and twenty dead bowmen kept him company. The wounded on both sides were many; and among the prisoners taken by the Scots were the English Warden, Sir James Ogle, Sir Cuthbert Collingwood, Sir Francis Russell (son of the Earl of Bedford), several Fenwicks, and other leading men from the English side of the Border. Carmichael took his prisoners to Edinburgh—not greatly to the comfort of the Scottish Regent, the Earl of Morton; for England and Scotland were then, for once in a way, at peace, and such an incident as this Raid of the Reidswire was but too likely to result in further war between the nations. Therefore, after a day or two's detention, or rather, perhaps, after a day or two's entertainment, Morton, with every expression of regret and of regard, sent all the prisoners back to England, apparently not ill pleased with their treatment. No international complications followed the affair. Carmichael was sent to York to explain matters, and he seems to have been able to show satisfactorily that the Scots were within their rights throughout; that, in fact, as the ballad says :

> " .   .   .   . pride, and breaking out of feuid
> Garr'd Tindaill lads begin the quarrel."

Some years ago, a very handsome silver mounted sword, and a fine specimen of a dagger, were unearthed by a man employed in cutting drains on the hillside where the battle was fought that July day of 1575. The sword was a beautiful weapon, of fine temper, and it probably belonged to one of the English leaders. Unfortunately it has been lost. Both it and the dagger have, as I understand, mysteriously disappeared from the house in which they were kept. Somebody too greatly admired them, one may suppose, and followed the example set by the men of Tynedale in the heat of battle that day.

The scene of the fight is that fairly level bit of moorland to the left of the road just after you quit the Carter Bar, going south.

Bridge over Jed Water at old Souden Kirk.   The Cheviots behind.

Harking back now for a moment to Jed,—five or six miles above the bridge at Camptown where we quitted the line of river to follow the old coach-road over Carter Fell, we come to Southdean. Here are the ruins of an ancient church, (the foundations, at least, and part of the walls and tower,) which have lately been dug out from the great green mound with its big ash trees atop, which lay these two hundred years and more between hillside and river, down by the little grey bridge. This is the "churche in a fayre launde called Zedon," wherein, says Froissart, Douglas and the other Scottish leaders met on the eve of that expedition into England which ended with the glorious fight of Otterbourne. "I never heard the old song of Percy and Douglas," wrote Sir Philip Sidney, "that I found not my heart more moved than with a trumpet;" and who is there to-day, in spite of lapse of centuries, whose blood does not quicken at the very sound of the word "Otterbourne.

It used to be said that the "Zedon" of Froissart was more applicable to Yetholm than to Southdean. Some, indeed, still maintain that, as far at least as *sound* is concerned, "Zedon" (the "Z", as was formerly not uncommon, being treated as a "Y") bears a much greater resemblance to "Yetholm" than to "Southdean." One may readily admit that as it is spelled, "South-dean" is not in the least like "Zedon." But it is an entirely different affair when we come to a matter of local pronunciation. In this case the pronunciation is, as near as may be, "Seuden." If we very slightly soften the sound of the letter "Z," and allow for the fact that the "e" of Zedon would naturally be used by Froissart with the same value that it bears in his own language, we arrive absolutely at the local pronunciation of the name—"Seuden."

In any case, it seems most unlikely that the point of assembly could have been Yetholm, if only for the reason that when marching from there into England,—presumably by way of the Bowmont valley, and so past Wooler and through Northumberland,—Douglas would have exposed himself to be struck in rear and on his left flank from the adjacent vantage points of Roxburgh and Wark, both of which formidable strongholds were then in English hands, and, (seeing that the intention of the Scots to make an invasion had long been known in Northumberland,) probably held in force. And certainly, if the column came by way of Ottercops and Rothely Crags, as it is said to have done, its starting point was not

Yetholm. Obviously, too, a Scottish army concentrated at Southdean was in a much better strategical position than any that it could have occupied in the neighbourhood of Yetholm. From Southdean it could strike either way at will, either over the easy, and necessarily well known, pass by Catcleuch Shin, or across the hills by the old Roman way, the Whele Causeway, into Liddesdale, and thence on to Carlisle.

This Scottish plan, to assemble an army here at Southdean, was the outcome of a meeting held some time previously at Aberdeen, a city " on the fronter of the Wylde Scottes," and, so far as was possible, the business had been kept secret ; even to the King himself no hint was given of what the Nobles designed, " for," said they among themselves, "the King is no manne of warre." But "the Scottes coude nat do their maters so secretly, but the lords of Englande knewe howe men rose in Scotland, and how they shulde mete agayne at Gedeours." Spies brought word to Northumberland of what was afoot, and the English took all necessary steps to upset the Scottish plan of campaign. If the Scots decided to come by way of Carlisle, then the English resolved that they, on their part, would burst into Scotland by way of Berwick, or by Dunbar. Thus, said they, " we shall do them more dommage than they can do us, for their countrey is all open ; we maye go where we lyst, and our countre is strong, and the townes and castelles well closed."

Now the Scots had gathered at Southdean this August of 1388 so vast an army that "in threscore yere before there was nat assembled toguyder in Scotlande suche a nombre of good men ; there were xii hundred speares and xl thousande men besyde with their archers ; but in tyme of nede the Scottes can lytell skyll with their bowes ; they rather beare axes, wherwith they gyve great strokes." And this army, "whan they were thus mette togyder in the marchesse of Gedours. . . . were mery, and sayd, they wolde never entre againe into their owne houses tyll they had ben in Englande, and done suche dedes there that it shulde be spoken of xx yere after."

To this gathering at Southdean came an English spy, one who "knewe right well the marchesse of Scotlande, and specially the forest of Gedeours." Without arousing suspicion, this man made his way into the church, and overheard the Scottish leaders discuss their plans. And when he had picked up information enough for his purpose, he withdrew quietly from the building and went to get his horse, which he had left in a convenient spot, tied to a tree. But never a trace of horse nor of harness was there now, "for a Scotte, who be great theves, had stollen hym awaye." It was a very tight corner for the spy. He durst make no great outcry, lest he betray himself; so, in default, he started "forthe afote, boted and spurred," thinking maybe to slip out of the camp unobserved and make over the Cheviots into Rede valley. In any other place but the Border, perhaps he might have got clear away. But the Borderers have ever been horse lovers, and now the unwonted sight of a man, booted and spurred, footing it, at once drew eyes to him that might have taken little heed had he been mounted. "A filthie thing," says Bishop Leslie, writing of the Borderers in the sixteenth century, "a filthie thing thay esteime it, and a verie abjecte man thay halde him that gangis upon his fete, ony voyage. Quhairthrough cumis that al are horsmen." So the spy had not gone many furlongs ere he was stopped by two mounted men.

"Felowe," said one of the two to the other, "I have sene a marveyle; beholde yonder a man goeth alone, and as I thynke, he hath lost his horse, for he came by and spake no worde; I wene he be none of our company; lette us ryde after hym to prove my saying." So, says Froissart, they went after him. And "whane he sawe them commynge, he wolde gladly have ben thens." The spy's answers to questions not being satisfactory, "they brought hym againe to the church of Zedon and presented him to the Erle Duglas and to other lordes." And there "they handled hym in suche wise that he was fayne to shewe all the mater." Their methods were not gentle in

those days; one wonders what they did. Anyhow, "they knew by
hym that the lordes of Northumberland had sent hym thyder,
to know the estate of their enterprise, and whiche waye they
wolde drawe. Hereof the Scottes were right joyous, and wolde
nat for a great good but that they had spoken with this
squyer."

Scottish arguments proved too strong for the unhappy Englishman : "Sirs," said he at last, "sithe it behoveth me to saye the
truthe, I shall." So he gave information of the whereabouts of
the English army, and disclosed the whole of the English plans,
telling how, the force at the disposal of the Northumbrian lords
not being strong enough to stand up against the Scottish host,
the intention of the English leaders was that if the Scots should
"take the waye into Gales [Cumberland] they wyll go by
Berwike, and so to Dunbare, to Edinborowe, or els to Alquest
[Dalkeith]; and if ye take nat that waye, then they wyll go by
Carlyle, and into the mountayns of the countrey. Whan the
lordes herde that, eche of them regarded other." As indeed
they had excellent cause, for this information put into their
hands a card that could most effectually trump their adversary's
strongest suit. They were " ryght joyfull," says Froissart, and
" demannded counsayle what way was best for them to
take."

Accordingly, the main army was despatched over the hills,
probably, and most naturally, up Jed and the Raven Burn, and
across into Liddesdale by the old Roman road that leaves
Carlin Tooth and Wheelrig Head on its left, and follows down
Peel Burn to Liddel Water; thence down the Liddel Valley
the marching would be easy to Longtown and on to Carlisle ;
whilst Douglas, with a flying column consisting of "thre hundred
speares of chosen men, and of two thousande other men and
archers," went up the Carter Burn and over the easy pass at
Catcleuch Shin into Redesdale, with intent to "drawe towardes
Newcastell upon Tyne, and passe the ryver and entre into the
bysshoprike of Durham, and burne and exyle the country."

"Thus these two hoostes departed eche from other, eche of
them prayenge other, that if the Englysshmen folowed any of
their armyes, nat to fyght with them tyll bothe their armyes
were joyned toguyder. Thus in a mornyng they departed fro
Gedeours, and toke the feldes."

Down the Rede valley—all fairly easy going in the dry
August weather, even at that day, one may suppose; Froissart
says the weather was "fayre and temperate,"—and across Tyne,
Douglas pushed rapidly, pausing neither to burn nor to slay,
until he came into Durham, "where they founde a good countrey.
Than they beganne to make warre, to slee people, and to brinne
vyllages, and to do many sore displeasures." Everyone knows
what happened after this; how at length, having skirmished
right up to the walls of Durham, and beyond, Douglas and his
men turned again northward and halted two days before Newcastle, where lay Percy, and English knights so many that
"they wyst not where to lodge"; how, whilst the Scots remained
here, Douglas and Percy fought, and Douglas overthrew Percy
and took from him a trophy which the latter swore to redeem
before it could be carried from Northumberland; and how
Percy, coming up with the Scots at Otterburne, strove to
regain that which he had lost at Newcastle, and was defeated
and made prisoner; how the fight raged throughout the moon-
lit night far into the morning, and the trampled heath lay red
with more than the bloom of heather; and how Earl Douglas
was slain. It is all told in the ballad, and how valiantly each
fought where cowards had no place.

> It fell about the Lammas tide,
>   When the muir-men win their hay,
> The doughty Douglas bound him to ride
>   Into England to drive a prey.
>
> He chose the Gordons and the Graemes,
>   With them the Lindsays, licht and gay,
> But the Jardines wald not with him ride,
>   And they rue it to this day.

And he has harried the dales o' Tyne
    And half o' Bambroughshire ;
And three good towers on Reidswire fells,
    He left them a' on fire.

And he march'd up to New Castel,
    And rade it round about :
" O, wha is the lord o' this castel,
    Or wha is the ladie o't ? "

But up spak proud Lord Percy then,
    And O but he spak hie !
" It's I am the lord o' this castel,
    My wife's the ladie gay."

" If thou art the lord o' this castel,
    Sae weel it pleases me !
For ere I cross the Border fells,
    The ane o' us shall dee."

He took a lang spear in his hand,
    Shod with the metal free ;
And forth to meet the Douglas there,
    He rade right furiouslie.

But O, how pale his ladie look'd
    Frae aff the castel wall,
When down before the Scottish spear
    She saw proud Percy fa' !

" Had we twa been upon the green,
    And never an eye to see,
I wad hae had you, flesh and fell,
    But your sword shall gae wi' me."

" But gae ye up tae Otterbourne,
    And bide there dayis three ;
And gin I come not ere they end,
    A fause knight ca' ye me."

" The Otterbourne's a bonny burn,
    'Tis pleasant there to be ;
But there is nought at Otterbourne
    To feed my men and me.

"The deer rins wild on hill and dale,
   The birds fly wild frae tree to tree;
But there is neither bread nor kail
   To fend my men and me.

"Yet I will stay at Otterbourne,
   Where you shall welcome be;
And, if you come not at three dayis end,
   A fause knight I'll ca' thee."

"Thither will I come," proud Percy said,
   "By the micht of Our Ladye!"
"There will I bide thee," said the Douglas,
   "My troth I plight to thee."

They lichted high on Otterbourne,
   Upon the brent sae brown;
They lichted high on Otterbourne,
   And threw their pallions down.

And he that had a bonnie boy,
   Sent out his horse to grass;
And he that had not a bonnie boy,
   His ain servant he was.

Then up and spak a little page,
   Before the peep of dawn:
"O waken ye, waken ye, my good lord,
   For Percy's hard at hand."

"Ye lie, ye lie, ye liar loud!
   Sae loud I hear ye lie;
For Percy had not men yestreen
   To fight my men and me.

"But I hae dreamed a dreary dream,
   Beyond the Isle of Skye:
I saw a dead man win a fight,
   And I think that man was I."

He belted on his gude braid sword,
   And to the field he ran;
But he forgot the helmet good
   That shou'd have kept his brain.

When Percy with the Douglas met,
    I wat he was fu' fain !
They swakkit swords till sair they swat,
    And the blood ran down like rain.

But Percy, wi' his good braid sword,
    That could sae sharply wound,
Has wounded Douglas on the brow,
    Till he fell till the ground.

Then he call'd on his little foot-page,
    And said—" Run speedilie,
And fetch my ain dear sister's son,
    Sir Hugh Montgomerie."

" My nephew good," the Douglas said.
    " What recks the death o' ane !
Last nicht I dream'd a dreary dream,
    And I ken the day's thy ain.

" My wound is deep; I fain would sleep;
    Take thou the vanguard of the three,
And hide me by the bracken bush
    That grows on yonder lily lee.

" O, bury me by the bracken bush,
    Beneath the blooming brier ;
Let never living mortal ken
    That a kindly Scot lies here."

He lifted up that noble lord,
    With the saut tear in his ee ;
He hid him in the bracken bush,
    That his merrie men might not see.

The moon was clear, the day drew near,
    The spears in flinders flew ;
But mony a gallant Englishman
    Ere day the Scotsmen slew.

The Gordon's gude, in English bluid
    They steep'd their hose and shoon ;
The Lindsays flew like fire about,
    Till a' the fray was dune.

The Percy and Montgomerie met,
  That either of other was fain ;
They swakkit swords, and they twa swat,
  And aye the bluid ran down between.

"Now yield thee, yield thee, Percy," he said,
  " Or else I vow I'll lay thee low ! "
"To whom must I yield," quoth Earl Percy,
  " Sin' I see that it maun be so ? "

" Thou shalt not yield to lord or loun,
  Nor yet shalt thou yield to me ;
But yield ye to the bracken bush
  That grows upon yon lilye lee ! "

" I will not yield to a bracken bush,
  Nor yet will I yield to a brier ;
But I would yield to Earl Douglas,
  Or Sir Hugh Montgomerie if he were here."

As soon as he knew it was Montgomerie,
  He stuck his sword's point in the gronde ;
Montgomerie was a courteous knight,
  And quickly took him by the hond.

This deed was done at Otterbourne,
  About the breaking o' the day ;
Earl Douglas was buried by the bracken bush,
  And the Percy led captive away.

    .   .   .   .   .   .

Froissart says he was told by two English squires who took part in the fight, " how this batayle was as sore a batayle fought as lyghtly hath been harde of before of such a nombre, and I believe it well. For Englysshmen on the one partye and Scottes on the other party are good men of warre : for whan they mete there is a hard fight without sparynge ; there is no hoo bytwene them as long as speares, swordes, axes, or dagers wyll endure, but lay on eche upon other, and whan they be well beaten, and that the one parte hath optaygned the victory, they than glorifye so in their dedes of armes and are so joyfull, that suche as be taken they shall be raunsomed or

they go out of the felde, so that shortly eche of them is so
contente with other that at their departynge curtoysly they wyll
saye, God thanke you.   But in fyghtynge one with another
there is no playe nor sparynge ; and this is trewe, and that shall
well apere by this sayd rencounter, for it was as valyauntly
foughten as coulde be devysed."

With hand to hand fighting so close and so fierce as here
befell at Otterburne, the slaughter could not fail to be very
great.   According to Godscroft, the English alone lost one
thousand eight hundred and forty killed, and over a thousand
wounded.   The total Scottish loss in killed, wounded and
missing appears to have been less than half that of the enemy
in killed alone. The English lost also over a thousand men who
were captured by the Scots ; indeed, the latter had so many
prisoners that they were greatly put to it to know what to do
with them at the moment when the Bishop of Durham with his
ten thousand fresh troops came on the scene and seemed
likely to renew the battle.   Many of the prisoners were men of
distinction.   Percy himself was taken by the Earl of
Montgomery ; his brother, Ralph Percy, by Sir John Maxwell ;
Sir Matthew Reedman, governor of Berwick, by Sir James
Lindsay.   And many another Scottish knight or squire held
his brother of England to ransom.

Froissart describes more than one picturesque incident of
the fight, and none, surely, is more vivid and alive than that in
which he tells how Sir Matthew Reedman, Governor of
Berwick, fled from the field, pursued by Sir James Lindsay.
When all was done that man could do, and all was done in
vain, Sir Matthew turned to save himself.   Lindsay chanced
to be near at hand, and saw him gallop out from the stress
of battle.   "And this Sir James to wyn honour, followed
in chase . . . . and came so nere hym that he myght have
stryken him with his speare if he had lyst.   Than he said,
'Ah, sir knyght, tourne, it is a shame thus to flye : I am James
of Lindsay : if ye wyll nat tourne I shall stryke you on the backe

with my speare.' Sir Matthew spake no worde, but strake his
horse with the spurrs sorer than he dyde before. In this
manner he chased hym more than thre myles, and at laste sir
Mathue Reedman's horse foundred and fell under hym. Than
he stept forth on the erthe, and drewe oute hys swerde, and
toke corage to defende hymselfe; and the Scotte thought to
have stryken hym on the brest, but sir Mathewe Reedman
swerved fro the stroke, and the speare poynt entered into the
erthe: than sir Mathue strake asonder the speare with his
swerde. And whan sir James Lynsay sawe howe he had loste
his speare, he caste awaye the trounchon and lyghted afote, and
toke a lytell batayle axe that he caryed at his backe, and
handeled it with his one hande, quickely and delyverly, in the
whiche feate Scottes be well experte. And than he sette at sir
Mathue, and he defended hymselfe properly. Thus they
tourneyed toguyder, one with an axe, and the other with a
swerde, a longe season, and no man to lette them. Fynally,
sir James Lynsay gave the knyght suche strokes, and helde hym
so shorte, that he was putte out of brethe, in such wyse that he
yelded hymselfe, and sayde : 'Sir James Lynsay, I yelde me to
you.' 'Well,' quod he, 'and I receyve you, rescue or no rescue.'
'I am content,' quod Reedman, 'so ye deale with me lyke a good
campanyon.' 'I shall not fayle that,' quod Lynsay, and so put
up his swerde. 'Well, sir,' quod Reedman, 'what wyll you nowe
that I shall do? I am your prisoner, ye have conquered me ; I
wolde gladly go agayn to Newcastell, and within fyftene dayes
I shall come to you into Scotlande, where as ye shall
assigne me.' 'I am content,' quod Lynsay : 'ye shall promyse by
your faythe to present yourselfe within this iii wekes at
Edenborowe, and wheresoever ye go, to repute yourself my
prisoner.' All this sir Mathue sware and promysed to fulfyll.
Than eche of them toke their horses and toke leave eche of
other."

They were to meet again, however, in less than the stipulated
time. Sir James turned his horse towards Otterburne,

intent on rejoining his friends. But a mist came down over the hills and blotted out the moorland ; he could only feel his way in the direction he desired to go. And when at length through the haar and thickness there came to his ears the muffled sound of voices, the ring of bridles and snort of horses, in full assurance that the sounds came from a body of his own men returning from pursuit of the broken English, he rode confidently forward, it was to find himself face to face with five hundred horse under the Bishop of Durham. And said the Bishop to Lindsay : " ' Ye shall go with me to Newcastell.' ' I may nat chose,' quod Lynsay, ' sithe ye wyll have it so ; I have taken, and I am taken, suche is the adventures of armes.' ' Whom have ye taken ' : quod the bysshop. ' Sir,' quod he, ' I toke in the chase sir Mathue Redman.' ' And where is he ? ' quod the bysshop. ' By my faythe, sir, he is returned to Newcastell ; he desyred me to trust hym on his faythe for thre wekes, and so have I done.' ' Well,' quod the bysshop, ' lette us go to New- castell, and there ye shall speke wyth hym.' Thus they rode to Newcastell toguyder, and sir James Lynsay was prisoner to the Bysshop of Durham." So the twain met again, and " ' By my faythe, sir Mathewe,' said Lindsay, ' I beleve ye shall nat nede to come to Edenborowe to me to make your fynaunce : I thynke rather we shall make an exchaunge one for another, if the bysshoppe be so contente.' " Whereupon, Reedman—as has ever been the wont of Englishmen—proposed that they should mark the occasion by a dinner ; and, says Froissart, " thus these two knyghts dyned toguyder in Newcastell."

He was not a valiant person, apparently, this Bishop of Durham. Had he been a very militant Prince of the Church, it had surely gone hard now with the Scots, for, outnumbered as they had been throughout the fight, they were sore spent ere ever the Bishop hove in sight with his ten thousand fresh troops, and it could scarcely have taken very much to drive them from the field in headlong rout. But the English leader was not a very intrepid man ; and when he found the Scots drawn together in a position so defended by swamp and morass that entry could be forced only by the one way, the Bishop hesitated. Then the Scottish leaders ordered their "mynstrels to blowe up all at ones, and make the greatest revell of the worlde"; for, as Froissart says, "whan they blowe all at ones, they make suche a noyse that it may be herde nighe iiii myles of; thus they do to abasshe their enemyes, and to rejoyse themselfes."

The instruments used were horns, we are told. Had they been bagpipes, one might perhaps have understood the consternation of the English. Says Froissart: "Whan the bysshoppe of Durham, with his baner, and XM men with hym, were aproched within a leage, than the Scottes blew their hornes in suche wise that it seemed that all the devyls in hell had been amonge them, so that such as herde them, and knewe nat of their usage, were sore abasshed." Nevertheless, the Bishop, with his host in order of battle, advanced to within about two bow-shot of the Scots, and there came to a halt in order to reconnoitre their position. The more he looked at it, the less he liked it; losses were certain to be heavy, victory by no means assured. So the English drew off; and the Scots, we are told, "wente to their lodgynges and made mery."

Then, the next day, having burned their camp, they marched unmolested back up the Rede valley into Scotland; and with them they bore the honoured bodies of Douglas and of others who had fallen in the fight. Percy went with them, a captive, and many another distinguished Englishman against his will sadly followed the victors. But those prisoners who were too badly hurt to endure the march into Scotland were sent under parole back to Newcastle, among them Sir Ralph Percy, who was returned in a horse litter. Huge sums are mentioned as having been paid in ransom by the English prisoners, the estimate of some writers reaching the extravagant figure of £600,000, a sum that in those days would have enriched the entire Scottish nation beyond the dreams of avarice. Even that number of pounds

M

Scots (equal to £50,000) seems beyond reason. Froissart's 200,000 francs (£8,000 in our money) is probably about what was paid—in that day a most handsome sum.

A cheerful little village is the Otterburne of the present day, —even though there are not wanting evidences that some part of it, down by the inn, for example, has planted itself in too close proximity to a river and a burn which still, as in those early

Otterburne.

eighteenth century days of "Mad" Jack Hall, are capable of sudden and vindictive flood. As regards the battlefield, however, there is not a great deal to see. The so-called Percy's Cross, which stands in a thin clump of trees to the east of the road three-quarters of a mile on the Scottish side of the village, is a comparatively modern erection. The true site of the original "Battle Stone," according to maps of date 1769, was about a couple of hundred yards more to the east, and there it stood, or rather, lay, till 1777, when the then proprietor of the land, a

Mr. Ellison, put up the cross now standing, within view of the new turnpike road which was then being made up the valley of the Rede. Mr. Ellison used the ancient socket of the original cross, but the rough pedestal on which the socket stands has nothing to do with the old memorial. Nor has the present shaft, which, says Mr. Robert White in his " History of the Battle of Otterburne" (1857), was nothing but " an old architrave which had been removed from the kitchen fireplace at

Otterburne.

Otterburne Hall. This stone, the cross-section of which is fifteen and a half by eight inches, still shows a bevelled corner throughout its length ; besides, two small pieces of iron project from one of its sides, which, in its former period of usefulness, were probably connected with some culinary apparatus. On its top is another stone, tapering to a point, which completes the erection. The entire length of the shaft above the base is nine and a half feet. The socket is a worn, weather-beaten

M 2

sandstone, about two feet square, without any tool-marks upon it, and appears to have been in use much longer than any of the stones connected with it."

A still more modern memorial of the battle is a large semi-circular seat cut in freestone, bearing on darker coloured panels various inscriptions, which stands by the road-side a little farther to the north. This was erected in 1888 by Mr. W. H. James, then M.P. for Gateshead. It may be noted that one of the panels gives the date of the battle as *tenth* August, 1388, which is almost certainly a mistake.

Douglas, of course, had satisfactory reasons for camping that night where he did,—reasons not unconnected probably with the question of shelter from English arrows. A wood protected him, it is said. Had he gone four or five miles farther on up the valley, he might have occupied the old Roman camp of Bremenium, a strong position, not sheltered from arrow-flight by trees, it is true, but protected on two sides by what in old days must have been swamps, and surrounded by a heavy wall which, even in its present condition, would be, to a defending force, a considerable protection in hand to hand fighting. Five hundred years ago, before the day of agricultural improvement and the custom of using ancient monuments as a quarry, such a defence must have made the camp a place of very considerable strength. Portions only now remain of the formidable wall which originally protected Bremenium, but enough stands to show what its strength must have been in the days when the Roman Legions manned it. The face is composed of great blocks of hewn freestone, accurately fitted ; in height it must have been about fourteen feet, in thickness something like seventeen,—the inner portion, of course, being rubble work ; outside there were two or more fosses. One of the gateways is still intact to a very considerable height, but the camp as a whole has to a most pitiable extent been used as a quarry, perhaps for hundreds of years. Even yet, one doubts if it is held quite sacred from vandal raids. As late as 1881, when members of the Berwickshire Naturalists' Club visited the camp they found masons deliberately quarrying stones from one corner of the wall, in order to build a hideous modern cottage, and I daresay some of the houses in the immediate neighbourhood may be composed entirely of stones taken from the old walls. The writer has not seen the Roman tombs which exist about half a mile to the east of the camp. The largest of these is said to have still two courses of stones standing, besides the flat stones of the foundation. This tomb has in front a small carving, regarding which Dr. Collingwood Bruce, in " The Roman Wall," suggests that it may have been intended to represent " the head of a boar—the emblem of the twentieth legion." The writer is given to understand that the carving bears no resemblance whatever to the head of a boar. A coin of the Emperor Alexander Severus was found in this tomb, together with a jar containing calcined bones, and a coin of the Emperor Trajan was found in the camp.

How many of Douglas's wounded, one wonders, were carried from the field of battle over to Southdean, and, succumbing there to their wounds, were buried at the church? Two or three years ago, when the ash-trees were cut down and the grassy mound carted away that had so long concealed the ruins of the old building, quantities of human bones were dug up within and about the walls, some of the skulls showing unmistakably that the owners had died no peaceful death. No doubt the main body of the Scottish army would follow the dead Douglas to his tomb in Melrose Abbey, and would therefore never come so far west as Southdean, but the severely wounded would naturally be left wherever they could be attended to. It is certain that the Southdean district was in old days much less sparsely populated than is now the case; two important yearly fairs, for instance, used formerly to be held at Lethem, (three miles nearer the Border than Southdean,)—where also, on a knoll still called the Chapel Knowe, was a chapel, subsidiary to the church of Southdean. These fairs were for the sale of "horse, nolt, sheep, fish, flesh, malt, meal," and all sorts of merchandise, and in the permit to hold the Fairs Lethem is described as being "by reason of its situation, lying near the Border, a very convenient and fit place for traffic and trade." The church of Southdean, therefore, as its ruins indicate, was probably of considerable importance, surrounded by a settlement of some size, where wounded men might well be left to take their chance of recovery. Whether the Scots returned from

Souden Kirk.

Otterburne up Rede valley and over the pass by way of Catcleuch Shin, or (as is more probable) followed the Roman Road which passes Bremenium Camp and runs over the Cheviots some miles to the east of Carter-fell, and thence crossing Kale, Oxnam, Jed, and Teviot, goes in more or less direct line towards Newstead and Melrose, it would be easy and natural for them to detach a party with the wounded, and perhaps with the bodies of some of the more notable dead, to

Southdean. And those of them who died there would of course
be buried in or close to the church.

During the excavations, it is of interest to note that numbers
of skulls were found all together at one spot, pointing to the
probability of many bodies having been, from some common
cause, buried in a common grave. The inference seems not
illegitimate that this cause was the fight at Otterburne. The
English appear to have carried away from the field many of
their dead, as well as their wounded :

> " Then on the morne they mayde them beerys
>   Of birch and haysell graye ;
>   Many a wydowe with wepynge teyrs
>   Ther makes they fette awaye."

It is not unlikely that the Scots also brought away some, at
least, of their dead, and, as Southdean was the nearest spot in
their own country where they could find consecrated ground,
the probability is that these bodies, as well as those of the
wounded who died later, would find rest there.

In his "History and Poetry of the Scottish Border," Professor
Veitch mentions that "a recent discovery made at Elsdon
Church, about three miles from the scene of conflict, may be
regarded as throwing some light on the slaughter. There skulls
to the amount of a thousand have been disinterred, all lying
together. They are of lads in their teens, and of middle-aged
men ; but there are no skulls of old men, or of women. Not
improbably these are the dead of Otterburne."

The length of the old building at Southdean, including tower
and chancel, was ninety-seven feet, and the nave was about
twenty-three feet in width. Many notable things were unearthed during the work of excavation, those of most interest
possibly being a massive octagonal font, cut from one block of
stone, and a small stone super-altar incised with the usual five
crosses.

At Southdean, as elsewhere, the old church has for generations
been used as a quarry. The retaining wall of the adjacent

Newcastle road is full of dressed stones taken from the building, and others, some of them carved, have been built into the
walls of an adjoining barn.   Certainly our ancestors in this
instance had more excuse than usual to offer for their depreda-
tions, for the building was a hopeless ruin.   The roof of the
church fell in one Sunday in the year 1689, and the walls—not
unhelped by human hands—speedily followed suit.   Stones
from the principal doorway seem to have been used in 1690 in
the building of a new church at Chesters.   That too is now in
ruins.

CHAPTER VI

ALE, RULE WATER, TEVIOT, HAWICK

As we ascend Teviot, after Jed its next important tributary is the Ale, not so named from the resemblance of its waters, when flooded, to a refreshing beverage. Sir Herbert Maxwell says that the name was originally written "Alne" (as in Aln, Alnwick) and this form survives in the place-name in Ale, Ancrum, the site of a desirable Scottish victory. The word would at first be *Alne crumb*, the crook of Alne or Ale." *Crom* does mean "crook" in Gaelic, I understand, and Ale does make a crook or bend round Ancrum, so the names are tokens of the possession of the dale by Gaelic-speaking people, very long ago. In Timpendean, the name of a ruined tower opposite the point where Ale enters Teviot, we have the English "dene" or "den," as in the neighbouring Hassendean

The places of most historical interest on lower Ale are Ancrum Moor and Lilliard's Edge, the scene of a battle in which the Scots partly avenged the incessant burnings and slayings by the men of Henry VIII, inflicted while the prince was furious at his failure to secure the hand of the baby Queen, Mary Stuart, for his puny son, later Edward VI. Henry first hoped, by the aid of these professional traitors, chiefs of the Douglases,—the Earl of Angus and his brother, Sir George —to obtain the Royal child and the great castles, and the

Crown of Scotland, without drawing sword. Baffled in this by the adroitness and patriotic courage of Cardinal Beaton, he sent his forces to rob, burn, and slay through all the eastern and central Marches. In February 1545, Hertford had finished his own work of ruin, despite which the Earl of Angus declared that he loved Henry VIII "best of all men." There followed a breach in this tender sentiment, *amantium irae.* Hertford's lieutenants, Evers and Laiton, with "assured Scots" of Teviotdale, wearing St George's cross, were harrying the Border. The Scottish Regent, the fickle, futile, good-humoured Earl of Arran, called for forces, but met little response, for, as a contemporary diarist writes, all men suspected the treachery of Henry's lover, and of the Douglases, "ever false, as they alleged." Yet Scott, in his ballad of "The Eve of St John," speaks of "the Douglas true and the bold Buccleugh"; the Scotts of Buccleuch, in fact, were ever loyal. The Laird, approached with bribes in English gold, rejected them in language of such pardonable profanity as frightened and astonished the English envoy, accustomed to buy Scottish traitors by the gross.

So mixed were affairs that while Wharton was trying to kidnap Sir George Douglas for Henry, Sir George was endeavouring to betray Arran to the English. They worsted the pacific Regent near Melrose, burned town and abbey, and desecrated the ancestral graves there of the Douglases, among them the resting place of the Earl who fell, when "a dead man won a fight," at Otterburne. The English clearly did not understand that Angus and his brother were eager to make their peace with Henry by renewing their treacheries to their country.

The ruining of his ascestors' tombs aroused the personal fury of Angus, moreover Henry had made large gifts of Angus's lands to Evers and Laiton. Angus therefore gathered his forces, breathed out threats, and joined hands with Arran, who was also supported by a very brave man, Norman Leslie,

presently to be one of the assassins of Cardinal Beaton—in
Henry's interest.   Norman, however, was patriotic for the
moment, and the bold Buccleuch was ever trusty.   As Angus
and Arran followed the English, Leslie and Buccleuch "came
lightly riding in" and the Scots united on the wide airy moor
of Ancrum.

The English saw their approach, and saw their horses
moving to the rear.   Supposing that the Scots were in retreat,
(they meant to fight on foot, and only sent their mounts to the
rear,) the lances of Evers and Laiton galloped gaily in pursuit.
But what they found was "the dark impenetrable wood" of
stubborn spears.   With the sun and the wind and blown
smoke in their faces, the English cavalry charged, and were
broken on the *schiltroms* or serried squares as they were
broken at Bannockburn.   Hereon the clan Ker, the men of
Cessford and Ferniehirst, "assured Scots," tore off their crosses
of St. George, and charged with Leslie, the Douglases, and
Buccleuch.   The English were routed, the country people rose
against them ; Evers and Laiton lost their new lands with their
lives, eight hundred of the English were slain, and two
thousand were taken alive—which is rather surprising.   The
English evacuated Jedburgh, and the Scots recovered
Coldingham.

Meanwhile the good-natured, false, feckless Regent Arran
wept over the dead body of Sir Ralph Evers.   "God have
mercy on him, for he was a fell cruel man, and over-cruel.
And welaway that ever such a slaughter and blood-shed should
be among Christian men," sobbed the Regent.   His heart was
better than his head.   Even George Douglas had warned
Henry VIII of what would result from "the extreme war that
is used in killing women and young children."   In my childhood I heard and never forgot, the country rhyme on an
Amazon of a girl, who, to avenge her lover, took arms at
Ancrum moor.   She fell, and on her tomb, which has been
many times restored, the following epitaph is engraved :

" Fair Maiden Lilliard
    Lies under this stane ;
Little was her stature,
    But muckle was her fame.
Upon the English loons
    She laid many thumps,
And when her legs were cuttit off
    She fought upon her stumps."

Clearly this is a form of

" For Widrington I must bewail as one in doleful dumps,
    For when his legs were cutten off he fought upon his stumps."

Lilliard's Edge, the ancient name of the scene of this fair lady's fall, must have suggested the idea of a girl styled Lilliard, and her story was thus suggested to the rhymer and became a local myth.

About Ancrum the Ale, like the Jed, and, over the Border, the Eden and Coquet, beautifies itself by cutting a deep channel through the fine red sandstone of which Melrose Abbey is built.   These channels are always beautiful, but Ale, otherwise, as we ascend its valley, is a quiet trout stream "that flows the green hills under."   In my boyhood, long, long ago, Ale abounded in excellent trout, and was my favourite among all our many streams.   It does not require the angler to wade, like Tweed and Ettrick ; it is narrow and easily commanded. The trout were almost as guileless as they were beautiful and abundant ; but I presume that they are now almost extermin- ated by fair and unfair methods.   The Scot, when he does not use nets, poisons, and dynamite, is too often a fisher with the worm, and, as I remember him, had no idea of returning even tiny fish to the water, as James Thomson, author of *The Seasons*, himself a Border angler, advises us to do.

Guileless, indeed, since old time has been the character of the trout of Ale.   Sir Thomas Dick Lauder tells how in his boyhood he went once with a chance-met "souter" from Selkirk to the long pool in Ale above Midlem bridge, and how there, by a most unsporting device, they captured the innocent trout almost by the sack-load. "We came," he says, "to a very long gravelly-bottomed pool, of an equal depth all over of from three to four feet. Here the souter seated himself; and, shortening both our rods, and fitting each of them with the three hooks tied back to back, he desired us to follow him, and then waded right into the middle of the pool. The whole water was sweltering with fine trouts, rushing in all directions from the alarm of our intrusion among them. But after we had stood stock still for a few moments, their alarm went off, and they began to settle each individually in his own place. 'There's a good one there,' said the souter, pointing to one at about three yards from him; and throwing the hooks over him, he jerked him up, and in less than six seconds he was safe in his creel. We had many a failure before we could succeed in catching one, whilst the souter never missed; but at length we hit upon the way; and so we proceeded with our guide, gently shifting our position in the pool as we exhausted each particular spot, until the souter's creel would hold no more, and ours was more than half filled with trouts, most of which were about three-quarters of a pound in weight; and very much delighted with the novelty of our sport, we made our way back to Melrose by the western side of the Eildon hills, and greatly astonished our companion with the slaughter we had made, seeing that he had been out angling for a couple of hours in the Tweed, without catching a single fin." A slaughter of the innocents, indeed! But the most inveterate poacher could not now, in any Border stream, hope to rival a feat so abominable in the eyes of present-day fishers. Nor, if he did attempt it, would he be likely to find trout so utterly devoid of guile as to submit thus quietly to be hooked out of the water one by one till the pool was emptied. Trout are better educated, if fewer in number, than they appear to have been eighty or ninety years ago. It is difficult, too, to see where the fun of this form of fishing comes in, after the rather

cheap excitement of catching the first one or two. But they
did curious things in the name of Sport in the earlier half of
last century. Many of the methods of catching salmon that
are written of approvingly by Scrope, that great angler of Sir
Walter's day, are now the rankest of poaching, and are prohibited by law.

The mid course of Ale is through "ancient Riddel's fair
domain," as Scott says in the great rhymes of William of
Deloraine's midnight ride from Branksome Tower to Melrose.
There is now no Riddel of Riddel.

Here I shall mercilessly quote the whole of William of
Deloraine's Itinerary from Branksome Tower till he rides Ale
when "great and muckle o' spate."

> " Soon in his saddle sate he fast
> And soon the steep descent he past,
> Soon cross'd the sounding barbican,
> And soon the Teviot side he won.
> Eastward the wooded path he rode,
> Green hazels o'er his basnet nod ;

> " He pass'd the Peel of Goldiland,
> And cross'd old Borthwick's roaring strand ;
> Dimly he view'd the Moat-hill's mound.
> Where Druid shades still flitted round ;
> In Hawick twinkled many a light ;
> Behind him soon they set in night ;
> And soon he spurr'd his coarser keen
> Beneath the tower of Hazeldean.

> " The clattering hoofs the watchmen mark :—
> ' Stand, ho ! thou courier of the dark.'—
> ' For Branksome, ho !' the knight rejoin'd,
> And left the friendly tower behind.
> He turn'd him now from Teviotside,
>   And guided by the tinkling rill,
> Northward the dark ascent did ride,
>   And gained the moor at Horsliehill ;
> Broad on the left before him lay,
> For many a mile, the Roman way.

" A moment now he slack'd his speed,
A moment breathed his panting steed ;
Drew saddle-girth and corslet-band,
And loosen'd in the sheath his brand.
On Minto-crags the moonbeams glint,
Where Barnhill hew'd his bed of flint ;
Who flung his outlaw'd limbs to rest,
Where falcons hang their giddy nest,
Mid cliffs, from whence his eagle eye
From many a league his prey could spy ;
Cliffs, doubling, on their echoes borne,
The terrors of the robbers' horn ;
Cliffs, which, for many a later year,
The warbling Doric reed shall hear,
When some sad swain shall teach the grove,
Ambition is no cure for love !

" Unchallenged, thence pass'd Deloraine,
To ancient Riddel's fair domain,
   Where Aill, from mountains freed,
Down from the lakes did raving come ;
Each wave was crested with tawny foam,
   Like the mane of a chestnut steed.
In vain ! no torrent, deep or broad,
Might bar the bold moss-trooper's road.

" At the first plunge the horse sunk low,
And the water broke o'er the saddlebow ;
Above the foaming tide, I ween,
Scarce half the charger's neck was seen ;
For he was barded from counter to tail,
And the rider was armed complete in mail ;
Never heavier man and horse
Stemm'd a midnight torrent's force.

" The warrior's very plume, I say,
Was daggled by the dashing spray ;
Yet, through good heart, and Our Ladye's grace,
At length he gained the landing place."

Above the point where William rode the water, the scenery
is quiet and pastoral ; about Ashkirk and Synton we are in the

lands of lairds whose genealogies are recounted in the rhymes
of old Satchells, who

> " can write nane
> But just the letters of his name."

Further up, Ale rests in the dull deep loch of Alemuir, which
looks as if it held more pike than trout.   And so we follow her
into the hills and the water-shed that, on one side, contributes
feeders to the Ettrick.   It is a lofty land of pasture and broken
hills, whence you see the airy peaks of Skelfhill, Penchrise, the
Dunion, and the ranges of "mountains" as Scott calls the hills
through which the Border Waters run, Yarrow, Ettrick, Borthwick
Water and Ale Water.   A "water" is larger than a "burn," but
attains not to the name of a river.

Rule, the next tributary as we ascend Teviot, is but a "Water,"
a pretty trout stream it would be if it had fair play.   The
question of fishing in this country is knotted.   Almost all the
trout streams were open to everybody, in my boyhood, when I
could fish all day in Tweed or Ale, and never see a rod but my
own.   The few anglers were sportsmen.   "Duffer" as I was, I
remember a long summer day on Tweed at Yair, when, having
come too late for the ten o'clock "rise" of trout, I had an almost
empty creel.   Just before sunset I foregathered with old Adam
Linton, his large creel three-quarters full of beauties.   "What
did you get them with?" I asked.   At the moment he was
using the tiniest midges, and the finest tackle.   "Oh, wi' ae
thing and another, according to the time o' day," he answered.
I daresay he used the clear water worm, fished up stream ;
deadly sin in Hampshire, but not in the Forest.   Since these
days the world has gone wild on angling, the waters are crowded
like the Regent's canal with rods.   Now I am all for letting
every man have his cast ; but the only present hope for the
survival of trout is in the associations of anglers who do their
best to put down netting and dynamiting.   A close time when
trout are out of season, we owe to Sir Herbert Maxwell, opposed
as he was by the Radical Member for the Border Burghs.   I

am not sure that there is a rule against slaying trout under, shall
we say, seven inches? However it may be, I had my chance
and wasted it; being a duffer. Trout may become extinct like
the Dodo; it makes no odds to me. I never cast fly in Rule,
nor even examined "the present spiritless parish church," on
the site of a Norman church of the early twelfth century. The
few relics of carved stone fill Sir Herbert Maxwell's heart with
bitterness against the dull destroyers. Our Presbyterian forefathers, as far as in them lay, destroyed every vestige of the
noble art whereof these glens were full, when, in the twelfth
century, the Border was part of a civilised country. For all that
I know, they were innocent of ruin at Bedrule; the English of
Henry VIII may here, as all through this region, have been the
destroyers. They were Protestants of a sort. Moreover in
Rule dwelt the small but fierce clan of Turnbull, who, between
Scotts and Kers, fought both of these great clans, and now, as
a power, "are a' wede awa'." Perhaps an enemy of theirs took
sanctuary in the church, and they "burned the chapel for very
rage," as the Scotts burned St. Mary of the Lowes shortly before
the Reformation.

Somewhere about 1620, Rule Water had her minstrel, named
Robin, nick-named "Sweet-milk," from the place of his residence. In my opinion these singers of the late days of James
VI and I, were the survivors of the Border minstrels who, says
Queen Mary's Bishop of Ross, Lesley, the historian, made their
own ballads of raids and rescues, such as *Jock o' the Cow*, and
as much as is not Scott's of *Kinmont Willie*. There was a rival
minstrel, Willie Henderson, whom I take to have sided with
the Scotts, while Robin was the Demodocus of the Eliotts of
Stobs. The pair met, drank, fought, and Willie pinked "Sweet-
Milk" Robin, the Eliotts' man.

> "Tuneful hands with blood were dyed,"

says Sir Walter, but what was the cause of the quarrel? I have
a hypothesis. The famous ballad of *Jamie Telfer* exists in two

N

versions. In one the Scotts are covered with laurels, while
Martin Eliott plays the part of a cur. In the other, the Eliotts
gain all the glory, while Scott of Buccleuch acts like a mean
dastard. One of these versions is the original, the other is a
perversion. The ballad itself, which takes us all through the
Border, from Bewcastle on the English side, to the fair Dodhead
on Upper Ettrick, is not of the period of the incidents described.
As far as these are historical, the date is about 1596. The
author of the ballad does not know the facts, and makes
incredible statements. Consequently he is late, writes years
after the Union of the Crowns (1603) and the end of Border
raids. I guess that either Will Henderson was the author
of the ballad in favour of the Scotts, and that Robin,
the minstrel of the Eliotts, perverted it into the Eliott version,
or *vice versâ*, Robert was the original author, Will the
perverter. Here, in any case, was infringement of copyright
and deadly insult. The poets fought. Certainly, Robin fell,
and the Eliotts hanged Will, gave him " Jeddart justice." To
the ballad we shall return ; it is, though inaccurate, full of the
old Border spirit, and is in itself an itinerary of the Marches.

These high powers, the Scott and Eliott clans, like the States
of Europe, were now allies, cementing their federacy by inter-
marriages ; and again were bitter foes. The strength of the
chief of the Eliotts was in Liddesdale, of the Scotts, in
Teviotdale. They were allies for young James V against his
Keepers, the Douglases,

> " When gallant Cessford's life-blood dear
> Reeked on dark Eliott's Border spear,"

at " Turn Again," a spot on Scott's estate of Abbotsford. They
were foes in 1564–66, in Queen Mary's reign, when Martin
Eliott, chief of his clan, plotted with the Armstrongs to betray
her strong fortress of Hermitage to the English.

In this feud the Eliotts attacked Scott of Hassendean in his
tower on Hassendean burn, the next tributary of Teviot, but

the ballad of *Kinmont Willie* makes Gilbert Eliott of Stobs
ride with the bold Buccleuch to the rescue of Willie from
Carlisle Castle (1596). Unluckily, in 1596 Gilbert Eliott was not
yet the Laird of Stobs. This Gilbert, at all events, married the
daughter of the Flower of Yarrow, the wife of Auld Wat Scott
of Harden, himself the neighbour and foremost fighting man of
the laird of Branksome in Teviot, the bold Buccleuch. His
descendant, Sir Walter, has made Auld Wat's name immortal,
and, in *Jamie Telfer*, has certainly interpolated a spirited stanza
to his praise.

John Leyden's birthplace, Denholm.

In the village of Denholm, on Teviot, opposite to
Hassendean, was born John Leyden, the great friend of Scott,
a poet in his way, but much more remarkable as a man of
amazing energy of character, an Orientalist, and a collector of
ballads. But few now know what

> " distant and deadly shore
> Holds Leyden's cold remains."

His memory is twined with that of Sir Walter, and he is one of the most living figures in Lockhart's Life of Scott. Leyden had the poetic quality, not judiciously cultivated, of the old Border minstrels, while the energy which the clans expended in war was given by him to omnivorous studies.

Below Denholm, but on the other side of the river, nearly opposite the junction of Rule Water with Teviot, is Minto, in the fourteenth century a property owned by one of that unruly clan, the Turnbulls. Later, it passed to the family of Stewart, and finally, somewhere about the beginning of the eighteenth century, it was bought by Sir Gilbert Elliot, ancestor of the Minto branch of that family. The present house dates only from 1814, but it has a curious legend attached to it, which is mentioned in Sir Walter Scott's diary, under date 23rd December, 1825. He says: "It is very odd that the common people about Minto and the neighbourhood will not believe at this hour that the first Earl is dead." [He died in June, 1814.] "They think he had done something in India which he could not answer for—that the house was rebuilt on a scale unusually large to give him a suite of secret apartments, and that he often walks about the woods and crags of Minto at night, with a white nightcap and long white beard. The circumstances of his having died on the road down to Scotland is the sole foundation of this absurd legend, which shows how willing the public are to gull themselves when they can find no one else to take the trouble. I have seen people who could read, write, and cipher, shrug their shoulders and look mysterious when this subject was mentioned. One very absurd addition was made on occasion of a great ball at Minto House, which it was said was given to draw all people away from the grounds, that the concealed Earl might have leisure for his exercise."

To the east of Minto House are Minto Crags, towering precipitous to a height of over seven hundred feet. On the summit is the ruin called Fatlips Castle, which is said to have been the stronghold of the fourteenth-century owner of Minto,

Turnbull of Barnhill, a notorious Border freebooter. A small grassy platform, or level space, a little below the ruin, is called Barnhill's Bed, "Where Barnhill hew'd his bed of flint,"—a convenient spot, no doubt, in old days on which to station a sentry or look-out.

The third Sir Gilbert Elliot of Minto was apparently in his own way something of a poet, but the ever tolerant Sir Walter Scott, to whom he used to read his compositions, confesses that the verses were "but middling." Sir Gilbert had, however, a better title, at least to collateral fame; he was the brother of the Jean Elliot who wrote that undying lament, the "Flowers of the Forest."

It is curious to note that in 1374 the church of Minto belonged to the diocese of Lincoln.

Here at Minto, if credence in the reality of Fairies no longer lingers amongst the people,—one of the writers of this volume records, some chapters back, that he found traces of the belief not very many years ago still surviving at Flodden Edge,—at least but a very few generations have passed since it died. Throughout Teviotdale, perhaps to a greater extent than in any other part of the Border, tales still are told which show how strong was once this belief in the existence of the Little Folk, and many of the customs that, we are told, were followed by country dwellers in order to propitiate the Good People, or to thwart their malevolence, are very quaint. Should it chance, for instance, that at the time a child was born the blue bonnet usually worn by the husband was not kept continually lying on the mother's bed, then there would be the most imminent danger of that child being carried off by the Fairies, and a changeling being left in its place. Many a fine child has been lost through neglect of this simple precaution. Generally, if the abduction took place before the child had been christened, a pig or a hedgehog, or some such animal, was substituted for the infant; but if the Fairies did not succeed in their design till after the child's baptism, then they left another bairn in its

place, usually a peevish, ill-thriven, wizen-faced little imp.   A
tale is told of a woman who lived at Minto Cragfoot, and
whose child, in consequence of some trifling lack of precaution
in the matter of the blue bonnet, was carried off, and in the
end was rescued only by the superior knowledge and power of
a Presbyterian minister.   Whilst she herself was engaged one
day in gathering sticks for her fire, the woman had laid her
child beside a bush on the hill side.   She neither heard nor
saw anything unusual, but on going to pick up her child at the
close of her task, instead of her bonny, smiling little son she
found only a thin, wasted, weird little creature, which "yammered" and wept continually.   Recourse was had to the
Reverend Mr. Borland, (first Presbyterian minister of Bedrule
after the Reformation,) and that gentleman at once unhesita-
tingly pronounced that this was no mere human child.   The
mother must go to the cliffs, said Mr. Borland, and there gather
a quantity of the flowers of the fox-glove, (locally called " witches
thimbles,") and bring them to him.   These Mr. Borland boiled,
poured some of the extract into the bairn's mouth, scattered
the boiled flowers all over its body, then put it in its cradle
wrapped in a blanket, and left it all night alone in the barn.
Mr. Borland took the key of the door away with him, and gave
instructions that under no circumstances was anybody to enter
the barn until he returned next day.   The anxious mother
watched all night by the door, but heard no sound ; never once
did the child wail.   And next morning when Mr. Borland
arrived he was able to hand to the mother her own child, fat
and smiling as when carried off by the fairies.   It was a heroic
remedy, but probably the sick child did not swallow much of
that decoction of *digitalis*.   In any case, they did not have
coroners' inquests in those days, and had the worst come to
the worst, the uncomplaining fairies would have borne the
blame.

It was up Teviot, in the days when witches flourished, that
a poor woman lived, whose end was rather more merciless than

that inflicted on most of her kind. A man's horse had died suddenly,—elf-struck, or overlooked by a witch, of course. To break whatever spell the witch or elf might have cast over other animals the owner of the dead horse cut out and burnt its heart. Whilst the fire was at its fiercest and the heart sizzling in the glow, there rushed up a large black greyhound, flecked all over with foam and evidently in the last stage of fatigue, which tried persistently to snatch the heart from the fire. One of the spectators, suspecting evil, seized a stick and struck the animal a heavy blow over the back, whereupon, with a fearful yell, it fled, and disappeared. Almost at that instant, a villager ran up, saying that his wife had suddenly been taken violently ill; and when those who had been engaged in burning the heart went in to the man's cottage, they found his wife, a dark-haired, black-eyed woman, lying, gasping and breathless, with her back, to their thinking, broken. She, poor woman, was probably suffering from a sudden and particularly acute attack of lumbago. But to those wise men another inference was only too obvious. She was, of course, a witch, and it was *she* who, in the guise of a greyhound, had tried to snatch the horse's heart from the fire, and who had then got a stroke across her back that broke it. They insisted that she should repeat the Lord's prayer,—an infallible test, for if she were a witch she would be sure to say : " lead us into temptation, and deliver us not from evil." And so, when the poor woman in her pain failed to get through the prayer to their satisfaction, they bound her, carried her away, and burnt her alive in the fire where the horse's heart had been roasted.

Two or three miles across the river from Minto is Ruberslaw, a rugged hill, towering dark and solitary, a land-mark for half the Border. More than any of its distant neighbours in the Cheviot range, it seems to draw to itself the hurrying rain-clouds, more than any other it seems to nurture storms. About its grim head all Teviotdale may

"see with strange delight the snow clouds form
When Ruberslaw conceives the mountain storm—
Dark Ruberslaw, that lifts his head sublime,
Rugged and hoary with the wrecks of time ;
On his broad misty front the giant wears
The horrid furrows of ten thousand years."

Like many another wild Border hill, Ruberslaw was a favourite lurking place for the persecuted Covenanters, and near its top is a craggy chasm from which, it is said, Wodrow's "savoury Mr. Peden" used to preach to his scattered congregation. It was on this hill that the pursuing dragoons all but caught the preacher and his flock one day ; they were caught, indeed, like rats in a trap, had it not been for Ruberslaw's well-known character for breeding bad weather. The soldiers were advancing in full view of the conventicle. Way of escape there was none, nor time to disperse ; mounted men from every quarter were scrambling up the steep face of the hill, and in that clear light what chance was left now to hide among the rocks and boulders !" "O Lord," prayed Peden with extreme fervour, "lap the skirts of thy cloak ower puir auld Sandy." And as if in answer to his petition, there came over the entire hill a thick "Liddesdale drow," so dense that a man might not see two feet around him. When the mist cleared again, there was no one left for the dragoons to take.

Above Hassendean, but on the other side of Teviot, is one of the few remaining possessions in this country, namely Cavers, of the great and ancient House of the Black Douglases. The relics are a very old flag ; its date and history are variously explained by family legend and by antiquaries. It is not a pennon, therefore not Hotspur's pennon taken by the Earl of Douglas before the battle of Otterburne. It is nothing of the Percys', for it bears the Douglas Heart and a Douglas motto. On the whole it seems to have belonged not to the Black, but to their rivals and successors, the Red Douglases, who were as unruly, and "ill to lippen to" by Scottish kings, as the elder branch.

The lady's embroidered glove, with the letters K.P., ought to
have belonged to Hotspur's wife, who is Kate in Shakespeare,
a better authority than your mere genealogists.

As we ascend, the water of Teviot becomes more and more
foul ; varying, when last I shuddered at it, from black to a most
unwholesome light blue. It is distressing to see such a fluid

Cavers.

flowing through beautiful scenes ; and possibly since I mingled
my tears with the polluted stream, the manufacturers of Hawick
have taken some order in the way of more or less filtering their
refuse and their dyes.

Hawick, to the best of my knowledge, contains no objects of
interest to the tourist who " picturesques it everywhere." A

hotel is called the Tower Hotel, and contains part of an ancient keep of the Douglases—" Doulanwrack's (Douglas of Drumlanrig's) Castell," which Sussex spared in 1570 when he " made an ende of the rest " of Hawick,—but " you would look at it twice before you thought " of a castle of chivalry. The people of Hawick have retained many of the characteristics of

Hawick.

the old Borderers ; they are redoubted foes at football ; and are said to be not very scrupulous raiders—of mushrooms. Their local patriotism is fervid, and they sing with passion their song of " Teribus and Teriodden," which refers to " Sons of heroes slain at Flodden,"—among other Flowers of the Forest. And, like their neighbours at Selkirk, they cherish a banner, said to have been captured from the English. The Hawick

trophy, however, is not attributed to Flodden, but to a slightly
later fight at Hornshole, near Hawick, when those who were

The Tower Inn, Hawick.

left of the townsfolk fell on, and defeated with great slaughter,
an English raiding party. That the mysterious words Teribus

and Teriodden, or Odin, are a survival of a pious ejaculation imploring the help of Thor and Odin, I can neither affirm nor deny. It would be a gratifying thing to prove that the memory of ancient Scandinavian deities has survived the sway of the mediæval Church and the Kirk of John Knox. But I have not heard that the words occur in documents before the

Hornshole Bridge.

eighteenth century. The town has a site naturally beautiful, as Slitrig, a very rapid stream, here joins Teviot, which, above the mills of Hawick is *electro clarior*; not of a pure crystal translucency, but of a transparent amber hue.

Slitrig takes its rise on the Windburgh Hill, on the northern side of the Liddesdale watershed, a hill of old the known resort of the Good People, whose piping and revels might

often be heard by the solitary shepherd. The rivulet is
said to well out from a small, black, fathomless little loch high

St. Mary's, Hawick.

up on the hill. Here, as all knew, dwelt the Kelpie, or other
irritable spirit prone to resent human intrusion, and if a stone
should chance to be thrown into the depths of the lakelet,

resentment was pretty sure to be expressed by a sudden
dangerous overflow of water into the burn, whereby destruction
would be carried down the valley.   That, tradition tells, is how
Hawick came to be devastated, and all but swept away, early
in the eighteenth century.   A shepherd, it was said, had quite
accidentally rolled a large stone into the lake, and had thus
roused the Spirit of the mountain to ungovernable fury.
Leyden thus writes of the tradition :

> " From yon green peak, black haunted Slata brings
> The gushing torrents of unfathomed springs :
> In a dead lake, that ever seems to freeze,
> By sedge enclosed from every ruffling breeze,
> The fountains lie ; and shuddering peasants shrink
> To plunge the stone within the fearful brink ;
> For here, 'tis said, the fairy hosts convene,
> With noisy talk, and bustling steps unseen ;
> The hill resounds with strange, unearthly cries ;
> And moaning voices from the waters rise.
>
> .   .   .   .
>
> Nor long the time, if village-saws be true,
> Since in the deep a hardy peasant threw
> A pondrous stone ; when murmuring from below,
> With gushing sound he heard the lake o'erflow.
> The mighty torrent, foaming down the hills,
> Called, with strong voice, on all her subject rills ;
> Rocks drove on jagged rocks with thundering sound,
> And the red waves, impatient, rent their mound ;
> On Hawick burst the flood's resistless sway,
> Ploughed the paved streets, and tore the walls away,
> Floated high roofs, from whelming fabrics torn ;
> While pillared arches down the wave were borne."

Borthwick Water, too, as well as Slitrig, was famed for its
fairies—and for worse than fairies, if one may judge by the
name given to a deep pool ; the Deil's Pool, it is called, a
place to be shunned by youthful fishers.   But probably the
youthful fisher of the twentieth century cares neither for deil
nor for fairy.   Higher up the stream than this pool is the
Fairy Knowe, where a shepherd was once flung into the flooded

burn by the fairies,—at any rate he was carried down the burn one evening, late, and he *said* it was the fairies, and no other spirits, that had flung him in.

One very odd relic hard by Hawick is a mote, or huge *tumulus*, of the kind so common in Galloway. Probably above

Vale of the Borthwick Water looking towards Hawick.

it was erected a palisaded wooden fortress, perhaps of the twelfth century. The area, as far as an amateur measurement can determine, is not less than that of the tower of Goldielands, an old keep of the Scotts, some two miles further up the water, almost opposite to the point where Borthwick Water flows into Teviot on the left. If we cross the bridge here and follow the pretty wandering water through a level haugh, and then turn off to the right, we arrive at a deep thickly-wooded dene, and from the crest above this excellent hiding place of raided cattle looks down the old low house of Harden, (the Stammschloss of Sir Walter Scott,) now the property of Lord Polwarth, the head of this branch of the Scotts of Buccleuch. The house is more modern than the many

A glimpse of Harden.

square keeps erected in the old days of English invasions and family feuds. The Borthwick Water turns to the left, and descends from the heights of Howpasley, whence the English raiders rode down, "laigh down in Borthwick Water," in the ballad of *Jamie Telfer*. A mile or a little more above Goldielands Tower, on the left side of Teviot is Branksome Tower, the residence of the Lady of Branksome in *The Lay of the Last Minstrel*.

At Branksome Tower we are in the precise centre of the Scottish Border of history and romance, the centre of Scott's country. Yet, looking at Mr. Thompson's excellent sketch, you

Goldielands Tower and the Teviot.

would scarce guess it. The house stands very near the Teviot, but still nearer the public road. Thanks to the attentions of the English at various periods, especially when the bold

o

Buccleuch stood for the fairest of ladies, Mary Queen of Scots, against preachers, presbyters, puritans, and their southern allies, perhaps no visible part of the edifice older than 1570 remains except the tower. The Lady of Branksome who finished the actual house after the old stronghold had been burned, appears

Branksome.

to have thought that square keeps and barmkyns were obsolete in war, owing to the increasing merits of artillery ; and she did not build a house of defence. Manifestly " nine and twenty Knights of fame " never " hung their shields in " *this* " Branksome Hall," and never were here attended by " nine and twenty Squires of name," and " nine and twenty yeomen tall."

There is no room for them, and at Branksome, probably,
there never was. It is not to be credited that, at any period,
ten of the knights went to bed "sheathed in steel," to be
ready for the English, or

> " Carved at the meal, with gloves of steel,
>   And drank the red wine through the helmet barred." [1]

The minstrel gave free play to his fancy. The Laird of Branksome, though Warden of the Marches, never had, never needed,
so vast a retinue, and was so far from " Warkworth or Naworth,
or merry Carlisle" that no Scrope, or Howard, or Percy, could
fall on him at unawares.

The Scotts, in the reign of James I, already owned the wild
upland pastoral region of Buccleuch between Teviot and Ettrick,
and Eckford in Teviotdale; also Murdiestone on the lower
Clyde, a place now too near the hideous industrial towns and
villages near Glasgow. Meanwhile a pacific gentleman named
Inglis was laird of Branksome. He grumbled, it is said, to Sir
Walter Scott of Murdiestone about the inconveniences caused
by English raiders; though, as they had a long way to ride,
Inglis probably suffered more at Branksome from the Kers,
Douglases, and ferocious Turnbulls. Scott was not a nervous
man, and he offered to barter Murdiestone for half of Branksome,
which came into his pastoral holdings at Buccleuch. Inglis
gladly made the exchange, and Scott's son obtained the remaining half of the barony of Branksome, in reward of his
loyalty to James II, during his struggle with the Black
Douglases, (during which he dirked his guest, the Earl, at
the hospitable table.) The Scott lands, carved out of those of
the fallen Douglases, extended from Lanarkshire to Langholm;
and as they were loyal to their country, (at least till the reign
of Charles I,) and withal were fighting men of the best, they
throve to Earl's estate, the dukedom coming in with the ill-

---

[1] The conjectural reading of Schlöpping, " Carved at the *veal*," though
ingenious (for, as he observes, " the ancient Scots did not carve oat-meal "
has no manuscript authority.

fated marriage of the heiress to James, son of Charles II, Duke of Monmouth. Of course if Charles II really married Lucy Walters, (as Monmouth's pious Whiggish adherents asserted,) the Duke of Buccleuch would be our rightful king. But the good king, Charles II, firmly denied the marriage, fond as he was of his handsome son by Lucy Walters; and the good House of Buccleuch has never believed in the Whig fable of the black box which contained the marriage lines of Lucy

Branksome.

Walters and Charles II. The marriage of Monmouth with the heiress of Buccleuch was made in their extreme youth and was unhappy. Monmouth was in love, like Lord Ailesbury, with Lady Henrietta Wentworth, whom he (according to Ailesbury,) spoke of as "his wife in the sight of God," which means that she was not his wife at all.

The house of Branksome makes a picturesque object in the middle distance of the landscape; but is not otherwise

interesting.   In front of the door lies, or used to lie, a rusty iron
breach-loading culverin of the fourteenth century ; of old, no
doubt, part of the artillery of the castle, when it was a castle.

Returning from Branksome Tower to the right bank of
Teviot, now a clear and musical stream, we cross one of the many
Allan Waters so common in Scotland, and arrive at Caerlanrig,
where there is a tablet with an inscription bitterly blaming
James V, for his treachery to Johnny Armstrong of Gilnockie

Looking down Teviotdale from Caerlanrig.

in Eskdale, hanged in 1530. The Armstrongs, being next
neighbours of England on the Border, were a clan of doubtful
allegiance, given to intermarrying with the English, and sometimes wearing the cross of St. George as "assured Scots."
They were the greatest of reivers on both sides of the Border.
In 1530, James V, who had escaped from the Douglases,
and driven Angus, their chief, into the service of Henry VIII,
tried to bring the country into order. He first arrested
the chief men—Bothwell (Hepburn), Ferniehirst (Ker), Max-

well, Home, Buccleuch (his old ally), Polwarth, and Johnston ;
and, having kept them out of mischief, led a large
force into their region.   He caught Scott of Tushielaw in
Ettrick, and Cockburn of Henderland on Meggat Water.
Cockburn was tried in Edinburgh for theft and treason, and
beheaded ; *not* hanged at his own door as legend fables.   He
was in the conspiracy of Henry VIII and Angus, and had
sided with invaders.   Tushielaw suffered for oppression of his
tenants.   Numbers of lairds, Kers, Douglases, Rutherfurds,
Turnbulls, Swintons, Veitches, put themselves on the King's
mercy and gave sureties for quiet behaviour.   Gilnockie,
according to the ballad, came to the King at Caerlanrig in royal
array, with forty retainers.   I find no contemporary account
of the circumstances, for Lindsay of Pitscottie gives but late
gossip, as he always does.   Calderwood, still later, says that
Johnie "was enticed by some courtiers."   Calderwood adds
that one of the sufferers with Johnie had burned a woman and
her children in her house.   The evidence for Royal treachery
is that of the ballad of *Johnie Armstrang*, which may have
been the source and authority of Pitscottie.   We may quote it.
It was a favourite of Sir Walter Scott.

JOHNIE ARMSTRANG.

Sum speikis of lords, sum speikis of lairds,
  And sik like men of hie degrie ;
Of a gentleman I sing a sang,
  Sum tyme called Laird of Gilnockie.

The King he wrytes a luving letter,
  With his ain hand sae tenderly,
And he hath sent it to Johnie Armstrang
  To cum and speik with him speedily

The Eliots and Armstrangs did convene ;
  They were a gallant cumpanie—
"We'll ride and meit our lawful King,
  And bring him safe to Gilnockie.

" Make kinnen[1] and capon ready, then,
    And venison in great plentie ;
We'll wellcum here our royal King ;
    I hope he'll dine at Gilnockie ! ".

They ran their horse on the Langholme howm,
    And brak their spears wi' mickle main ;
The ladies lukit frae their loft windows—
    " God bring our men weel hame again ! "

When Johnie cam before the King,
    Wi' a' his men sae brave to see,
The King he movit his bonnet to him ;
    He ween'd he was a King as weel as he.

" May I find grace, my sovereign liege,
    Grace for my loyal men and me ?
For my name it is Johnie Armstrang,
    And a subject of yours, my liege," said he.

" Away, away, thou traitor strang !
    Out o' my sight soon may'st thou be !
I grantit never a traitor's life,
    And now I'll not begin wi' thee."

" Grant me my life, my liege, my King !
    And a bonny gift I'll gie to thee—
Full four-and-twenty milk-white steids,
    Were a' foal'd in ae yeir to me.

" I'll gie thee a' these milk-white steids,
    That prance and nicker at a speir ;
And as mickle gude Inglish gilt,
    As four o' their braid backs dow bear."

" Away, away, thou traitor strang !
    Out o' my sight soon may'st thou be !
I grantit never a traitor's life,
    And now I'll not begin wi' thee ! "

" Grant me my life, my liege, my King !
    And a bonny gift I'll gie to thee—
Gude four-and-twenty ganging mills,
    That gang thro' a' the yeir to me.

[1] Rabbits.

"These four-and-twenty mills complete
　Sall gang for thee thro' a' the yeir ;
And as mickle of gude reid wheit,
　As a' their happers dow to bear."

"Away, away, thou traitor strang !
　Out o' my sight soon may'st thou be !
I grantit never a traitor's life,
　And now I'll not begin wi' thee !"

"Grant me my life, my liege, my King !
　And a great great gift I'll gie to thee—
Bauld four-and-twenty sisters' sons,
　Sall for thee fecht, tho' a' should flee !"

"Away, away, thou traitor strang !
　Out o' my sight soon may'st thou be !
I grantit never a traitor's life,
　And now I'll not begin wi' thee !"

"Grant me my life, my liege, my King !
　And a brave gift I'll gie to thee—
All between heir and Newcastle town
　Sall pay their yeirly rent to thee."

"Away, away, thou traitor strang !
　Out o' my sight soon may'st thou be !
I grantit never a traitor's life,
　And now I'll not begin wi' thee !"

"Ye lied, ye lied, now King," he says,
　"Altho' a King and Prince ye be !
For I've luved naething in my life,
　I weel dare say it, but honesty—

"Save a fat horse, and a fair woman,
　Twa bonny dogs to kill a deir ;
But Ingland suld have found me meal and mault,
　Gif I had lived this hundred yeir !

"She suld have found me meal and mault,
　And beef and mutton in a' plentie ;
But never a Scots wyfe could have said,
　That e'er I skaithed her a puir flee.

"To seik het water beneith cauld ice,
　　Surely it is a greit folie—
I have asked grace at a graceless face,
　　But there is nane for my men and me ! [1]

"But had I kenn'd ere I cam frae hame,
　　How thou unkind wad'st been to me !
1 wad have keepit the Border side,
　　In spite of all thy force and thee.

"Wist England's King that I was ta'en,
　　O gin a blythe man he wad be !
For ance I slew his sister's son,
　　And on his breist bane brak a trie."—

John wore a girdle about his middle,
　　Imbroidered ower wi' burning gold,
Bespangled wi' the same metal,
　　Maist beautiful was to behold.

There hang nine targats [2] at Johnie's hat,
　　And ilk ane worth three hundred pound—
"What wants that knave that a King suld have
　　But the sword of honour and the crown ?

"O where gat thou these targats, Johnie,
　　That blink sae brawly abune thy brie ?"
"I gat them in the field fechting,
　　Where, cruel King, thou durst not be.

"Had I my horse, and harness gude,
　　And riding as I wont to be,
It suld hae been tauld this hundred yeir,
　　The meeting of my King and me !

"God be with thee, Kirsty, my brother,
　　Lang live thou Laird of Mangertoun !
Lang may'st thou live on the Border syde
　　Ere thou see thy brother ride up and down !

"And God be with thee, Kirsty, my son,
　　Where thou sits on thy nurse's knee !
But an' thou live this hundred yeir,
　　Thy father's better thou'lt never be.

[1] This and the three preceding stanzas were among those that Sir Walter Scott most delighted to quote.   [2] Tassels.

"Farewell! my bonny Gilnock hall,
  Where on Esk side thou standest stout!
Gif I had lived but seven yeirs mair,
  I wad hae gilt thee round about."

Teviothead Kirk.

John murdered was at Carlinrigg,
  And all his gallant companie;
But Scotland's heart was ne'er sae wae,
  To see sae mony brave men die—

> Because they saved their country deir
>   Frae Inglishmen ! Nane were sa bauld,
> Whyle Johnie lived on the Border syde,
>   Nane of them durst cum neir his hauld.

It will be observed that Gilnockie puts forward as his claim to respect the very robberies in England for which, says the poet, he was hanged.   The only sign of treachery is that Johnnie did come to Caerlanrig, probably in hope of making his peace like many other lairds.   Whether he were "enticed by some courtiers," or whether he risked the adventure is not manifest.   According to Pitscottie he had held England as far as Newcastle under blackmail.

Above Caerlanrig, Teviot winds through the haughs and moors and under the alders to its source at Teviot-stone.

CHAPTER VII

TWEED, ST. BOSWELLS, DRYBURGH, NEWSTEAD, AND THE LEADER

WE now return from Teviotdale to Tweed, which we left at Kelso. The river passes through one of its rock-fenced and narrow defiles at the Trows of Makerstoun, (accent the penultimate,) itself the home from ancient days of a branch of the once great Argyll clan—and generally western clan—of Macdougal. How they came so far from their Celtic kindred, potent in Dalriadic Scotland before the Campbells came to the front as allies of Robert Bruce, is not known to me. As foes of Bruce, the Macdougals of Lorne suffered much loss of lands after the king's triumph. At the Trows the river splits into very deep and narrow channels, and to shoot one of them in a canoe needs a daring and a fortunate paddler.

In former years there were four of these channels, two of very great depth—thirty feet and more, it is said—but so narrow that, with the river at summer level, it was possible for an active man to jump from stone rib to stone rib, across the swift rushing stream. The feat was attempted once too often, however, with fatal result, and since then the middle rib has been blasted out, so that it is no longer possible for any one to tempt fate in this manner. Even an expert and powerful swimmer, falling in there, would have but a slender chance of coming out alive, for if he were not sucked under by the eddies of that boiling current and jammed beneath some sunken ledge, the odds would be very great on his brains being knocked out amongst the rocks that thrust their ugly fangs here and there above the surface of the stream. Both below and above the Trows, the trout fishing—for those who may fish—is extremely good, but the wading is ticklish; pot-holes, ledges, and large boulders are apt to trap the unwary to their undoing. There are, too, some excellent salmon casts in the Makerstoun Water, and it was in one of them that the famous Rob o' the Trows—Rob Kerss, a great character in Sir Walter's day,—nigh on a hundred years ago landed a fish so huge, that even a master of the art so skilled as Rob,—Stoddart says he had few equals as a fisher—was utterly spent when at length his silvery prize lay gasping on the bank. Before taking the fly from its mouth, Rob turned half aside to pick up a stone which might conveniently be used as a "priest"; but even as he turned, out of the tail of his eye he saw the monster give a wallop. Rob leapt for the fish. Alas! as he jumped, his foot caught the line and snapped it, and walloping fish and struggling man plunged together off a shelf into the icy water,—from which Rob emerged alone. The rod with which Kerss killed so many hundreds of fish is still in the possession of one of his descendants, near Beattock. Compared with present-day masterpieces of greenheart or split cane, it is a quaint and clumsy weapon, of extraordinary thickness in the butt, and of crushing weight. The writer has handled it, and he is convinced that one hour's use could not fail to choke off for the rest of the day even the most enthusiastic of modern salmon fishers.

It is not often that ancient weapons are found in Tweed, but some years ago, when the river was unusually low, a moss-trooper's spear was recovered at a spot a little above Makerstoun. It was lying at the bottom, below what used to be a ford of sorts across the river. Curiously enough, shaft and head were both intact, and in fair preservation after their long immersion. If the spear was not used by some trooper in days when fighting was the Borderer's chief delight and occupation, it is difficult to imagine to what use it could have been put. Salmon cannot be successfully speared with a single-pointed unbarbed weapon; so that it is certain this was no poacher's implement.

Above Makerstoun is Rutherford, once the home of the Rutherfurds of that Ilk, but now it knows them no more. A like doom, as I write, hangs over Mertoun, long the beautiful home of the Scotts of Harden, Lord Polwarth's family.

> " And Minstrel Burne cannot assuage
> His grief, while life endureth,
> To see the changes of this age,
> That fleeting Time procureth ;
> For mony a place stands in hard case,
> Where blythe folk ken'd nae sorrow,
> Wi' Homes that dwelt on Leader-side,
> And Scotts that dwelt in Yarrow ! "

Mertoun is a modern house ; hard by it, across the river, the strong ruins of Littledean tower (once the Kers') speak of old Border wars.

Following the curves of Tweed we reach St. Boswells, named after an Anglo-Saxon saint to whom St. Cuthbert came, laying down his spear, and entering religion. At St. Boswells are sheep fairs ; Hogg preferred to attend one of these festivals rather than go to London and see the Coronation of George IV. My sympathies are with the shepherd ! The paths near Lessudden, hard by, are haunted by a quiet phantasm, in costume a minister of the Kirk of the eighteenth century. I know some of the percipients who have seen him individually and collectively. There is no tradition about the origin of this harmless appearance, a vision of a dream of the dead ; walking "in that sleep of death."

Above Lessudden the Tweed winds round and at the foot of the beautiful ruins of Dryburgh Abbey, softly mourning for him who lies within that sound "the dearest of all to his ear," Sir Walter Scott. The great Magician lies, with Lockhart at

his feet, within the ruined walls, in the place which, as he
wrote to his bride that was to be, he had already chosen for
his rest. The lady replied with spirit that she would not
endure any such sepulchral reflections. This is one of the

Tomb of Sir Walter Scott, Dryburgh.

most sacred places, and most beautiful places in broad
Scotland.

Approaching Dryburgh, not from the riverside but from the
road, we come by such a path through a beautiful wood as

that in which proud Maisie was "walking so early," when "bold Robin on the bush singing so rarely," spaed her fortune. The path leads to a place of such unexpected beauty as the ruinous palace where the Sleeping Beauty slumbered through the ages. The beauty is that of Dryburgh itself, delicately fair in her secular decay ; fallen from glory, indeed, but still the last home of that peace which dwelt in this much harried Borderland in the days of the first White Friars, and of good St. David the king. They were Englishmen out of Northumberland, teachers of good farming and of other good works. What remains of their dwellings is of the age when the round Norman arch blended with the pointed Gothic, as in the eastern end of the Cathedral of St. Andrews. Thrice the English harmed it, in the days of Bruce (1322) during a malicious and futile attack by Edward II ; again, under Robert II, when Richard II played the Vandal ; and, lastly, during the wasting of the Border in 1544, which was the eighth Henry's rough wooing for his son, of the babe Mary Stuart. The grounds, the property of a member of the House of Scott's eccentric Earl of Buchan, are kept in charming order. The Earl was the only begetter of a huge statue of Sir William Wallace, who used Ettrick Forest now and again in his guerilla warfare, and from the Forest drew his archers, tall men whom in death the English of Edward I admired on the lost field of Falkirk.

The said Earl of Buchan rather amused than consoled Scott, during a severe illness, by promising to attend to his burial in the place so dear to him, which, till the ruin of his paternal grandmother, had belonged to the Haliburtons, also in old days the lords of Dirleton castle. Readers of Lockhart remember the great Border gathering at the funeral of the latest minstrel, and how his horses, which drew the hearse, paused where they had been wont to rest, at a spot where it had been Sir Walter's habit to stop to admire the landscape. His chief, the young Duke of Buccleuch, was prevented by important business from being an attendant. You would never guess what the business was! No man knows but I only; and if Scott could have known, I doubt whether he would have drawn his shaggy brows into a frown, or laughed; for the business was——but I must not reveal so ancient a secret!

Moving up the river on the left bank, we reach that ancient House concerning which Thomas of Ercildoune's prophecy is still unbroken.

> " Betide, Betide, whate'er betide,
> There shall aye be a Haig in Bemersyde."

The family were at home in Bemersyde in the days of Malcolm the Maiden. One of them was condemned to pay a dozen salmon yearly to the monastery of Melrose, for some scathe done to the brethren. It must have been an ill year for the angler when Haig expressed a desire to commute the charge for an equivalent in money as he could not get the fish. There was scarce a Border battle in which the Haigs did not leave a representative on the field of honour. Here, too, befell " the Affliction of Bemersyde," when the laird, after a long fight with a monstrous salmon, lost him in the moment of victory. The head of the fish would not go into the landing net, his last wallop freed him; he was picked up dead, by prowlers,—and he weighed seventy pounds. Probably no salmon so great was ever landed by the rod from Tweed. Only the Keep of the mansion is of great antiquity.

It may be worth while to leave the river and climb to Smail-holme Tower, where Scott's infancy was passed. The tower, standing tall and gaunt above a tarn, is well known from Turner's drawing, and is the scene of Scott's early ballad, *The Eve of St. John*. Perhaps the verses which have lingered longest in my memory are those which tell how

> " The Baron of Smailholme rose with day,
> And spurred his charger on,
> Without stop or stay down the rocky way
> That leads to Brotherton."

P

1911

Smailholme Tower.

He did not go, as we remember, to Ancrum fight, but he returned with armour sorely dinted, having slain in private quarrel a knight whose cognisance was

> " A hound in a silver leash bound
>   And his crest was a branch of the yew."

And that same eve the dead man was seen with the lady of Smailholme. The story is a version of that ancient tale, the

The Eildons from Bemersyde Hill.

Beresford ghost story, which can be traced from the chronicle of William of Malmesbury to its Irish avatar in the eighteenth century—and later. Do ghosts repeat themselves? It looks like it, for the Irish tale is very well authenticated.

It was not actually in the tower, but in the adjacent farm-house of Sandyknowe, his grandfather's, that Scott, at first a puny child, passed his earliest years, absorbing every ballad and legend that the country people knew, and the story of every battle fought on the wide landscape, from Turn Again to Ancrum Moor.

We have reached the most beautiful part of Tweed, dominated by the triple crest of the pyramidal Eildons, where the river lovingly embraces the woods of Gladswood and Ravenswood, and the site of Old Melrose, a Celtic foundation of Aidan, while as yet the faith was preached by the Irish missionaries of St. Columba. This is the very garden of Tweed, a vast champaign, from which rise the Eildons, and far away above Rule Water "the stormy skirts of Ruberslaw," with the Lammermuir and Cheviot hills blue and faint on the northern and southern horizons.

On the ground of Drygrange, above Bemersyde, but on the right bank of Tweed at Newstead, the greatest stationary camp in Scotland of Agricola's time has been excavated by Mr. Curle, who also describes it in a magnificent and learned volume. Here were found beautiful tilting helmets, in the shape of heads of pretty Greek girls, and here were the enamelled brooches of the native women who dwelt with Roman lovers. But these must be sought, with coins, gems, pottery, weapons and implements of that forgotten day, in the National Museum in Edinburgh.

The chief tributary on the northern side as we mount the stream is Leader Water, "where Homes had aince commanding."

> Sing Erslington and Cowdenknowes,
>   Where Humes had aince commanding ;
> And Drygrange, with the milk-white yowes,
>   Twixt Tweed and Leader standing :
> The bird that flees through Redpath trees
>   And Gladswood banks ilk morrow,
> May chant and sing sweet Leader Haughs
>   And bonnie howms of Yarrow.

It is scarcely possible to conceive a scene more beautiful than that where Leader winds her cheery way through the woods of Drygrange. When the Borderland is starred thick

with primroses, and the grassy banks of Leader are carpeted
with the blue of speedwell and the red of campion ; when
a soft air and warm sun hatch out a multitude of flies at which
the trout rise greedily, then is the time to see that deep, leafy
glen at the bottom of which sparkles the amber-clear water
over its gravelly bed.   In cliff or steep bank the sides tower up
perhaps to the height of a couple of hundred feet, thick clad
with rhododendrons and spreading undergrowth, and with
mighty larch, beech, elm, or ash, and everywhere the music of
Heaven's feathered orchestra smites sweetly on the ear.   It is,
I think, to this Paradise that good birds go when they die,
where the ruthless small boy's raiding hand is kept in check,
and every bird may find ideal nesting place.

The district is most famous in ballad, song and story,
Leaderdale, being apparently equivalent to Lauderdale, giving
a title to the Earl of Lauderdale, the chief of the Maitlands.
" They call it Leader town," says the enigmatic ballad of *Auld
Maitland*, speaking of the stronghold of a Maitland of the days
of Wallace, a shadowy figure still well remembered in the folk
lore of the reign of Mary Stuart.   The ballad has some good
and many indifferent verses.   It was known to the mother and
uncle of James Hogg, the Ettrick Shepherd.   He copied it
out for Will Laidlaw, Scott's friend and amanuensis, and this
began the long and valuable association of Hogg with the
Sheriff.   The authenticity of the ballad has been impugned,
Hogg and Scott, it has been asserted, composed it and Scott
gave it to the world as genuine.   This is demonstrably an
erroneous conjecture, (as I have shown in *Sir Walter Scott and
the Border Minstrelsy*).   Letters which had not been published
refute all suspicions of forgery by Hogg or Scott or both.   But
the ballad had, apparently, been touched up, perhaps in the
seventeenth or eighteenth century, probably by one of the witty
and literary family of Maitland.   It came to Hogg's mother
from " auld Babby Metlan," (Maitland,) housekeeper to the
last of the Scotts of Tushielaw ;   herself perhaps a reduced

member of the impoverished family of " the flower of the wits of
Scotland," Queen Mary's Secretary of State, Maitland of
Lethington.

Though the legendary " Maitland or auld beard grey " may
have stoutly held his house of Thirlestane against Edward I,
(as he does in the ballad of *Auld Maitland*), I have found no
record of the affair in the State Papers of the period. Thereafter the Maitlands of Lethington, though a family of ancient
origin, play no conspicuous part in Scottish history, till we
reach old Sir Richard, who died at the age of ninety in 1586.
He was not openly recalcitrant against, but was no enthusiast
for, the new doctrines of Knox and his company. A learned,
humorous, peaceful man, he wrote Scottish verses and collected
and preserved earlier poetry in manuscripts.

Of his sons the eldest, William, was—setting Knox aside—
the most extraordinary Scott of his time. Knox was essentially Scottish in the good and not so good of his character,
and was essentially an extreme Calvinist of his period ; " judged
too extreme," he says, by his associates. Young Maitland of
Lethington, on the other hand, might have been French or
Italian, hardly English. He was an absolutely modern man.
In religion, even before the revolution of 1559, he was in favour
of the new ideas, but also in favour of compromise and, if
possible, of peace. We first meet him in private discussion
with Knox,—pleading for compromise, but yielding, with a
smile, or a sigh, to the amazingly confident fallacies of the
Reformer. . He serves the Queen Mother, Mary of Guise, a
brave unhappy lady, as Secretary of State, till he sees that her
cause is every way impossible, and goes over to the Reformers,
and wins for them the alliance of England, and victory. He
had a great ideal, and a lofty motive, a patriotic desire for
honourable peace and alliance with England. On all occasions
when he encountered Knox, he met him with the " educated
insolence " of his wit, with the blandest *persiflage* ; Knox
writhed and reports his ironies, and—Knox, in the long run,

had the better of this smiling modern man, no fanatic, no believer in any preacher's infallibility.

Maitland served Queen Mary loyally, while he might; when things went otherwise than he wished, was behind the scenes of the murder of Riccio; but was frankly forgiven as the husband of the dearest of the Four Maries, Mary Fleming, and as indispensable. He and his brother John, later the able minister of James VI, were in the conspiracy to murder Darnley; that is the central mystery in his career, his part in that brutal, blundering needless crime. He was partner with the violent Bothwell, a brute of culture, who hated, captured, bullied, and threatened him; for Maitland discountenanced, with remarkable and solitary courage, Bothwell's marriage. Escaping from Bothwell's grip, he fled to the nobles who had risen against Bothwell; he corrupted Mary's commander in Edinburgh Castle; when she was a captive, he is said, by the English agent, Randolph, to have urged that she should be slain,—for, as she said, "she had that in black and white which would hang Lethington." She escaped, and his policy was, in his own interests, to appear to prosecute her, and secretly to advise and aid her; to win, if not her forgiveness, an amnesty, if she returned to power, which he believed to be inevitable. She hated no man more bitterly, but she needed no man so much. As he had lost for her Edinburgh Castle, he gained it for her once more by winning to her cause the gallant Kirkcaldy of Grange, commanding therein for her enemies. He lived, a disease-stricken man, through the siege of the castle, meeting Knox once or twice with the old insolent smooth-spoken disdain of the prophet. He escaped the gibbet by a natural death, when the castle surrendered and Kirkcaldy was hanged. This "Michael Wiley," (Scots for Macchiavelli,) had trusted too absolutely to his own wit, his own command over violent men,—trusted too much to sheer intellect; been too contemptuous of honour. There is no one who at all resembles him in the history of Scotland; he fascinates and repels us; one likes so much in him, and detests so much.

From a brother's descendants came the notorious Lauderdale of the Covenant and the Great Rebellion; a scholar; at one time professedly godly; the natural and deadly opposite of the great Montrose, the coarse voluptuary and greedy governor of Scotland, and the servile buffoon of Charles II during the Restoration. He paid a trifling pension to the descendants of Lethington, who are so impoverished that I guess at one of them in "auld Babby Metlan," "other than a gude ane," who handed on the ballad of *Auld Maitland* and was housekeeper to the last Scott of Tushielaw on upper Ettrick.

These two are the great men of Leader Water (an ideal trout stream if not poached out), Lethington and — St. Cuthbert! It was while he watched his flocks by night on the braes of Leader that Cuthbert saw, either some meteoric phenomenon which he misconstrued, or the soul of Bishop Aidan passing heavenward in glory. Next day he walked or rode to Old Melrose, leaned his spear on the wall at the portal, and confided to Boisil (St. Boswells) his desire to enter into religion. From his noble biography by the Venerable Bede (he has "got his step" now, I think, and is Blessed Bede, *beatus*), we know this great and good man, Cuthbert, chief missionary on the violent Border, who sleeps in Durham Cathedral. The English have captured him, the great glory of Leader Water, but in his region, in his day, the people were already English by blood to a great degree, and in language. Cuthbert, despite the Reformation, continued to be a favourite Christian name north of Tweed, witness Cuddie Headrig, whose mother, Mause, had nothing papistical in her convictions!

By a burn that takes its rise far up Leader near a summit of the Lammermuirs called Nine Cairn Edge, is the Well of the Holy Water Cleuch. It was here that St. Cuthbert spent his shepherd boyhood; here that he saw the vision which sent him to Mailros. And here, after Cuthbert's death, they built in his honour, beside the Holy Well, the Childeschirche, the name of which survives to us now as Channelkirk.

Were one of Border birth to quit "sweet Leader Haughs," leaving unnoticed "True Thomas," Thomas of Ercildoune, I do not know how he might again face his fellow Borderers. For, though Thomas may not have been a great man, in the same sense that St. Cuthbert and Lethington were great, yet to most of his countrymen he is better known than either. For one at the present day to whom the name of Cuthbert is familiar, or one to whom "Lethington" conveys any very definite idea, you will find a hundred who take an intelligent interest in Thomas the Rhymer, and who believe with Spottiswoode, who wrote of him early in the seventeenth century: "Sure it is that he did divine and answer true of many things to come." Fact regarding the Rhymer is so vague, and so beautifully blended with fiction, that I doubt if most Borderers do not more than half persuade themselves still to accept as fact much of the fiction that they learned of him in childhood. To Border children, not so very long ago, nothing was more real than the existence of a tree, still alive and growing somewhere about the enchanted land of Eildon, which must necessarily be *the* Eildon Tree:

> " Syne he has kissed her rosy lips
> All underneath the Eildon Tree ; "

nothing was more certain than that True Thomas, at the call of the Queen of Faëry, rose and obediently followed the hart and the hind into the forest, and returned no more.

> " First he woxe pale, and then woxe red,
> Never a word he spake but three ;—
> ' My sand is run, my thread is spun,
> This sign regardeth me.' "

No spot was looked on, in early youth, with more awe than that Bogle Burn whose stony bed crossed over the St. Boswells and Melrose road in the cheerless hollow beside a gloomy wood; it was here that True Thomas beheld things unseen by mere mortal eye.   Who could doubt? Was there not still standing in Earlston the remains of his old tower to confute all scoffers!

> " The hare sall kittle on my hearth stane,
>   And there never will be a Laird Learmont again."

Earlston.

And, a hundred years ago and more, did not a hare actually produce its young on the shattered, grass-grown hearth-stone of the Rhymer's dwelling? So everybody believed. But if doubt yet lingered anywhere regarding some portion of True Thomas's story, it was easily set at rest by the words

cut on that old stone built into the wall of the church at
Earlston.

> " Auld Rymer's race
> Lyes in this place,"

it says ; and somehow it gave one a peg to hang one's faith
upon.   The whole, or at least a sufficient part of it, is quite
real in that countryside by the Rhymer's Glen where True
Thomas lay "on Huntlie bank," and where flourished the Eildon
Tree ; and that True Thomas's still unfulfilled prophecies will
yet one day come to pass, is a sound article of belief.   Though
how the ruthless prediction is to come about regarding the
house of Cowdenknowes, (which is not far removed from the
Rhymer's old tower,) one does not quite see.   But it was a
doom pronounced against a pitiless Home who there "had aince
commanding."   And the Homes are gone.

> " Vengeance ! Vengeance ! when and where ?
> On the house of Coldingknow, now and ever mair ! "

Perhaps, too, that was not of True Thomas's foretelling.
One prefers rather to think of Cowdenknowes in connection
with the ballad :

> " O the broom, and the bonny, bonny broom,
>   And the broom of the Cowdenknowes !
> And aye sae sweet as the lassie sang,
>   I' the bught, milking the ewes."

CHAPTER VIII

ST. BOSWELLS GREEN, MELROSE, DARNICK, ABBOTSFORD, AND THE ELLWAND

ALL the way up Tweed from a mile below Mertoun Bridge, up past the cauld where the pent water spouts and raves ceaselessly, along the bank where lies St. Boswells Golf Course, round that noble sweep where the river holds Dryburgh lovingly in the crook of its arm, up by the boulder-strewn streams above, and round the elbow by the foot suspension-bridge, past the lofty red scaurs and the hanging woods to the Monk's Ford, trout fishing—at least from the right bank—is free. And though it goes without saying that pool and stream are "sore fished," yet it is not possible by fair angling to spoil Tweed. Many a fisher may depart, empty and downcast, but if he persevere, some day he shall have his reward. To him who patiently teaches himself to know the river and the whims of its inhabitants, to him who studies weather and time of day— or, may be, of night—there must at length come success, for many are the trout, and large. The writer has known a yellow trout of 8 lbs. 12 ozs. to be killed with fly hard by the golf course. The weight is of course exceptional, but many a beauty of 2 lbs. and over is there to be taken by him who is possessed of skill and patience ; and to me is known no more enticing spectacle than one of these long swift pools of a summer evening, in the gloaming, when the water is alive with the dimples of rising trout.

And what a river it is, however you take it! What a
series of noble views is there for him who can withdraw his
attention from the water. Let him climb, in the peaceful evening
light, to the top of the red and precipitous Braeheads behind the
long single street of St. Boswells Green, pleasantest of villages,
and there gaze his fill at the beautiful Abbey far beneath his
feet, sleeping amongst the trees across the river.   Or let him go
farther still, up by the leafy path that overhangs the rushing
water, till he come to the little suspension-bridge.   And let him

The River at Dryburgh Abbey.

stop there, midway across, and face towards the western sky
and the three peaks of Eildon that stand out beyond the trees
clear-cut against the warm after-glow. At his feet, mirroring
the glory of the dying day, a broad shining sweep of quiet water
broken only by the feeding trout ; on his left hand, high in air
the young moon floating like lightest feather ; above the fretful
murmur of some far-off stream, a bird piping to his mate.   And
over all, a stillness that holds and strangely moves the very soul.
I think that if there be one with him attuned to his mood,
an hour may pass and the gloaming have deepened almost to

dusk, and neither of them shall have spoken a word, or noticed that the time has sped. And still they will linger, unwilling to break the spell.

At Leaderfoot the river is crossed by two stone bridges, one, the lofty naked viaduct of the Berwickshire Railway; the other, older and more pleasing, carries the picturesque road that, breaking out from the leafy woods of Drygrange and leaving on its left hand the hallowed site of Old Melrose, leads past St. Boswell's Green and the Kennels of the Buccleuch Hunt, over by Lilliard's Edge to Jedburgh. Between, and immediately above, the bridges at Leaderfoot are some glorious salmon casts, where nigh on a century ago Scrope was wont to throw a fly. Strange that during twenty years, in all that magnificent water fished by him, from Kelso to Caddonfoot, he never once landed a salmon of thirty pounds, and but few as heavy as twenty. There may have been more fish in his day,—one cannot judge; they *got* more, but then they took them not only with fly, but by "sunning" and by "burning" the water, and by many another means that now is justly considered to be poaching. But they seldom caught a salmon approaching in weight those which are now commonly taken in Tweed every season. Thirty pounds is a weight by no means noticeable now-a-days, and scarcely a year passes that fish of forty pounds ànd over are not taken by some fortunate angler; even above Melrose cauld, an obstruction that checks the ascent of many big fish, they have been got, far up the river, as heavy as thirty-eight pounds. Floors Water, at Kelso, I believe holds the record as regards size; in 1886 a fish of fifty-seven and a half pounds was captured. And as to numbers, though it is of course possible to labour for a week or more in Tweed—as elsewhere—even with the water apparently in good order, and with plenty of fish up, fresh from the sea, and meet with no manner of success, on the other hand there is on Makerstoun Water the pleasing record of twelve, fourteen, fifteen and sixteen salmon killed by one rod on four consecutive days; fifty-seven fish in all, and

seventy-three for the week.   And in a similar period in
November, 1903, Upper and Lower Floors Water produced

Eildon Hills and Gorge of the Tweed from Lessudden.

between them one hundred and forty-three fish, the average
weight for Lower Floors being nineteen pounds.

A little above Leaderfoot, on the opposite bank, is Newstead with its Roman camp,—though the visitor will be disappointed with what he may now see; there are no walls, no remains of buildings, such as exist at Bremenium, or down on the Roman Wall in Northumberland. Behind Newstead, high on the nearest peak of Eildon, are well-defined remains of a Romo-British station. Where they got a sufficient supply of water at that elevation is puzzling: it is a large camp, and could not possibly be held by a numerically weak body of men.

Melrose from Newstead.

From the head of that "brae" by Newstead that overhangs the river, you will look on a scene typical of Tweed. Far through the broad and smiling valley the river winds towards you, like a ribbon shot with silver; a mile away, across green fields, lies the venerable abbey, dreaming in the sunshine— "thy ruins mouldering o'er the dead." And, up stream, the distant belching chimneys of Galashiels cause one fervently to thank Heaven that beside the old monastic pile there are no tweed mills to foul the air, and to pollute the lovely stream more even than is now the case.   Mercifully, as regards trade, it is still at Melrose as it was when the "solemn steps of old departed years" paced through the land with youthful vigour. The little town is yet guiltless of modern iniquities—except as regards the railway and the inevitable Hydropathic, both of which are no doubt necessary evils (or blessings?) of these

Melrose Cross.

latter days.   And except, also, that the modern villa is overmuch in evidence.   A hundred years ago, when there was little of a town but the open Market Place hedging round the Old Cross of Melrose, it must have been a better, or at least a more picturesque place.   On to the Abbey itself now the town's houses jostle, treading on its skirts, pertly encroaching.   Therefore it lacks the charm and solitude of Dryburgh.   Yet is its own charm irresistible, its beauty matchless,—"was never

Q

scene so sad and fair." To the halting pen, it is the indescribable. In the deathless lines of the Wizard himself, its

East Window, Melrose Abbey.

beauty lives to all time. But a thousand years of purgatory
might not suffice to wipe from their Record of Sin the guilt

incurred by Hertford, and Evers, and Laiton, in 1544 and 1545
when they wantonly profaned and laid waste this dream in
stone and lime, wrought by "some fairy's hand." Nor in later
days were our own people free from offence in this respect.
The number of old houses in the immediate neighbourhood
is probably very small into which have not been built stones
from the ruined abbey. Even across the river they are found;
in the walls of a mouldering old farm house there, pulled down
but a few years ago, were discovered many delicate bits of
scroll work and of finely chiselled stone.

A mile to the west of Melrose lies the village of Darnick.
Here is a fine old tower dating from the sixteenth century, the
property still of the family that originally built it. Fain would
Sir Walter Scott have bought this picturesque old building
after he moved to Abbotsford, and many another has looked
on it with longing eyes, but no offer has succeeded in divorcing
it from the stock of the original owner, though the surrounding
lands have melted away. Somewhere about 1425 a Heiton
built the earliest tower. That, naturally, could not stand
against the all-destroying hand of Hertford in 1544, but the
Heiton's descendant repaired, or rebuilt, it in 1569, and ever
since it has remained in the possession of the family, still, I
believe, is occasionally inhabited by them. It is now probably
the finest existing specimen of the old bastel-house. From its
watch-tower may be had a glimpse of Tweed at Bridgend, where
Father Philip, Sacristan of St. Mary's, took his involuntary bath.
This is the Bridgend mentioned in Sir Walter's Notes to *The
Monastery*. The ancient and very peculiar bridge over Tweed
which gave to the hamlet its name is described in the text of
the novel. There is now no trace of such a bridge, but in the
early part of the eighteenth century the pillars yet stood.
They are described in Gordon's *Itinerarium Septentrionale*
(1726), and in Milne's account of the Parish of Melrose
published in 1794, there is a full description. Those pillars
yet stood, he says. "It has been a timber bridge; in the

Q 2

middle pillar there has been a chain for a drawbridge, with a little house for the convenience of those that kept the bridge and received the custom.   On this same pillar are the arms of

Darnick Tower.

the Pringles of Galashiels." In Sir Walter's day, only the
foundations of the piers existed. He tells how, "when drifting
down the Tweed at night, for the purpose of killing salmon by
torch light," he used to see them.

A Heiton of Darnick fell at Flodden. His successor
played no inconspicuous part in the bitter fight by his
own tower side, on Skirmish Field, scene of that memorable
encounter in 1526 between Angus and Buccleuch, when
the stake was the person of the young king, James V.
Turn-Again, too, is in the immediate neighbourhood, on the
lands of Abbotsford, where the Scotts turned fiercely on
their pursuers, and Ker of Cessford was slain. It is curious
to note that beneath what is now a lawn at Darnick Tower
many skeletons were dug up some years ago, and beside them
were swords. Doubtless the skeletons were those of men
slain in this fight; but why were their swords buried with
them? Over the hill, at Holydene, an ancient seat of the
Kers of Cessford, there was also unearthed years ago within
the walls of the old castle, a gigantic skeleton, by its side a
very handsome sword. Were their weapons, in the sixteenth
century, laid convenient to the grasp of the dead warriors, as
in Pagan times they were wont to be?

Bowden Moor and Halidon are but over the hill from
Darnick. It was from this direction, by the descent from
Halidon (or Halyden, modern Holydene), that Buccleuch
came down on Angus, after Cessford and Fernihirst and
Home had ridden off. But the Homes and the Kers returned,
and spoiled the play for the outnumbered Scotts.

> " Now Bowden Moor the march-man won,
>   And sternly shook his plumed head,
>   As glanced his eye o'er Halidon ;
>   For on his soul the slaughter red
>   Of that unhallowed morn arose,
>   When first the Scott and Carr were foes ;
>   When royal James beheld the fray,
>   Prize to the victor of the day ;

When Home and Douglas, in the van,
Bore down Buccleuch's retiring clan,
Till gallant Cessford's heart-blood dear
Reek'd on dark Elliot's border spear."

Less than a couple of miles to the west from Darnick, we come to that which Ruskin pronounced to be "perhaps the most incongruous pile that gentlemanly modernism ever

Abbotsford.

designed." I fear that even the most devoted Borderer must admit that Abbotsford *is* an incongruous pile. Nevertheless it is hallowed ground, and one may not judge it by common standards. It reminds only of the gallantest struggle against hopeless odds that ever was made by mortal man; it speaks only of him whom everyone loved, and loves. "The glory dies not, and the grief is past."

But what a marvellous change has been wrought over all

that countryside since "the Shirra" bought Abbotsford, a hundred and two years ago. Undrained, unenclosed, tree-less and bare, covered for the most part only with its rough native heath—that was the character of the country. And the house; "small and poor, with a common *kail-yard* on one flank, and a staring barn on the other; while in front appeared a filthy pond covered with ducks and duckweed, from which the whole tenement had derived the unharmonious designation of *Clarty Hole*." It does not sound enticing; and already offers had been made to him of a property near Selkirk, where, among fields overhanging the river, was a site unsurpassed for natural beauty of prospect, whence Ettrick could be viewed winding past "sweet Bowhill," far into the setting sun. It was Erskine, I think, who urged him to buy this property—land which then belonged to the writer's grandfather and great-grandfather. But it was too far from Tweed, Scott said; "Tweed was everything to him—a beautiful river, flowing broad and bright over a bed of milk-white pebbles," (pebbles, alas! that, there at least, are no longer milk-white, but rather grey with sewage fungus and the refuse of mills). In spite of all its manifest drawbacks, "Clarty Hole," appealed to Scott. It was near the beautiful old abbey, and the lands had been abbey-lands. An ancient Roman road led through the property from Eildon Hills to that ford over Tweed which adjoined the farm, (and with this ford for sponsor, he changed the name from "Clarty Hole" to "Abbot's Ford.") Over the river, on the rising ground full in his view was the famous Catrail; and through his own land ran the Rhymer's Glen, where True Thomas foregathered with the Queen of Faëry. Bit by bit, Scott added to his land, bit by bit to his cottage, regarding which his first intention was "to have only two spare bedrooms, with dressing-rooms, each of which will on a pinch have a couch-bed." And his tree-planting had begun at once. When the property was first acquired from the Reverend Dr. Douglas of Galashiels, there was on it but one solitary strip of firs, "so long and so narrow that Scott likened it to a black hair-comb. It ran," says Lockhart, "from the precincts of the homestead to near Turn-Again, and has bequeathed the

The Rhymer's Glen.

name of *the Doctor's redding-kame* to the mass of nobler trees amidst which its dark, straight line can now hardly be traced." I do not think that "the Doctor's redding-kame" now survives as a name, even if the original trees be still to the fore.   In any case they would attract no attention, for what Sir Thomas Dick Lauder says was then "as tame and uninteresting a stretch of ground as could well be met with in any part of the world," is now rich in woods, and everywhere restful and pleasing to the eye—though it may be conceded that Galashiels has stretched a villa-bedecked arm farther up Tweed's left bank than might have been quite acceptable to Sir Walter.

At Boldside, of whose "ruined and abandoned church-yard" he writes in his introduction to the *Monastery*, there is now a railway station, and suburban villas, large and small, dot the landscape ever the more plentifully as one approaches that important manufacturing town which a century back was but a tiny village peopled by a few industrious weavers. No longer, I fear, can it be said that Boldside's "scattered and detached groves," combining with "the deep, broad current of the Tweed, wheeling in moonlight round the foot of the steep bank . . . . fill up the idea which one would form in imagination for a scene that Oberon and Queen Mab might love to revel in."

The Fairy Folk have fled from scenes tainted by an atmosphere of railway and modern villa.   Even the Water-bull has ceased to shake the hills with his roar around Sir Walter's "small but deep lake" at Cauldshiels.   Yet as late as the time of our grandsires people told gravely how, one warm summer's day, a lady and her groom, riding by the sullen shore of this "lochan," ventured a little way from the edge in order to water their thirsty horses, and were immediately engulfed in the Kelpie's insatiable maw.   If such a tragedy ever did happen, no doubt the explanation is simple enough. Without any warning the hard upper crust would give way beneath the horses' feet, and, struggling vainly, they would sink in the fathomless, spewing, inky slime below.   Once trapped in that, no power on earth could ever bring them out

again, dead or alive.   A like fate nearly befell the writer when
fishing alone one day in a gloomy, forsaken, kelpie-haunted
Border hill loch.   Dense fog came down, wreathing over the
quiet water, hiding the dripping heather and the benty hill.
A bird of the bittern kind boomed dismally at intervals, and a
snipe bleated.   It was a cheerless prospect; and the tem-
perature had fallen with the coming of the fog.   But through
the mist could be heard the sound of trout rising in the little
loch, and one bigger than his fellows persisted in rising far out.
The sound was too tempting.   The fisher waded out, and still
out ; and ever the big trout rose, luring him on.   Another
step, and another ; it was no longer stony under foot, and the
bottom began to quake.   Still the footing was hard enough,
and nothing happened ; and again the big fish rose just out of
casting distance.   One more step would do it; and what
danger could possibly be added in so small a distance ?   So
one more step was taken, and—without a second's warning the
crust broke.   Only one thing saved the fisher ; instinctively,
as he sank through the fetid slime, he threw himself on his
back, striking vigorously with his arms.   But it took many an
agonised, almost despairing, stroke ere his legs *sucked* out of
that death trap.   Nor, as long as there was water shoreward
deep enough to swim in, did he again attempt to wade.   His
rod had not been abandoned—which was matter for gratula-
tion ; but, soaked to the skin, chilled to the very marrow, and
reeking with the stench of putrid swamp, it was no thing of
joy that day to make his devious way home over an unfamiliar
hill that was wrapped in impenetrable folds of dense mist.

There is an origin, likely enough, for the Water-Bull.   A
great volume of marsh-gas, bursting from the bottom of a
swampy loch, might be seen some still, foggy day, or in the
uncertain evening light, suddenly to boil up on the surface
far out.   The wallowing upheaval caused by the belching gas
would readily suggest the part-seen back or side of some
formless monster, whose gambols were agitating the water and

causing billows to surge upon the weed-fringed shore; and a bittern's hollow boom quivering on the still night air, would easily be construed by the credulous and ignorant as the bellow of this fearsome monster that they thought they had seen wheeling and plunging. If he was anything more substantial than gas, what a beast he would have been to troll for!

One should not forget that it was by the shore of Cauldshiels Loch that Scott wrote the exquisitely sad lines that yet so vividly paint the scene:

> " The sun upon the Weirdlaw Hill,
>   In Etrrick's vale is sinking sweet ;
> The westland wind is hushed and still,
>   The lake lies sleeping at my feet.
> Yet not the landscape to mine eye
>   Bears those bright hues that once it bore ;
> Though evening with her richest dye,
>   Flames o'er the hill of Ettrick's shore.
>
> With listless look along the plain,
>   I see Tweed's silver current glide,
> And coldly mark the holy fane
>   Of Melrose rise in ruined pride.
> The quiet lake, the balmy air,
>   The hill, the stream, the tower, the tree,
> Are they still such as once they were,
>   Or is the dreary change in me ?

It is only a little above "the holy fane of Melrose" that there enters Tweed on the northern side an interesting little burn, the Ellwand, or Allen. Up the glen—the Fairy Dene, or Nameless Dene—formed by this stream, lies Glendearg, the tower described in the opening scenes of the *Monastery*. There are, in fact, three towers in the glen, Hillslap (now called Glendearg), Colmslie, and Langshaw. Over the door of the first is the date 1595, and the letters N. C. and E. L., the initials of Nicolas Cairncross and his wife. Colmslie belonged to the family of Borthwick; their crest, a Goat's Head, is still on the

ruin,—or was some years ago.   But who in old days owned
Langshaw is not known to me.   For mutual protection, Border
towers were very commonly built thus, in groups of three—as
is instanced, indeed, at the neighbouring village of Darnick,
where formerly, besides the present existing bastel-house, there
stood two others.   "In each village or town," says Sir Walter,
"were several small towers, having battlements projecting over
the side-walls, and usually an advanced angle or two with shot-
holes for flanking the door-way, which was always defended by
a strong door of oak, studded with nails, and often by an
exterior grated door of iron.   These small peel-houses were
ordinarily inhabited by the principal feuars and their
families ; but, upon the alarm of approaching danger, the
whole inhabitants thronged from their own miserable cottages,
which were situated around, to garrison these points of defence.
It was then no easy matter for a hostile party to penetrate into
the village, for the men were habituated to the use of bows and
fire-arms, and the towers being generally so placed that the
discharge from one crossed that of another, it was impossible
to assault any of them individually."

The Nameless Dene is famed for the "fairy" cups and
saucers that are still to be found in the streamlet's bed after a
flood, little bits of some sort of soft limestone which the wash-
ing of the water has formed into shapes so fantastic and delicate
that one hardly needs the imagination of childhood to believe
they are the work of fingers more than mortal.   Up this valley
ran the ancient Girthgate, a bridle-way over the hills used of
old by the infrequent traveller, and always by the monks of
Melrose when duty took them to visit the Hospital which
Malcolm IV founded in 1164 on Soltre, or Soutra, Hill.   As
late as the middle of last century the grassy track was plainly
to be seen winding through the heather ; perhaps in parts it is
not even yet obliterated.   Nature does not readily wipe out
those old paths and drove roads that the passing of man and
beast traced across the hills many centuries back.

CHAPTER IX

GALASHIELS AND THE GALA, LINDEAN

AND now we come to a once beautiful stream, of which, in the present condition of its lower stretches, it is not easy to speak with due moderation.

> " Deil take the dirty trading loon
> Wad gar the water ca' his wheel,
> And drift his dyes and poisons down
> By fair Tweed side at Ashiesteel."

It is not the Tweed at Ashiesteel, however, that in this instance is injured, but the Gala at Galashiels, and Tweed below that town. "It would," says the Official Report issued in 1906 by H.M. Stationery Office, "be impossible to find a river more grossly polluted than the Gala as it passes through Galashiels,"—a verdict with which no wayfarer along the banks of that dishonoured stream will be inclined to disagree. The grey-blue liquid that sluggishly oozes down the river's bed among stones thick-coated with sewage fungus, is an outrage on nature most saddening to look upon. He does wisely who stands to windward of the abomination. It is true that of late years much has been done, much money spent, in the praiseworthy effort to bring purity into this home of the impure; but to the lay eye improvement is yet barely perceptible. "Fools and bairns," however, they tell us, "should never see half-done work." The filter-beds of the extensive sewage works

237

are said to be not yet in working order, and so one may not despair of even yet living long enough to see Gala as Gala should be.

In the meantime, and till the entire sewage scheme is in full working order, there are—if one may judge from reports in the daily Press,—a few minor improvements not quite out of reach of the inhabitants. On 15th July, 1912, an evening paper published the account of "another" dead pig

Galashiels, the Eildons in the distance.

which at that date was lying in the river "immediately in front of the main entrance to the Technical College." The carcase, we are told, was "much decomposed, and attracted huge swarms of flies." This paper, in commenting on the corpse of an earlier defunct pig, which a few days before had reposed in the same tomb, remarks that "it has been the custom up to now for all kinds of objectional matter to be deposited on the river banks or thrown into the bed of the river to await the first flood to carry it down to the Tweed." "The river," the journal continues, "is at present at its lowest summer ebb, and during the heat wave the smells arising from decomposing matter have been overpowering." In an arctic climate, there may perhaps be some excuse for the proverb : "the clartier the cosier," but it seems scarcely applicable to Gala ; and there might, one would imagine, be other and more modern methods of dealing with decomposed pigs than that of floating them into outraged Tweed. The condition of "fishes that tipple in the deep" and quaff cerulean dyes in every stream, is not likely to be improved by a diet of sewage fungus and decayed pig, any more than is the health of human dwellers by the banks likely to benefit by the proximity of decomposing animal matter.

The history of Galashiels is mainly industrial, mainly the history of the "Tweed" trade. There were mills of a sort in the town as early as 1622, but even a hundred and fifty years later the trade cannot have greatly harmed the river ; only 170 cwt. of wool were then used in all the mills of Galashiels, and there was no such thing as the manufacture of modern "tweeds." All the wool then used was made into blankets, and "Galashiels Greys," (whatever fearful fowl *they* may have been). The term "tweeds" came later, one is given to understand, and arose through the mistake of an English correspondent of one of the Galashiels manufacturers. This gentleman misread a letter, in which the Scottish writer spoke of his "tweels." The Englishman, having read the letter somewhat carelessly, and knowing that Galashiels was somewhere near the river Tweed, hastily concluded that the goods under discussion were termed "tweeds," and gave his order accordingly. The name was universally adopted in the trade, and now—as the professional cricketer said about "yorkers,"—"I don't see what else you *could* call them."

Galashiels has a tradition to which it clings, that it was once a royal hunting seat. Mr. Robert Chambers says that the lodge or tower used by the Scottish monarchs when they came here a-hunting was pulled down only so recently as about the

year 1830. It was called the Peel, a strong square tower with
small windows, "finer in appearance than any other house in
the whole barony, that of Gala alone excepted." From it a
narrow lane called the King's Shank led to the. town.   I
cannot say if the name survives in Galashiels.

But there is another tradition in which perhaps Galashiels
takes greater pride, the tradition connected with the plum tree in
the Town's Arms. (Though what the little foxes are doing at the
foot of the tree, and what they have to do with the legend, none
can say. Perhaps they are English foxes ; and they *got* the plums
—sour enough, as it turned out.) The incident commemorated
is said to be this : During one of the invasions of Edward III,
a party of his soldiers had taken up their quarters in Galashiels.
The country no doubt had been pretty well harried and laid
waste—Edward's men had plenty of practice—and they may
have been careless, with the carelessness begotten of over-
confidence.   Anyhow, they straggled through the woods,
looking for wild plums, the story goes—though one would
imagine that the only plums they would be likely to find there
would be sloes, not a fruit that one would expect to tempt them
far afield.   But perhaps, as some say, they were robbing an
orchard—if there *were* orchards in Scotland in the fourteenth
century.   In any case, a party of Scots, either a passing armed
band, or, as Galashiels would fain believe, the inhabitants of
the town themselves, swearing that they would give the southern
swine sourer plums than any that had yet set their teeth on
edge, fell on the English, drove them in headlong rout to the
banks of Tweed opposite to where Abbotsford now stands—
the Englishmen's Dyke, they call the spot—and slew them to
a man.   "Soor Plums in Galashiels" has for centuries been a
favourite air in the town, though the words of the song have
perished.

Gala as a stream has been badly misused by man—at and
below the town poisoned by sewage and mill refuse, above the
town overfished, and poached, almost to the extinction of its

trout. Matters now, however, are, I believe, vastly improved as
regards sport; the Galashiels Angling Association works with a
will to make things what they should be in a stream once so
famed, and one hears that its efforts are meeting with the
success they deserve.   But it can never come back to what it
must have been "lang syne," say in Sir Thomas Dick Lauder's
day.   That gentleman records that he and a friend fished one
day from Bankhouse down to Galashiels, and turning there,
fished Gala up to its junction with the Ermit Burn, then

The Tweed from the Ferry, Abbotsford.

followed the latter to its source on Soutra Hill, and found
at the end of the day that they had filled three creels; their
total catch was over thirty-six dozen trout.   A good many were
caught in the burn with worm, of course, and most of the
trout taken were probably very small, but it shows what
possibilities these small Border streams might hold if they
were well treated.   Nobody, however, one may hope—no
reasonable mortal out of his teens, that is—now wants to
catch over four hundred trout in a single day under any
circumstances.   Even to the very juvenile schoolboy there can

R

be but the very minimum of sport in jerking fingerlings on to the bank. If a fixed limit of size could be imposed ; if the close season were continued for another fortnight or three weeks in Spring ; and, above all, if the sale of trout could be prohibited by law until at least the beginning of April, our Border fishing would be improved beyond recognition. Great takes are made now, with worm, early in the season, when the waters are discoloured and the trout lean and ravenous ; and long before they are in anything like condition either to give sport or to be decently fit for food, vast quantities of fish from the Border streams are sent off to the English markets. If those markets were kept closed a few weeks longer, many a trout would have a chance to reach maturity that is now sacrificed in extreme youth to put a few "bawbees" into a poacher's pocket. The great takes at the season's opening are not made by fair fishing. The writer was informed, three or four years ago, by the solitary porter of a very small Tweed-side railway station—himself a keen and skilful fisher—that on 2nd March of that year two men had consigned to Manchester from that one little station *one hundred and ten pounds weight* of trout. How were *they* caught ? Certainly not by fair means. They are not *fishers* who take trout after this fashion. These are the men who, to suit their immediate wants and their own convenience, would deplete every stream in the Border and put a speedy end to all sport. As things are at present there is practically nothing to prevent them from taking what they please from any water.

However, to return to Gala. Here, as everywhere in the Border, vast are the changes that the past sixty or seventy years have wrought on the face of nature. Even at a time so comparatively recent as that when the present North British line of railway from Edinburgh to Carlisle was being constructed down the valley, Sir Thomas Dick Lauder remarks on the revolution that in his own experience a few years had made. "We know of no district," says he, "which has been so com-

pletely metamorphosed since the days of our youth as that of
Gala Water." In his boyhood, "the whole wore a pastoral
character. Crops were rare, and fences hardly to be met with.

Torwoodlee.

Not a tree was to be seen, except in the neighbourhood of one
or two old places, and especially at and around Torwoodlee
and Gala House, near the mouth of the river. Everything
within sight was green, simple, and bare." Then he contrasts

R 2

this with the appearance of the valley at date of his writing, when "the whole country is fenced, cultivated, and hedged round. Thriving and extensive plantations appear everywhere." Could he see it, he would find the change even more marked now, with the "thriving plantations" grown and extended, countless trains thundering up and down the line day and night, and above all with his little village of "two thousand

Abbotsford from the left bank of the Tweed.   The Eildon Hills behind.

two hundred and nine inhabitants" grown into a great and busy town.

In ancient days, this valley through which Gala flows was called Wedale,—the Dale of Woe, the Valley of Weeping, for here says Professor Skene, was fought one of King Arthur's great battles against the Pagans.   At what is now the village of Stow—the Stow (old English, " place,") of Wedale—the Bishops of St. Andrews had a palace ; and here, by the Lady well at Torsonce, stood in Arthurian days a church famed for its possession of fragments of the True Cross, bestowed, it was

said, by King Arthur himself.   Here, too, were preserved in
great veneration, long years after Arthur had passed away "to
be king among the dead," portions of that miraculous image of
the Blessed Virgin which, the old historian Nennius tells us, the
king   bore   into   the   stress   of   battle   that   day   among
the hills of Wedale.   And here, till about 1815, lay a
very large stone on whose face was the well marked impression
of a foot, said by tradition to have been the imprint of the foot
of the Virgin.   To be converted into road-metal has doubtless

Where Tweed and Ettrick meet.

been its fate.   There are still, I believe, in Stow, the remains of
a very old church, not, however, those of the original church of
Wedale.

Leaving Galashiels by road past Boldside, with a glimpse of
the Eildons and Abbotsford to the left, three miles from the
town and immediately above the junction of Tweed with its
tributary the Ettrick we cross the former river.   Hard by, to
the right, in a wood on top of Rink Hill, are the remains of a
very fine British camp.

Here for the time we again quit the banks of Tweed, and proceed up Ettrick. A mile from the junction of the rivers, we pass near the old churchyard of Lindean, where once stood the ancient church in which, the night after his assassination in 1353, lay the bloody corpse of Sir William Douglas, the Knight of Liddesdale, slain by his kinsman.

In connection with this churchyard, there used to exist a belief that greatly troubled the minds of country folk in the surrounding district. Away back in those evil times when the Plague raged through Scotland, very many of its victims were buried in a common grave in Lindean churchyard. But the church was demolished after the Reformation, and the churchyard gradually fell out of use as a place of burial. There came a time when the people had no farther need for it; why, thought some practical person, should it not be ploughed up and cultivated? There was but one thing that saved it from this fate;—not reverence for the ashes of the rude fore-fathers of the hamlet that lay here at rest, but the sure and certain belief in the minds of their descendants that in the event of the soil being disturbed, there must inevitably be a fresh outbreak of the dreaded Plague. It is curious and interesting to read of the blind horror with which our ancestors in their day regarded this scourge; but their horror is not hard to understand. Sanitation did not exist in those times, medicine as a science was impotent to curb the ravages of the dreaded pestilence. The people were helpless; to save themselves there remained only flight. And in what remote spot might flight avail them in a Plague-swept land! In that outbreak during the seventeenth century, temporary houses, or shelters, were erected in many parts of the Border, and into them were hurried persons smitten by the pestilence—and often, no doubt, persons suffering from some very minor ailment which their panic-stricken neighbours diagnosed as Plague. It is not to be supposed that once there, they would get much, if any, attention; they would simply take their

chance—a slender one—of recovery.   And if they died, so
great was the dread in the minds of the living that, in many
instances, to save unnecessary risk, the authorities merely pulled
down the building over the dead bodies, and heaped earth on
top.   At a period even so late as in the writer's boyhood, there
were many spots—perhaps in very remote districts there may
yet be a few—where the Plague was said to be buried, and
where to disturb the soil was believed to be a matter of extreme
danger ; the pestilence, like some malevolent fiend long held
down, would inevitably break loose, and again Grim Death
would hurl his darts broadcast at old and young, rich and poor.
In his *Scenes of Infancy* Leyden alludes to the belief:

> " Mark, in yon vale, a solitary stone,
>   Shunned by the swain, with loathsome weeds o'ergrown !
>   The yellow stonecrop shoots from every pore,
>   With scaly sapless lichens crusted o'er :
>   Beneath the base, where starving hemlocks creep,
>   The yellow Pestilence is buried deep.
>
>   .   .   .   .
>
>   Here oft, at sunny noon, the peasants pause,
>   While many a tale their mute attention draws ;
>   And, as the younger swains, with active feet,
>   Pace the loose weeds, and the flat tombstone mete,
>   What curse shall seize the guilty wretch, they tell,
>   Who drags the monster from his midnight cell."

All manner of precautions were adopted to hinder the
spreading of the pestilence.   Orders were even issued forbidding
the assembling together of more than three or four persons at
any one place, but the Privy Council Records of the time show
that this regulation was obeyed only when it suited the people
to observe it.   There were limits to the dread in which the
pestilence was held, and even fear of the consequences did
not always reconcile the Borderers to such an interference with
their liberty.   It is on record that, in 1637, when, in the
execution of his duty as Convener of the Justices of his
county, Sir John Murray of Philiphaugh went to Selkirk, he

found that a marriage was about to take place, and that most part of the community had been invited to be present. Sir John at once forbade the assemblage, and, later, he sent for the father of the bride, a man named James Murray, and informed him that on no account would more than four or five guests be permitted. But James was not to be thus coerced. "Na, na!" he cried, "If ye be feared, come not there. But the folk are comin'."

So Sir John called on the bailies to commit the offender at once to prison. The bailies, however, were probably included in the number of the wedding guests, and were looking forward to the "ploy" with as great pleasurable anticipation as was even the most irresponsible of those invited. They paid no heed to Sir John's demand; "there was no obedience given thereto," say the Records. And next day, when the postponed wedding took place, "there was about four or five score persons who met and drank together all that day till night." Whether Sir John remained to take any part in the festivities we are not told, but of this at least we may be very sure: his interference did not tend to lessen the amount of liquor consumed on the occasion.

CHAPTER X

SELKIRK

Two miles up the river from Lindean you come to Selkirk. But this is not the route by which that town should be approached; by the Galashiels road, one is in the heart of Selkirk almost before one is aware of any streets. To see properly the old royal burgh clinging to the steep side of its hill, and to realise the beauty of its situation, it is necessary to come from Galashiels up Tweed by the road diverging at Rink. Thence cross Yair Bridge, go by that beautiful highway through the shaggy woods of Sunderland Hall, past Ettrick-bank and the Nettley Burn, down by Linglie, across Ettrick by the old bridge, and so up into the Market Place of Selkirk by the Green, (which is not anything in the nature of a lawn, but, on the contrary, a rather steep road).

This is a route longer, but to those not pressed for time, one infinitely more pleasant and beautiful than the direct way between the two towns. By it you see the exquisite bit of Tweed valley that lies between the junction and Yair Bridge, and, pausing as you cross that bridge, you have on either hand a prospect infinitely fair of heathery hill, green, leafy wood, and glorious river, the latter, above you on the right, hurrying down from Yair Cauld, a glittering sheet of eddying water, sweeping in magnificent curve past its elms at the foot of a mighty tree-clad brae ; then passing beneath your feet, chafing and hoarsely roaring, it plunges through between imprisoning

rocks, till once more comparative peace is gained in reaches
dear to the heart of salmon fishers. Then you leave the
bridge at Yair, and climbing an easy gradient, pass along by a
pleasant, shady road through rich woods, over the hill to
Ettrickbank, where tradition says Queen Mary crossed the
Ettrick on her way to Jedburgh in 1566.

In itself, Ettrickbank possesses no feature of interest,
but it recalls to mind the fact that here, in 1818, two

Selkirk from the Heatherlie.

harmless-looking hawkers with a cart were wont to call
at intervals, ostensibly to sell fish. Had their real errand
been known, it is little fish they would have sold, and short
would have been their shrift at the hands of the roused
and horrified country-folk. They were Burke and Hare,
the notorious body-snatchers, and the real purpose of
the cart in which they brought fish was to carry back to
Edinburgh the bodies they might procure in the country.

Burke and Hare ! Still, after the lapse of close on a century their memory is held in execration in the Border, still is their name a kind of vague horror even to those to whom it may convey little else, and who are almost wholly ignorant of what hideous crimes were committed by the pair. It was, of course, not only *dead* bodies that they took. These they ravished from new made graves ; but they took also living men, drugged or filled with drink, and murdered them for the sake of the price their corpses would bring as subjects for dissection by some of the doctors of that day. Hare turned king's evidence. After the trial and execution of his accomplice, he was smuggled away to the United States. There his identity was discovered, and an infuriated mob threw him into a lime-kiln, where he was badly burned and his eye-sight destroyed. After a time, when the rage and horror aroused by his mis-deeds might to some extent be supposed likely to have died away, he returned to England, and as late as 1855 he was alive and in London. A blind, white-haired, frouzy, ragged old man, led by a dog, used daily to slouch up Oxford Street, turn at the Circus towards Portland Place, post himself near where the Langham Hotel stands, and beg there from charit-able passers-by. How many of them would have given, had they known that this old man was Hare, a ruffian stained with the blood of perhaps half a score of victims ? How many of them, shrinking aside, would have stepped into the foulest gutter rather than be contaminated by even brushing against the hem of his filthy old garments? Few then knew who he was ; but there are men yet alive who may possibly remember having seen him. An eminent London surgeon, who died, comparatively speaking, but the other day, very well re-membered, and occasionally spoke of, the grizzly old ruffian who stood, with tapping stick, holding a bowl for alms. The late Mr. Serjeant Ballantine, too, in his *Reminiscences* describes the appearance of the man.

Immediately after passing Ettrickbank, the road, coming

suddenly out from a clump of trees, breaks into view of a wide
and pleasant valley, with a goodly prospect of wood and
heathery hill stretched far to the west and south. Down this
valley sweeps the gravelly bed of Ettrick ; on its farther bank,
on the flat haugh, stand a long line of mills and the station of
a branch line of railway. Above, rising abruptly, tier upon tier
in cheerful succession, trees and houses that blend into the
smiling face of Selkirk. And perhaps it is by reason of the
width of the setting in which they are placed, or because down
the mighty funnel of the valley comes rushing the west wind
that sweeps all smoke away, but somehow it seems that the
mills on the haugh below the town give no air of squalor or of
dirt to the landscape.

Would that one could say the same with regard to the effect
of their dyes and refuse on the condition of the river. By a
steep red "scaur" below Linglie there once was a pool clearer
than amber, across which in summer weather small boys,
breathless but greatly daring, essayed to swim. Farther down,
at the back of Lindean Flour Mill, was another, where in the
long twilights of June,

> " . . trout beneath the blossom'd tree,
> Plashed in the golden stream,"

and whence many a pounder and half-pounder was drawn by
eager young fishers. Where is that seductive amber-clear water
now? Alas ! in these days it is of a sickly blue tint, smelling
evilly ; and the stones in its bed, that once were a clear, warm
grey, with yellow boulders interspersed that flashed in the
stream of a sunny day like burnished copper,—they are
slime-covered and loathsome, things to be shunned. Surely
more can be done to check this pollution of our beautiful
streams. So far as can be ascertained, there is but one of the
mills of Selkirk that strives (and I believe it strives
successfully,) so to deal with its refuse that the water it uses
may be returned to Ettrick in a condition that does not defile
that stream.

Nevertheless, it has to be admitted that during the autumn floods salmon do run the gauntlet of Ettrick's lower reaches, and in countless numbers congregate below Selkirk Cauld (or weir), where the difficulty of ascent acts as a partial check on their continued migration. On a day in the month of November, if there should happen to be a considerable flood in the river, this cauld is a sight worth going a long way to look at. A wide rushing sea of tawny, foaming water— a hundred yards from bank to bank—races over the sloping face of the cauld, and, where it plunges into the deep pool at foot, rears itself in a mighty wave, with crest that tosses in the wintry breeze "like the mane of a chestnut steed." From daylight till dark you may watch the fish,—big and little, from the thirty-pound leviathan to the little one or two-pound sea trout—in their eagerness to reach the spawning-beds of the upper waters, hurl themselves high in air over this great barrier-wave, then, gallantly struggling, continue for a while their course up the rushing torrent, till gradually they lose way and come tumbling back, head over tail, into the pool from which half a minute before they had emerged. It is like standing by one of the jumps in an endless kind of finny Grand National Steeple-chase ; so many fish are in the air at once at any given moment that one becomes giddy with watching them. Probably a good many do in time accomplish the ascent, or perhaps get up by the salmon-ladders in mid-stream, but the great majority are swept back, over and over again. Those that make their attempt near the side, in the shallow water out of the main force of the current, are frequently taken in landing-nets (by water-bailiffs stationed there for the purpose), and are carried up and set at liberty in the smooth water above the cauld. It must be confessed that a considerable number are also taken in this way, or with the help of a "cleek," by poachers. The bailiffs cannot be everywhere ; and a salmon is a temptation before which (in the Border) almost the most virtuous of his sex might conceivably succumb. The average

Borderer, indeed, I believe would cheerfully risk his life sometimes, rather than forego his chance of "a Fish."— "The only crime prevalent [in Selkirk] is that of poaching," says the Rev. Mr. Campbell, minister of the parish for fifty years, writing in 1833. There was one, greatly sinning in this respect, of whom nevertheless, because of his gallant end, I cannot think without a feeling almost of affection. He—with a fish where no fish should have been—was hopelessly outmanœuvred by the bailiffs, escape cut off on every side, and only the river, red, swollen, and cold as ice, open to him. "Here's daith or glory for Jockie!" he cried, and plunged into a torrent from which he came no more alive.

A little higher up than the cauld is the Piper's Pool, where, until he was hit by a chance bullet that brought him rolling like a shot rabbit down the brae into the water, a piper stood piping that September morning of 1645, when Montrose and Leslie were striving for the victory. On the bank above, those inhabitants of Selkirk who cared to run some risk—which was probably the whole community—took up their position and watched the fight as from a grand stand. There is no better vantage point imaginable.

Leslie, I suppose, crossing opposite the gap called Will's Nick, (not far from Lindean), came up the left bank of Ettrick and, hidden by the fog, skirted along the edge of the hills till he was within striking distance of the Royal camp, when he took them, no doubt, both in flank and in rear. But how did a man of Montrose's experience allow himself to be thus fooled? Montrose passed the night in Selkirk, and he received no information whatever of any hostile movement. It was too late when he and what mounted men he could hastily collect came thundering and foaming through the shallow stream next morning, and went spurring over the flat haugh against the enemy. Someone besides Traquair must have played him false. It is inconceivable that he had no pickets out, or employed none of his cavalry on outpost duty. If they were out, in spite of the fog they could not fail to have got in touch with some part of Leslie's force. No large body of troops could have come undetected by a route so obvious, if those on the look-out for them were doing their duty.

Selkirk on this occasion saw war, as it were from the dress circle. The town was burned to the ground by the English after Flodden, and at various other odd times, but I do not think that it ever saw much actual street fighting such as was the experience of Jedburgh again and again. Selkirk was out of the main current of invasion, and it was only odd " spates " that came her way, such as when, in 1304, Edward I passed through the town on his march back to England ; and again when in 1309 Edward II, following an unexpected route to the north, took her on his way. Still, Selkirk had always been familiar with at least the pomp and circumstance of war. The town was old when Earl David founded its abbey in 1113 ; probably it had always been a headquarters of the Scottish Kings and their retinue, when hunting in the Forest. Certainly William the Lion, Alexander II, and Alexander III all passed a good deal of time in its castle, which of old stood on an eminence in what are now the grounds of Haining, near the " head " of the town. Probably the Court came here chiefly for the purpose of hunting ; the Forest of Ettrick was famed for its deer, as its men—unlike the majority of their countrymen— were famed for their archery. At Falkirk, in 1298, the English themselves bore witness to the warlike prowess of the men of Selkirk, as well as to their stature and fine appearance. At Bannockburn the sons of the forest distinguished themselves. And again at Flodden.

Regarding the part borne by her sons in the last-named great struggle, there are many traditions to which the inhabitants of Selkirk cling tenaciously. Some, I fear, will not bear too close investigation. Traditions are mis-chancey things to handle ; it does not always do to enquire too closely if one would retain one's faith. A large body of the men of

Selkirk and the Forest went to Flodden, and they fought as
they always did fight. That much, at least, is certain. But
who shall say how many returned from that fatal field? . The
Burgh Records are silent. There is a mournful gap of two
months in the history of the town; not an entry of any sort
for eight weeks in the autumn of 1513. And, says Mr. Craig-
Brown in his History of Selkirkshire, "Quite as mournful and
significant are the frequent services of heirs recorded after the
battle." Selkirk suffered severely at Flodden. There, as elsewhere, her sons did their duty ; and they fell gloriously. One
could wish that that might suffice; it is an ungrateful task to
rake among the dead cinders of time-honoured traditions.
But it is the detestable habit of the day to leave none of our
ancient beliefs unassailed ; the more beloved the tradition, the
more likely is some one to remain unsatisfied till he has upset
it. Yet it must be admitted that few of our cherished legends
emerge triumphant when assailed by the scoffer. That, for
instance, of Fletcher and the English standard captured at
Flodden, which has been revered in Selkirk by so many
generations of Souters, I fear, when it is investigated, must
crumble into dust.

Certainly the tradition regarding the origin of the town's
Arms is impossible of maintenance. The figures are so
obviously those of the Virgin and Child ; the halo and the
glory round their heads forbid any other interpretation. But
it is easy to imagine that after the Reformation no Scottish
town would care to acknowledge any connection, however
remote, with the detested Church of Rome. Hence probably
the legend of the dead woman and her still living baby
who were found at the Lady-wood Edge by the Selkirk
survivors of Flodden. Such a body, of course, may quite
possibly have been discovered, and the tradition would be
used later to account for the figures that appear in the town's
Arms. Just in the same way is a gargoyle in Melrose Abbey,
beside the reputed grave of Michael Scott, now pointed out to

American and English tourists as an authentic representation in stone of that mighty Wizard.

As to the "Souters of Selkirk," there can be no proof either way; but I prefer to believe that the song is old, almost as old as Flodden. Perhaps I have misread Mr. Craig-Brown, and am wrong in believing that he regards it as commemorating a famous football match played in 1815 between Souters and men under the leadership of Lord Home. If that were so, it could not have been sung at Dalkeith in 1804, when the Selkirkshire Yeomanry were present at a banquet there after the False Alarm. We read that Lord Home called for the song on that occasion, but that none of the Yeomanry cared to sing it before a man on whose ancestor it reflects, whereupon, amid rapturous applause, Lord Home sang it himself. If it refers to a football match, it must be to one of very ancient date, but one that surely could not fail to have left some mark on the minds of the Souters. Mr. Plummer, of Sunderland Hall, Sheriff Depute of the county prior to Sir Walter Scott, writing in 1793 says that though he had lived all his life within two miles of Selkirk and had known the song from his boyhood, there was not in his day, and he believed there never had been, any tradition connecting the song with anything of the nature of a football match. The verses may not have been written, probably were not written, immediately after the battle, but I am confident that it refers to Flodden—in spite of the fact that there was then no *Earl* of Home. No doubt the song has had variants from time to time; probably there was no allusion to an "Earl" in the original verses. Popular calumny shortly after Flodden taxed Lord Home with having been the cause of James's defeat and death; he was unable, as we know, to come to his Sovereign's aid. This popular belief, coupled with the fact that Selkirk's representatives suffered more cruelly than did Lord Home's men—and therefore, of course local prejudice would infer, did their duty

s

better—would be quite sufficient to give rise to the sentiment:
"Down wi' the Merse to the Deil." In his letter of 1793,
referred to above, Mr. Plummer says: "At election dinners,
etc., when the Selkirk folks begin to get *fou*' they always call
for music, and for that tune in particular. At such times I
never heard a Souter hint at the football, but many times speak
of the battle of Flodden." So far as it goes, there is nothing
in the evidence to suggest a football origin for "The Souters
of Selkirk."

It has always seemed to me, (who, being a native, am on
that account possibly no impartial witness,) that the people of
Selkirk have ever possessed in greater degree than their neighbours the true Spirit of the Sportsman. Of the inhabitants of
Yarrow and Selkirk, a seventeenth-century writer recorded that
"they are ingenuous, and hate fraud and deceit; theft or
robbery are not heard among them, and very rarely a Ly to be
heard in any of their mouths, except among them of the baser
sort." There has always been in them, I think, little of that
"win, tie, or wrangle" disposition which is usually to be found
among small communities; and they were never of the sort
who "heave half a brick at the head" of the outland wayfarer.
In their dealings with the French officers, prisoners of war on
parole, who were quartered in the old town from 1811 to 1814,
the Selkirk people displayed an admirable generosity and a
gratifying amount of good feeling,—though in that respect none
of our Border towns can be said to have been lacking. One of
these French prisoners afterwards, when an old man, published
most interesting reminiscences of his stay, and he writes of his
involuntary hosts with appreciation, and almost with affection.
In 1811, when the accumulation of prisoners of war in England
had become very great, it was decided to distribute a large part
of them throughout Scotland. To Selkirk, as its share, came a
hundred and ninety men.

How it may be now, I cannot say, but in the writer's boyhood
the memory of these prisoners still lived, and old people told

innumerable tales of the strange habits of "thae Frainch."
"They made tea oot o' dried whun (furze) blossoms, an' they
skinned the very paddas (frogs)," said one old man. The writer
of the reminiscences referred to above makes no allusion to
"paddas," but he does mention that "a lake in the neighbourhood supplied abundance of very delicate pike." This lake
may have been the Haining Loch, a picturesque sheet of water
over which, however, there is, or used to be, at times a nasty
vegetable scum. "One of the most beautiful and peaceful
lakes that ever was seen," is Sir Thomas Dick Lauder's description of it as it was in his day. I think, however, that the
French writer probably refers to the Pot Loch, a small and once
very deep lochan, or pond, nestling in a hollow at the foot of
the pleasant heathery hills on which is now the Selkirk Golf
Course. It is a much more likely spot than the Haining for
the prisoners to frequent. The former is on the town's property,
the latter on an estate in private hands. And in the former
there are, or at least there certainly used to be, many pike of
no great size. It was here, too, that tradition told us the
prisoners went to catch frogs? That Frenchmen in their own
land lived chiefly on a diet of frogs was the firm belief of a
majority of the town's inhabitants, ("French frogs" of course
was a term of contemptuous reproach,) and that the prisoners
went to the Pot Loch for any other purpose than to obtain
supplies of what seemed to the townsfolk to be a very loathsome
dainty, would never occur to them. The fact that the edible
frog did not exist there, would make no difference in their
belief. That was no difficulty; frogs were frogs all the world
over; and frogs of course included toads. The French ate
them all.

The writer of the reminiscences, M. Doisy de Villargennes,
tells us that some of the prisoners were "passionately fond
of fishing, and excelled in it,"—national prejudice of course
forbids that we should accept the latter part of the statement as correct!—and that they used to fish in Ettrick and

S 2

Tweed. Part of the former, close to the town, would be within their "bounds," but the Tweed is far outside the mile radius which was their limit of liberty. On every road, one mile from the town, was placed a post bearing the words "Limit of the Prisoners of War"; down the road which leads towards Bridgelands there is still a memorial of these unfortunates,—a thorn bush, called the Prisoner's Bush, which marked their limit in that direction. Any prisoner found outside the boundary was liable to be fined one guinea—a process, one would imagine, something akin in certain cases to getting blood

The Ettrick from the outskirts of Selkirk.

from a stone—and the fine was supposed to go to the person who informed on the delinquent. To the credit of Selkirk it must be recorded that no one ever claimed this reward; even when a prisoner uprooted a notice post and carried it a mile farther along the road, it was, we are told, only "to the amusement of the inhabitants," who, M. Doisy adds, "never on any occasion took advantage of a regulation in virtue of which whoever might see us outside the fixed limits was entitled to one guinea, payable by the delinquent." He himself, he says, "frequently went fishing several miles down the Tweed," and

awaited us, which took us at a good pace to Abbotsford, where
we were most graciously received by our host. We only saw
Mrs. Scott during the few moments before the announcement
of dinner, at which she was not present. Mrs. Scott was, as
we supposed, French, or of French extraction; in fact, she
spoke French perfectly : Mr. Scott had married her at Carlisle.
Our host appeared to us in quite a different aspect to that
under which we had known him passing in the streets of
Selkirk. There he gave us the impression of being a cheery
good-natured man, whose face was rather ordinary, and whose
carriage somewhat common, and halting in his gait, this
probably due to his lameness. At Abbotsford, on the contrary,
we found him a gentleman full of cordiality and gaiety, receiving
his guests in a fashion as amicable as it was delicate. The
rooms were spacious and well lighted ; the table, without being
sumptuous, was on the whole *recherché*. One need not expect
me to describe very exactly the surroundings of Abbotsford, as
on the occasions I was privileged to be there, we arrived in the
twilight, and we returned when it was quite dark by the same
means of locomotion. Thus, with the exception of the dining
room, and a short glimpse of the salon, all that I know about
Abbotsford has been derived from publications which everyone
has read. Neither should it be expected that I can give
details of repasts to which I was invited sixty-five years ago.
But the general theme of our conversation has remained
immutably fixed in my memory. The principal subject of our
discussion did not ordinarily turn on politics, but on minute
details concerning the French army. All that particularly
referred to Napoleon, and above all, traits and anecdotes,
appeared to interest our host in the highest degree, who always
found the means, we observed, to bring round the conversation
to this subject if it happened to have diverged in any way. As
can be imagined, we took good care to repeat nothing
unfavourable regarding the character of our beloved Emperor.
We little suspected that our host was gathering material for a

work published ten years later under the title of 'A Life of
Napoleon Bonaparte.'"   That Sir Walter's estimate of the
Emperor greatly displeased M. Doisy, goes almost without
saying.   It will be remembered, also, that the French General,
Gourgaud, was so bitterly incensed by some statements in this
book that a challenge to Sir Walter was fully expected ; and
assuredly it would have been accepted if given.

Selkirk in the time of the French prisoners was a small place
of two thousand inhabitants or less, the houses nearly all
picturesquely thatched, very few roofed with slate as at present.
It must have been matter of no small difficulty in such a
community suitably to house a sudden influx of strangers.
Indeed there *was* very great difficulty, until it was discovered
that the Frenchmen were to pay for their accommodation, and
then the difficulty vanished.   But it would be hard at the
present day to find in Selkirk lodgings of any sort at the
rate (2s. 6d. a week) which then satisfied owners of
houses.

The following is the French prisoner's description of Selkirk :
"The town is encircled by beautiful hills on all sides ; in the
centre it had a large square adorned with a fountain ; a very fine
bridge crossed the Ettrick.   An ordinary-looking building
belonging to the National Church and a much larger one
owned by the Presbyterians, or rather the sect known by the
name of Anti-Burghers, who had for their pastor an excellent
and venerable man named Lawson, were the only two buildings in Selkirk worthy of notice."

The hills are still beautiful ; perhaps, owing to extensive tree
planting, more beautiful now than then ; still within a step of
Selkirk is the purple heather, and the heartsease and blue-bell
a-swing in the summer breeze ; still on every side the view lies
wide and glorious.   And even in the winter, when snow first
"grimes" the hills, or when the northern blast has wrapped
them in its winding sheet, one can gaze, and repeat with
heartfelt and perfect sincerity :

" By Yarrow's stream still let me stray,
　Though none should guide my feeble way ;
　Still feel the breeze down Ettrick break,
　Although it chill my wither'd cheek."

" In the centre it had a large square adorned with a fountain."
The " square " of Selkirk is, in effect, a triangle, (in which now

Selkirk.

stands Sir Walter Scott's monument,) but as to the "fountain,"
I should have doubts ; it was probably what used to be called
the " Pant Well," whence was drawn water (supplied from the

Haining Loch) of a body and bouquet indescribable. "Hoots!" scornfully cried, in later days, an old woman, apropos of a new and irreproachable supply which had been got for the town from another source, "Hoots! It has naether taste nor smell!" Alas! that one should record the fact,—in old days the drainage of the upper town (what there was of drainage in those times, that is to say), fell into the Haining Loch not a hundred yards from the spot where the town's supply was drawn off! And yet people lived in Selkirk to unusually great ages. Our ancestors were hardy persons; but perhaps it was only the very fit who then survived.

It must have been a dull, uneventful, depressing life, that of the prisoners in Selkirk, more especially in those months between October and March, when darkness comes early and the days are chill and grey. What news they got was chiefly of fresh disasters to their country's arms in Spain, and the rejoicing of the townsfolk over Wellington's victories was of necessity exceedingly bitter to the Frenchmen. It was execrable taste on the part of the inhabitants of Selkirk thus to show their joy, says the writer of the Reminiscences— "indelicate," he calls it. But the chances are that they were chiefly mannerless schoolboys who thus misbehaved. I fear he looked for more than poor fallen human nature is prepared to give, if he expected the townspeople entirely to suppress their pleasure. Many a heart in Selkirk was then following with dire anxiety the movements of our Army in the Peninsula, dreading the news that any hour might bring of mishap or death to son, brother, or friend; every soul in the place took the profoundest interest in the welfare of those men who had gone from their little community "to fecht the Frainch" and, however desirable it might be that the feelings of prisoners should not be lacerated, it seems too much to expect that the townsfolk should go apart in secret places in order to express, without offence, the joy they must feel when those they loved were covering themselves with glory.

Provided that no one was ill-mannered enough to jeer at or to taunt the prisoners, I hardly think they had a right to complain, more especially as they themselves had already sinned in respect of rejoicing openly over victory.   On a certain occasion they heard of a great French success in Russia. Two prisoners concealed themselves and were locked up in the church one Sunday after evening service ; about midnight these men admitted their comrades, and together they roused sleeping Selkirk by a terrific joy-peal of bells.   Honours were easy between the two nations, I think.   Both acted under strong feeling ; those were strenuous days, and feeling naturally ran high.

In the writer's possession are letters sent from Spain to Selkirk at this period by his grand-uncle, an ensign in the Scots Brigade, now the 94th Regiment.   One, which gives a vivid picture of the storming and capture of Ciudad Rodrigo on 19th January, 1812, could not have failed to arouse intense enthusiasm in the town.   In so small and friendly a community, no doubt everybody was in possession of the chief details of this letter, (and of any other that might chance to come from a soldier at the front,) within a few hours of its receipt, and that a towns-man's regiment should be the first to enter the besieged town would be legitimate ground for extreme pride.   The following is an extract from the letter : " About 5 in the afternoon orders came that we were to make the attack at 7 in the Evening, the Light Division at one Breach and ours at another.   Picks and axes were given to the front rank of the Grenadiers, and to the first Company of our Regt., and also Ropes to swing us down into the Ditch, which we were to clear of any obstructions that were supposed would be laid in our way.   Accordingly we moved off about dusk, and got under cover of a Convent, to a short distance from the Ditch ; there we remained till the hour of attack ; it being come, and everything ready, we rushed forward as fast as our legs could carry us, cheering all the way.   On reaching the Ditch, we found it only about six feet high, so we leaped down as quick as possible and made to the Breach with all possible speed, and met with no obstacles.   After getting to it, we found ourselves to be the first there; on the front rank getting to the top of it, the Enemy saluted us with a volley of grape shot and shells (the latter they had laid across the top in rows) the explosion of which was so dreadful that I thought we should have been all blown up in the air together. . . . Some of the Men that had got up to the top came tumbling down, dead as herrings.   It stunned us for a moment, but we gave another cheer and rushed on, scrambled to the top and drove the fellows from the Guns opposite the Breach.   Our Reg^t. was about five minutes in the Town (and it is only 200 Men strong) before any other Reg^t. came to its support; at last the 5th came, and the others followed.   The French dogs kept peppering at us with Musketry and Hand-grenades at such a rate that I well thought we would all have been slain together.   At last we drove them from the Ramparts into the Town, and then they threw down their Arms and surrendered. . . . I went down from the Ramparts into the Town, but such a scene of confusion I never beheld; there were our troops plundering the houses as fast as they were able, one fellow to be seen with two or three Loaves stuck on his Bayonet, another with as much Pork, and in another place a parcel of fellows knocking out the end of a Wine Cask with their Firelocks and drinking away with the greatest fury; some ravishing the Women, others breaking open doors, and into all such a noise, altogether inconceivable.   This continued four or five hours, and our Brigade was shortly after moved out of the Town, at which I was very glad. . . . We had two Captains killed, but immediately on their falling a Sentry was placed over them, to guard them from being strip't, and had them afterwards brought to the Camp and decently buried. . . . The Enemy that night blew up the Mines, which killed a great many, both of their own Men and ours. It was a shocking spectacle, the sight of the dead bodies lying at the place where it happened, all bruised and burnt quite black, some wanting both Legs, others blown all to pieces, Legs and Arms mixed together in confusion ; it was there where Genl. M'Kinnon was killed. You were always wishing to hear of our Reg^t. doing something great ; Now I think it has done a great deal, but I fear much it will not receive the praise due to it, as it was not intended that it should be the first that should enter the Breach, it was only meant that it should clear the way for the other Brigade ; but somehow or other we got to it before them, and of course did not wait their coming."

Except on this occasion of the bell-ringing, and one other, when the French officers with some difficulty had induced certain of the townsfolk to drink to the health of the Emperor, and to shout " *Vive l'Empereur,*" friendly relations were unbroken. But the latter unpleasantness at one time had threatened to ripen into a very ugly affair. Bloodshed was narrowly averted. Friendship, however, was restored, and the prisoners continued to make the best of their situation. They obtained a billiard table from Edinburgh ; they started a café, they opened a theatre, with an excellent orchestra of twenty-five performers "superior to all those to which the echoes of our Scottish residence had ever till then resounded." This theatre was established in a barn which then belonged to the writer's grandfather. Frescoes on the walls, which had been painted by the prisoners, were still fairly fresh in colour though hopelessly obscure as to design, when the writer saw them in his early boyhood.

In connection with the time when Peace was proclaimed and the prisoners were being sent back to France, it is pleasant to have to record an incident greatly to the credit of Selkirk. The pockets of the Frenchmen were naturally, in their situation, not very well filled ; indeed, amongst the hundred and ninety they could raise no more than £60, a sum not nearly

sufficient to provide transport to the sea-port of Berwick for
the entire party.   They resolved, therefore, to march on foot,
using what money they had to hire carriages for the few among
them who were in bad health.   After an excited night (spent by
most of the ex-prisoners in the Market-place, where they shouted
and sang till daylight, like a pack of schoolboys), just as they
were preparing to set out on their long tramp to Berwick, "an
altogether unexpected and pleasant sight met our view," writes
M. Doisy.   "Vehicles of all kinds came pouring in by the
streets converging on the centre of the town, carriages, gigs,
tilburys, carts, and a few saddle-horses, all of which had been
sent by the inhabitants of the surrounding parts to convey us
free of expense as far as Kelso, about half-way to Berwick.
This delicate attention had been so well calculated, and so
neatly accomplished, that we could not do otherwise than avail
ourselves of it with many thanks.   We therefore separated
from our Selkirk friends without carrying away on the one part
or the other any particle of grudge that might previously have
existed between us."

Similar good feeling, however, appears to have been very
general between the French prisoners and the people of the
many Border towns where the former were quartered—though
it was almost too much to expect that no unpleasantnesses
should ever occur, when we remember how great a bogie the
Emperor Napoleon then was to the majority of British people,
and how to hate the French was looked on as almost a virtue.
"Bless us, and save us, *and keep the French from us*," was a
common form of invocation, then and later.   Persons more
ignorant or prejudiced than their neighbours were sure, sooner
or later, to overstep the mark, and bring disgrace on their
nation by boorish or brutal conduct to the defenceless
prisoners.   Thus, at Jedburgh for instance, not only did
schoolboys sometimes jeer at and stone the Frenchmen, but
one bitter old man, who no doubt thought that in hating the
French he was only carrying out a manifest duty, actually

pointed his gun at, and threatened to shoot, a prisoner whom he found outside the mile limit. A very regrettable incident occurred, too, in the same town during rejoicings over a great British victory. An effigy of the Emperor, mounted on a donkey, was paraded by torchlight through the streets and was then publicly burned, in full view of the deeply-pained French officers. Whatever the faults of the Emperor, he was at least adored by his army, and such instances of brutal ill-manners were bound to lead to bad blood and to reprisals.

Amongst themselves, the prisoners do not seem to have been quarrelsome, nor were duels common—for which fact, of course, the lack of suitable weapons may probably have been responsible. There was, however, a duel at Lauder between two of the prisoners quartered in that town, and one cannot help thinking that it must have suggested to Stevenson the duel in "St. Ives," between prisoners in Edinburgh Castle. In Stevenson's novel, they fought with the separated blades of scissors, securely lashed to sticks. At Lauder, they used the blades of razors secured in similar fashion. But, whereas in "St. Ives" the result was the death of one combatant, in the real duel at Lauder no greater harm came of it than slashed faces. It might be bloody enough, a duel with razor-blades, but it could not be very dangerous, except to the tips of noses.

It might perhaps be unseemly to quit the subject of Selkirk without making at least some mention of a custom which has prevailed there for something like four centuries. The great day of the whole year in Selkirk is that of the Common Riding, the Riding of the Marches of the town's property. The custom as yet gives no sign of waning in popularity; indeed, as the years pass, it seems to rise steadily in favour, and where one rode fifty years ago there must now be a good half dozen who follow the cavalcade. It is a cheerful ride and a beautiful, in the sweet air of a sunny June morning. Selkirk needs no awakening that day by the shrill fifes that are so early afoot in the streets; even the old and the scant of breath rise from their beds betimes, and make a push to see the muster of riders in the Market Place. Then it is through the shallows of the gushing river, and away over the breezy hills, for horsemen all filled with enthusiasm if not in all cases very secure of seat. It is a pleasant ride,—away over the hill by "Tibbie Tamson," the lonely grave of a poor eighteenth century Suicide, a Selkirk woman, the victim of religious despair. Of unpardoned sinners the chief, as she imagined, in a pious frenzy she took her own life ; therefore must her body be denied Christian burial and the poor privilege of lying beside her friends in "the auld Kirk yaird." Bundled into a pauper's coffin, she was carted out of Selkirk under a hail of stones and of execrations from her righteous neighbours, and here, on the quiet hill, her body found rest.

Then the route runs across the heather—where whaups wail eerily and the grouse dash out with sudden whir that sets some horses capering—and away to the cairn of the Three Brethren, overlooking Tweed and Fairnilee ; then down by the Nettley Burn and across Ettrick where Queen Mary is said to have forded it, and so home by the Shawburn, to see the Colours "cast" in the Market Place. And then to breakfast with an appetite that in ordinary circumstances comes only "when all the world is young." It is two hundred years and more since it was ordained that the Marches be ridden on the first Tuesday of June in each year— formerly, August had been the month—and that the Deacons of all the Crafts in Selkirk were not only to attend themselves, with their horses, but that they were to see that every man of their trade who had a horse should also ride, "all in their best equipage and furniture." Why the change was made from August to June, I do not know,—unless it was to permit of the introduction of those immense and very famous gooseberry-tarts which are so conspicuous a feature in Common Riding rejoicings. The day's arrangements then and earlier, were much as they are now, no doubt. But there are no Kers now to slay the Provost, as in the sixteenth century days of Provost Muthag. The only danger in these times is that some of the horsemen—unseasoned vessels—may be induced to swallow one or more of the glasses of raw whisky which are passed round with liberal hand as the cavalcade sets out from Selkirk. Whether this is a practice ordained of old with the laudable object of counteracting any possible risk of chill from the nipping air of the early morning, or whether it is done in order to inspire courage in the possible John Gilpins of the assemblage, I know not. Yet of those who partake, the major part seem to thrive well enough on it; they are none the worse in the afternoon, when the great body of the townsfolk stream out southward over the hill to the Gala Rig. Here horse races are run, over a course most gloriously situated, where a matchless view lies widespread to the Cheviots and down to far Liddesdale, and away up among the dim blue hills of Ettrick and Yarrow. There were races held here at least as early as 1720, and I suppose races of a sort have probably taken place annually on the same ground ever since.

CHAPTER XI

AND now we shall go—as they say in Selkirk—" up the Watters," a phrase which, to us of " the Forest," used of old to convey the idea of going on a vast journey. " Did ye see the Eclipse, on Monday ? " asked a Selkirk man of his crony. " Man, *No!* I was up the Watters that day." Which reply conveyed, perhaps not so much the feeling that an eclipse was a frivolous affair pertaining to geographically remote Selkirk alone, as that the answerer had been too deeply engaged up the waters with other business to have leisure to attend to such petty trifles as solar phenomena. Business " up the Watters," one used to understand, was not seldom protracted far into the night, and at times there were lunar phenomena observable, such as double moons, and stars whose place in the heavens was not definitely fixed.

Leaving Selkirk by the Ettrick road, in about a couple of miles we come abreast of the spot where Yarrow drowns herself in Ettrick. And here below Bowhill, on the sunny, wooded peninsula formed by the two rivers, lies Carterhaugh, scene of that famous fairy tale " The Young Tamlane." Tamlane when a boy of nine was carried off by the Fairies.

> " There came a wind out of the north,
>   A sharp wind and a snell ;
> And a deep sleep came over me,
>   And frae my horse I fell."

T

The Queen of the Fairies "keppit" (caught) him as he fell, and bore him off to dwell in Fairyland. There he remained, neither increasing in years nor in stature, but taking at will his human shape, and returning to earth for a time when it pleased him. Carterhaugh was his special haunt, and here, if they did not altogether shun that neighbourhood, young women too often had cause to repent having met him.

The Ettrick at Bowhill.

> "O I forbid ye, maidens a',
>   That wear gowd on your hair,
>   To come or gae by Carterhaugh,
>   For young Tamlane is there."

"Fair Janet," however, was one who would take no warning :

> "I'll cum and gang to Carterhaugh,
>   And ask nae leave o' him,"

said she.   And she went.   But

> " She hadna pu'd a red red rose,
>   A rose but barely three ;
> Till up and starts a wee wee man,
>   At Lady Janet's knee."

" He's ta'en her by the milk-white hand, amang the leaves sae
green,"—and Janet rued her visit.   Later, Tamlane tells her
how he may be rescued from Fairyland, and the ballad relates
Janet's successful venture :

> " The night it is good Hallowe'en,
>   When fairy folk will ride ;
> And they that wad their true love win
>   At Miles Cross they maun bide.

> " Gloomy, gloomy, was the night,
>   And eiry was the way,
> As fair Janet in her green mantle,
>   To Miles Cross she did gae.

> " The heavens were black, the night was dark,
>   And dreary was the place ;
> But Janet stood, with eager wish
>   Her lover to embrace.

> " Betwixt the hours of twelve and one,
>   A north wind tore the bent ;
> And straight she heard strange elritch sounds,
>   Upon that wind which went.

> " About the dead hour o' the night,
>   She heard the bridles ring ;
> And Janet was as glad o' that
>   As ony earthly thing.

> " Their oaten pipes blew wondrous shrill,
>   The hemlock small blew clear ;
> And louder notes from hemlock large,
>   And bog-reed, struck the ear.

" Fair Janet stood, with mind unmoved,
    The dreary heath upon ;
And louder, louder wax'd the sound,
    As they came riding on.

" Will o' the Wisp before them went,
    Sent forth a twinkling light ;
And soon she saw the Fairy bands
    All riding in her sight.

" And first gaed by the black, black steed,
    And then gaed by the brown ;
But fast she grip't the milk-white steed,
    And pu'd the rider down.

" She pu'd him frae the milk-white steed,
    And loot the bridle fa' ;
And up there raise an erlish cry—
    ' He's won among us a' ! '

" They shaped him in fair Janet's arms,
    An esk, but and an adder ;
She held him fast in every shape—
    To be her bairn's father.

" They shaped him in her arms at last
    A mother-naked man :
She wrapt him in her green mantle,
    And sae her true love wan ! "

A mile or two up the river from Carterhaugh, on Ettrick's right bank, stands the interesting and well-preserved old tower of Oakwood, the property of the Scotts of Harden, in whose possession it has been since 1517. Locally, the belief is implicitly held that this tower was, in the thirteenth century, the residence of the great Michael Scott, the Wizard, out of whose tomb in Melrose Abbey William of Deloraine took

" From the cold hand the Mighty Book,
    With iron clasp'd, and with iron bound :
    He thought as he took it the dead man frowned."

There *was* a Michael Scott who once owned Oakwood, but that was long after the Wizard's day. In spite of all tradition—for whose birth Sir Walter is probably responsible—it is not likely that the veritable Michael (Thomas the Rhymer's contemporary, and a Fifeshire man) ever was near Oakwood. Certainly he never lived in the tower that stands now on the steep bank hard by the river. That is no thirteenth century building. I fear, therefore, that the story of Michael and the

Oakwood Tower.

Witch of Fauldshope, and of how, bursting one day from her cottage in the guise of a hare, he was coursed by his own dogs on Fauldshope Hill, can no more be connected with Selkirkshire than can the legend of his embassy to Paris, to which city he journeyed in a single night, mounted on a great coal-black

steed, who indeed was none other than the Foul Fiend himself.
There is, however, a Witchie Knowe on Fauldshope; perhaps the
Michael who really did live at Oakwood, sometime about the
beginning of the seventeenth century, may have had dealings
with the woman, which in some way gave rise to the legend.
This " witch," by the way, was an ancestress of Hogg, the Ettrick
Shepherd.

Oakwood Tower is not very old, and it never was very
strong—as the strength of peel towers is reckoned; its walls
are little more than four feet in thickness, which is almost
flimsy compared with those of its near neighbour, Newark.
Above the dungeons, Oakwood is three stories in height, and
its external measurements are thirty-eight by twenty-three and
a half feet.   Into one wall is built a stone on which are the
initals R·S· L·M·, initials of Robert Scott and his wife, probably
a Murray.   Between them is the Harden crescent ; and below,
the date, ANO. 1602, which is no doubt the true year of the
present tower's erection.   Tradition tells of a haunted chamber
in Oakwood ; the " Jingler's Room," it was called, but what
the story was, the writer has not been able to learn.   The
tower now is used chiefly as a farm building, and if there are
any hauntings they probably take the unpleasant form of rats.

Following up the Ettrick, presently we come to the village of
Ettrickbridgend, near to which are the picturesque Kirkhope
Linns and Kirkhope Tower, a well preserved Border peel.   In
this tower in old days at times dwelt Auld Wat of Harden, or
one of his family.   Tradition tells that it was Wat who first
spanned Ettrick with a bridge.   It was a penance, self-inflicted,
because of a mishap that occurred at the ford here to a young
boy, heir of the Nevilles, whom Wat had carried off from his
home in Northumberland.   Wat's bridge stood a little way
above the site of that which now crosses Ettrick at Ettrickbridgend, and I am told—though I have not seen it—that a
stone from the old bridge, with the Harden coat of arms carved
on it, may now be seen built into the present structure.   A

Kirkhope Tower.

little higher up, there falls into Ettrick the Dodhead Burn, at the head of which is "the fair Dodhead," the reputed residence of Jamie Telfer, hero of the famous ballad. These Border hills have produced from time to time many a long-distance runner of immense local celebrity,—such for instance, as the far-famed Will of Phaup—but few of them, I imagine, could have "lived" with Jamie Telfer in that burst of his across the trackless heather and the boggy moors from the Dodhead, over by the headwaters of Ale, across Borthwick, across Teviot, on to Slitrig at "Stobs Ha'," and from there back again to Teviot at

Looking up Ettrickdale from Hyndhope.

Coultercleuch. It must be a good sixteen miles at the least, across a country over which no runner could travel at a pace so fast as that with which the ballad credits Jamie. But if anyone did this run, I fear it was no Jamie Telfer. At least in "the fair Dodhead" up Ettrick there was at the supposed date of the ballad, and for generations before, no Telfer, but a Scott. The Dodhead of the ballad must be some other place of the same name, possibly that near Penchrise, by Skelfhill.

Following up Ettrick, past Hyndhope and Singlie, we come to Deloraine, an ancient possession of the Scotts, for ever

famed through its association with William of Deloraine and the
"Lay of the Last Minstrel":

> "A stark moss-trooping Scott was he,
> As e'er couch'd Border lance by knee."

There are various theories as to the derivation of the name
"Deloraine." One, in accord with the local pronunciation of
the word—"Delorran," with the accent on the second syllable
—gives its origin as from the Gaelic, "dal Orain," the place or
land of Orain, who, I understand, was a Celtic saint. There is
also the explanation given by the Rev. Dr. Russell of Yarrow,

Ettrick Water at the Deloraines.

in the Statistical Account of the Parish of 1833. "In 1503,
James IV endowed his Queen, the Lady Margaret of England,
with the Forest of Ettrick and Tower of Newark, which had
formerly been the dowry of Mary of Guelders. Hence,
probably, our two farms of Deloraine (de la reine) received
their name, or afterwards perhaps from Mary of *Lorraine*." One
would prefer to adopt Dr. Russell's interpretation of the name,
but probably the place was called "Delórran" long before the
day of any of the historical characters mentioned.

Higher still up Ettrick is Tushielaw, with its fragment of

a ruined tower, the home in old days of that formidable
freebooter Adam Scott, "the king of the Border," or "king
of thieves." Local tradition tells that he was hanged by
James V to the branch of an ash tree that grew within his
own castle walls—retributive justice on a man who had himself,
in like manner, sent to their doom so many poor wretches
from the branches of that same tree. The ash no longer
stands, but in *Chambers' Gazetteer* for 1832 there is this note
concerning it : "It is curious to observe that along its principal
branches there are yet visible a number of nicks, or hollows,
over which the ropes had been drawn wherewith he performed
his numerous executions."

Like too many local traditions, however, the story of his
execution will not bear examination. Adam Scott was arrested
and hanged in Edinburgh, a full month before the King set
out on his memorable expedition to pacify the Border.
James certainly laid a heavy hand on the freebooters ; and
he appears also to have very materially altered the face of
things in other ways in these Border hills. The timber which
clothed them began from this time to disappear—birch and
oak it appears to have been for the most part, interspersed
with ash, mountain-ash, thorn, and hazel, to judge by the
numbers of stumps and pieces of decayed trees still found
in mossy ground. They mostly suggest timber of no great
size, but now and again the remains of a fine tree are come
upon, even in exposed and high-lying situations. The remains
of a very large oak, for instance, were discovered some years
ago during draining operations among the wild hills right at
the head of Jed.

Probably James destroyed a great deal of timber in his
efforts to convert the country into a sheep-run. According
to Pitscottie, the king soon had "ten thousand sheep going
in the forest, under the keeping of Andrew Bell, who made
the King as good an account of them as if they had gone
in the bounds of Fife."

James V no doubt was a good husbandman,—it was his boast that in these wilds he "made the rush bush keep the cow,"—but he was a better husbandman than he was a sportsman, at least as we now understand the word. We should now probably call him a pot-hunter. It was early

The bridge at Tushielaw.

in June when he started on his expedition; young calves are then with the hinds, and the harts are yet low in condition, and "in the velvet" as to their horns. Yet Pitscottie says: "I heard say he slew in these bounds eighteen score of harts." However, if his expedition had to be made then, his army—and it was an army—must necessarily be fed; and no doubt if he wanted to run sheep there, the stock of deer had to be cleared out. But what a place for game of all kinds this forest must then have been. One may learn from the place-names which still linger among the hills what manner of beasts formerly inhabited this part of the Border : Ox-cleuch, Deer-law, Hart-leap, Hynd-hope, Fawn-burn, Wolf-cleuch, Brock-hill, Swine-brae, Boar-cleuch, Cat-slack. The Hart's-leap is said to have got its name owing to an incident that

Ettrick Vale from Hyndhope.

occurred during King James's expedition in 1530; a deer, in sight of the king, is said to have cleared at one bound a distance so remarkable that James directed his followers to leave a memorial of the leap. Two grey whinstones here, twenty-eight feet apart, are said to be those which were then set up. Ox-cleuch was probably so named from some ancient adventure with a Urus, or wild bull, or possibly because it was a favourite haunt of those formidable beasts. Their skulls are still occasionally dug up during the process of draining swampy lands among our Border hills. There is a very fine specimen

now at Synton (between Selkirk and Hawick), home of one of
the oldest branches of the Scott family. If one may judge

Buccleuch.

from that skull, the horns must have been something like twice
the size of the ox of the present day. He was the ancestor, I
suppose, of the fierce wild cattle of Chillingham.

Half a mile, or a little more, above the inn at Tushielaw—a comfortable hostelry, and a good fishing centre—the Rankle Burn flows into Ettrick. Up this burn's right bank, through the lonely vale and over the hills runs a road leading to Hawick, and on your right, as you head in that direction, a few miles up is Buccleuch, one of the earliest possessions in the Border of the great Scott clan. Near the road, in a deep ravine or cleuch, is pointed out the spot where, they say, the buck was slain from which originated the title of the present ducal

A glimpse of Clearburn Loch.

house. Farther on, just upon the water-shed between Ettrick and Teviot, is Bellenden, which became the Scotts' mustering place and whose name was the clan's slogan. As Mr. Thomson's sketches show, it is a wild country enough ; in winter its bleakness at times is surely past the power of words to tell. It must be a hardy race that can live and thrive here. A land of swamp, and sullen, dark, moss-hag, this must have been in days of old. Still among the hills, bogs and lochs innumerable are scattered ; of the latter, Clearburn, Kingside, Crooked Loch, Windylaw, Hellmuir, Alemuir, and various others, all within a few miles, but not many, I think, such as need tempt the wandering fisher.

A couple of miles up Ettrick, above Tushielaw, is Thirlestane, the seat of Lord Napier of Ettrick, surrounded by its woods. It is a mansion built something less than a hundred years ago, but close to it are the remains of the old Thirlestane Castle. I do not know if Hertford's long arm was responsible in 1544 for its ruin. It is probable enough. The stronghold belonged then to Sir John Scott, a prominent man in those days, and the only Scottish baron at Fala-muir who did not refuse to follow James V into England, for which reason the king charged " our lion herauld and his deputies for the time beand, to give and to graunt to the said John Scott, ane Border of ffleure de lises about his coatte of armes, sik as is on our royal banner, and alsua ane bundell of launces above his helmet, with thir words, *Readdy, ay Readdy*, that he and all his after-cummers may bruik the samine as a pledge and taiken of our guid will and kyndnes for his true worthines." Lord Napier is this John Scott's descendant.

Across the river from Thirlestane are the ruins of another castle—Gamescleuch, built by Simon Scott, named Long Spear, a son of John of Thirlestane. Tradition says that Games-cleuch was never occupied, but was allowed to fall into decay because its owner, Simon of the Spear, was poisoned by his step-mother the night before he should have been married and have taken up his abode there.

We are getting far into the wild hills now, near to the head of Ettrick, by Ettrick Pen, Wind Fell, and Capel Fell, all hills considerably over two thousand feet in height. But before crossing over to Yarrow and St. Mary's, there remain to be noticed Ettrick Kirk, and James Hogg's birthplace, Ettrick Hall. Ettrick Kirk, of course, is inalienably associated with the Rev. Thomas Boston, " Boston of Ettrick," minister of the parish for a quarter of a century, a man who left a deep mark on the religious life of Scotland. He died here in 1732, and his monument stands in the little graveyard by the kirk, not far from the head-stone to the memory of the Ettrick Shepherd, and near to the spot where, as the stone tells us, "lyeth William Laidlaw, the far-famed Will of Phaup, who for feats of Frolic, Agility, and Strength, had no equal in his day." Laidlaw was Hogg's grandfather.

Ettrick Kirk.

How many persons now-a-days are familiar with, or indeed, perhaps, ever heard of, Boston's "Fourfold State," or his "Crook in the Lot"?   Perhaps in Ettrick there may yet be, in cottages, an odd copy or two, belonging to, and possibly yet read by, very old people.   But Boston, who as a theologian had once so marked an influence, is now little more than a name, even to the descendants of his flock in Ettrick, and his books, which formerly were to be found in almost every peasant's house in Scotland, are unknown to later generations. Nor, perhaps, is that great matter for wonder. It must be confessed that these writings, which, up to even quite a recent date, had so great a hold on the Scottish peasant, and which, indeed, with the Bible formed almost his only reading, do not appeal to present day readers. The plums in the pudding to modern eyes seem few and far between. But there *are* plums to be found, and many a forcible expression. In "The Crook in the Lot," for instance, where his theme is profligacy, the expression is a happy one whereby he warns the vicious man against the possibility of a "leap out of Delilah's lap into Abraham's bosom."

Like most of his class and creed in those days, Boston was stern and unbending in his Calvinism, and when he came to Ettrick in 1707, he was faced by a state of affairs that bred for a time great friction between minister and congregation. The flock had been for a while without a shepherd, and laxity had crept into their church-going. Boston had to complain of the "indecent carriage of the people at the kirk, going *out* and *in*, and *up* and *down* the kirkyard the time of divine service." But he speedily drilled them into a line of conduct more seemly; and whereas when he dispensed the Sacrament for the first time in 1710 there had been present only fifty-seven communicants, in 1731 when he dispensed it for the last time, there were no fewer than seven hundred and seventy-seven. Crowds of people from other parishes came vast distances over the pathless mountains in order to be present. Where did they all find food and accommodation, one wonders. The farmers, then as now the most hospitable and kindly of human beings, fed and housed numbers, as a matter of course, but they could not accommodate all, and there was then no inn at Tushielaw, none indeed nearer than Selkirk. Great must have been the fervour of those many scores of men and women who resolutely tramped so far over

U

the wild hills to be present at " the Sacrament." There were no
roads in those days, or practically none.   Even at late as 1792,
the Statistical Account of the Parish says : " The roads are
almost impassable.   The only road that looks like a turnpike
is to Selkirk, but even it in many places is so deep as greatly
to obstruct travelling.   The distance is about sixteen miles,
and it requires four hours to ride it.   The snow also at times
is a great inconvenience ; often for many months we can have
no   intercourse   with   our   neighbours. . . . Another   great

Mill gang at Ettrick.

disadvantage is the want of bridges.   For many hours the
traveller is obstructed on his journey when the waters are
swelled."   Such was the condition of the hill country sixty
years after Boston's death.   In his day it must have been even
worse ; probably the only road that resembled a road in 1792
was a mere track earlier in the century.

Close by Ettrick Kirk is Ettrick Hall, where Hogg was
born.   Though in name suggestive of a lordly mansion, it
was in reality but a mean, and rather damp, little cottage, or
" butt and ben," of which there are now no remains.   I understand that the walls fell down about the year 1830.   There is

now a monument to "the Shepherd" where the cottage stood;
and there is of course the commemorative statue over by
St. Mary's, hard by "Tibbie Shiels." Hogg was, as the late
Professor Ferrier said: "after Burns (*proximus sed longo
intervallo*) the greatest poet that has ever sprung from the
bosom of the common people." But to how many of those
who visit his birth-place, or look on his monument over in
Yarrow, are his works now familiar? How many of us, indeed,
have any but the merest nodding acquaintance even with
"Kilmeny"? And of his prose writings, who of the general
public, except here and there a one, knows now even the
"Brownie of Bodesbeck," a Covenanting story that used to
thrill every Scottish boy?

Hyndhope Burn.

U 2

CHAPTER XII

YARROW

In whatever part you take the vale of Ettrick, there is about it, and about its scenery and its associations, a charm, different perhaps from that of the more widely famed Yarrow, yet almost equally powerful. There is in the summer season a solemnity and a peace brooding over these "round-backed, kindly hills," that act like a charm on the body and mind that are weary. Each vale has its distinctive peculiarities, yet each blends imperceptibly into the other.

From the head of Ettrick by Ettrick Kirk over to Yarrow is but little more than a step across the hills, either by the bridle track by Scabcleuch and Penistone Knowe over to the Riskinhope Burn and the head of the Loch of the Lowes, for those afoot; or by the road up Tushielaw Burn, for those on whom time, or years, press unduly, and who prefer to drive. It is not a very good road, but it serves, though the descent to St. Mary's is something of the abruptest,—one in ten, I think. If the bridle track has been followed, as one comes down towards Riskinhope, there, on the opposite side of the valley, is Chapelhope, for ever associated with Hogg's "Brownie of Bodesbeck." And at Riskinhope itself, Renwick, last of the Scottish Covenanting Martyrs, preached no long time before his execution at the Grassmarket in Edinburgh in February, 1688. "When he prayed that day, few of his

hearers' cheeks were dry," says the Ettrick Shepherd.   It was
here

> " Where Renwick told of one great sacrifice,
>   Ere he himself had borne in full his cross,
>   And hearts sublimed were round him in the wild,

St. Mary's Loch and the Loch of the Lowes.

And faces, God-ward turned in fervent prayer,
For deeply smitten, suffering flock of Christ ;
And clear uprose the plaintive moorland psalm,
Heard high above the plover's wailing cry,
From simple hearts in whom the spirit strong
Of hills was consecrate by heavenly grace,
And firmly nerv'd to meet, whene'er it came,
In His own time, the call to martyrdom."

"The plover's wailing cry."—It is curious to note how even to
this day the peewit, or plover, is hated in the Border hills,
because its incessant complaining wail when disturbed so often
betrayed to the dragoons the presence of lurking Covenanters,
or the whereabouts of some Conventicle of the persecuted
people. The shepherd or the peasant of to-day will stamp on
the eggs of the peewit wherever he comes on them, muttering
to himself curses on the bird as it wheels and plunges overhead,
wailing dolefully.

But of Yarrow, how is one to write? The task is hopeless,
whether it be to speak of its beauty, of its legend, its poetry, or of
its associations. From Scott and Wordsworth downwards, what
poet has not sung its praises? However halting may be his pen,
what writer in prose has not tried in words to picture its scenes?
It is left to one now only to repeat what has been said by
better men; at the best, one may but paraphrase the words of
another. There is nothing new to be said of Yarrow, no fresh
beauty to be pointed out. Its charm affects each one differently; each must see and feel for himself. But whether the
season be sweetest summer-tide, or that when winter's blast
comes black and roaring down the glens, fiercely driving before
it sheets of water snatched from the tortured bosom of lone
Saint Mary's,—there, still, abides the indescribable charm of
Yarrow. Yet on the whole, I think almost that I should prefer
my visit to be in the winter time, if a few fine days might be
assured, or days at least without storm. In the summer
season now, and especially since the advent of the motor car,
from morning till night so constant a stream of visitors and

tourists passes through the vale, and along the lake side, that even Yarrow's deathless charm is broken, her peace disturbed; one's soul can take no rest there now, far from the clamour of the outer world. No longer may one quote Alexander Anderson's beautiful lines:

> "What boon to lie, as now I lie,
>   And see in silver at my feet
> Saint Mary's Lake, as if the sky
>   Had fallen 'tween those hills so sweet.

St. Mary's Loch.

> " And this old churchyard on the hill,
>   That keeps the green graves of the dead,
> So calm and sweet, so lone and still,
>   And but the blue sky overhead."

And yet, even in summer, if one can betake oneself to the old churchyard of St. Mary of the Lowes, at an hour when the chattering, picnic-ing tourist is far from the scene, one may still lie there and dream, unvexed by care; and, if fate be kind, one may yet spend long restful days among the hills, beside some crooning burn that

> "   .   .   .   half-hid, sings its song
> In hidden circlings 'neath a grassy fringe ";

still rejoice in the unspoilt moorlands and the breezy heights :

> " There thrown aside all reason-grounded doubts,
> All narrow aims, and self-regarding thoughts,
> Out of himself amid the infinitude,
> Where Earth, and Sky, and God are all in all."

And in these hills, what fitter place can there be for dreams than St. Mary's chapel, overlooking the silent lake, with

Site of St. Mary's Church.

Yarrow gliding from its bosom ?   Here you will find a Sabbath peace, as placid as when

> " . . . on sweet Sabbath morns long gone,
> Folks wended to St. Mary's Forest Kirk,
> Where mass was said and matins, softly sung,
> Were borne in fitful swell across the Loch ;
> And full of simple vision, there they saw
> In Kirk and Quire, the brier and red rose,
> That fondly meet and twin'd o'er lover's graves,
> Who fled o' night through moor up Black Cleuch heights
> Pass'd through the horror of the mortal fight,
> Where Margaret kiss'd a father's ruddy wounds."

The ballad of the Douglas tragedy is known to everyone; it need not be quoted. This is the kirk where the lovers lie buried, almost within distant sight of the ancient tower from which they had fled, and whose ruins are still to be seen near Blackhouse, on the Douglas Burn. The Douglas stones, which, tradition tells us, mark the spot where Lady Margaret's seven brothers fell under the sword of her lover, are out high on the moor; but there are eleven, not seven, stones, though only three are left standing. It was at Blackhouse, one may

The Douglas Burn and Blackhouse Tower.

remember, that Sir Walter first made the acquaintance of Willie Laidlaw, whose father was tenant of the farm. James Hogg was shepherd here from 1790 to 1800, but he had left before Sir Walter's visit, though the two met very shortly after. It was whilst Hogg was in service here that there came the tremendous snow storm of 1794, of which he gave so vivid a description in Blackwood's Magazine of July, 1819.

There are now no remains of the chapel of St. Mary;

"O lone St. Mary of the waves,
    In ruin lies thine ancient aisle."

It was destroyed about the year 1557, and was never rebuilt. A Cranstoun, flying from the Scotts, sought sanctuary in the holy building, and the Scotts, heedless of the terrors of excommunication, burnt it down. "They burned the Chapel for very rage," says The Lay, because Cranstoun escaped them. The churchyard is little used now, but a few privileged families do still, I understand, bury their dead in that quiet spot. It is an enviable place in which to lie at rest, where the lark sings high in air, and the free wind comes soughing over the hill.

Near to the burial ground is the mound called Binram's Corse, the grave, they say, of a wizard priest, whose bones might not find rest in hallowed ground.

> " Strange stories linger'd in those lonely glens,—
> Of that weird eve when wizard Binram old,
> Was laid in drear unrest, beyond hallow'd ground ;
> How, at bell-tolling by no mortal hand,
> And voices saying words which no man knew,
> There rose such shrieks from low depths of the lake,
> And such wild echoes from the darken'd hill,
> That holy men fled from the scant fill'd grave,
> And left bare buried that unholy priest."

Across the loch from the quiet grave-yard on the hill, lies " Bowerhope's lonely top," and Bowerhope farm, so loved of its tenant of many years ago. In his " Reminiscences of Yarrow," the late Rev. Dr. Russell mentions that " Bowerhope farmhouse was so low in the roof that my father at the exhortations had to stand between two of the rafters, so that the Kitchen full of people and full of smoke was not the most pleasant place to speak in. Yet old Sandy Cunningham, the tenant, used to say : " Ministers may talk o' Heevin' as they like ; commend me to Bowerhope ; I cud tak a tack [lease] o't to a' eternity."

On our right, on the same side of the loch with us as we stand facing Bowerhope, is Henderland, where, on a spot called the Chapel Knowe, is a grave-slab, and on it, sculptured, a sword and what appear to be armorial bearings, with the inscription :

"Here lyis Perys of Cokburne and hys wyfe Marjory." This, we used to be told, was the grave of a famous freebooter, whom King James V, (dropping in, as it were, one day while the unsuspecting reiver sat at dinner,) took, and hanged over the gate of his own castle, the tower whose weather-battered fragments are still to be seen here. His wife, it was said, fled to the adjacent Dow Glen, a rocky chasm through which rushes

Cokburne's grave.

the Henderland burn, and there, says Sir Walter Scott, cowering on what is still called the Lady's Seat, she strove "to drown amid the roar of a foaming cataract, the tumultuous noise which announced the close of his existence." But Cokburne of Henderland, like Adam Scott of Tushiealaw, was executed in Edinburgh, before King James set out on his expedition. Moreover, that Cokburn of Henderland's Christian name was

William.   This, therefore, cannot be the grave of James' victim
in 1530.   But whatever the real story of " Perys Cokburne and
hys wyfe, Marjory," their fate has given rise to a ballad fuller of
pathos than all the countless pathetic ballads of Yarrow.

> " My love he built me a bonny bower,
>   And clad it a' wi' lilye flower,
>   A brawer bower ye ne'er did see,
>   Than my true love he built for me.

> " There came a man, by middle day,
>   He spied his sport and went away ;
>   And brought the King that very night,
>   Who brake my bower, and slew my knight.

> " He slew my knight, to me sae dear ;
>   He slew my knight, and poin'd his gear ;
>   My servants all for life did flee,
>   And left me in extremitie.

> " I sewed his sheet, making my mane ;
>   I watch'd the corpse, myself alane ;
>   I watch'd his body, night and day ;
>   No living creature came that way.

> " I took his body on my back,
>   And whiles I gaed, and whiles I sat ;
>   I digged a grave, and laid him in,
>   And happ'd him with the sod sae green.

> " But think na ye my heart was sair,
>   When I laid the moul' on his yellow hair ;
>   O think na ye my heart was wae,
>   When I turn'd about, away to gae ?

> " Nae living man I'll love again,
>   Since that my lovely knight is slain,
>   Wi' ae lock of his yellow hair
>   I'll chain my heart for evermair."

Just by Henderland is Coppercleuch, (called Cappercleuch
in my boyhood,) and below it, Megget, flowing into the loch—a
troutful stream, at least in earlier days.   Pike used to bask in

the shallows here of a hot summer's day ; perhaps even yet
they do so.   But I think these fish are more numerous now in
the Loch of the Lowes than in St. Mary's.   Up Megget's left
bank runs a hill road leading over into Tweedsmuir.   It has
been negotiated by motors, but it is far from being a desirable
road for that form of traffic, or indeed for any except foot traffic.
The surface is rough and hilly, and where it plunges down past
Talla Linns it is exceedingly steep, and in places very soft.

Coppercleuch Post-office and a glimpse up Meggetdale.

Higher up the loch than Coppercleuch is the Rodono Hotel,
and beyond, on the isthmus at the very head of St. Mary's,
"Tibbie's," that famous little hostelry, haunt lang syne of
Christopher North and Hogg ; "Tibbie's," with its queer little
antiquated box-beds, that I believe even yet exist.   But it is
not the "Tibbie Shiels" of North's day, or even of much later

days; it has not the same simplicity; it has grown, and is no
longer the simple little cottage into which Tibbie and her
husband entered just ninety years ago this year of 1913.
Robert Chambers described it in 1827 as "a small, neat
house, kept by a decent shepherd's widow . . . It is scarcely
possible to conceive anything more truly delightful than a
week's ruralizing in this comfortable little mansion, with the
means of so much amusement at the very door, and so many
interesting objects of sight and sentiment lying closely around."

Tibbie Shiel's.

Perhaps in some ways it is as delightful now as ever; but motors
and bicycles have changed its air, and its aspect. They seem
as inconsistent with the air of "Tibbie's" as would be a railway
train, or penny steamers on the loch. Necessarily, there is now
about the place a more commercial air; it is no longer the mere
cottage, with its simple fare of oatmeal porridge,—cooked as
nowhere now it is cooked; milk, rich and frothy; of ham and
eggs, the mere whiff of which would bring you in ravenous from
loch or hill; of fresh caught trout fried in oatmeal and still
sizzling as they were brought in. There are trout now as of

old, no doubt, and hens yet lay eggs, and pigs are turned to
bacon; but you eat now with a sense of having a train to
catch, or a motor hurriedly to jump into; your eye seems to be
ever on the clock, and the old air of leisure and of peace is
gone.   Tibbie Shiel herself departed in time.   She who, when
all the world was young, listened many a time to that Shepherd
who had

> " Found in youth a harp among the hills,
>   Dropt by the Elfin people,"

I think could ill have brooked this twentieth century rush and
hurry; she was spared the trial of finding the pure air of St.
Mary's poisoned by the stench of petrol fumes.   A native of
Ettrick, born in 1782, Tibbie lived at her home in Yarrow till
the summer of 1878, and she lies in the same kirk-yaird
that "haps" all that is mortal of James Hogg.   And here by
the loch, almost at her door, with plaid around him, the Shepherd sits in effigy, as Christopher North predicted to him in
1824, with "honest face looking across St. Mary's Loch and
up towards the Grey Mare's Tail, while by moonlight all your
own fairies will weave a dance round its pedestal."

They were weird things, those box-beds, that have been
mentioned as still existing in Tibbie Shiel's cottage, weird, and
responsible for much ill-health, more especially one would
suppose, for consumption.   They were built into the wall of
a room, and they had wooden doors that could be drawn close
at night, entirely cutting them off from the room, and jealously
excluding every breath of fresh air.   Some had a very small
sliding trap, or eyelet hole, in one of the doors, opening at the
side just above the pillow, but the custom was, as I understand, to shut even that.   The box-bed was of old almost
universal in peasants' cottages in the Border.   No doubt it
gave a certain amount of privacy to the occupant or occupants,
but what countless forms of disease it must have fostered !
The present writer can remember the case of a young man of
twenty-five or so, who, to the puzzled wonder of his friends,

died of a galloping consumption. "I canna think hoo he
could hae gotten't," said his sister to the daughter of her
mistress. "He was aye *that* carefu' o' himsel'. Od! he wad
hap himself up that warm, an' he aye drew the doors o' his bed
close, an' shuttit the verra keek-hole. Na! I canna think
hoo *he* could hae catched it." To add to the sanitary joys of

Dryhope Tower.

those homes of disease germs, it was, too, the almost universal
custom to use the space below the bed as a kind of store
house. The writer can remember as a boy to have seen in
one of the most decent and respectable of such cottages, bags
of potatoes stowed under the sleeping place occupied by a
husband and wife!

Quitting now the Loch, and following the road that leads down Yarrow to Selkirk, on our left, half a mile or so from the road and overhanging the burn, stands the massive little tower of Dryhope.   This was the birthplace, about the year 1550, of the beautiful Mary Scott, the Flower of Yarrow, bride of Scott of Harden.   I suppose that Harden must have succeeded his father-in-law in the possession of Dryhope, for in 1592, James VI issued orders to demolish the tower of Dryhope, "pertaining to Walter Scott of Harden who was art and part of the late treasonable act perpetuate against His Highness' own person at Falkland."   James' instructions, however, cannot have been carried out very effectually, if at all, for Dryhope, though roofless, is in rather better preservation than are the majority of Border peels.

And now, on the far side of Yarrow, we pass Altrive, the farm which, from 1814 till his death in 1835, Hogg leased from the Duke of Buccleuch, at a merely nominal rent.   Here, as Allan Cunningham said, he had "the best trout in Yarrow, the finest lambs on its braes, the finest grouse on its hills, and as good as a *sma' still* besides."   Indeed he must almost have needed a "sma' still," in order effectually to entertain the crowds of people who came here unasked, to visit him, once he had established his reputation as a lion.   The tax on him must have been even heavier in proportion than it was on Sir Walter at Abbotsford.

Farther down, by the intersection of the cross road that leads over to Traquair and Tweed, there is the Gordon Arms, snuggest of fishing quarters, where in the endless twilights of June and July you may lie long awake, yet half steeped in sleep, listening contentedly to the wavering trill of whaups floating eerily over the hill in the still night air ; or in the lightest dreamland you forecast the basket of tomorrow.   It was here, at the Gordon Arms, that Scott and Hogg parted for the last time in the autumn of 1830, when the waters were already rising high that were so soon to close over Sir Walter's head.   Slowly they

X

walked together a mile down the road, Scott leaning heavily on
Hogg's shoulder, and " I cannot tell what it was," wrote the latter
afterwards, "but there was something in his manner that dis-
tressed me.   He often changed the subject very abruptly, and
never laughed.   He expressed the deepest concern for my
welfare and success in life more than I had ever heard him do
before, and all mixed with sorrow for my worldly misfortunes.
There is little doubt that his own were then preying on his
vitals."   In truth Sir Walter then might well "never laugh."

The Gordon Arms.

He had already had a slight paralytic stroke, and he could not
but realise that the end of his titanic labours was approaching.

A few miles down stream from the Gordon Arms, we come
to Yarrow Kirk, and Yarrow Manse, smiling in a valley that to
me in some strange way always speaks of sunshine and of peace.
Perhaps it is due to thoughts of those who laboured here so
long, and who gave to everyone

> " That best portion of a good man's life—
> His little, nameless, unremembered acts
> Of kindness and of love."

I think I am not mistaken in saying that in this Parish of Yarrow there have been during a hundred and twenty-two years only three ministers. From 1791 to 1883 there were the Russells, father and son,—the Reverend Dr. Robert Russell and the Reverend Dr. James Russell, whose names were household words far beyond the bounds of Yarrow, and at whose manse old and young, rich and poor, were equally made

Looking up the Vale of Yarrow—the Gordon Arms in the distance.

welcome. And after them came the Reverend Dr. Borland, who died in 1912, and whose "Raids and Reivers" is a Border classic. It is a remarkable record, and a wonderful testimony to the pure air of Yarrow. During his long life Dr. Robert Russell never spent a single day in bed, nor until three days before his death was he ever prescribed for by a doctor.

Yarrow Kirk was built in 1640, and the first minister of the

Parish after the Revolution was the Reverend John Rutherford, maternal great-grandfather of Sir Walter Scott. Dr. James Russell gives a quaint account of the church as it was in 1826, in the time of his father. "The interments," he says, "which had taken place in the course of nearly two hundred years, and the wish for proximity to Church walls, had had the effect of raising the ground of the graveyard around the church considerably above its level. In front, the earth outside was two feet, and at the corner of the aisle fully four feet higher. In consequence, the lower walls were covered with a green damp, and the rain water flowed into the passages. In winter the water froze, and my father used to say that he often got a slide to the pulpit." This matter, however, was remedied in 1826, when many improvements were made in and around the church. One improvement which Dr. Russell mentions had to do with the shepherds' dogs, which then invariably accompanied their masters to church—a practice which I think died out but recently. "There were no doors on the seats," says Dr. Russell, "and nothing but a narrow deal in each as a footboard, and no separation below between them. The planking on the passages was very deficient, and a great deal of the earthen floor was thus exposed, and it can easily be imagined that when the shepherds from Ettrick, as well as from Yarrow, came to church, each shepherd as regularly accompanied by his dog as encased in his plaid—no matter what the weather or the season—what frequent rows there were. On the slightest growl they all pricked up their ears. If a couple of them fell out and showed fight, it was the signal for a general *mêlée*. The rest that were prowling about, or half asleep at their masters' feet, rushed from their lairs, found a way through below the pews, and among the feet of the occupants, and raised literally such a *dust* as fairly enveloped them. Then the strife waxed fierce and furious, the noise became deafening, the voice of the minister was literally drowned, and he was fain to pause, whether in preaching or in prayer. Two or three shepherds had to leave their places and use their *nibbies* unmercifully before the rout was quelled, and the service of the sanctuary resumed." Such a scene as the above was quite an ordinary occurrence in a country church in Scotland, early in the nineteenth century—and in remote districts even later than that; minister and congregation were accustomed to it, and took it as a matter of course. The shepherd's dogs could not be left behind to their own devices; and it was a matter of necessity that their master should go to church. There was no more to be said, not even when the dogs (as they often did) with long-drawn howls joined in the singing of the psalms. And when the benediction was pronounced, (which "to cheat the dowgs," was always done with the congregation seated,) then, at the first movement after it, a perfect storm of barking broke out as the dogs poured out of the building ahead of the people.

Just below Yarrow Church are the ruins—I think not much more than the foundations—of Deuchar tower, a Scott stronghold, perhaps, like so many others, or maybe a holding of some descendent of the Outlaw Murray. And hard by Deuchar Mill is the picturesque old bridge with its broken arch stretched, like the stump of a maimed arm, towards the farther shore of Yarrow. It is a bridge that dates from about the year 1653. The burgh records of Peebles for that year show that the magistrates then ordained "that all in the town who have horses shall send the same for a day, to carry lime for the said brig, under a penalty of forty shillings." That bridge stood till 1734, when the south arch was wrecked by a great flood. To restore the arch was a task at that time beyond the means of the district, and for some years those who lived on the south side of Yarrow and who wished to attend Yarrow Church, could do so only at the cost of wading the water, a feat in flood time impossible, and in the winter season a trial to be endured with difficulty even by the most hardy. The dead, in many instances, could not be buried beside their friends in the

old churchyard; children born in parts of the parish south of
Yarrow could be baptised only at uncertain times and after indefinite delay; and marriages frequently had to be postponed.
Finally, of the money required for repair of the bridge, owing
to various circumstances only the half could be raised, and the
arch put in after a delay of several years was of such peculiar
construction, and so steep and causeway-like on the south side

Deuchar Bridge.

that it was not without difficulty that even an empty cart could
cross.   "Besides," says Dr. Russell, "there was little earth on
the stones that formed the arch to steady and protect it."
Nevertheless, it held together for the best part of a century,
and then, suddenly, it collapsed one winter's afternoon, just
after the roadman's cart had crossed.   A new bridge had been
erected just opposite the church, and no farther attempt was

made to repair the old one. There it stands, a pathetic and picturesque memorial of old days.

It seems always to me that these old broken bridges—there are two in Yarrow—strike a note fittingly attuned to the dirge murmured by the water as it wanders through the vale, strikingly in keeping with its mournful traditions and with the inexplicable sadness that for ever broods here. This is the very heart of the Dowie Dens of Yarrow. Here is the scene of the so-called

The Dowie Dens.

"duel" between John Scott of Tushielaw and his brother-in-law, Walter Scott, third son of Robert Scott of Thirlestane.

> " Late at e'en, drinking the wine,
>   And ere they paid the lawing
>   They set a combat them between,
>   To fecht it in the dawing."

Assassination, however, rather than duel, seems to have been the word applicable to the combat.

> " As he gaed up the Tinnies Bank,
>   I wot he gaed wi' sorrow,
>   Till, down in a den he spied nine armed men,
>   On the dowie houms of Yarrow."

" ' Oh, come ye here to part your land,
    The bonnie Forest thorough ?
Or come ye here to wield your brand
    On the dowie houms of Yarrow ?'

' I come not here to part my land,
    And neither to beg nor borrow ;
I come to wield my noble brand
    On the bonnie banks of Yarrow.'

' If I see all, ye're nine to ane,
    And that's an unequal marrow ;
Yet will I fight while lasts my brand,
    On the bonnie banks of Yarrow.'

Four has he hurt, and five has slain,
    On the bludie braes of Yarrow ;
Till that stubborn knight came him behind
    And ran his body thorough.

' Yestreen I dreamed a doleful dream ;
    I fear there will be sorrow !
I dreamed I pu'd the heather green,
    Wi my true love on Yarrow.

' O gentle wind that bloweth south,
    From where my Love repaireth,
Convey a kiss frae his dear mouth,
    And tell me how he faireth ! '

' But in the glen strove armed men ;
    They've wrought me dule and sorrow ;
They've slain—the comeliest knight they've slain—
    He bleeding lies on Yarrow.'

As she sped down yon high, high hill,
    She gaed wi' dule and sorrow,
And in the glen spied ten slain men
    On the dowie banks of Yarrow.

She kissed his cheek, she kaimed his hair,
    She searched his wounds all thorough ;
She kissed them till her lips grew red,
    On the dowie houms of Yarrow."

Here too, a little above Deuchar Bridge, and beyond the church, is the famous "inscribed stone" of Yarrow, on the merits of which, as on the question of its age, I am not qualified to express an opinion. The place where it stands was waste moorland about the beginning of last century, and the stone was uncovered when the first attempts were being made to reclaim it. In his "Reminiscences of Yarrow," Dr. James Russell says on this subject: "On more than twenty different spots of this moor were large cairns, in many of which fine yellow dust, and in one of which an old spear-head, was found. Two unhewn massive stones still stand, about a hundred yards distant from each other, which doubtless are the monuments of the dead. The real tradition simply bears that here a deadly feud was settled by dint of arms: the upright stones mark the place where the two lords or leaders fell, and the bodies of followers were thrown into a marshy pool called the *Dead Lake*, in the adjoining haugh. It is probable that this is the locality of "the Dowie Dens of Yarrow." About three hundred yards westward, when the cultivation of this moor began, the plough struck upon a large flat stone of unhewn greywacke bearing a Latin inscription. Bones and ashes lay beneath it, and on every side the surface presented verdant patches of grass." The inscription is difficult to decipher, and readings differ; all, however, seem to agree as to the termination: "*Hic jacent in tumulo duo filii Liberalis* ;" and it is supposed to date from about the fifth century.

Still following the stream downwards we come to Hangingshaw, in ancient days home of the Murrays. In Hangingshaw tower—long demolished—dwelt the Outlaw Murray, who owned "nae King in Christentie."

> " Fair Philiphaugh is mine by right,
>   And Lewinshope still mine shall be ;
> Newark, Foulshiells, and Tinnies baith,
>   My bow and arrow purchased me.

> " And I have native steads to me,
>   The Newark Lee and Hanginshaw."

Of the bold Outlaw's stock there remains now in the Border not one representative, and the last of their lands has passed from them.

At Foulshiels, a couple of miles farther down, by the roadside stand the walls of the modest dwelling in which was born Mungo Park, the famous African explorer of the late eighteenth and early nineteenth centuries, a man of whom another traveller of our own day, himself among the greatest, has said : " For actual hardship undergone, for dangers faced, and difficulties overcome, together with an exhibition of the virtues which make a man great in the rude battle of life, Mungo Park stands without a rival." His dauntless spirit stands out conspicuous in the last words he ever sent home : " Though the Europeans who were with me were dead, and though I myself were half dead, I would still persevere, and if I could not succeed in the object of my journey, I would at last die on the Niger." That, I think, is the same fearless spirit that has so recently touched to the core the inmost heart of the Nation, the spirit displayed in the last message home of another dauntless explorer and his comrades, who have perished also for duty's sake.

But Park was less heard of then—more than a century back ; news filtered slowly in those days ; he did not at the moment become a national hero. And if a man is seldom a prophet in his own country, it is surely from members of his own family that he is apt last of all to receive the honour which is his due. When Mungo came home in 1797 from his first African expedition, his elder brother, then tenant of Foulshiels, ("a man," says Lockhart, "remarkable for strength both of mind and body,") chanced to be in Selkirk when the explorer arrived there. That night, as the worthy farmer lay asleep in bed, he was awakened by his mother, who told him to get up ; there was "a man chappin' (knocking) at the door." "Oh, ay !" drowsily muttered the disturbed sleeper, weary from a long day passed at the market, turning himself over in bed, "I daursay that'll be oor Munga. I saw him gettin' aff the coach in Selkirk the day." It was this Archibald Park who was riding one day with Sir Walter Scott—"the Shirra"—when, in a desolate part of the country, they came unexpectedly on a desperate gang of gipsies, one of whom was "wanted" for murder. Park did not hesitate an instant, but seized the man and dragged him away from under the very noses of his lawless, threatening comrades.

Opposite to Foulshiels, on the farther bank of Yarrow, stands "Newark's stately tower," the most famous, and I think, from

Newark.

its situation, the most beautiful of all the Border strongholds. Situation and surroundings are perfect; I know of no scene more captivating, whether you view it from Foulshiels, or stand by the castle itself, or, climbing high up on its ramparts, gaze around where wood and hill and stream blend in a beauty that is matchless. And from far below comes the voice of Yarrow, chafing among its rocks and boulders, moaning perhaps as it moaned that cruel day after the battle of Philiphaugh, when, on Slain Man's Lea, hard by the castle, Lesly's prisoners were butchered in cold blood.

Newark is the best preserved of all the famous Border

towers. And this we owe to the House of Buccleuch. Writing of the ancient towers of Ettrick and Yarrow, the Reverend Dr. James Russell says: " Some of them were burned down when clans were in conflict with each other; but what was allowable in the period of Border warfare was without excuse in our times of peace. Even the grim grey ruins were interesting features of the landscape, and worthy of being spared. But, worse than 'time's destroying sway,' the ruthless hand of vandalism has swept the greater part of them away, as standing in the way of some fancied improvement, or to employ the material for building some modern dyke or dwelling. Even Newark Castle, the stateliest of them all, was thus desecrated through the bad taste of the factor of the day, so recently as the beginning of this [the nineteenth] century, and the best of the stones from the walls and enclosing fence pulled down for the building of a farmhouse immediately in front on the Slain Man's Lea. The present noble proprietor [the fifth Duke of Buccleuch, who died in 1884], was so displeased and disgusted with the proceedings, that when he came into power he swept the modern houses away, and restored stones that in an evil hour had been abstracted, and put the ancient pile into a state of perfect preservation."

Built sometime before 1423—it is referred to as the " new werke " in a charter of that date to Archibald, Earl of Douglas, —Newark Castle was a royal hunting seat; the royal arms are carved on a stone high up on its western wall. But in its time it has seen war as well as sport; in 1548 Lord Grey captured it for Edward VI, and in 1650 it was garrisoned for a while by Cromwell's men after Dunbar. It is of peace, however, rather than of war that one thinks when wandering here; and one recalls how Anne, Duchess of Monmouth and Buccleuch, quitting the throng of men and the hideous later turmoil of her life, retired here with her children after the execution of her unhappy husband in 1685. To what more beautiful and restful scene could she have carried the burden of her sorrows?

It is she to whom, in Newark, the "Last Minstrel" recites his Lay.

> " The Duchess mark'd his weary pace,
> His timid mien, and reverend face,
> And bade her page the menials tell,
> That they should tend the old man well :
> For she had known adversity,
> Though born in such a high degree ;
> In pride of power, in beauty's bloom,
> Had wept o'er Monmouth's bloody tomb ! "

Yair Bridge.

Turning away now from sight of Newark, and from Foulshiels, the road sweeps winding down the Yarrow, high over wooded banks, and

> " . . . .sweet in Harewood sing the birds,
> The sound of summer in their chords ; "

past Harewood, its braes shimmering in the summer sun, Yarrow far below, plunging through deep black pools that seem fathomless, and boiling angrily where hindering rocks essay to check its course. This, I think, is the most beautiful part of all Yarrow, as beautiful as the stream's higher reaches, but .

wilder, with higher,—almost precipitous—banks, rich draped in woods.   Away far over to the right across the river, among the trees lies Bowhill; and down past the "General's Brig" we leave Philiphaugh House on the left, and the cairn that commemorates the battle, pass near the junction pool of Yarrow and Ettrick; then quitting Yarrow, we rejoin the Tweed road opposite Selkirk, and once more come to Yair Bridge.

> " Sweet smells the birk, green grows, green grows the grass,
>   Yellow on Yarrow's braes the gowan,
>   Fair hangs the apple frae the rock,
>   Sweet the wave of Yarrow flowan."

> " Flows Yarrow sweet ? as sweet, as sweet flows Tweed,
>   As green its grass, its gowan yellow,
>   As sweet smells on its braes the birk,
>   The apple frae the rock as mellow."

CHAPTER XIII

UPPER TWEED, YAIR, FAIRNILEE, ASHIESTEEL, ELIBANK, INNERLEITHEN, TRAQUAIR

SWEET in truth flows Tweed here, as all will own who leisurely wend their way—it is too beautiful to justify hurried progress— under leafy boughs where the sun slants down in fairy pattern on a road divorced by but a narrow edge of greenest grass from the clear, hurrying river. Here, at your very hand, you may see countless "ripples of the rising trout, that feed beneath the elms of Yair." There over against you on the far bank of Tweed is Yair itself; and on the hither side, nestling above a lofty bank among its grand old trees, the beautiful ruin of Fairnilee, with its hospitable modern mansion hard by. It was in this fine old seventeenth-century Scottish mansion that Alison Rutherfurd wrote her exquisite version of the "Flowers of the Forest." In the old ruined house the little room in which she wrote is still intact, and now is carefully preserved from farther possibility of decay. But why, one wonders vainly, why was a place so fair ever abandoned, and allowed so long to crumble away as if it had been a thing accursed?

> " Gin ye wad meet wi' me again,
>   Gang to the bonny banks o' Fairnilee,"

said the Queen of Faery to True Thomas. And were she here now in the Border land, to no more enchanting spot could she tryst him;—the sunny slope above the river, the giant limbs of

mighty trees green with the leafy crown of June, or flushed with
the blood-red and orange of autumn ; the ceaseless song of
water gushing over the cauld and dashing among the boulders
below ; the wide expanse that carries the eye through the

Fairnilee.

waving boughs over the gleaming belt of water, and away far
up the hill purpling with the bloom of heather,—or, late in the
season, "grymed" with the new fallen snow,—up and over to
the broad summit of the Three Brethren Cairn.   In very truth
it is itself a fairyland, and, standing here, to the mind comes,

Caddonfoot, looking towards Yair.

irresistibly, thought of the hidden Gold of Fairnilee that in
boyhood one sought for so diligently.   Then, higher up the
river a mile or thereby, at the foot of Neidpath Hill, the long
deep, swift-hurrying stream in which, when autumn floods have
done their work, there is not a yard where a lordly salmon may
not be hooked.   And higher still, there is Caddonfoot, and
Clovenfords, in whose little inn Sir Walter used to stay before he
lived at Ashiesteel ; and the Nest, snug quarters of a famous
Edinburgh Fishing Club, among whose members in old days

The Inn at Clovenfords.

was included the name of many an eminent Scot.   Then
opposite the Nest, across the river, Ashiesteel, which, almost
more eloquently than even Abbotsford itself, speaks of Sir
Walter.   Here were spent the seven happiest years of his life ;
here he wrote the " Lay of the Last Minstrel," " Marmion," and
" The Lady of the Lake " ; here came into his service those
most faithful of followers, Mathieson (his coachman) and Tom
Purdie, the latter, before the good fortune that brought him to
the notice of " the Shirra," a most accomplished poacher of

salmon. Who has not read, and smiled over, the tales that
Scrope tells of him in his " Days and Nights of Salmon Fishing
in Tweed ? "

Purdie's eccentricities were many, his tongue free and out-
spoken to an extent that one would suppose might at times
have ruffled the temper even of a man so tolerant and sweet-
tempered as Scott. Yet the attachment that sprang up
between the three, Sir Walter, Mathieson, and Purdie, was

Thomas Purdie's grave, Melrose Abbey.

of the deepest and most abiding, ending only with their lives.
All men—all living things, one might say—loved Scott; these
two adored him, and their master's affection for them, and his
trust in them, were profound. Mathieson outlived the others;
Purdie was the first to go. The end was very sudden, and the
blow affected Sir Walter as if the death had been that of a
near and dear relative. A niece of Mungo Park used to tell
afterwards of Sir Walter's visit to the widow, as related by Mrs.

Y 2

Purdie herself. There came a tap at the door, she said, and he came silently in, sitting down without a word in the chair that Mrs. Purdie handed to him. And, " he juist grat, an' better grat, the tears rinnin' doon his cheeks." At last the poor woman said brokenly ;

" Ye mauna tak' on that way, Sir Walter. Ye mauna tak' on. Ye'll maybes get some other body juist as guid as Tam."

" *No*, my dear old friend," he said, at length mastering his emotion. " No. There can never be but one Tom Purdie."

In truth no one could, and no one ever did, replace him. A very few years, and Mathieson drove his master for the last time, that memorable drive in September, 1832, when the horses of their own accord stopped at his favourite view above Bemersyde ; that September when the whole world mourned for him who was gone, who yet lives for ever, not alone in Border hearts, but in the affection of all humanity.

In Sir Walter's day, no bridge spanned the river at Ashiesteel, and the ford was not always a safe one; Sir Walter and his horse on at least one occasion, when the water was heavy, had to swim when crossing. But " the Shirra " was always the most reckless of riders, and would plunge in where none dared follow. " The deil's in ye, Shirra," said Mungo Park's brother to him—not on one occasion only—" the deil's in ye. Ye'll never halt till they bring ye hame with your feet foremost." It was at this Ashiesteel ford that Leyden, when Sir Walter's guest, came to grief. He and " the Shirra," and Mr. Laidlaw of Peel were riding one day. Leyden was talking, as one having authority, of the paces and good manners of Arab horses, and telling tales of the marvellous skill with which their owners managed them. " Here," said he, gathering up his reins, " is one of their feats "——; but just at that moment the pony on which he rode (*not* a docile Arab steed) took it into its head to bolt down the steep bank into Tweed, and Leyden disappeared over its head into the stream. " Ay, ay, Dr. Leyden, is *that* the way the Arabs ride ? " said Laidlaw gravely, when the rider reappeared, dripping like a river-god.

The Tweed at Ashiesteel.

Up the Glenkinnon Burn from Ashiesteel, at Williamhope Ridge, is the spot where Scott said his last farewell to Mungo

Park. At the open drain which then separated moor from road, Park's horse stumbled badly. "A bad omen, Mungo, I'm afraid," said Sir Walter. "Freits (omens) follow them that fear them," cried Park, gaily, setting off at a brisk canter. "I stood and looked after him; but he never looked back," Scott used to tell, afterwards. And they met no more. Ere

The Tweed between Ashiesteel and Thornilee.

very many months had passed, Park lay dead, somewhere by that great African river with whose name his own will be for ever linked. But Williamhope has older memories than this; "William's Cross" was the name given to a great stone on the hill here, which marked the spot where the Knight of Liddesdale fell, slain by his kinsman's sword one August day in 1353.

Quitting the neighbourhood of Ashiesteel, the road, in close company now with the railway from Galashiels to Peebles, still winds up the beautiful banks of Tweed, past Thornilee and Holylee, past boulder-strewn reaches and pleasant streams where big trout lie,—"a chancier bit ye canna hae," I think Stoddart says,—on past where, high on the farther side, over-hanging the river, stand the crumbling ruins of Elibank Castle. This was a stronghold built—or possibly only enlarged—in 1595 by Sir Gideon Murray, father of Muckle Mouthed Meg, heroine of the story which tells how young Scott of Harden, caught reiving the Murrays' cattle, was given his choice between matrimony and the rope and "dule-tree." Harden, it is said, at first chose the latter, but at the last moment, as a mate scarcely to be preferred to death, took the lady. There was probably a good deal of bravado and "bluff" about Harden's wavering—if indeed the story is a true one. But in any case it was a wedding in which the proverb: "Happy the Wooing that's not long adoing," was well exemplified. All went well with bride and with reluctant bridegroom; they "lived happy ever after," as in the most orthodox fairy tale. And of their descendants, one was our own Sir Walter.

And now we come to Walkerburn and Innerleithen, manu-facturing townships. The latter, with its famed medicinal well, has been identified, or identifies itself, with St. Ronan's of the Waverley Novels. It is prettily situated on the Leithen, by wide spreading haughs, and the surroundings, like all in Tweedale, cannot fail to attract. But what may be said of Innerleithen, on top of that terrible Report issued in 1906 by H. M. Stationery Office? It will take some living down, if all that was then said by the Tweed Pollution Commission is without exaggeration, and if—as one is informed—nothing has yet been done to sweep away, or at least greatly to improve, the conditions revealed. Here is what the Report says of the river Leithen, a stream in former days called by Sir Thomas Dick Lauder "a fine trouting river." "Occasionally, in time of

Tower of Elibank.

heavy rainfall, severe floods occur on the Leithen; when these occur, a large amount of water flows down the bed of the stream, which is usually dry, carrying with it all the rubbish and filth to the Tweed . . . The mills are supplied with water from the mill-lade, and one of them obtains water from the

Innerleithen.

Tweed when necessary. The people of the town are entirely engaged in the woollen industry; wool scouring, weaving, and dyeing are all carried on here. The town is sewered. All the sewage is collected in an outfall sewer, which discharges into the mill-lade below the lowermost mill, and about three hundred yards from the Tweed; there is no attempt at purification of the sewage. The liquid refuse from the mills is discharged into the lade. The water of the lade where it discharges to the Tweed is very foul with sewage and dye water . . . Below the point at which the lade discharges to the Tweed the water of this river is greatly fouled, the bottom of the river is covered with sewage deposit and the stones coated with sewage fungus. The river here contains also a large amount of refuse of all kinds, such as pots and pans, old linoleum, old iron-work, and such like. Although there is a daily collection of rubbish in the town, a great deal of large sized rubbish is thrown into the bed of the Leithen, and the tip to which all refuse is taken, together with offal from the slaughter houses, is situate just where the Leithen falls into the Tweed. In times of flood the water of the Leithen excavates this refuse tip, and carries the refuse into the Tweed. Some of the mill-owners here have tanks for settling the spent liquids after dyeing, and in this way some of the solid refuse is retained, but the coloured liquid is allowed to enter the river." One is thankful for small mercies; "*some* of the solid refuse is retained." But the "offal from the slaughter houses," and the "tip" to which all refuse is taken! And the sewage which there is "no attempt to purify"! What grizzly nightmare could be more grizzly than this?

However, we get soon now above the range of pollution by mill or town. Peebles only remains; thereafter we have really a river as it used in its entirety to be, and, above Peebles, as it may still be called, "the silver Tweed." Before reaching Peebles, however, there is, over against Innerleithen, on the angle between Quair Burn and Tweed, Traquair House to notice; and, nearer to Peebles, on its green knoll the old riven tower of Horsburgh, ancient seat of an ancient family.

Of old, Traquair was a royal residence. In the twelfth century, William the Lion hunted from its tower; and other of the Scottish monarchs visited it in later days, the last, I suppose, being Mary and Darnley in August, 1566. The original tower,

or some part of it, I believe stands now in the north-east
corner of the building, but the house has, of course, been
greatly added to at different periods, mostly, however, during the reign of Charles I. It is a very fine specimen of
the old Scottish château, with walls of immense thickness.
Probably it is the oldest inhabited mansion house in Scotland;
a place full of interest. And not least interesting, the picturesque old gates at the end of the avenue, that have remained
so long unopened. The tale used to run that they had been

A road beside the Tweed, near Caddonfoot.

closed after the '45, by an Earl loyal to the Stuart cause, who
swore that they should never be opened till the rightful king
came back to his own again. As a matter of fact, however, the
misfortunes of Prince Charlie and his family had nothing to do
with it. The gates were not closed till 1796, when the seventh
Earl of Traquair, after the death of his countess, declared that
they should remain shut till they opened to admit one worthy
to take the dead lady's place. That, at least, is the story.

The Earl who lived in the latter part of the seventeenth
century belonged to the Church of Rome. "A quiet, inoffensive

man," he is said to have been. But that in no way protected him from the unwelcome attentions of those zealous Presby-

The closed gates at Traquair House.

terians who at that time "thought it someway belonged to us to go to all the popish houses and destroy their monuments of idolatry, with their priests' robes, and put in prison [the

priests] themselves." So a pious mob set out from Edinburgh
one grim December day in 1688, and trudged through the
snow to Traquair House. Earl and priest, having got word
of their coming, had fled before the arrival of this gentle band
of Reformers, and though they ransacked all Traquair for
"Romish wares," they did not find all they expected. Much
had been hidden away. The vestments of the priest this,

Traquair House.

that, and the other popish emblem could not be found.
However, they did get a good deal—an altar, a large brazen
crucifix, and several small crucifixes, "a large brodd opening
with two leaves, covered within with cloth of gold of Arras work,
having a veil covering the middle part, wherin were sewed
several superstitious pictures," a eucharist cup of silver, boxes
of relics, "wherin were lying, amongst silk-cotton, several

pieces of bone, tied with a red thread, having written on
them the Saint they belonged to," "a harden bag, near full
of beads," "Mary and the Babe in a case most curiously
wrought in a kind of pearl," a hundred and thirty books—
silver-clasped many of them.   No doubt the books, Popish or
otherwise, excited to frenzy those pious but illiterate persons,
almost as effectually as the "pot of holy oil," and the "twelve
dozen of wax candles" that they seized.

Not content with all this, however, a detachment of the
mob invaded the house of a neighbouring clergyman "who
had the name of a Presbyterian minister."   The orders
given by their ringleaders were that this house should be
narrowly searched, but that they themselves were to "behave
discreetly," advice the latter part of which one might give
with equal propriety and effect to the proverbial bull in a
china shop.   The Reverend Thomas Louis and his wife
apparently did not treat the inquisitors with the kindness
and consideration to which they thought themselves entitled;
they "mocked them," it is complained; and indeed the
minister and his wife carried their resentment so far as to
offer them "neither food nor drink, though"—it is
naïvely added—"they had much need of it."   Undaunted,
however, by this shabby conduct on the part of the reverend
gentleman, the mob hunted about till they came on two
locked trunks, which they demanded should at once be
opened.   This modest request not being complied with, they
"broke up" the trunks—to "behave discreetly," is no doubt
when desired, capable of liberal interpretation—and therein
"they found a golden cradle, with Mary and the Babe in her
bosom; in the other trunk, the priest's robes."   So they made
a pile of the articles found here and in Traquair House, carried
them a distance of seven miles to Peebles, and had them "all
solemnly burned at the cross."   Such were the enlightened
methods of our seventeenth century progenitors.   But, one
sometimes wonders, is the toleration of the mob now-a-days

greatly in advance of what it was in 1688 ? However, they did not also " solemnly burn " Traquair House, though it *was* a "nest o' paipery." But the last Countess of Traquair has gone through the old gates ; and her son, the eighth Earl, was the last of his line. He died, unmarried, in 1861 ; and the last of her race, the venerable Lady Louisa Stuart, died in 1875, in her hundredth year. Yet still, a pathetic link with days long dead, the old house stands brooding over the past ;

Where the Quair enters the Tweed above Innerleithen.

and still there sounds the music of the waters, and the sough of the wind in the trees of " the bush aboon Traquair." And perhaps he who has

> " . . . heard the cushies croon
> Thro' the gowden afternoon,
> And the Quair burn singing down to the vale o' Tweed,"

may come away steeped in sadness, yet it is a sadness without sting, not wholly unpleasing.

CHAPTER XIV

PEEBLES, NEIDPATH, MANOR, LYNE, DRUMMELZIER, DAWYCK

WRITING of Peebles in the year 1847 or 1848, Sir Thomas Dick Lauder speaks of "the singular air of decayed royalty that hangs over it, and which so strangely blends with its

On the road to Peebles.

perfect simplicity and rurality." More than any other of the Scottish Border towns, Peebles has a right to talk of "royalty." A royal poet has sung of her Beltane Feast;—the evidence is at least as much for, as against, acceptance of the time-honoured

belief that King James I was author of "Peblis to the Play."
Professor Veitch strongly favours that conclusion. And unbroken tradition points to the King as the author.

From earliest times the town was a favourite residence of the
Scottish monarchs, and to this day its place-names, such as
King's Meadows, King's House, King's Orchards, for example,
suggest royal traditions. The Burgh Records of Peebles, go
back very far—to October 1456, in the reign of James II.
It is a town of much interest and of much beauty, beautiful
especially as regards its situation and surroundings, and there
are still in it many remains that speak eloquently of the past.
There is the old five-arched stone bridge, dating from about
1467, altered, of course, and widened since that date, but still
the same old bridge. Until the erection of the bridge at
Berwick early in the seventeenth century, I suppose that this
was the only one spanning Tweed in all its course. Then
there is the ancient Cross of Peebles, which, after various
vicissitudes and excursions, at length stands once more on the
spot where it was originally placed. It is said by the writer of
the Statistical Account of the Parish to have been "erected by
one of the Frasers of Neidpath Castle, before the time of
Robert the Bruce, and bears the arms of the Frasers."

There are still to be seen within the burgh the ruins of the
Cross Church, and of the Church of St. Andrew. The former
got its name from the fact that in May, 1261, "a magnificent
and venerable cross was found at Peblis," which was supposed
to have been buried close on a thousand years before that
date. Shortly after the unearthing of this cross, there was found
near the same spot a stone urn, containing ashes and human
bones, and on a stone the words carved: "The place of St.
Nicholas the Bishop." On account of the miracles which were
reputed to have been wrought where the cross was discovered,
Alexander III caused a church to be erected on the spot, "in
honour of God, and of the Holy Rood." This Cross Church
in some unexplained way escaped practically unscathed during

z

the English invasion of 1548–49, and from 1560 till 1784 it served as the Parish Church—deprived, no doubt, of many an interesting relic of the past.   At the last-named date, our zealous forefathers, *more majorum*, pulled it down—all but a fragment—in order, out of the material so obtained, to build a new Parish Church. (They had in those times a perfect genius for wrecking the beautiful and interesting, and for erecting the ugly and the dull.)

The other old church, that of St. Andrew, was founded about the year 1195. It, however, unlike its neighbour, suffered badly at the hands of the English in 1548, after which it gradually fell into ruin, and met the fate that was wont to wait on most of our venerable Scottish buildings. The tower alone remained, impervious to wind and weather, defiant of man's destroying hand. Thirty years ago, it was restored by the late Dr. William Chambers,—"more honour to him had he been less successful in concealing the old work," says Sir Herbert Maxwell, in his "Story of the Tweed." It was in the Church of St. Andrew, tradition says, that Cromwell's troopers stabled their horses in 1650 when siege was being laid to Neidpath Castle.

Peebles at one time was a walled town, and I believe that some fragments of fortification remain. But the names: "Northgate," "Eastgate," "Portbrae," still recall former days. There was a castle also, a royal residence ; but though it yet stood in the end of the seventeenth century, or even a little later, there is now not a vestige of it to be found. Again, no doubt, the ruthless hand of our not very remote ancestors !

An interesting and very ancient custom continues to be observed in the town. Annually, on the second day of May, there is chosen from among the youthful beauties of Peebles one who is styled the "Beltane Queen"; and Beltane Sports and Festivities are held. Chambers says: "The festivities of Beltane originated in the ceremonial observances of the original British people, who lighted fires on the tops of hills and other places in honour of their deity Baal; hence Beltane or Beltien, signifying the fire of Baal.   The superstitious usage disappeared . . . but certain festive customs on the occasion were confirmed and amplified, and the rural sports of Beltane at Peebles, including archery and horse-racing . . . drew crowds not only from the immediate neighbourhood, but from Edinburgh and other places at a distance."   " Peblis to the Play " is a description of the Festival as it was held in the day of the author; "a picture of rustic life and festivities, of the humorous and grotesque incidents of a mediaeval Feast Day in an old provincial town, the centre of a rural district," says Professor Veitch.

> " At Beltane, when ilk bodie bownis [1]
> To Peblis to the Play,
> To heir the singin and the soundis,
> The solace, suth to say ;
> Be firth [2] and forest furth they found,[3]
> They graythit [4] them full gay ;
> God wot, that wald they do, that stound,[5]
> For it was their Feist Day,
>   They said,
> Of Peblis to the Play."

Space does not permit me to quote more than the opening verse.

Before moving on up the valley, one may recall the fact that at the Old Cross Keys Inn at Peebles Sir Walter found, in its then landlady, the original of his " Meg Dods " of " St. Ronan's Well."   Guests arriving now-a-days at this Inn—which is as often called " the Cleikum " as the Cross Keys—still drive into the yard under the " old-fashioned archway " of the novel ; still there is shown " Sir Walter's room," overlooking the yard ; and still, it may perhaps be noted, there is to be found at the head of affairs one who, while leaving out Meg's " detestable

---

[1] Makes ready to go.   [2] Enclosed wood, or place.
[3] Issue, or go forth.   [4] Dressed.
[5] Time : German *stunde*.

bad humour" and asperity of tongue, in all essentials is worthy
to rank as her successor. "Her kitchen was her pride and
glory; she looked to the dressing of every dish herself, and
there were some with which she suffered no one to interfere. . . . Meg's table-linen, bed-linen, and so forth, were
always home-made, of the best quality, and in the best order;
and a weary day was that to the chambermaid in which her
lynx eye discovered any neglect of the strict cleanliness which
she constantly enforced." The most fervent patriotism cannot,
I fear, blind one to the sad fact that a majority of Scottish
country inns do not strive very successfully to vie with Meg in
those qualities which made her so shining an ornament of her
sex. Too often one is left to the greasy attentions of a waiter
of foreign tongue, whose mercies it might be desired were more
tender than the scrag-end of the cold beef to which, in a
parlour of the lethal-chamber variety, he somewhat tardily
introduces tired wayfarers. And the beef itself might in many
cases taste none the less of beef, if it were served on table-
linen not quite so elaborately decorated with outlines of
mustard pots and Worcester Sauce bottles, left by the day-before-
yesterday's commercial traveller.

This Cleikum, or Cross Keys Inn, is a building of more than
respectable age; it dates from the year 1653, when it was the
town house of the Williamsons of Cardrona, a tower a few
miles down Tweed, nearly opposite to Horsburgh. Probably
both the Cross Keys and its neighbour the Tontine Hotel—
Meg's "Tomteen," the "hottle" of which she spoke so
wrathfully—were in Sir Walter's mind when he wrote the
novel.

And now we may set out once again up Tweed—not forgetting, however, that Peebles with its mills also contributes
no small share to the pollution of that much-injured river. A
mile or so out of the town, there is the old castle of Neidpath,
in very remote days a stronghold of the Frasers of Fruid and
Oliver Castle, in Tweedsmuir. A Hay of Yester, ancestor of

Lord Tweeddale, succeeded the Frasers in 1312, by marriage
with the daughter of Sir Simon Fraser; and after the Hays,
by purchase came the Queensberry family, of whom, the fourth
Duke, "Old Q.," Wordsworth's "Degenerate Douglas,"

Neidpath Castle.

"unworthy lord," did his best to wreck the estate in 1795.
What he could spoil and disfigure, he did spoil and disfigure.
And here at Neidpath he swept off the face of nature every
stick of timber, old and young, that could be felled or
destroyed, leaving, as far as lay in his power, the landscape
bare almost as it was when primeval chaos ended. Replanting
could not be set about as long as "Old Q." lived, and a
hundred years scarce repaired the damage he did. It is
curious to note how one who in all respects during his life was
so very far removed from grace, at the end wished to lie
(where I believe his body does lie), under the Communion
Table of St. James's Church, Piccadilly—in his estimation
perhaps a sort of side-gate or private entrance to Heaven. The
path is steep and the way thorny to most of us. And how
fares "Old Q."? I hardly think that the inhabitants of
Peebles, had they been Roman Catholics at the time of his
death, would have paid for Masses for the soul of the dead
"Old Q.," as they did lang syne for the soul of the dead King
James the First.

Neidpath Castle is said by old Dr. Pennecuick to have been
in reality the stronghold which was anciently called the Castle
of Peebles. But there are allusions to the "Castel of Peebles"
in the Earl of Tweeddale's Rental book for 1685, and Neidpath
was Neidpath centuries before that date.   On this subject,
Professor Veitch, writing about 1877, says : "The Castle of
Peebles was standing and inhabited in the early part of last
century.   It was afterwards pulled down, and the materials
converted, according to the morality and taste of the time, into
one of the least architecturally attractive parish edifices in
Christendom."   As to Neidpath's age, there is no sure record,
but as it was a seat of that Sir Simon Fraser who defeated the
English three times in one day at Roslin Muir in 1303, its
antiquity must be very great.   And what a place of immense
strength it must originally have been, before the days of
artillery.   Its walls are ten feet thick, put together with that

ancient form of cement which, when dry, became hard as the
stones it bound together ; and it stands on a high rock overhanging an elbow of Tweed where the water is deep, and was
therefore on the river face unassailable.   But the day of
artillery came too soon for Neidpath.   It fell before the guns
of Cromwell in 1650, after a most gallant resistance under the
young Lord Yester,—father, I suppose, of the Lord Yester who
wrote the fine old ballad "Tweedside."

Peebles from Neidpath.

Like every other part of the Vale of Tweed, here also it is
beautiful.   Looking back towards Peebles from above Neidpath
the view is very fine, though perhaps an eyesore may be found
in the unwholesome speckled appearance given to the castle
by the way in which the "facing" of its walls has been done.

Little more than a mile from here, Tweed is joined by
Manor Water, a stream now probably best known as that beside
which stands the cottage of "Bowed Davie," the original of
Scott's "Black Dwarf" of Mucklestane Muir.   Sir Walter was
staying at Hallyards, on Manor Water, in 1797, with his friend
Adam Ferguson, and it was on that occasion that he first saw

David Ritchie, a poor mis-shapen dwarf, embittered by the derision which his extraordinary personal appearance everywhere brought on him, and who had retired to this unfrequented valley, where he built himself a cottage of dimensions in keeping with his own stature. The cottage still stands, " where from his bole the awsome form peer'd grim on passer-bye," but at least the exterior has been modernised, and an addition has

The " Black Dwarf's" cottage in the Manor Valley.

been made ; his garden wall, with its ponderous stones, is much as Bowed Davie left it. The "Black Dwarf" was not written till a good many years after Ritchie's death. His grave is in Manor Kirkyard, not, as he himself originally meant it to be, in a secluded spot of his own choice, surrounded by the rowan-trees that it comforted him to think could be relied on to keep witches, and evil spirits generally, at a respectable distance. Poor Davie ! There were worse things than witches to be taken

into account.   It is said—Dr. John Brown mentions it—that
his body proved a temptation too great to be resisted by
resurrectionists.   They dug him up, and carried the poor
"thrawn" frame to where it could be sold.   ·Perhaps in death
he still excites that derision or pity which in life so angered
him ; his bones may now lie in some city anatomical museum.

Within the Vestry of Manor Parish Kirk, there is, according to the Ordnance Gazetteer of Scotland edited by
Mr. F. H. Groome, "a table made of oak that had been used
for church building not later than the thirteenth century ; and
a bell in the belfry bears the Latin inscription : 'In honore
Sanct. Gordiani MCCCCLXXVIII.'"   And far up the vale,
near Kirkhope, is the site of this St. Gordian's Kirk, "marked
by a granite runic cross, with the old font stone at its base."

Manor Valley in days of old must have been a "mischancey"
spot for any stranger whose intentions were, so to speak, not
"strictly honourable."   There were, in and about it, not fewer
than nine or ten peel towers, two at least of which—Barns
and Castlehill—belonged to the Burnets, than whom none bore
higher reputation as reivers and· men of action.   In 1591 no
Borderer was more renowned for his exploits and for his
conduct of midnight forays, than William Burnet, the "Hoolet
of Barns."   His tower, Barns, is rather nearer Tweed than
Manor, but it is included in the strongholds of Manor Valley.
It is still in excellent preservation, but the roof is modern,
and the upper part of the tower has been greatly altered
from what it was originally.   The accommodation in such
towers must have been something of the most cramped ; in
this instance the outside dimensions of the tower (three stories)
are only twenty-eight by twenty feet.   On the lintel of the door
is the date 1498, but there appears to be some uncertainty as
to whether the figures were not added at a later time.
Castlehill, now a ruin, "hollow-eyed, owl-haunted," was
somewhat larger and stronger than Barns.   Higher up the
valley is Posso, now mere fragments of walls.   It was of old a

seat of the Bairds, who were succeeded in the sixteenth century by the Naesmiths. At Posso Craigs was the eyry whence Henry Ashton in the "Bride of Lammermuir" got his hawks. And here under the craigs is the Ship Stone. The whole valley teems with objects of antiquarian interest—the tumulus called the Giants' Grave, up Glenrath Burn; the "cup-marked fallen monolith," that was once an old woman whom the devil turned into stone; the old Thief's Road, trodden of old by many a mob of "lifted" cattle; numerous hill forts. And from the bosom of the wild hills springs Manor; a tiny rivulet

Looking up the Manor Valley.

from Dollar Law—(is "Dollar" a corruption of "Dolour," the Hill of Sorrow?)—from Notman Law another; infantile rills from Shielhope Head, Black Law, Blackhouse Heights, grim round-shouldered hills that rise all of them to a greater altitude than two thousand feet. And everywhere is the music of running water.

> " In its far glen, Manor outspreads its arms
> To all the hills, and gathers to itself
> The burnies breaking from high mossy springs,
> And white streaks that fall through cleavings of the crags
> From lonely lochans where the curlews cry."

Cademuir, by the way, the hill on Manor's right at its junction with Tweed, is the supposed scene of Arthur's seventh battle against the Pagans. *Cad* is Welsh for battle,—Gaelic, *cath*, hence *Cad-more*, the " great battle." Professor Veitch hesitates between this site and that of the neighbouring pre-historic hill fort, the Lour, near Dawyck, but thinks the former the more probable. Just below the height of the Lour, till the beginning of the nineteenth century there stood, he says, an almost perfect *cromlech*, consisting of " two or more upright stones, and one flat stone laid across as a roof, all of remarkable size." This *cromlech* was known in the district as Arthur's Oven. It is humiliating to have to confess that it, the neighbouring old peel tower of Easter Dawyck, the Tower of Posso, and the ancient Kirk of St. Gordian, were all made into road metal, or used as material for building walls or farm buildings, by Sir Walter Scott's father, of all people in the world. One may wonder what were Sir Walter's thoughts when he came to know.

A little way up from Manor Valley, and joining Tweed from the northern side, is Lyne Water. It is not possible to pursue all Tweed's tributaries to their source, however full of interest each may be, for their name is legion. But Lyne cannot be passed without note being taken of its little—very little—early seventeenth century Parish Church. And adjoining it are remains of a great Roman camp—Randall's Wa's, it has been called locally from times long past. Perhaps it was here—at least it was on Lyne Water—that Sir James Douglas captured Randolph before the time came when the latter finally cast in his lot with the Bruce. Farther up, on an eminence at the junction of Lyne and Tarth Waters, stands the massive ivy-clad ruin of Drochil Castle. Built by the Regent Morton in the sixteenth century, Drochil was never completed, and never occupied. Just before the building approached completion, Morton, judged guilty of complicity in the murder of Darnley, was executed, beheaded by " the Maiden "—a sort of Scottish

guillotine—on 2nd June, 1581; and the home of a Regent of
Scotland, "designed more for a palace than a castle of defence,"
is now a ruin, of use only as a shelter for cattle!

Happrew, on Lyne, is the scene of the defeat "wrought by
the lords William de Latymer, John de Segrave, and Robert
de Clifford, upon Simone Fraser and William le Walleys at
Hopperowe," in 1304. And on the elevated heathy flat below
which Tweed and Lyne meet, there is what is called the
Sheriff's Muir, of old a mustering place for Scottish forces
during the wars with England.

Bridge over the Lyne Water.

And now, as we run up Tweed's left bank, we have on the
one side Stobo, with its ancient church—of which mention has
been made earlier in this volume—and its fine woods; on the
other bank, Dawyck, and the castles of Tinnies and
Drummelzier. From the thirteenth well on into the seventeenth century, Dawyck was the home of a distinguished
Tweedside family, the Veitches, once the Le Vaches, of
Gascony, of whom one, William le Vache, signed the Ragman
Roll at the Castle of Peebles in 1296. At the same time that

the Veitches held Dawyck, Drummelzier was the headquarters of another powerful Border family, the Tweedys; and for the delicate questions involved in the origin of this family's name, readers may consult Sir Walter's introduction to "The Betrothed." Of necessity, as things went in those days, these two families quarrelled, and from the quarrel emerged a feud long and bloody, in which, ere it ended, half the countryside was involved. Wherever a Veitch and a Tweedy met, they fought, and fought to kill. On the haughs of the river one summer's day, young Veitch and young Tweedy, each, perhaps, looking for trouble, came together face to face. The grey of next morning saw of the latter but

> " A face upturned to the breaking dawn,
>   Dead by the Tweed, but honour sav'd."

He lay beside the quiet water, and over him, it is said, like a snowy pall drooped the clustering May-blossom.

> " His mother sought him on the haugh,
>   She found him near the white flower'd thorn ;
> The grass red wet ; the heedless birds
>   Pip'd sweet strains to the early morn."

In 1590, the head of the Veitches, "the Deil o' Dawyck," an immensely powerful man, had for his ally William Burnet, "the Hoolet o' Barns," a man equally powerful. These two daunted the Tweedy of that day; the feud for a space lay dormant. But, most unhappily for the Veitches, it chanced that "the Deil's" son rode into Peebles alone one morning. And that was the end of young Veitch. For nine Tweedys, in two parties, trapped him near Neidpath, came on him in front and from the rear as he rode towards home ; and it was no fight, but bloody murder that reddened the grass that day. Four days later, two Veitches met John Tweedy, Tutor of Drummelzier, in the High Street of Edinburgh, and young Veitch's bloody death was avenged ; "a tooth for a tooth," no matter how many were concerned in its drawing. And so it went on *ad nauseam*, a Veitch killing a Tweedy, a Tweedy a Veitch. The feud was alive even as late as 1611 ; and for anything that I know to the contrary, it endured as long as the two families were there to neighbour each other on Tweedside.

Of Drummelzier Castle only an angle of the tower and a portion of the main building now stand. It was here that there dwelt that arrogant bully, Sir James Tweedy, who of old was wont to exact homage from every passing traveller ; and the traveller who omitted to, so to speak, "lower his tops'ls" as he passed the castle, had cause to rue the day the fates took him that way. It was a pretty enough game from Tweedy's point of view. But, as the saying is, one day he "bit off more than he could chew." A stranger, attended by a very small retinue, passed up the valley without taking the smallest notice of the castle or its formidable owner. Foaming with rage, spluttering dire threats, Tweedy and his men went thundering in pursuit ; truly, the back of that stranger should smart to some tune. But, just as you may see the birses and tail of a vicious, snarling cur drop when he finds he has inadvertently rushed out against a bigger dog than himself, so here, Tweedy's mood changed with astonishing celerity when he jumped from his horse beside the man he had been cursing and bawling at to stop, and found that the fugitive he was vowing to flog was his king, James V.

Tinnies Castle was also a holding of the Tweedys, possibly before the building of Drummelzier. This castle is believed to date from the thirteenth century, or perhaps earlier, and it seems to have been a place of considerable size and of great strength. "In no part of Scotland was there any feudal keep so like a robber's castle on the Rhine, as that of Tinnis," says Chambers. The building was destroyed under royal warrant in 1592, at the time when the King issued orders to raze Dryhope and Harden. The position of Tinnies is immensely strong. Perched on a lofty eminence, three of whose sides are almost perpendicular and the fourth a long steep slope, the castle in its day must have been almost unassailable. Any approach to the walls could only be made in force by a narrow winding pathway, within shot of, and fully exposed to, the castle bowmen, and the building itself, as may even yet be noted, was of a solidity truly formidable. Immense portions of the walls and flanking towers, yet bound by the old imperishable cement, still lie where they were bodily hurled by the exploding gunpowder when James VI's orders were carried out.

Of Dawyck and its magnificent woods one must not forget to take note. Here in 1725 were planted the first larches introduced into Scotland, anticipating it is said, by a few years those planted at Dunkeld. And while on the subject of natural history, one may perhaps quote that most notable fact regarding Dawyck which Dr. Pennecuick, writing in the early eighteenth century, vouches for in his "Shire of Tweeddale." "Here," says he, "in an old Orch-yard did the Herons in my time build their Nests upon some old Pear-trees, whereupon in the Harvest time are to be seen much Fruit growing, and Trouts and Iles crauling down the Body of these Trees. These fish the Herons take out of the River of Tweed to their Nests, and as they go in at the Mouth, so they are seen squirt out again at the Draught. And this is the remarkable Riddle they so much talk of, to have Flesh, Fish, and Fruit at the same time upon one tree." There is still a heronry at Dawyck, but not, I think, in an "Orch-yard."

In the neighbourhood of Drummelzier there is a spot that takes us back in thought to those dim, far off days when the world was in its infancy. Near to where Powsayl Burn, the "burn of the willows," joins Tweed, you may see the grave of Merlin the Seer, the Wizard Merlin. Fleeing from the field of Arderydd (Arthuret, near Carlisle), after the terrible defeat of the Pagans by the Christians in 573, Merlin found refuge among the hills of Upper Tweed, and there lived for many years, half-crazed, a homeless wanderer. Finally, the fear

raised by his supposed possession of supernatural powers, and
the dread of his enchantments, caused a mob of ignorant
country-folk to club and stone him to death, and he was buried
where he fell, by the Powsayl burn. In a poem still extant,
Merlin tells how he wandered long in the wild wood of
Caledon.

> " Sweet apple tree, growing by the river !
> Whereof the keeper shall not thrive on its fruit ;
> Before I lost my wits I used to be around its stem
> With a fair sportive maid, matchless in slender shape.
> Ten years and forty, the sport of the lawless ones,
> Have I been wandering in gloom among sprites,
> After wealth in abundance and entertaining minstrels.
>
> .   .   .   .   .   .
>
> After suffering from disease and despair in the forest of Caledon."

The place of the "apple tree" was Tal Ard—Talla of to-day ;
and somewhere between Drummelzier and Talla, Merlin and
St. Kentigern foregathered for a time. High up on the mighty
shoulder of Broadlaw, too, there is a spring that gushes out
from the hillside clear and cool, that may be the fountain—
fons in summo vertice montis—beside which Geoffrey of
Monmouth in 1150 tells that Merlin was wont to rest. And
the "fair sportive maid"—that is Nimiane, Tennyson's
"Vivien." A Romance of the fifteenth century tells how
"Thei sojourned together longe time, till it fell on a day that
thei went thourgh the foreste hande in hande devysing and
disportynge, and this was in the foreste of Brochelonde, and
fonde a bussh that was feire and high of white hawthorne, full
of floures, and ther thei sat in the shadowe ; and Merlin leide
hys heed in the damesels lappe, and she began to taste softly
till he fill on slepe ; and when she felt that he was on slepe
she aroos softly, and made a cerne (circle) with hys wymple all
aboute the bussh and all aboute Merlin, and began hir
enchantementes soche as Merlin hadde hir taught, and made
the cerne ix tymes, and ix tymes her enchantementes ; and
after that she wente and satte down by hym and leide hys heed

in hir lappe, and hilde hym ther till he dide awake; and then
he looked aboute hym, and hym semed he was in the feirest
tour of the worlde, and the most stronge, and fonde hym leide
in the feirest place that ever he lay beforn . . . . Ne never
after com Merlin out of that fortresse that she hadde hym in
sette; but she wente in and oute whan she wolde." Not far
from the churchyard of Drummelzier to this day they
point out the grave where Merlin lies beneath a thorn tree.
And to everyone is known Thomas the Rhymer's prediction:

> " When Tweed and Powsayl meet at Merlin's grave
> Scotland and England shall one monarch have,"

and how the prophecy was fulfilled that same day on which
James of Scotland was crowned King of England. For Tweed
then so overflowed its banks that burn and river joined beside
the spot where Merlin lies, which, as Dr. Pennecuick says, " was
never before observed to fall out, nor since that time."

Over against Drummelzier, Biggar Water falls into Tweed,
and a curious circumstance about this stream is this, that " on
the occasion of a large flood . . . the Clyde actually pours a
portion of its water into one of the tributaries of Tweed." The
whole volume of Clyde at Biggar, says Sir Archibald Geikie,
could without any difficulty be made to flow into Tweed by
way of the Biggar Water. The latter at one point is separated
from Clyde by but one and a half miles of almost level ground.

All this region of Biggar Water is rich in remains of old
towers and camps; but of the most important, that of Boghall
Castle at Biggar, seat of the great Fleming family, Lords Fleming in 1460, there is now practically nothing left standing; the
customary fate, the fate that so long dogged most Scottish historical buildings overtook it about sixty or seventy years ago.
It was a place of strength in 1650, when Cromwell's men held
it; a sketch done in 1779 by John Clerk of Eldin, shows that
it was then entire, or almost entire, and it stood, a fine ruin, as
lately as 1831, when Sir Walter and Lockhart were at Biggar.

A A

With what devilish energy since then must the wreckers have laboured to destroy ! Of Biggar Moss, Blind Harry tells the wondrous tale of how Wallace, with a diminutive Scottish force, smote here in 1279 a large English army led by Edward I ; eleven thousand Englishmen were slain, says the veracious poet. And if corroboration of Blind Harry be needed, why is there not standing here, as witness to this very day, the Cadger's Brig, over which, as local tradition vouches, Wallace, disguised as a hawker, crossed on his way to spy out the weak points in Edward's camp ! As with most Border places, there is no lack of interest about Biggar, but considerations of space forbid any attempt to treat of its history. Yet it must not be omitted that here was born a man greatly loved in Scotland, Dr. John Brown, best known to the outside world, perhaps, as the author of " Rab and his Friends."

CHAPTER XV

BROUGHTON, TWEEDSMUIR, TALLA, GAMESHOPE, TWEED'S WELL

Returning to the neighbourhood of Tweed, on the bank of a little burn tributary to Biggar Water stands the village of Broughton, reminiscent of Mr. "Evidence" Murray, the Prince's Secretary, who saved his own life after the '45 by turning King's Evidence. Broughton House, his old home, was burned to the ground about 1775, (a couple of years prior to Murray's death on the Continent,) and the estate was afterwards sold to the famous Lord Braxfield, the original of Stevenson's "Weir of Hermiston." Higher up Tweed, on the farther bank, is Stanhope, in the eighteenth century the property of Murray of Broughton's nephew, Sir David Murray, who lost his all in the '45 ; and not many miles farther up the river is Polmood, where the dishonoured uncle lay hid, and was taken, in June 1746, losing thereafter more than the life he saved—honour and the respect of his fellow men. "Neither lip of me nor of mine comes after Mr. Murray of Broughton's!" cried Sir Walter Scott's father as he threw out of window the cup from which the apostate had but then drunk tea. And :—"Do you know this witness?" was asked of Sir John Douglas of Kelhead, a prisoner after the '45, before the Privy Council at St. James's, when Murray was giving evidence. "Not I," said Douglas, "I once knew a person who bore the designation of Murray of Broughton,—but that was a gentleman and a man of honour, and one that could hold up his head!"

355   A A 2

Of old, Polmood—the name, I believe, means the "wolf's burn," or stream—was a hunting seat of Scottish kings; in times more modern it was chiefly remarkable for an interminable law plea which dragged its weary length along for forty years and more, probably in the end with ruin to both parties to the suit. Before coming to Polmood, however, we pass Mossfennan, sung of in two ballads, one of the seventeenth century, the other (of which but a fragment remains) of much more ancient date. On the roadside a little further up is a sign-post that points dejectedly towards a dilapidated-looking tree which stands solitary on the haugh below. Here, says the legend on the post, was the site of Linkumdoddie, whereof Burns wrote a song. But to find any point of interest in the scene, or in the identity of Linkumdoddie or of the lady celebrated, it requires, I think, that the gazer should be possessed of a most perfervid admiration of the poet.

And now we begin to open up the wilder part of Tweed's valley, where not so many years ago you might go a long way, and for miles see no human being but a passing shepherd. It is different now, in these days when motor-cars, leaving behind them a trail of dust as ugly as the smudge of a steamer's smoke low down on the horizon, rush along what used to be the finest of old grass-grown coach-roads, smooth as a billiard-table and free from any loose metal—swept bare now to the very roots of the stones by the constant air-suction of passing cars. But even now, in the winter-time, when the rush of the tourist troubles no more, if one trusts oneself in these wilds, there is a reward to be gleaned in the fresh, inexpressibly *clean* air, and in the sense of absolute freedom that one gains. You have left civilisation and its cares behind ; here is peace. And in the great hills lying there so solemn and still, black as blackest ink where the heather stands out against the wintry grey sky, or deep-slashed on their sides with heavy drifts of snow from the latest storm, there is rest to the wearied soul and the tired

mind. And if the day be windless, what sweeter sound can anywhere be heard than the tinkling melody of innumerable burns
blending with the deeper note of Tweed? Nowhere in the
world, as it seems to me, is there any scene where Nature lays
on man a hand so gentle as here in Tweedsmuir. It is all one,
the season; no matter if the air is still, or the west wind
bellows down the valley, life is better worth living for the being
here. And the glory of it, when snow lies deep over the wide
expanse, and the sun shines frostily, and Tweed, black by
contrast with the stainless snow, goes roaring his hoarse song
seaward !

All burns up this part of the valley used to teem with nice,
fat, lusty yellow trout—Stanhope Burn, Polmood, Hearthstane,
Talla and Gameshope, Menzion, Fruid, Kingledores (with its
memories of St. Cuthbert), and the rest. Doubtless the trout
are there still, but most of the burns are now in the hands of
shooting tenants, and the fishing, probably, is not open to all
as of old. Talla and Gameshope (of which more anon) are
now the property of the Edinburgh Water Trust Commissioners,
and a permit from them is necessary if one would fish in these
two streams or in Talla Reservoir.

Before reaching Talla, almost equidistant between the Polmood and Hearthstane burns, but on the opposite side of
Tweed, we come to what used to be the cheery, clean little
Crook Inn, standing in its clump of trees. But its history of
two hundred years and more as an inn is ended; modern
legislation has seen to that. And there is now on this high-
road between Peebles and Moffat—a distance of something
like thirty miles—not a single house where man and beast may
find accommodation and reasonable refreshment. It is not the
so-called "idle rich" who are thus handicapped; fifteen or
sixteen miles are of small account to the man who owns a
motor-car. It is they who cannot afford the luxury of a car,
but who yet desire to be alone here with nature, or to fish in

Tweed and in such burns as may yet be fished, it is they who find themselves thus left out in the cold.[1]

Of old, when the mail-coaches running between Dumfries and Edinburgh came jingling cheerily along this smooth Tweed-side road, it was at the Crook Inn that they changed horses. But I doubt it was not then a spot so inviting as it certainly became in the 'seventies of last century. Sir Thomas Dick Lauder speaks of it as it was in 1807 as "one of the coldest-looking, cheerless places of reception for travellers that we had ever chanced to behold. . . . It stood isolated and staring in the midst of the great glen of the Tweed, closed in by high green sloping hills on all sides. . . . No one could look at it without thinking of winter, snow-storms, and associations filled with pity for those whose hard fate it might be to be storm-stayed there." But Sir Thomas Dick Lauder's visit in 1807 was paid in the month of November, when snow hung heavy in the air, threatening the traveller with wearisome and indefinite delay. And the hind wheels of his chaise collapsed like the walls of Jericho as the postillion, having changed horses here, started with too sudden a dash from the door of the inn; and Sir Thomas was bumped most grievously along the road for some hundreds of yards ere the post-boy (who perhaps had made use at the Crook of some far-seeing device to keep out the cold) discovered that anything was amiss. Not unnaturally the nerves of the occupants of the chaise were a trifle ruffled; no doubt the place then looked less cheerful than it might otherwise have appeared. Forty years later, he writes that it had, "comparatively speaking, an inviting air of comfort about it. . . . The road, as you go along, now wears altogether an inhabited look, and little portions of plantations here and there give an air of shelter and civilisation to it." It was a cheerless place enough, no doubt, in the Covenanting

[1] Since this was written, the Crook has reopened its doors as an inn. But they are not any longer content with the homely word "inn"; the place asserts itself now in large letters as the Crook "Hotel."

days of the seventeenth century, when the dour hill-men were flying from Claverhouse's dragoons, lurking in the black, oozing "peat-hags," hiding by the foaming burns, sheltering on the wild moors, amongst the heather and the wet moss. It was the landlady of this same Crook Inn who found for one fugitive a novel hiding-hole; she built him safely into her stack of peats. There has been many a less comfortable and less secure hiding place than that; and where could one drier be found?

It was at the Crook that William Black makes his travellers in the "Strange Adventures of a Phaeton" spend a night, and the fare to which in the evening he sets his party down was certainly of the frugalest. But when this present writer knew the inn in the 'seventies, it was far from being only on "whisky and ham and eggs" that he was obliged to subsist. It was then an ideal angler's haunt; and no more gentle lullaby can be imagined than the low murmur of Tweed, and the quiet *hus-s-s-sh* of many waters breathing down the valley on the still night air.

A mile or more beyond the Crook, there is the Bield, also once an inn. "From Berwick to the Bield," is the Tweedside equivalent of the Scriptural "From Dan even to Beer-sheba." It was here at the Bield that the Covenanters thought once to trap Claverhouse; but that "proud Assyrian" rode not easily into snares. On the hill above is the site of Oliver Castle, home of the Fraser family, once so powerful in this part of the Border—the site, I think, but nothing more.

And now, to reach that part of Tweedsmuir which more than any other casts over one a spell, it is necessary to branch off here to the left and follow the road shown in Mr. Thomson's charming sketch. Straight ahead of you, as you stand by the little Tweedsmuir post-office, you look up the beautiful valley of the Talla, where the steep hills lie at first open and green and smiling on either hand, but gradually changing their character, close in, gloomy and scarred, and frowning, as the distant Talla Linn is neared. But before you leave the little hamlet of Tweedsmuir—it can scarcely be

Looking up Talla from Tweedsmuir Post-office.

called a village—by the old single-arched bridge that is thrown here across Tweed, where he roars and chafes among his rocks

ere plunging down into the deep, black pool below, you will
see on your left a spire peering out over the tree-tops.   That is
the church of Tweedsmuir, on its strange, tumulus-like mound

Bridge over Tweed at Tweedsmuir.

by the river's brink. And here you will find in the green grass,
under the clustering trees, the graves of some who fell for
"The Covenant," one headstone, at least, relettered by "Old

Mortality" himself. This is the grave of one John Hunter; but doubless there are others, less noticeable, who rest with him in this quiet spot, far from the world's clash and turmoil, where no sound harsher than the Sabbath bell that calls to prayer or the sighing of the wind in the trees, can ever break the silence. Here is Hunter's epitaph:

HERE LYES JOHN HUNTER
MARTYR WHO WAS CRUELY
MURDERED AT COREHEAD
BY COL: JAMES DOUGLAS AND
HIS PARTY FOR HIS ADHERANCE
TO THE WORD OF GOD AND
SCOTLAND'S COVENANTED
WORK OF REFORMATION
1685

Erected in the year 1726.

" When Zion's King was Robbed of his right
His witnesses in Scotland put to flight
When popish prelats and Indulgancie
Combin'd 'gainst Christ to Ruine Presbytrie
All who would not unto their idols bow
They socht them out and whom they found they slew
For owning of Christ's cause I then did die
My blood for vengeance on his en'mies did cry."

And on a stone in another part of the churchyard—perhaps the grave of a grandfather and grandchild—are the quaint words:

" Death pities not the aged head,
Nor manhood fresh and green,
But blends the locks of eighty-five
With ringlets of sixteen."

The old Session Records of this church are full of references to the troubled times of the Covenant. Here are one or two entries, which I quote from the Rev. W. S. Crockett's "Scott Country." Mr. Crockett is Minister of the Parish.—"No session kept by reason of the elders being all at conventicles." "No public sermon, soldiers being sent to apprehend the minister, but he, receiving notification of their design, went away and retired." "No meeting this day for fear of the

enemy." "The collection this day to be given to a man for
acting as watch during the time of sermon." And so on.—
Sometimes it strikes one as strange, that passion for listening
to a sermon which is inherent in one's countrymen. It is but
a sombre pleasure, as a rule.

Talla, up to a recent period, flowed through a deep valley,
whose bottom for some distance was of a treacherous and
swampy nature ; its trout, therefore, (in marked contrast to
those of the tributary Gameshope,) were dark-coloured and
"ill-faured." I do not know that they are anything else now,

Tweedsmuir.

but there is not much of Talla left. A mile above the church
you come to a great barrier thrown across the valley, and
beyond that for three miles stretches a Reservoir which supplies
distant Edinburgh with water. Picturesque enough in its way
is this Reservoir, especially when all trace of man and his work
is left behind, and nothing meets the eye but the brown, foamflecked water, and the hills plunging headlong deep into its
bosom. Even more picturesque is the scene when storms
gather on the far heights, and come raging down the wild glen
of Gameshope, swathing in mist and scouring rain-squall the

deep-scarred brows of those eerie hills by Talla Linn-foot. What a spot it must be on a wild December day, when blinding snow drives down the gullies before the icy blast!

This Reservoir has been stocked with Loch Leven trout. But the fishing is not, and never will be, good. There is insufficient food; the water is too deep, and except at the extreme head of the loch there are no shallows where insect life might hatch out. The trout are long and lank, and seldom fight well. Nor are they even very eager to rise to the fly. Yet, it is true, some large fish have been taken. But they have a suspiciously cannibal look, and I think an insurance company would be apt to charge a very high premium on the chances of long life of troutlings now put in.

I do not know where Young Hay of Talla lived. If his peel tower was here, no doubt the site is now sixty or seventy feet under water, but I cannot remember any traces of a building, or site of a building, in pre-Reservoir days. Men born and brought up lang syne on the gloomy slopes of Talla, might well be such as he, fierce and cruel, ready for treason and murder, or any crime of violence.

> " Wild your cradle glen,
>   Young Hay of Talla,
> Stern the wind's wild roar
> Round the old peel tower,
>   Young Hay of Talla.
>
> " Winter night raving,
>   Young Hay of Talla,
> Snowy drift smooring,
> Loud the Linn roaring,
>   Young Hay of Talla.
>   .   .   .
>
> " Winterhope's wild hags,
>   Young Hay of Talla,
> Gameshope dark foaming,
> There ever roaming,
>   Young Hay of Talla.
>   .   .   .

" Night round Kirk o' Field,
    Young Hay of Talla,
Light faint in the room,
Darnley sleeps in gloom,
    Young Hay of Talla.

            .   .   .   .

" Shadow by bedside,
    Young Hay of Talla,
Noise in the dull dark,
Does sleeper now hark,
    Young Hay of Talla?

            .   .   .   .

" Ah ! the young form moves,
    Young Hay of Talla,
Hold him grim,—hold grim,
Till quivers not a limb,
    Young Hay of Talla.

" Now the dread deed's done,
    Young Hay of Talla,
Throw the corpse o'er the wall,
Give it dead dog's fall,
    Young Hay of Talla."

Hay was one of two executed on 3rd January 1568 for the
murder of Darnley.

If you would gain a good idea of this part of Tweedsmuir,
climb by the steep, crumbling sheep-path that scales the Linn-
side, till you reach the spot where Mr. Thomson has made his
sketch of the Reservoir. There, lying on the heather by the
sounding waters, or beneath the rowan trees where blaeberries
cluster thick among the rocks, you may picture to yourself a
meeting that took place by this very spot two hundred and
thirty-one years ago. On commanding heights, solitary men
keeping jealous watch lest Claver'se's hated dragoons should
have smelled out the place of meeting ; below, where the
Linn's roar muffles the volume of other sounds, a company of
blue-bonneted, stern-faced men, singing with intense fervour
some militant old Scottish Psalm, followed by long and earnest

extempore prayer, and renewed Psalms ; and presently then
falling into dispute as vehement as before had been their

Talla Reservoir from Talla Linn.

prayer and praise. This was that celebrated meeting of
Covenanters in 1682, of which Sir Walter Scott, writing in

"The Heart of Midlothian," says: "Here [at Talla] the
leaders among the scattered adherents to the Covenant, men
who, in their banishment from human society, and in the recollection of the severities to which they had been exposed,
had become at once sullen in their tempers, and fantastic in
their religious opinions, met with arms in their hands, and by
the side of the torrent discussed, with a turbulence which the
noise of the stream could not drown, points of controversy as
empty and unsubstantial as its foam."   Dour men they were,
and intolerant, our old Covenanting forebears, ready at any
moment to

> "prove their doctrine orthodox
> By apostolic blows and knocks."

Yet who can withhold from them his respect, or, in many
points, deny them his admiration?

If, as Sydney Smith has said, "it is good for any man to be
alone with nature and himself"; if "it is well to be in places
where man is little and God is great"; then assuredly it is well
to be alone, or with a friend "who knows when silence is more
sociable than talk," up in the great solitude by Gameshope
Burn.   Nowhere in Scotland can one find a glen wilder or
more impressive, nowhere chance on a scene which more
readily helps the harassed mind to slip from under the burden
of worldly cares.   For half a mile or more from its mouth but
a commonplace, open, boulder-strewn mountain burn, above
that point the broken, craggy hills fall swiftly to the lip of a
brawling torrent, which drops foaming by linn after linn deep
into the seething black cauldrons below, lingers there a minute,
then hurries swiftly onward by cliff and fern-clad mossy bank.
Above each pool cling rowan trees, rock rooted, a blaze of
scarlet and orange if the month be September, but beautiful
always at whatever season you may visit them.   Everywhere
the air is filled with the deep murmur and crash of falling
waters; yet, clamber to that lonely old track which leads to the
solitary cottage of a shepherd, and around you is a silence

almost oppressive, emphasised rather than broken by the ill-omened croak of a raven, or by the thin anxious bleat of a ewe calling to its lamb from far up the mountain side.

A sketch on the Gameshope Burn.

A mile past the shepherd's substantially built little house—it had need be strong of frame to stand intact up here against the winter storms—on your left is Donald's Cleuch, reminiscent of the Reverend Donald Cargill, a hero of the Covenant, Minister of the Barony Church in Glasgow in 1655, who was afterwards deprived of his benefice for denouncing the Restoration. The legend is, I presume, that Cargill hid somewhere in the wild moorland hereabout, up the Donald's Cleuch burn perhaps, or a long mile further on, by Gameshope Loch. A man might have lain long, in the summer time, amongst these rugged hills, safe hidden from any number of prying dragoons ; but Heaven help him if he lay out there in the winter season. All is wild, broken country, peat-hags, mosses, and deep cleuchs, over which one goes best a-foot—and, of necessity, best with youth on one's side if the journey be of any great length.

From the height at the head of Donald's Cleuch burn, one looks down on that gloomy tarn, Loch Skene, lying but a few short miles on the Yarrow side of the watershed. Mr. Skene of Rubislaw tells—it is in Lockhart's Life—how when Sir Walter Scott and he visited this loch, a thick fog came down over the hills, completely bewildering them, and " as we were groping through the maze of bogs, the ground gave way, and down went horse and horsemen pell-mell into a slough of peaty mud and black water, out of which, entangled as we were with our plaids and floundering nags, it was no easy matter to get extricated." Savage and desolate are perhaps the words that best describe Loch Skene ; yet, in fine summer weather, how beautiful it may be ! How beautiful, indeed, all this wild waste of hills where those dour old Covenanters were wont to lurk, never quite free from dread of the dragoons quartered but a few miles away over the hills at Moffat. Tales of the Covenanting times, such, for instance, as " The Brownie of Bodesbeck," used to possess an intense fascination for Scottish boys ; every Covenanter was then an immaculate hero, and, I suppose, few boys took any but the worst view of Claverhouse, or refused credence to any of the countless legends of him, and of his diabolical black charger, of which we firmly believed the story that it could course a hare along the side of a precipice. A point in some of those tales that used to interest and puzzle at

B B

least one boy, was the mysterious fashion in which a fugitive would at times disappear from ken when hard pressed on the open moor, and when apparently cut off from all chance of escape. A possible explanation presented itself to me one day, a summer or two back, when making my way across the bleak upland that lies between Gameshope Loch and Gameshope Burn. As I walked over the broken peaty surface of the plateau, but not yet arrived where the land begins to drop abruptly into the Gameshope Glen, a covey of grouse got up almost at my feet. The day was windless and very still, and as I stood watching the flight of the birds, the faint melodious tinkle of underground water somewhere very near to me fell on my ear. Glancing around, I saw on the flat ground in front of me within a yard of my feet, what appeared to be a hole, almost entirely concealed by heather. It was from this direction that the sound of the drip, drip of falling water seemed to come. Kneeling down, I pulled the heather aside, and found a hole two or three feet in diameter, and beneath it a roomy kind of chamber hollowed out of the peaty soil. It was a place perhaps five feet deep, big enough at a pinch to conceal half a dozen men ; a place from which—unless there was a way out from below—a man might never find exit, if inadvertently he fell in and in his fall chanced to break a limb. In that wild region the prospect of his ever being discovered by searchers would be very small. Unseen of man, he might lie in that peaty grave till his bones bleached, rest in that lonely spot till the last dread trump called him forth to judgment.

The day after I had chanced on this strange cavern, I returned with a friend to whom I wanted to show it, and though we knew that we must be often within a few yards of the spot, search as we might we never again found that hole. Was it in some *cache* such as this—perhaps in this very spot—that Covenanters sometimes lay hid? Here two or three might have lain for days or weeks at a time, sheltered from wind or rain and secure from hostile eyes ; it would be warm enough, and the drip of water into it is so slight as to be hardly worth naming.   Doubtless if one took careful landmarks it would be easy to find again, once knowledge of its whereabouts was gained.   And so the lurking Covenanters would have had small difficulty; but without such landmarks, to find it except by chance seems hopeless.   None of the shepherds knew of the hole, save one old man who said he had heard there was some such place.   But one might go a hundred times across that moor, passing close to the hidden mouth, and unless the faint tinkle of water betrayed it, or by remote chance one blundered in, its existence would never even be suspected.   It is a place worthy to be the abode of the Brown Man of the Muirs; and the district is wild and lonesome enough to breed the most eerie of superstitions.

Harking back now to the Tweed,—a little way above the bridge at Tweedsmuir on the right bank there is a huge standing stone, called the Giant's Stone, of which various legends are told.   Two other stones lie close at hand, but these appear to be mere ordinary boulders.   According to the Statistical Account of the Parish of 1833, this Giant's Stone is the sole survivor of a Druidical Circle; all its fellows were broken up for various purposes, and carted away; and we may be sure it was from no feeling of compunction that even the one was spared.   Residents tell us that it was from behind this stone that a wily little archer in days of old sent an arrow into the heart of a giant on the far side of Tweed.   The range is considerable; it must have been a glorious fluke.   But I rather think the place that is credited with this event, and with the veritable grave of the slain giant, is higher up Tweed, opposite the Hawkshaw burn.   Somewhere up this burn stood Hawkshaw Castle or Tower, home of that Porteous who gained unenviable notoriety for his feat of capturing at Falla Moss, with the aid of some of the moss-trooping fraternity, one of Cromwell's outposts, sixteen horse in all, and in cold blood afterwards executing the unfortunate troopers.   A contemporary historian relates that : " The greatest releiff at this tyme was by some gentillmen callit moss-trouperis, quha, haiffing quyetlie convenit in threttis and fourties, did cut off numberis of the Englishes, and seased on thair pockettis and horssis." The " pockettis and horssis" were all in the ordinary way of business ; it is another affair when it comes to cutting the throats of defenceless captives.

A few miles further on, the road we follow passes Badlieu, a place famed as the home, away back in the eleventh century, of Bonnie Bertha, who captured the roving heart of one of our early Scottish Kings as he hunted here one day in the forest. Unhappily for Bertha, there was already a Scottish Queen, and when news of the King's infatuation came to that lady's ears, she—queens have been known to entertain such prejudices— disapproved so strongly of the new *ménage*, that one afternoon when the king (who had been absent on some warlike expedition) arrived at Bertha's bower, he found the nest harried, and Bertha and her month-old babe lying dead. And ever after, they say, to the end the King cared no more to hunt, nor took pride in war, but wandered disconsolate, mourning for this Scottish Fair Rosamond. But how the rightful Queen fared thereafter, tradition does not say.

And now we come to Tweed Shaws, and Tweed's Well, the latter by popular repute held to be the source of Tweed. But there is a tributary burn which runs a longer course than this, rising in the hills much nearer to the head-waters of Annan. As is well known,

> "Annan, Tweed, and Clyde
> Rise a' oot o' ae hill-side,"

a statement which is sufficiently near the truth to pass muster. Near Tweed's Well of old stood Tweed's Cross, "so called," says Pennecuick, "from a cross which stood, and was erected there in time of Popery, as was ordinary in all the eminent places of public roads in the kingdom before our Reformation." It is needless to say that no trace of any cross now remains.

Up here, on this lofty, shelterless plateau, we find one of the few spots now left in Scotland where the old snow-posts still stand by the wayside, mute guides to the traveller when snow lies deep and the road is blotted from existence as effectually as is the track of a ship when she has passed across the ocean. Heaven's pity on those whom duty or necessity took across that wild moorland during a heavy snow-storm in the old coaching days! Many a man perished up here, wandered from the track, bewildered; stopped to rest and to take his bearings, then slid gently into a sleep from which there was no wakening. In 1831, the mail-coach from Dumfries to Edinburgh left Moffat late one winter's afternoon. Snow was falling as for years it had not been known to fall, and as the day passed the drifts grew deeper and ever more deep. But the guard, MacGeorge, an old soldier, a man of few words, could not be induced to listen to those who spoke of danger and counselled caution. He had been "quarrelled" once before for being behind time with the mail, said he; so long as he had power to go forward, never should "they" have occasion to quarrel him again. A matter of three or four miles up that heart-breaking, endless hill out of Moffat the coach toiled slowly, many times stopping to breathe the horses; and then it stuck fast. They took the horses out, loaded them with the mails, and guard and driver in company with a solitary passenger started again for Tweedshaws, leading the tired animals. Then the horses stuck, unable to face the deep drifts and the·blinding storm.

MacGeorge announced his intention of carrying the mail-bags; they *must* be got through. The driver remonstrated. "Better gang back to Moffat," he said. "Gang ye, or bide ye, *I gang on*!" cried MacGeorge. So the horses were turned loose to shift for themselves, and the two men started on their hopeless undertaking, the passenger, on their advice, turning to make his way back to Moffat. That was the last ever seen alive of the two who went forward. Next

day, the mail-bags were found beyond the summit of the hill,
—the most shelterless spot of the entire road,—hanging to a
snow-post, fastened there by numbed hands that too apparently
had been bleeding.   But of guard and coachman no trace till
three days later, when searchers found them, dead, on Mac-
George's face "a kind o' a pleasure," said the man who discovered the body in the deep snow.   Some such fate as that
ever trod here on the heels of foot passengers who wandered
from the track during a snow-storm.

In his "Strange Adventures of a Phæton," William Black
writes of these hills as "a wilderness of heather and wet
moss," even in the summer time; and he speaks of the
"utter loneliness," the "profound and melancholy stillness."
There is no denying that it is lonely, and often profoundly still.
And no doubt to many there is monotony in the low, rolling,
treeless, benty hills that here are the chief feature in the
scenery.   But I do not think it is melancholy.   The sense of
absolute freedom and of boundless space is too great to admit
of melancholy creeping in.   The feeling, to me at least, is more
akin to that one experiences when standing on the deck of a
full-rigged ship running down her Easting in "the Roaring
Forties," with the wind drumming hard out of the Sou'West.
From the haze, angry grey seas come raging on the weather
quarter, snarling as they curl over and leap to fling themselves
aboard, then, baffled, spew up in seething turmoil from beneath
the racing keel, and hurry off to leeward.   There you have a
plethora of monotony; each hurrying sea is exactly the mate of
his fellow that went before him, twin of that which follows
after.   Day succeeds day without other variety than what may
come from the carrying of less or more sail; hour after hour,
day after day, the same gigantic albatrosses, with far-stretched
motionless wings soar and wheel leisurely over and around the
ship, never hasting, never stopping,—unhasting and relentless
as Death himself.   Monotony absolute and supreme, but a
sense of freedom and of boundless space, and no touch of

melancholy. So it is here among these rolling hills where the
infant Tweed is born. There is no melancholy in the
situation, or at worst it can be but of brief duration. Who
could feel melancholy when, at last on the extreme summit and
beginning the long descent towards Moffat, he sees spread out
on either hand that glorious crescent of hills, rich in the purple
bloom of heather ; Annan deep beneath his feet wandering far
through her quiet valley, and dim in the distance, the English
hills asleep in the golden haze of afternoon. For my part, I
would fain linger, perched up here, late into the summer
gloaming, watching the panorama change with the changing
light when the sun has long set and the glow is dying in the
west ; —

> " For here the peace of heaven hath fallen, and here
> The earth and sky are mute in sympathy."

And this ground is classic ground. It was at Errickstane,
not far below, where, more than six hundred years ago, the
young Sir James Douglas found Bruce riding on his way to
Scone, to be crowned King of Scotland.

And to the left of the road shortly after leaving its highest
point on the hill, there yawns that tremendous hollow, the
Devil's Beef Tub, or, as it is sometimes called, the Marquis of
Annandale's Beef Stand. It was here in the '45 that a
Highland prisoner, suddenly wrapping himself tight in his
plaid, threw himself over the edge and rolled like a hedgehog
to the bottom, escaping, sore bruised indeed, but untouched
by the bullets that were sent thudding and whining after him
by the outwitted prisoners' guard. He is a desperate man who
would attempt a like feat, even minus the chance of a bullet.
It is a wild place and a terrible. The reason of its being
called the Marquis's Beef Stand is given by Summertrees in
" Redgauntlet." It was, said he, " because the Annandale
loons used to put their stolen cattle in there." And Summer-
tree's description of it is so truthful and vivid that it behoves
one to quote it in full : " It looks as if four hills were laying

their heads together to shut out daylight from the dark hollow space between them. A d—d deep, black, blackguard-looking

The Devil's Beef Tub.

abyss of a hole it is, and goes straight down from the road-side, as perpendicular as it can do, to be a heathery brae. At the bottom there is a small bit of a brook, that you would think could hardly find its way out from the hills that are so closely jammed round it."

And so, finally, having overshot the limits of Tweed and her tributaries, we cast back to the hills on the immediate border-line of the two kingdoms, and pass into the country of Dandie Dinmont.

CHAPTER XVI

LIDDESDALE, HERMITAGE, CASTLETON

COMING into Liddesdale by the route followed by Prince Charlie, over the hills by Note o' the Gate, one finds, a few miles past that curiously-named spot and no great distance from the road, the scene of a momentous battle of ancient times. It is claimed that it was here on Dawstane Rig the mighty struggle took place in the year 603 between Edelfrid, King of the Northumbrians, and Aidan, King of the Scots, the result of which, says Bede, writing a century and a quarter later, was that "from that time no king of the Scots durst come into Britain to make war on the Angles to this day." As written by Bede, the name of the place where the battle was fought is Daegsastan,—a "famous place" he calls it. Dalston, near Carlisle, also claims the honour of being the true site of this great defeat of the Scots; But Dawstane Rig seems the more probable spot, for, judging from the number of camps in the immediate vicinity, it must assuredly in old days have answered the description of a "famous place." There are numerous signs, also, that a great fight did at some remote period take place here; traces of escarpments are numerous on the hill side, arrowheads and other suggestive implements have frequently been picked up, and over all the hill are low cairns or mounds of stones, probably burial places of the slain. So far as I am aware, no excavations have ever been made here; the dead—

if these stones do indeed cover the dead—sleep undisturbed where they fell. But if the work were judiciously done, it would be interesting and instructive to make a systematic search over the reputed battle ground.

Not far distant from this ancient field of battle, but a little closer to the base of Peel Fell, runs a Roman road, the old Wheel Causeway, and into, or almost into, this road comes the Catrail, here finally disappearing. I have never heard any suggestion made of a reason why this Picts' Work Dyke should stop abruptly in, or at least on the very verge of, a Roman high-way. It is difficult to accept the theory that the Catrail was a road, because, in places where it crosses streams, no attempt is made to diverge towards a ford, or even to an easy entrance to the river bed ; it plunges in where the bank is often most inconveniently precipitous, and emerges again where it is equally steep. Yet if it was not a road, why should it run into and end in a recognised road that must have been in existence when the Catrail was formed ?

Up the Wheel Causeway, a little distance beyond the spot where the Catrail disappears, and between the Wormscleuch and Peel burns, there stood at one time an ancient ecclesiastical building, the Wheel Chapel, of whose walls faint traces still remain. It was in this building that Edward I of England passed the night of 24th May 1296, during his Border Progress ; in the record of his expedition the chapel is spoken of as the " Wyel." When the Statistical Account of 1798 was written, probably a considerable part of the ruin yet stood, for the writer of that account speaks of it as being of " excellent work-manship," and " pretty large." And he remarks on the great number of grave-stones in the churchyard, from which he con-cludes that the surrounding population must at one time have been very considerable. Over all this district, indeed, that seems to have been the case. Chapels were numerous among these hills ; in this part of Liddesdale there were no fewer than five, and the Wheel Chapel itself is not more than six miles or

so, as the crow flies, from Southdean, where it is certain that
about the date of the battle of Otterburne the population was
much more dense than it is at the present day.

What changes little more than one hundred years have wrought
in this countryside.   Six years before the Statistical Account of
1798 was penned, there were neither roads nor bridges in Liddesdale; " through these deep and broken bogs and mosses we must
crawl, to the great fatigue of ourselves but the much greater
injury of our horses," pathetically says the reverend writer of
the account.   Every article of merchandise had to be carried
on horseback.   Sir Walter Scott himself—in August 1800—
was the first who ever drove a wheeled vehicle among the
Liddesdale hills, and we know from " Guy Mannering," and
from Lockhart's " Life," pretty well what a wild country it then
was.   There was not an inn or a public house in the whole
valley, says Lockhart; "the travellers passed from the shepherd's
hut to the minister's manse, and again from the cheerful
hospitality of the manse to the rough and jolly welcome of the
homestead."   Inns, to be sure, even now are not to be found,
and are not needed, by every roadside, but at least there are
excellent main roads down both Liddel and Hermitage, and a
main line of railway runs through the valley; the moors are
well drained, and the necessity no longer exists to " crawl "
through broken bogs and mosses.   Yet still the hills in appearance are as they were in Scott's day, still they retain features
which render them distinct from any other of the Border hills ;
they are "greener and more abrupt . . . . sinking their sides
at once upon the river."   "They had no pretensions to
magnificence of height, or to romantic shapes, nor did their
smooth swelling slopes exhibit either rocks or woods.   Yet the
view was wild, solitary, and pleasingly rural.   No enclosures,
no roads, almost no tillage,—it seemed a land which a patriarch
would have chosen to feed his flocks and herds.   The remains
of here and there a dismantled and ruined tower showed that
it had once harboured beings of a very different description

from its present inhabitants,—those freebooters, namely, to whose exploits the wars between England and Scotland bear witness." The description might almost have been written to-day. The wild, hard riding, hard living freebooter of Johnie Armstrong's day is gone, leaving but a name and a tradition, or at most the mouldering walls of some old peel tower. But Dandie Dinmont himself, I think may still be found here in the flesh, as true a friend, as generous, as brave and steadfast as ever was his prototype,—but no longer as hard drinking. The days of " run " brandy from the Solway Firth are over, and the scene mentioned by Lockhart is now impossible, where Scott's host, a Liddesdale farmer, on a slight noise being heard outside, the evening of the traveller's arrival, *banged* up from his knees during family prayers, shouting "By——, here's the keg at last!" On hearing the previous day of Scott's proposed visit, he had sent off two men to some smuggler's haunt to obtain a supply of liquor, that his reputation for hospitality might not be shamed. And here it was, to the great prejudice of that evening's family worship! I do not suppose that the present day " Dandie" leisters fish any longer,—though one would not take on oneself rashly to swear that such a thing is even now entirely impossible; but certainly within recent years fox hunts have taken place amongst these hills much after the fashion described in " Guy Mannering." In such a country, indeed, what other means can there be of dealing with the hill foxes ?

There is another road into Liddesdale from the north, that which comes from Hawick up the Slitrig, past Stobs camp, then through the gap in the hills by Shankend and over the watershed by Limekilnedge, where Whitterhope Burn—tributary of Hermitage Water—takes its rise. As you drop down to heights less elevated, you pass on your left the Nine Stane Rig, a Druidical Circle, but locally more famed as the spot where the cruel and detestable Sorcerer, Lord Soulis, came to his grisly end. "Oh, *BOIL* him, if you like, but let me be plagued no more," cried (according to tradition) a Scottish

Monarch, wearied by the importunities of those who endlessly brought before him their grievances against the wicked lord. So—as Leyden wrote—

" On a circle of stones they placed the pot,
    On a circle of stones but barely nine ;
They heated it red and fiery hot,
    Till the burnished brass did glimmer and shine.

" They rolled him up in a sheet of lead—
    A sheet of lead for a funeral pall ;
They plunged him in the cauldron red,
    And melted him, lead, and bones, and all.

" At the Skelf-hill, the cauldron still
    The men of Liddesdale can show ;
And on the spot, where they boiled the pot,
    The spreat and the deer-hair ne'er shall grow."

("Spreat" is a species of rush, and "deer-hair" a coarse kind of grass.) Not the least painful part of the operation one would think must have been the getting so large a body into so small a cauldron. Some necromancy stronger than his own must have been employed to get him into a pot of the dimensions of that long preserved at Skelf-hill and shown to the curious as the identical cauldron. Of the stones that still remain of the original nine, two used to be pointed out as those between which the muckle pot was suspended on an iron bar, gipsy-kettle fashion. In reality, I believe this last of the de Soulis family died in Dumbarton Castle, a prisoner accused of conspiracy and treason.

A little way up Hermitage Water from the junction of Whitterhope Burn, stands the massive and most striking ruin of Hermitage Castle. Externally, the walls of this formidable stronghold are said to be mostly of the fifteenth century, but in part, of course, the building is very much older. The first castle built here is said to have been erected by Nicholas de Soulis in the beginning of the thirteenth century, and on a map of about the year 1300 Hermitage is shown as one of the

great frontier fortresses.   There were, however, earlier
proprietors of these lands than the de Soulis's, who may,
presumably, have lived here in some stronghold of their own, to
which their successors may have added.   About the year 1180,
Walter de Bolbeck granted "to God and Saint Mary and
Brother William of Mercheley" the hermitage in his "waste"
called Mercheley, beside Hermitage Water—then called the
Merching burn.   But from a much earlier date than this,
possibly as early as the sixth century, the place had been
famed as the retreat of a succession of holy men, and probably
something in the nature of a chapel existed even then.   The
chapel whose remains still stand, close by the bank of the
tumbling stream, a few hundred yards higher up than the
castle, is, I understand, of thirteenth century origin.   It
measures a little over fifty-one feet in length and twenty-four in
width, and the ruins are of much interest, if it were only for
the thought of those who in their day must have heard mass
within its walls, and perhaps there confessed their sins.

And surely, if sinners ever required absolution, some of
those who must have knelt here had need to ask it.   On
the shoulders of de Soulis and Bothwell alone—among
those who from time to time held the castle of Hermitage
perhaps the chief of sinners,—there rested a load of iniquity
too heavy to be borne by ordinary mortal ; and of the others,
some perhaps did not lag far behind in cruelty and wickedness.   If the tale be all true regarding the last days of Sir
Alexander Ramsay in 1342, the Knight of Liddesdale had
a good deal to answer for during his tenancy of the castle.
The interior of the building is in so much more ruinous a state
than the outside, that it is not possible to follow with any degree
of accuracy incidents that took place within its walls.   It is
said that before death ended his pangs, Sir Alexander Ramsay
eked out a miserable existence for seventeen days on grains of
corn that dribbled down from a granary overhead into the
dungeon where he lay.   But the small dungeon where he is

said to have been confined has a vaulted roof, and the room
above was manifestly a guard room ; so that—unless there was
some other dungeon—probably this story too, so far at least
as the grains of corn are concerned, must go the way of other
picturesque old tales. Some interesting relics were found
among the rubbish on the floor when the dungeon was opened
early in the nineteenth century, but I do not know that there

Hermitage Castle.

was anything that could in any way be connected with Sir
Alexander's fate. Many an unhappy wretch no doubt had
occupied the place since his day. But what there was I
believe was given to Sir Walter Scott, who also, as readers may
see in Lockhart's "Life," got from Dr. Elliot of Cleuchhead
"the large old Border war-horn, which ye may still see hanging in the armoury at Abbotsford. . . . One of the doctor's
servants had used it many a day as a grease-horn for his scythe,

before they discovered its history. When cleaned out, it was never a hair the worse—the original chain, hoop, and mouth-piece of steel, were all entire, just as you now see them. Sir Walter carried it home all the way from Liddesdale to Jedburgh, slung about his neck like Johnny Gilpin's bottle, while I [Shortreed] was intrusted with an ancient bridle-bit which we had likewise picked up." The horn I think had been found in a marshy bit of land near the castle.

Since about 1594, Hermitage has been the property of the Scotts of Buccleuch, into whose hands it came through their connection with Francis Stewart, Earl of Bothwell. A sketch done in 1810 shows that at that date one wall of the castle was rent from top to bottom by an enormous fissure, seemingly almost beyond redemption. But about 1821, careful repairs were undertaken by order of the then Duke of Buccleuch, and, externally, the building now seems to be in excellent condition.

Many a warrior, no doubt, lies buried in the graveyard of Hermitage chapel, but I do not think any tombstones of very great age have ever been found. Outside, however, between the wall of the burial ground and the river, there is an interest-ing mound, the reputed grave of the famous Cout o' Keilder. Keilder is a district of Northumberland adjoining Peel Fell, and in the day of the wizard Soulis, that iniquitous lord's most noted adversary was the chief of Keilder, locally called, from his great size and strength and activity, "the Cout." In his last desperate fight with Soulis and his followers on the banks of Hermitage Water, the Cout was hewing a bloody path through the press of men, towards his chief enemy, when weight of numbers forced him, like a wounded stag, to take to the water. Here, at bay in the rushing stream, guarding him-self from the foes who swarmed on either bank, the Cout stumbled and fell, and, hampered by his armour, he could not regain his feet; for each time that the drowning man got his head above water, Soulis and his band thrust him back with their long spears. Finally, as he became more exhausted,

C C

they held him down. And so the Cout perished. Here on the grassy bank, hard by what is still called "The Cout o' Keilder's pool," is his grave. But one is disappointed to learn that when an examination of it was made some years ago, no gigantic bones were unearthed, nor indeed any bones at all.

There is in some of the hills near Hermitage a peculiarity which cannot fail to strike observers; and that is, the deep *gashes*— you cannot call them glens—that have been cut here and there

Meeting of the Hermitage and Liddel.

by the small burns. Scored wide and deep into the smooth sides of the hills, they are yet not so wide as to force themselves on the eye. It would be possible to drive into them, and there effectually to conceal for a time, large mobs of cattle, and I do not doubt that in old days these fissures were often so used when a hostile English force was moving up the valley.

As one goes down Hermitage Water towards its junction with the Liddel, the country, one finds, is plentifully sprinkled with the ruins of peel towers,—abandoned rookeries of the Elliot clan, I suppose, for the Armstrong holdings were a little lower down. But in old days, when the de Soulis's held all Liddesdale, there were other strong castles besides Hermitage. Near Dinlabyre there stood the castle of Clintwood, and not far from the meeting of the two streams, on the high bank of Liddel, stood one of their strongholds—Liddel Castle. It was from this castle that the old village of Castleton took its name: the village was at first merely a settlement of de Soulis's followers.

The old Statistical Account of the Parish gives an extract from the Session Records of Castleton church which is of interest. It is as follows: "17 January 1649. The English army commanded by Colonels Bright and Pride, and under the conduct of General Cromwell, on their return to England, did lie at the Kirk of Castleton several nights, in which time they brak down and burnt the Communion table and the seats of the Kirk; and at their removing carried away the minister's books, to the value of one thousand merks and above, and also the books of Session, with which they lighted their tobacco pipes, the baptism, marriage, and examination rolls from October 1612 to September 1648, all which were lost and destroyed."

Castleton as a village does not now exist, and the old church has disappeared, though the churchyard is still used. The other village, the present Newcastleton, is of course entirely a township of yesterday—to be precise, it dates only from 1793. But it is interesting from the fact that the present railway station occupies the site where once stood the tower of Park, the peel of that "Little Jock Elliot" who so nearly put an end to the life of Bothwell. What a difference it might have made if he had but stabbed in a more vital spot, or a little deeper.

Not far from Castleton was the home of the notorious Willie of Westburnflat, last of the old reivers, and—it almost goes without saying—an Armstrong; the last of those of whom it was written :—

> " Of Liddisdail the common thiefis,
> Sa peartlie stellis now and reifis,
> That nane may keip
> Horse, nolt, nor scheip,
> Nor yett dar sleip
> · For their mischeifis."

But Willie lived in degenerate days; the times were out of joint, and reiving as a profession had gone out of fashion. People now resented having their kye " lifted," and meanly invoked the new-fangled aid of the Law in redressing such grievances. Nevertheless, Willie did his best to maintain old customs, and consequently he was feared and. hated far beyond the bounds of Liddesdale.

Modern prejudice however at length became too strong for him. It so fell out that a dozen or so of cows, raided one night from Teviotdale, were traced to Westburnflat. In the dead of night, when Willie was peacefully asleep, tired perhaps, and soothed by the consciousness of a deed well done, the men of Teviotdale arrived, and, bursting in, before Willie could gather his scattered wits or realise what was happening he was overpowered by numbers, and they had bound him fast, hand and foot. His trial, along with that of nine friends and neighbours, was held at Selkirk, and though the lost cattle had not been found in his possession, and the evidence of this particular theft was in no way conclusive, on the question of general character alone the jury thought it safer to find all the prisoners guilty. Sentence of death was pronounced. Thereupon Willie arose in wrath, seized the heavy oak chair on which he had been seated, broke it in pieces by main strength, kept a strong leg for himself, and passing the remainder to his condemned comrades, called to them to stand by him and they would fight their way out of Selkirk. There is little doubt, too, that he would have succeeded had he been properly backed up. But his friends—

poor "fushionless," spiritless creatures, degenerate Armstrongs surely, if they *were* Armstrongs—seized his hands and cried to him to " *let them die like Christians.*" Perhaps it was a kind of equivalent to turning King's Evidence ; they may have hoped to

Millholme or Milnholm Cross.

curry favour and to be treated leniently because of their services in helping to secure the chief villain. But they might better have died fighting ; pusillanimity availed them nothing. They were all duly hanged.

A few miles down the Liddel from Westburnflat is the site

of Mangerton Castle, home of the chief of the Armstrong clan, Johnie of Gilnockie's brother. Nothing now is left of the building, but Sir Walter mentions that an old carved stone from its walls is built into a neighbouring mill. Near to Mangerton, in a field between Newcastleton and Ettletown Churchyard, is the interesting Milnholm Cross, said to have been erected somewhere about six hundred years ago to mark the spot where a dead chief of the Armstrongs lay, prior to

On the Liddel at Mangerton.

being buried at Ettletown. The tradition as given in the Statistical Account of 1798, is as follows: "One of the governors of Hermitage Castle, some say Lord Soulis, others Lord Douglas, having entertained a passion for a young woman in the lower part of the parish, went to her house, and was met by her father, who, wishing to conceal his daughter, was instantly killed by the Governor. He was soon pursued by the people, and, in extreme danger, took refuge with Armstrong of Mangerton, who had influence enough to prevail on the people to desist from the pursuit, and by this means saved his life. Seemingly with a view to make a return for this favour, but secretly jealous of the power and influence of Armstrong, he invited him to Hermitage, where he was basely murdered. He himself, in his turn, was killed by Jock of the Side, of famous memory, and brother to Armstrong. The cross was erected in memory of the transaction." Here, too, I fear tradition is untrustworthy. Jock of the Syde— "a greater thief did never ride"—lived long after the day of the de Soulis's or of Douglas ; he was, indeed, contemporary with the equally notorious " Johne of the Parke,"—Little Jock Elliot. This Milnholm Cross is a little over eight feet in height. The carving is worn, and not very distinct, but on a shield there is the heraldic device of the Armstrongs, a bent arm ; some lettering, I.H.S. ; below, the initials M.A., and what appears to be A.A. ; and on the shaft is cut a two-handed sword, about four feet in length. In his " History of Liddesdale," (1883). Bruce Armstrong says the shield was added " recently."

CHAPTER XVII

KERSHOPEFOOT, CARLISLE CASTLE, SOLWAY MOSS

A LITTLE further down the river we come to the Kershope Burn, here the boundary between Scotland and England. It was here, at "the Dayholme of Kershoup"—which I take to be the flat land on the Scottish side of Liddel, opposite to the mouth of the burn—that the Wardens' Meeting was held in 1596, which became afterwards so famous owing to the illegal capture by the English of Kinmont Willie. All the world knows the tale, and all the world knows how gallantly Buccleuch rescued the prisoner from Carlisle Castle. But until one goes to Carlisle, and takes note for oneself of the difficulties with which Buccleuch had to contend, and the apparently hopeless nature of his undertaking, it is not possible to appreciate the full measure of the rescuer's gallantry. Kinmont, I suppose, on the day of his capture was riding quietly homeward down the Scottish side of the river, suspecting no evil, for the day was a day of truce. "Upon paine of death, presentlie to be executed, all persones whatsoever that come to these meitings sould be saife fra any proceiding or present occasioun, from the tyme of Meiting of the Wardens, or their Deputies, till the next Day at the sun rysing." The English did not play the game; from their own side of Liddel they had probably kept Kinmont in sight, meaning to seize him if opportunity offered. And they made the opportunity. For the most part, the banks of

Liddel here are steep and broken, and the river is devoid of
any ford ; but a mile or two down from Kershopefoot the land
on the Scottish side slopes gently from the water, and it is
easily fordable.   Here probably began the chase which ended
in Willie's capture.   A very fine sword was found near this
ford a great many years ago, possibly a weapon lost by one
of the pursuers, hurrying to get across.

Carlisle Castle.

The night of Kinmont's release, the 13th of April, 1596, was
very dark, with rain falling, and a slight mist rising over the
river flats at Carlisle.   And the Eden was swollen.   It is not
possible to form any very definite idea of the initial difficulty
Buccleuch must have met with at this point, because the bed
of the river is now entirely different from what it was then.   In
former days, I believe, a long, low island lay in mid-stream, the
water flowing swiftly through two channels.   Even now there
is shallow water part way across, but the stream runs strong and

it would be ill to ford, especially on a dark night. Buccleuch, I take it, must have swum his horses across the Eden nearly opposite, but a trifle above, the mouth of the little river Caldew, "the water being at the tyme, through raines that had fallen, weill thick; he comes to the Sacray, a plaine place under the toune and castell, and halts upon the syde of a little water or burne that they call Caday." The "Sacray" is of course what now goes by the name of the Sauceries.

Carlisle and the River Eden.

Buccleuch's scaling ladders proved too short to enable him to get within the castle walls by their means; but there is a small postern gate in the wall (nearly abreast of the present public Abattoirs), and this was forced, or at least one or two men squeezed in here, possibly by removing a stone below the gate, and opened the postern to their comrades. This postern has recently been reopened. After Buccleuch's exploit it had been securely built up on both sides, outside and in; and later, a Cook's galley and other domestic offices were erected on the inner side, against the wall, effectually hiding the old gate. These buildings and the stonework blocking the postern have now been pulled down, and the identical little oaken gate through which Buccleuch and his men entered, once more has seen the light of day, and, I understand, is now being put in a state of thorough repair.

Having made his entry, Buccleuch placed one part of his force between the castle and the town, so that he might not be

Carlisle from the Castle Ramparts.

assailed in rear, and, leaving a few men to guard the postern and secure their retreat, the rest pushed towards Kinmont Willie's place of confinement in the Keep, all making as great a noise as possible, "to terrifie both castell and toune by ane imaginatioun of a greater force." Hitherto they had encountered only the castle sentinels, who were easily scattered and brushed aside; "the rest that was within doors heiring the noyse of the trumpet within, and that the castell was entered, and the noyse of others without, both the Lord

Scroope himself and his deputy Salkeld being thair with the
garrisone and hys awin retinew, did keep thamselffis close."

It was one thing, however, for the rescuers to have forced their
way inside the castle walls, but it should have been quite

A Byway in Carlisle.

another, to accomplish the feat of getting the prisoner out of
the dungeon. Through a female spy they knew in what part
of the castle he lay ; but his place of confinement,—inside the
Keep,—was quite a hundred yards from the postern gate, and

surely a few resolute men might have held so strong a post for
a time without much difficulty.   Lord Scrope, however, did
not emerge from his retreat; and to the others as well,
discretion seemed the better part of valour.   Meantime,
Buccleuch's trumpets were blaring out the arrogant old Elliot
slogan; " *O wha daur meddle wi' me ?* "; and his men, falling
to with energy, forced the gate of the Keep, burst in the
massive door of the outer dungeon, tore away that of the dark

The Market Cross, Carlisle.

and noisome inner prison, a rough, vaulted stone chamber to
which no ray of light ever penetrated even on the brightest
day, and there they found Kinmont, chained to the wall.   No
time now to strike off his fetters; they could but free him from
the long iron bar that ran along one side of the wall, and

> " Then Red Rowan has hente him up,
>   The starkest man in Teviotdale—
> ' Abide, abide now, Red Rowan,
>   Till of my Lord Scroope I take farewell.

" 'Farewell, farewell, my gude Lord Scroope !
  My gude Lord Scroope, farewell !' he cried—
'I'll pay ye for my lodging maill,
  When first we meet on the Border side.'

"Then shoulder high, with shout and cry,
  We bore him down the ladder lang ;
At every stride Red Rowan made,
  I wot the Kinmont's airns played clang !

.   .   .   .   .   .

"We scarce had won the Staneshaw-bank,
  When a' the Carlisle bells were rung,
And a thousand men on horse and foot,
  Cam' wi' the keen Lord Scroope along."

But still they held aloof, hesitating to attack the retreating little
Scottish band, and Buccleuch and his men, with Willie in their
midst, plunged in and safely recrossed the swollen river.

"He turned him on the other side,
  And at Lord Scroope his glove flung he—
'If ye likena my visit in merry England,
  In fair Scotland come visit me !' "

.   .   .   .   .

But Lord Scrope on this night scarcely merited the term,
"keen"; he went no farther towards Scotland than the water's
edge.

" 'He is either himself a devil frae hell,
  Or else his mother a witch maun be ;
I wadna have ridden that wan water
  For a' the gowd in Christentie,' "

cried he, according to the ballad. Was he, one cannot help
wondering, ashamed of the English breach of Border law
entailed in the matter of Kinmont's capture, and was he in a
measure wilfully playing into Buccleuch's hands? If that were
the case, he took on himself a heavy risk. Elizabeth was not
exactly the kind of Sovereign who would be likely to be tender
hearted and to make allowances for slackness in such an affair,
nor one with whom her servants might safely take liberties.

As safely might the gambolling lamb play pranks with the drowsing wolf.

Not far from Longtown, at a place called Dick's Tree, on the farther side of Esk, there still stands the "smiddy" (or smith's shop) where Kinmont's irons were struck off. In one of Sir Walter Scott's M.S. letters of 1826 it is told that: "Tradition preserves the account of the smith's daughter, then a child, how there was a *sair clatter* at the door about daybreak, and loud

Dick's Tree. The blacksmith's shop where Kinmont Willie's fetters were taken off.

crying for the smith ; but her father not being on the alert, Buccleuch himself thrust his lance thro' the window, which effectually bestirred him. On looking out, the woman continued, she saw, in the grey of the morning, more gentlemen than she had ever before seen in one place, all on horseback, in armour, and dripping wet—and that Kinmont Willie, who sat woman-fashion behind one of them, was the biggest carle she ever saw—and there was much merriment in the company." Except for this event, Dick's Tree is quite uninteresting, and quite unpicturesque ; it is merely a cottage like a thousand others to be seen in the Border, possessing no special feature, or even any indication of antiquity.   And no

The reputed grave of Kinmont Willie in Sark graveyard.

one works the "smiddy" now, except at odd times ; modern requirements have, I understand, taken the business away to Longtown.

What was the end of Kinmont Willie no one knows, but he

certainly lived to pay, to some small extent, for his "lodging maill;" he was engaged in a raid on Lord Scrope's tenants in the year 1600, and doubtless he did not forget the debt incurred at Carlisle. Later than this I think there is no record of him, but it would not be surprising to learn that at the last Lord Scrope was able to give a receipt in full. Many an Armstrong in old days danced at the end of a rope at "Hairribie." Not improbably, Kinmont was one of them. There is a grave in an old churchyard not far from the Tower of Sark, which is pointed out as his. But the date on the tombstone makes it impossible that the veritable Willie of Kinmont lies underneath. The name of "William Armstrong called Kynmount" is in Lord Maxwell's Muster Roll of 1585, together with those of his seven sons. Willie, therefore—if at that date he had seven sons fit to fight—could have been no youth. Now the William Armstrong to whose memory the Sark tombstone is erected died in 1658, which, if he had been the famous Kinmont, would give him an age of considerably over a hundred years. But in any case, it is an interesting old stone. Many years ago steps were taken to preserve it from further decay, and the lettering and other points were re-touched. Round the edges of the stone is cut: "HEIR . LYES . ANE . WORTHIE . PERSON . CALLIT . WILLIAM . ARMSTRONG . OF . SARK . WHO . DIED . ꝥE 10 . DAY . OF . JUNE . 16 . 58 . AETATIS . SVAE . 56." On the body of the stone:

"IENOT . IOHNSTON . RELEK .   "Man as grass to grave he flies .
  TO . ꝥE . SED . DESISED . PERSN   Grass decays and man he dies .
  ꝥEH . PVT . VP . HIS . MONEME   Grass revives and man doth rise .
  Nꝥ . IN . ANO . DOMO . 16 . 60."   Yet few they be who get the prise."

Below are the Armstrong bent arm holding a sword, a skull and crossed bones, an hour glass and other emblems, and below all, "MEMENTO . MORA." This William Armstrong, there-fore, who died in 1658, aged 56, was not born when Kinmont Willie was rescued by Buccleuch from Carlisle Castle.

Here, on the lower part of Sark, we are in a country world-

famed for its old fashioned run-away marriages, more famed
even than was Coldstream. Down the river is Sark Bridge,
with its toll-bar, and adjacent to it, Gretna Green. At the toll-
house alone in the early part of last century, within six years
thirteen hundred couples were married—a profitable business
for the " priest," (usually the village blacksmith,) for his fee

Sark Bridge and toll-bar.

ranged from half a guinea to a hundred pounds, according to
the circumstances of each fond couple. But what was charged
in a case such as that of Lord Erskine, Lord High Chancellor
of England, who, when he was nearly seventy years of age,
eloped with a blushing spinster and was married at Gretna—in
the Inn, I think—history does not tell. There is a something,
part comic, part pathetic, in the thought of the tired old gentle-

man gallantly propping himself in a corner of his post chaise, flying through the darkness of night on Love's wings, a fond bride by his side. And when grey dawn at length stole through the breath-dimmed glass of the closed windows, revealing the "elderly morning dew" on his withered cheeks and stubbly chin, with callous disregard emphasizing the wrinkles, the bags

The blacksmith's shop, Gretna Green.

below the puffy eyes—bloodshot from want of sleep—and the wig awry, did the young lady begin to repent her bargain, one may wonder.

Stretched between Sark and Longtown is the Debateable Land and Solway Moss; the latter "just a muckle black moss," they will tell you here, yet surely not without its own beauty under certain combinations of sun and cloud. "Solway Moss" is a name of evil repute to us of Scotland, for here on 24th

November 1542 took place the most miserable of all Border battles—if indeed "battle" is a term in any degree applicable to the affair. The encounter, such as it was, took place not so much in Solway Moss, however, as over towards Arthuret. The Scots—a strong raiding army, but disorganised, and in a state of incipient mutiny against their newly-appointed leader, Oliver Sinclair, (Ridpath says : "a general murmur and breach of all order immediately ensued" when his appointment was

Solway Moss.

made known,)—at dawn of the 24th were already burning northward through the Debateable Land. Wharton with his compact little English force watched them from Arthuret Howes and skilfully drew them into a hopeless trap between the Esk and an impassable swamp, where there was no room to deploy. Here the English—at most not a sixth part so numerous as the Scots—charging down on the Scottish right flank threw them into hopeless confusion, and from that minute all was over.

Panic seized the Scots : men cast aside whatever might hamper their flight, and, plunging into the water, scrambled for what safety they might find among the Grahams and the English borderers of Liddesdale—which, as it turned out, meant little better than scrambling from the frying pan into the fire.   Many

Ancient cross, Arthuret.

were driven into the swamp and perished there miserably, many were drowned in the river, and twelve hundred men—including a large percentage of nobles—were captured.   Out of a force variously estimated at from two to three thousand strong—Sir William Musgrave, who was with the cavalry, puts it at the higher figure—the English lost but seven men killed.   It was a

sorry business, a dreadful day for Scotland; and it ended the
life of James V as effectually as if he had been slain on the
field of battle.   I do not know if Arthuret church was injured
on this occasion; it is recorded in 1597 that it had then been
ruinous for about sixty years.   Perhaps the Armstrongs may
have been responsible; they made a big raid hereaway in 1528.
The present building dates, I believe, from 1609.

Gorge on the Liddel.

There was another calamity connected with Solway Moss,
later than the battle and local in effect, yet sufficiently terrible
to cast over the district a black shadow of tragedy, the memory
of which time has lightened but even yet has not entirely wiped
out.   November 1771 was a month of evil note for its storms
and ceaseless wet.   Day followed day sodden with driving
rain, and the country lay smothered under a ragged grey
blanket of mist.   Firm ground became a quagmire that
quaked under foot, pools widened into lakes, and the rivers

rose in dreadful spate that yet failed to carry off the superfluous
water.   Liddel roared through the rocky gorge of Penton Linn
with a fury such as had never been known ; Esk left her bed

Study in Carlisle Cathedral.

and wandered at will.   Many people living in the low-lying
flats surrounding the Moss, alarmed for the safety of their
cattle, were abroad in the dark of the morning of 16th
November, intent on getting the beasts to higher ground,

when a long-drawn muffled rumble, as of distant thunder, startled them. The Moss had burst, spewing out from its maw a putrid mass that spread relentlessly, engulfing house after house, in many cases catching the inhabitants in their beds. For weeks the horrible eruption spread, and ere its advance was stayed thirty families were homeless, their houses, furniture, and live-stock buried twenty feet deep under a black slime that stank like the pit of Tophet.

Brampton.

Harking back to Carlisle, (which we left in company of Kinmont Willie,) one would fain linger in that pleasant town, to dream awhile over its alluring past. But Carlisle is a subject too big to introduce at the close of a volume; there is a more than sufficient material in the story of the castle (with its wealth of warlike and other memories), and of the Cathedral, alone to make a fair-sized book. There is too much to tell; for, besides the story of the captivity here of Queen Mary of

Scotland, and that of the capture of Carlisle by Prince Charlie, there are a hundred and one other things, if once a beginning were made and space to tell them were available. (What used to be called Queen Mary's Tower, to save cost of repairs was pulled down by Government between 1824 and 1835, together with the Hall in which Edward I held Parliaments, and much else of surpassing interest. Vandalism in those days was a vice which affected not alone the private individual.) Moreover, there would be the question of where to stop, for if the history of Carlisle be touched upon, at once we are mixed up with that of half a score of places in the immediate neighbourhood, all of which are full of profoundest interest. There would be, for example, Naworth, not far from the quaint little town of Brampton, Naworth with its massive walls, and memories of the Dacres, and of Belted Will Howard—a name better known to Border fame, at least to the Borderer of to-day, than even that of his predecessors. Then there would necessarily be the fascinating subject of the Roman wall, of Bird-Oswald camp, of Lanercost, and of Gilsland, with its memories of Sir Walter. One must needs make an end somewhere, and it is hopeless to treat of such subjects in small space. But Bewcastle, perhaps, because of its connection with a subject mentioned earlier in this volume, must not be omitted.

CHAPTER XVIII

BEWCASTLE, LIDDEL MOAT, NETHERBY, KIRK ANDREWS, GILNOCKIE, LANGHOLM

A PILGRIMAGE to Bewcastle cannot be recommended to persons animated by curiosity alone; or even by a passion for the beauties of nature. From childhood the writer had a

Bewcastle Church and Castle.

desire to behold Bewcastle, because it was the Captain of Bewcastle who, in the ballad of *Jamie Telfer*, in *The Border Minstrelsy*, made such an unlucky raid on the cows of a farmer in Ettrickdale. The very word Bewcastle seemed to re-echo

the trumpets of the Wardens' Raids and the battles long ago.
But when you actually find yourself, after a long walk or drive
up a succession of long green ascents, in the broad bleak cup

Bewcastle Cross.

of the hills ; when you see the grassy heights, with traces of
ancient earthworks that surround the blind grey oblong of the
ruined castle ; the little old church, all modern within, and the

tiny hamlet that nestles by the shrunken and prosaic burn;
then, unless you be an antiquary and a historian, you feel as
if you had come very far to see very little. But if a secular
antiquary and a ballad lover, you fill the landscape with
galloping reivers, you restore the royal flag of England to the
tower, and your mind is full of the rough riding life of Mus-
graves and Grahams, Scotts, Elliots and Armstrongs. If, on
the other hand, your tastes are ecclesiastical, and you are an

Naworth Castle.

amateur of Runic writing, you can pass hours with the tall
headless Runic cross beside the church, a work of art dating
from the middle of the seventh century of our era, according
to the prevalent opinion.

Bewcastle is at least ten miles from the nearest railway at
Penton; twelve from Brampton; not easily approached by a
fell path from Gilsland; and is most easily if least romantically
reached by motor car from Carlisle, a drive of nearly twenty

miles. The Elliots and Scotts of the reiving days, got at
Bewcastle by riding down Liddel water, crossing it at the
Kershope burn ford, and then robbing all and sundry through
some four miles. The castle they could not take in a casual
expedition.

The oldest monument in the place, except the earthworks
said to be Roman, is the Cross, which much resembles the
more famous Cross of Ruthwell, near Dumfries, with the runes
from the Song of the Rood. More fortunate than the Ruthwell
relic of early Anglican Christianity, that of Bewcastle was never
broken up by the bigots of the Covenant as " a monument of
idolatry." The head, however, was removed by Belted Will of
Naworth, and sent to Camden the historian, in the reign of
James VI and I. The west face is the most interesting. The
top panel contains a figure of St. John the Baptist ; our Lord is
represented in the central panel, inscribed in runes, *Gessus
Kristtus.* The figure is noble and broad in treatment ; done
in the latest gloaming of classical art. Beneath is seated a
layman, in garb of peace, with his falcon. The runic
inscription on the central panel is black, painted black, it
seems, by a recent rector, the Rev. Mr. Maughan, who laboured
long at deciphering the characters. Professor Stephens read
them :

> This victory-column
> Thin set up
> Hwaetred Woth-
> gar Olfwolthu
> after Alcfrith
> Once King
> and son of Oswi
> Pray for the high
> sin of his soul.

Runes are difficult. Mr. Stephens once read a Greek epitaph
in elegiac verse, for a Syrian boy, at Brough, as a Runic lament,
in old English, for a martyred Christian lady. I have little
confidence in Hwaetred, Olfwolthu, and Wothgar : who were

they ; the artists employed in making the Cross ? *Eac Oswiung*,
"and son of Oswin," "the king," is said to be plain enough,
and to indicate Alchfrith, son of Oswin, who after a stormy

Bewcastle Cross.

youth accepted, as against the Celtic clerics, the positions of
St. Wilfred. The decorative work, knot work, vine scrolls,
birds and little animals among the grapes, is of Byzantine and

Northern Italian origin : like the decoration of the Ruthwell Cross.

Bewcastle must, it seems, have been a more important and populous place when this monument was erected, than even when the Royal castle was a centre of resistance to the Liddesdale clans in Queen Elizabeth's day.

Returning from Bewcastle by Penton, we strike the Liddel near Penton Linn, not distant from the vanished peel of that Judas, Hector Armstrong of Harelaw, who betrayed the Earl of Northumberland into the hands of the Regent Murray in 1569. A little way below, near the junction of Liddel and Esk, on a commanding height that overhangs railway and river, is Liddel Moat. Locally this moat is called "the Roman Camp," but to the average amateur there is certainly nothing Roman about it. No doubt the Romans may have had an outpost here ; the position is too strong not to have been held by them, especially as they had a station barely a couple of miles away, at Netherby. But the prominent remains of fortifications now to be seen here manifestly date from long after Roman days. It is, I believe, the site of the earliest Liddel Castle, erected by Ranulph de Soulis before either the Liddel Castle at Castleton, or Hermitage, was built. This Liddel Castle was razed to the ground, wiped out of existence, by the Scottish army under David Bruce, which invaded England in 1346 and was so totally routed at Neville's Cross a few weeks later. On his march southward, says Ridpath, Bruce "took the fortress of Liddel and put the garrison to the sword, . . . spreading terror and desolation all round him in his progress through Cumberland." Liddel Moat is well worthy of a visit, but it is somewhat out of the beaten track and can only be reached by walking a little distance, preferably from the station at Riddings Junction. The position, defended on the landward side by an immensely deep moat, and on the other dropping almost sheer into the river – or rather, now, on to the intervening railway line—is a magnificent one, and the view obtained from the

highest point is very fine,—at one's feet, just beyond the two
rivers, "Cannobie lea";

> "There was mounting 'mong Graemes of the Netherby clan,
>   Forsters, Fenwicks, and Musgraves, they rode and they ran,
> There was racing and chasing on Cannobie lea,
>   But the lost bride of Netherby ne'er did they see."

A short way farther down the Esk is Netherby, headquarters of that clan whose peel towers once dotted this part
of Cumberland and all the Debateable Land, and who in the
early seventeenth century were so hardly used by James VI
and I. They were no better, I suppose, than the others of
that day, but they were no worse, and the story of their banishment is not very pleasant reading. Lord Scrope believed that
the Grahams were "privy" to Buccleuch's rescue of Kinmont
Willie, and certainly the Grahams did not love Lord Scrope,
who, I suppose, was not likely to present the clan in a very
favourable light to Queen Elizabeth. Their reputation, in any
case, became increasingly black, and James I, when he came
to the throne, issued a proclamation against them. In fact, the
dog was given an exceedingly bad name—not of course wholly
without cause—and hung; or, rather, many of their houses
were harried, their women and children turned out to fend for
themselves in the wet and cold, and their men shipped off to
banishment in Ireland and in Holland. Certainly, in driblets
they made their way back to their own country again, after a
time—those who survived, that is,—but their nests had been
harried, their broods scattered down the wind, and, as a clan,
their old status was never regained.

As has already been told, Netherby was the site of a Roman
station, and it is rich in evidences of the old Legions—coins,
altars, and what not. The original peel at Netherby—
which still forms part of the present mansion—I take to have
been such another as the Graham tower of Kirk Andrews, its
near neighbour, which stands—still inhabited—just across the
Esk, perched on a rising ground overhanging the river.

From a sporting point of view at least, the Esk here is a beautiful stream, famous for its salmon, which are plentiful and often of great size. In his Notes to "Redgauntlet," Sir Walter Scott mentions that "shortly after the close of the American war, Sir James Graham of Netherby constructed a dam-dike, or cauld, across the Esk, at a place where it flowed through his estate, though it has its origin, and the principal part of its

Kirk Andrews Tower, Netherby.

course, in Scotland. The new barrier at Netherby was considered as an encroachment calculated to prevent the salmon from ascending into Scotland ; and the right of erecting it being an international question of law betwixt the sister kingdoms, there was no court in either competent to its decision. In this dilemma, the Scots people assembled in numbers by signal of rocket-lights, and, rudely armed with fowling-pieces, fish spears and such rustic weapons, marched to the banks of the river for the purpose of pulling down the dam-dike objected to. Sir James Graham armed many of his own people to protect his property, and had some military from Carlisle for the same purpose. A renewal of the Border wars had nearly taken place in the eighteenth century, when prudence and moderation on both sides saved much tumult, and perhaps some bloodshed. The English proprietor consented that a breach should be made in his dam-dike sufficient for the passage of the fish, and thus removed the Scottish grievance. I believe the river has since that time taken the matter into its own disposal, and entirely swept away the dam-dike in question." I do not think there is now any trace of the obstruction which so roused the good people of Langholm and their supporters. The question, of course, was not a new one. As early as the middle of the fifteenth century, Cumberland folks and Scots were at logger-heads over a " fish-garth " constructed by the former, which the Scots maintained prevented salmon from ascending to the upper waters. The dispute raged for something like a hundred years.

Leaving Kirk Andrews, we get at once onto the old London and Edinburgh coach road close to Scot's Dike, and in the course of two or three miles reach the village of Canonbie, where at a little distance from the bridge over Esk stands the comfortable old coaching inn, the Cross Keys, now favoured of anglers. Thence all the way to Langholm the road runs by the river-bank through very delightful scenery, said, in old days, indeed, to be the most beautiful of all between London and Edinburgh. In the twelfth century a Priory stood at Canonbie, and as late as 1576 there was still a resident Prior, but the building itself I think was wrecked by the English in 1542, after the battle of Solway Moss. A few of its stones are still to the fore, but I fear the ruin was used as a quarry during the building of Canonbie Bridge.

That also is a fate that waited on another famous building not far from Canonbie—Gilnockie Castle, the residence of the

notorious Johnny Armstrong.   Hollows Tower, a few hundred
yards above the village of Hollows, is often confounded with
Gilnockie, probably for the reason that no stone of the latter
has been left standing on another, and that Hollows Tower is

The Armstrong Tower on the Esk.

a conspicuous object in the foreground here.   Perhaps, too,
Sir Walter Scott was partly responsible for the belief prevalent
in many quarters that the Hollows is Gilnockie.   In " Minstrelsy
of the Scottish Border," he says :   " His [Johny Armstrong's]

E E 2

place of residence (now a roofless tower) was at the Hollows, a few miles from Langholm, where its ruins still serve to adorn a scene which, in natural beauty, has few equals in Scotland "

Gilnockie Bridge.

I am not certain, but I do not think that Sir Walter ever visited Gilnockie. If he had done so, it could scarcely have escaped his knowledge that another castle once stood less than half a

mile from Hollows Tower, and that towards the end of the
eighteenth century the stones from that castle were utilised in
the building of Gilnockie Bridge.   That they were so used is
well authenticated ; and I should think it is probable that the
ruin was found to be a convenient quarry also when houses in
the neighbouring village of Hollows were being built.

Hollows Tower is a very good example of the old Border
Keep, but it is small, much too small to have given anything
like sufficient accommodation for Johny Armstrong's " tail,"
which must necessarily have been of considerable strength.
The dining hall, for instance, measures roughly only a little
over twenty-two feet by thirteen, and the total outside length of
the tower is less than thirty-five feet.   I should imagine it to be
certain that Johny never lived here ; indeed, I should be
inclined to doubt if this particular Hollows Tower was even
built during Johny Armstrong's life-time.   Neither is the
position a very strong one,—though on that point it is perhaps
not easy to judge, because, in old days no doubt (as in the case
of Hermitage Castle,) impassable swamps probably helped to
protect it from assault on one or more sides.

The place where Gilnockie stood is without any doubt a little
lower down the Esk than Hollows Tower, at a point where
the river makes a serpentine bend and contracts into a narrow,
rocky gorge, impossible to ford.   Here, at the Carlisle end of
Gilnockie Bridge, on the high tongue of rocky land that
projects into the stream, are faint but unmistakeable outlines
of a large building, with outworks.   The position is magnificent
—impregnable, in fact, to any force of olden days unprovided
with artillery.   On three sides the rocky banks drop nearly
sheer to the water, and across the root of the tongue are
indications of a protecting fosse.   It is impossible to imagine
a site more perfect for a freebooter's stronghold.   To have
neglected it, in favour of such a position as that occupied by
the Hollows Tower, would have been on the reiver's part to
throw away the most obvious of the gifts of Providence.

Local tradition has it that Johny had a drawbridge by which, at will, he could cross the river. Certainly there is a projecting

On the Esk at Hollows.

nose of rock just at the narrowest part of the stream, immediately above the present stone bridge, but one would be inclined to doubt if the engineering skill of Scotland in the

sixteenth century was equal to the task of constructing a
serviceable drawbridge capable of spanning a width so great.

There is a curious stone that projects *inwards* from high up
in Hollows Tower, the original purpose of which forms to the
amateur lover of ancient buildings a quite insolvable puzzle.
The stone measures, roughly, from the wall to its tip about
three feet in length, and its diameter is perhaps ten or twelve
inches.   Towards the end farthest from the wall it has a well-
marked groove on the upper part and sides, as if heavy weights
had frequently been suspended from it by ropes or chains.   Its
position is on the right of a narrow door that opens two or
three feet above the floor-level of the room into which the
stone projects, and the stone itself must have been close to the
ceiling of the chamber.   What was its use?   An intelligent
but youthful guide, when the writer was at Hollows, suggested
with ghoulish delight that it was "a hangin'-stane."   But that,
surely, would have been wilful waste on the part of the
Armstrongs, so long as trees were available.   Nor is it likely
that they got rid of prisoners in this way with a regularity
sufficient to account for the well-worn groove in the stone.   It
does, however, recall Sir Thomas Dick Lauder's feelings, when
"at the top of the south-western angle of the Tower [of
Neidpath], a large mass of the masonry had fallen, and laid
open a chamber roofed with a Gothic arch of stone, from the
centre of which swung, vibrating with every heavy gust of wind,
an enormous iron ring.   To what strange and wild horrors did
this not awaken the fancy?"

From a little beyond Hollows Tower, all the way to
Langholm you catch through the trees glimpses of hurrying,
foamflecked streams that speak most eloquently of "sea-trout,
rushing at the fly."   It has never been the writer's fortune to
cast a line in this water, but if looks go for anything the sport
must be excellent.

It is impossible to imagine scenery more pleasing than
the woody banks that overhang the river as Langholm is

approached; and the position of the town itself, nestling
amongst beautiful hills, is singularly inviting.   Langholm
occupies the site of a famous old battle, that of Arkenholm,
where in 1454 the power of the Douglas's was finally broken.
In and about the town there is much to interest those whose
tastes lean towards archaeology ; the whole countryside, indeed,
is sprinkled with towers and the remains of towers.   In the

Langholm.

burgh itself for example, there is what appears to be the
remains of an old peel, now forming part of the wing of a hotel ;
just above the upper bridge are the ruins—the sorely battered
ruins—of Langholm Castle, once an Armstrong stronghold ;
and most beautifully situated on Wauchope Water, just
outside the town, is Wauchope Castle, long ago the seat of the
Lindsays.   Little now is left of the building, practically nothing,
indeed, but two small portions of the outer wall on the rocks

immediately overhanging the picturesque water of Wauchope. The position must in the days of its pride have been immensely strong, and the scene now is very beautiful.

In close proximity to the castle is an old graveyard, with remains—at least the foundations—of a pre-Reformation church and a few interesting old stones, two, at least, apparently very ancient, if one may judge from the style of sword cut on them. Not far from this are traces of the old Roman Road, and near at hand a stone bridge, also believed to be Roman, once crossed the stream. But it is said—with what truth I know not—to have been destroyed long ago by a Minister, whose care of his flock was such that, to prevent the lads of Langholm strolling that way of an evening, disturbing the peace of mind and pious meditations of his female domestics, he demolished it.

As in the case of Selkirk, and of Hawick, the great festival of the year at Langholm is on the occasion of the Fair and Common Riding. In the Proclamation of the Fair, after a statement of the penalties to be imposed on disturbers of the festival, the curious words occur: "They shall sit down on their bare knees and pray seven times for the King, and thrice for the Muckle Laird o' Ralton." The Laird of Ralton was an illegitimate son of Charles II, but what he had to do with Eskdale, or what is the origin of the words, I have been quite unable to learn.

To go, even superficially, into the history of Langholm and of the interesting and beautiful country surrounding it, would occupy much space, and neither time nor space is available.

Here, amongst the hills and the many waters, we must leave the Border. It is a country whose mountains are seldom grand or awe-inspiring, as in some parts of the Scottish Highlands they may be; its streams do not flow with the rich majesty of Thames, nor with the mighty volume of Tay; and there are, doubtless, rivers possessed of wilder scenery. But to the true Borderer, however long absent he be, into what part soever of the world he may have been driven by the Fates, there are no hills like the Border hills—they are indeed to him "the Delectable Mountains"; there are no waters so loved, none that sing to him so sweetly as Tweed and all the streams of his own land. "If I did not see the heather at least once a year, I think I should die," said Scott. To a greater or less extent it is so with all of us. One of her most loving sons (he who should have guided the course of this volume, and who, had he lived, would have made of it something worthy of the Border), once said, on his return from a visit to famed Killarney : "The beauty of the Irish Lakes is rather that of the Professional Beauty. When one comes back to the Border, there one finds the same beauty one used to see in the face of one's mother, or of one's old nurse." And : " I am never so happy as when I cross the Tweed at Berwick from the South," he writes in an Introduction to Mr. Charles Murray's "Hamewith." It was not only his own, but, I think, every Borderer's sentiments that he voiced when he wrote :

> "Brief are man's days at best; perchance
> I waste my own, who have not seen
> The castled palaces of France
> Shine on the Loire in summer green.

> " And clear and fleet Eurotas still,
> You tell me, laves his reedy shore,
> And flows beneath his fabled hill
> Where Dian drave the chase of yore.

> " And 'like a horse unbroken' yet
> The yellow stream with rush and foam,
> 'Neath tower, and bridge, and parapet,
> Girdles his ancient mistress, Rome !

> " I may not see them, but I doubt
> If seen I'd find them half so fair
> As ripples of the rising trout
> That feed beneath the elms of Yair.

" Unseen, Eurotas, southward steal,
    Unknown, Alpheus, westward glide,
    You never heard the ringing reel,
     The music of the water side !

" Though Gods have walked your woods among,
    Though nymphs have fled your banks along ;
  You speak not that familiar tongue
    Tweed murmurs like my cradle song.

" My cradle song,—nor other hymn
   I'd choose, nor gentler requiem dear
  Than Tweed's, that through death's twilight dim,
    Mourned in the latest Minstrel's ear ! "

His love of the Border hills, " the great, round-backed, kindly, solemn hills of Tweed, Yarrow, and Ettrick," his devotion to the streams beside whose banks the summers of his boyhood were spent, never lessened with the passing years. In prose and in verse continually it broke out. Tweed's song is the same that she has ever sung ; but now—

    " He who so loved her lies asleep,
     He hears no more her melody."

INDEX

INDEX

A

Abbey St. Bathans, 28
Abbot of Inchcolm, 93
Abbotsford, 178, 227, 230, 245, 261, 384
Agricola, 212
Aidan, Bishop, 216
Ale, 33, 126, 169, 172, 280
Alemuir, 176, 286
Alexander II., 4, 91, 255
   III., 4, 91, 255, 337
Allanbank, 8
Allanton, 8
Allan Water, 107, 197
Allen Water, 235
Allevard, 21
Altrive, 305
Ancrum, 33, 126, 129, 169
   Moor, 102, 169
Anderson, Alexander, 295
Angus, Earl of, 102, 169, 229
Annan, 375
"*Antiquary, The,*" 25, 84
Argyll, 53
Arkenholm, 424
Armstrong, Johnny, 197, 418
Armstrong of Harelaw, Hector, 415
Armstrongs, 144, 197, 388, 401, 406
Arran, Earl of, 102, 170
Arthuret, 351, 404
Arthur's Oven, 347
Arundel, Earl of, 92
Ashiesteel, 237, 322
Ashkirk, 174
Auld Babby Metlan, 213
"*Auld Maitland,*" 213
Auld Ringan Oliver, 136
Auld Wat of Harden, 278
Ayala, 52

B

Badlieu, 371
Bairds, 346
Baillie, Lady Grisell, 42
Bale-fires, 23
Ballad of Otterburne, 153
Ballantyne, James, 78
Balliol, 5, 6
   Edward, 92
Barmoor, 51
Barnhill's Bed, 181
Barns, 345
Battle Stone, 162
Bawtie's Grave, 20
Beaton, Cardinal, 170, 171
Beauté, Sieur de la, 20
Bedrule, 182
Bellenden, 286
Belted Will Howard, 409, 413
Bemersyde, 209
Berwick, 3, 25, 48, 98, 113, 150, 154, 269
Berwickshire Naturalists' Club, 69, 165
Bewcastle, 178, 410
   Cross, 413
Bield, The, 359
Biggar, 353
   Moss, 354
   Water, 353
Billie, 13
Billy Castle, 17
Binram's Corse, 298
Bird-Oswald, 409
Bishop Flambard, 47
Boghall Castle, 353
Bogle Burn, 217
Bohun, Humphrey de, 4
Boldside, 233, 245

Bonny Bertha, 371
Borland, Rev. Dr., 307
Borthwick Water, 170, 190, 280
    Castle, 106
Boston of Ettrick, 287
Bothan, 28
Bothwell (Hepburn), Earl of, 52, 85, 106,
    110, 215
    (Stewart), Earl of, 135, 385
    Brig, 137
Bowden Moor, 229
"Bowed Davie," 343
Bowerhope, 298
Bowhill, 231, 273, 318
Bowmont, 48
    Valley, 149
Box-beds, 303
Buccleuch, 2, 195, 286
    Duke of, 196, 208, 305, 316, 385
    Hunt, 222
    Lairds of, 134, 179, 194, 229, 392, 394,
        395
Buchan, Earl of, 208
Buchanan, George, 67, 106, 108, 110, 112
Bunkle, 13, 15
Burghley, 135
Buried Treasure, 56, 88
Burke and Hare, 250
"Burke, Sir Walter!" 90
Burns, Robert, 118, 123
Blackadder, 8, 32, 39
Blackcastle Rings, 39
Black Dwarf, 343
Black Hill of Earlstoun, 144
Blackhouse Heights, 346
    Tower, 297
Black Law, 144, 346
Black, William, 359, 374
Blair, Rev. Thos., 61
Blanerne, 13
Blind Harry, 354
Bloody Laws, 88
Braidley Burn, 107
Brampton, 409
Branksome, 2, 174, 179, 192
    Hall, 194
Branxton, 51
Braxfield, Lord, 355
Breamish, 48
Bremenium, 88, 142, 164, 166
Brewster, Sir David, 118
"Bride of Lammermuir," 346
Bridgelands, 260
Bridgend, 227
Broadlaw, 144, 352
Broadmeadows, 38
Broomhouse, 20
Brougham, Lord, 61
Broughton, 355
Brown, Dr. John, 354
Brownies, 31
"Brownie of Bodesbeck," 291, 369
Bruce, David, 68, 415
    Robert the, 67, 92, 208, 347, 375
Byrecleuch Ridge, 30

C

CADDONFOOT, 222, 322
Cademuir, 347
Caerlanrig, 197
Caledon, 352
Camps, 128
Camptown, 141
Cannobie Lea, 416
Canonbie, 418
Capel Fell, 287
"Capon Tree," 125
Cappercleuch, 300
Cardrona, 340
Carey, 135
Cargill, Rev. Donald, 137, 368
Carham, 3
    Burn, 48
Carlin's Tooth, 143, 152
Carlisle, 77, 115, 117, 150, 152, 392, 408
    Castle, 144, 392
Carmichael, Sir John, 144
Carter Bar, 141, 148
Carterfell, 129, 136, 143, 166
Carterhaugh, 273
Castlehill, 345
Castleton, 387
Catcleuch Reservoir, 141
    Shin, 141, 166
Catrail, 2, 41, 231, 379
Cauldcleuch Head, 107, 144
Cauldshiels Loch, 233
Cavers, 72, 184
Caves, 126, 134
Cecil, Sir W., 37, 134
Cessford, 86
Cockburn Law, 26
    Thomas, 22
    of Henderland, 198, 299
Cockburns, 20
Coldstream, 56
    Guards, 59
Collingwood Bruce, Dr., 165
Collingwood, Sir Cuthbert, 147
Collingwoods, 145
Colmslie, 235
Commonside Hill, 2
Cope, Sir John, 5, 35, 77
Corbridge, 5
Coultercleuch, 280
Cout o' Keilder, 385
Covenanters, 47, 85, 137, 293, 359, 365, 370
Cowdenknowes, 219
Ciudad Rodrigo, 266
Chambers, Dr. Robert 104, 302
    Dr. William, 338
Channelkirk, 217
Chapel Knowe, 165
Charles I., 77
Chesters (Berwickshire), 42
    (Roxburghshire), 168
Cheviot, 144
Cheviots, 1, 88, 142, 151, 212
Chillingham, 50

Chirnside, 7, 15
Chronicle of Lanercost, 4
Churchhill, 6
Clandestine Weddings, 60, 402
Clarty Hole, 231
Claverhouse, 359, 365, 369
Clearburn Loch, 286
Cleikum Inn, 339
Clerk of Eldin, John, 353
Clints Dod, 30
Clintwood, 387
Clovenfords, 322
Clyde, 353
Crab, 5
Craigmillar, 23, 113
Crailing, 87, 126
Cranshaws, 30
Crawford, 52
Cromwell, 22, 56, 316, 338, 343, 353, 371, 387
Crook-backed Richard, 5
Crook Inn., 357
Crooked Loch, 286
Cumberland, 25
Curle, Mr., 212

D

DACRE, 53, 74, 98, 130
Dalkeith, 25, 152, 257
Dandie Dinmont, 377, 381
D'Arcy, Sir Anthony, 20
Darnick, 227
Tower, 227
Darnley, 85, 111, 215, 330, 347, 365
D'Aussi, 52
David I., 66, 73, 81, 84, 91
David, Earl, 255
Dawstane Rig, 378
Dawyck, 347, 348
Woods, 351
Debateable Land, 403
De Beaugué, M., 131
De Bolbec, Walter, 383
" Degenerate Douglas," 341
De Grey, Sir Thomas, 48
Deil o' Dawyck, 349
De la Mothe Rouge, 133
Deloraine, 280
William of, 174, 281
Denham Tracts, 66
Denholm, 119, 179
De Soulis, 382, 387, 415
D'Espec, Walter, 66
D'Essé, Sieur, 129, 132
Deuchar Bridge, 309
Devil's Beef Tub, 375
Dick Lauder, Sir Thomas, 8, 17, 35, 59, 172, 233, 241, 259, 327, 336, 358, 423
Dick's Tree, 399
Differences with Prisoners, 266
Dinlabyre, 387
Dodhead, 178, 280
Dog Knowe, 115

Dogs in Church, 308
Dollar Law, 144, 346
Donald's Cleuch, 368
" Doo Tairts and Herrin' Pies," 83
Douglas, Archibald, 72
Douglas Burn, 72, 297
Douglas, Earl, 72, 149, 153
of Kelhead, Sir John, 355
Rev. Dr., 231
Sir George, 71
Sir George, 170
Sir James, 82, 92, 125, 128, 347, 375
Tragedy, 297
Douglas's Wounded, 165
Douglases, 72, 145
Dowie Dens of Yarrow, 72, 311
Drochil Castle, 347
Drumclog, 137
Drumlanrig, 118
Drummelzier, 348, 350
Dryburgh Abbey, 206, 220
Drygrange, 212, 222
Dryhope Tower, 305
Dunbar, 56, 101, 113, 150, 152
Castle, 20, 86
Earl of, 30
Dumbarton Castle, 382
Dunion, 144, 176
Dunkeld, 137
Duns, 15, 26, 44
Law, 46
Scotus, 44
Durham, 153
Bishop of, 158, 160
Cathedral, 216
Dussac, 133
Dye Water, 29

E

EARLSIDE MOOR, 107
Earlstoun, 16, 217
Eden (Carlisle), 393
Water, 8, 33, 57, 64
Edie Ochiltree, 84
Edgar, 35
Iurn, 35
Edgerston, 141, 144
Edinburgh, 56, 152, 159, 198, 212, 261, 292, 299, 333, 349
Edington, 8
Edinshall, 8, 27
Ednam, 8
Edrington Castle, 7
Edrom, 8, 15
Edward I., 56, 58, 69, 208, 214, 255, 379, 409
II., 5, 48, 69, 208, 255
III., 5, 68, 69, 92
VI., 169, 316
Eildon Hills, 142, 144, 212, 221, 224, 231, 245
Eildon Tree, 217
Eital Castle, 50

Elba, 27
Elcho, Lord, 118
Elibank, 327
Eliott of Stobs, Sir Gilbert, 119
Elizabeth, Queen, 398, 416
Elliot of Cleuchhead, Dr., 384
  Jean, 181
Elliots, 145
Ellison, Mr., 163
Ellwand, 235
Elsdon Church, 167
Emperor Alexander Severus, 165
Errickstane, 375
Errol, 52
Erskine, Lord, 402
Esk, 407, 416
Ettrick, 2, 176, 231, 245, 252, 263, 271, 288
  Bank, 249
Ettrickbridgend, 278
Ettrick Hall, 287, 290
  Kirk, 287
  Pen, 287
  Shepherd, 121, 213, 278, 288
Evelaw Tower, 35
Evers, Lord (Sir Ralph), 100, 170, 171, 227
Eye Water, 18

F

" Fair Maiden Lilliard," 172
Fairies, belief in, 56, 181
Fairnilee, 271, 319
Fairy Dene, 235
Falaise, Treaty of, 4
Falkirk, Battle of, 255
Falla Moss, 371
False alarm, 25
Fast Castle, 86
Father Ellis, 126
Fatlips Castle, 180
Faungrist Burn, 39
Fenwick, Sir Roger, 129
Fenwicke, Colonel, 22
Fenwicks, 145
Ferguson, Adam, 343
Fernihirst, 128, 130, 134, 137
  Mill, 136
Flemings, 353
Flodden, 49, 59, 255
Flodden Edge, 48, 50
Fogo, 33
Ford Castle, 49
Forest of Ettrick, 255
  Jedworth, 129, 131
Forster, Sir John, 144
Foulshiels, 39, 314
Floors Castle, 71
Flower of Yarrow, 305
Flowers of the Forest, 181, 319
Franck, Richard, 7
Fraser, Sir Simon, 341, 348
Frasers of Fruid and Oliver, 340
French Invasion, 24
  Prisoners in Selkirk, 258

Froissart, 115, 149, 157
Fruid, 357

G

Gala, 94, 237, 241
Gala Rig, 272
Galashiels, 94, 224, 233, 237, 245
" Galashiels Herons," 84
Galashiels Town's Arms, 240
Gamelshiel, 30
Gameshope Burn, 357, 370
  Glen, 363, 370
  Loch, 369, 370
Gamescleuch, 287
Garter, Countess of Salisbury's, 69
Gemmels, Andrew, 84
Giant's Stone, 371
Gibb's Cross, 35
Gilnockie, 197, 418
  Bridge, 421
Gilsland, 409
Girthgate, 236
Godscroft, 158
Goldielands, 191
Gordon Arms, 305
Glendearg, 235
Glengaber, 1
Glenkinnon Burn, 324
Glenrath Burn, 346
Graham, Sir James. 417
Grahams, 405, 416
Greatmoor Hill, 107
Greenlaw, 41
Gretna Green, 60, 402
Grey Friars, 141
Grey Mare's Tail, 303
Guizot, M., 59
" Guy Mannering," 380

H

Habbie Ker's Cave, 126
Haggiehaugh, 78
Haig of Bemersyde, 209
Haining, 255, 259, 265
Halidon Hill, 5, 55
Hall, Hobbie, 87
  Henry, 87, 137
Halliburton, Wm., 67
Hallyards, 343
Hangingshaw, 38, 313
Happrew, 348
Harden, 192
Harecleuch Hill, 32
Harehead, 30
Harelaw, 35
Harewood, 317
Hartlaw, 35
Hartshorn Pyke, 143
Hassendean, 178
Hawick, 16, 94, 107, 134, 185, 381
  " Minister's Man," 117
  Mote, 191

Hawkshead Burn, 371
  Castle, 371
Hay of Yester, 341
  of Talla, 85
Hearthstane Burn, 357
Hellmuir Loch, 286
Hemingburgh, 5
Henderland, 298
Henderson, Willie, 179
Henry I., 66
  III., 69
  VIII., 4, 49, 74, 99, 132, 169, 170, 177, 197, 208
Hepburn of Bowton, 85
  of Hailes, 30
Hermitage Castle, 72, 85, 107, 382
  Water, 107, 380, 381
Heron, Lady, 49
Heronry at Dawyck, 351
Herries, 53
Herrit's Dyke, 41
Hertford, Lord, 13, 37, 44, 74, 100, 102, 129, 132, 141, 170, 227, 287
Hexham, 45
Hielandman's Grave, 116
Hill Burton, 74
Hillslap, 235
Hindside, 35
Hirsel, The, 60
Hodgson, Richard, 69
Hogg, James, 206, 213, 278, 290, 297, 303, 305
Hollows Tower, 419
Holydene, 41, 126, 229
Holylee, 327
Home Castle, 20, 22, 23, 113
Home, Sir David, 20
  Family of, 17, 20, 212
  Grisell, 42
  Lord, 8, 20, 22, 51, 60, 229, 257
  of Haliburton, 44
  of Polwarth, Patrick, 41
Homildon Hill, 55
Hoolet of Barns, 345
Hornshole, 187
Horsburgh, 330
Hotspur's Pennon, 184
Howpasley, 192
Howard, Edmund, 53
  Edward, 53
Hundalee, 126
Hunsdon, Lord, 37, 134
Hunter, John, 362
Hunthill, 128, 129, 134
"Huntlie Bank," 219
Huntly, Earl of, 52, 106
Hutton Hall, 8
Hyndhope, 280

I

Illicit Stills, 116
Innerleithen, 327

J

James I., 337, 342
  II., 23, 67, 80
  III., 5
  IV., 48, 49, 281
  V., 178, 197, 229, 282, 287, 406
  VI. and I., 6, 67, 305, 353, 413, 416
"Jamie Telfer," 177, 192, 280, 410
Jed, 33, 78, 94, 124, 152, 166
Jedburgh, 23, 78, 90, 114, 119, 126, 131, 171, 222
  Abbey, 92, 95, 102, 113
  Castle, 92, 95
  Prison, 123
Jedforest Hunt, 129
"Jethart's here!" 100, 146
John, King, 4
John's Cleuch, 30

K

Kale Water, 84, 87, 126, 166
Kelso, 26, 33, 61, 64, 71, 113, 114, 126, 222, 267
  Abbey, 74, 84
Ker, Dand, 86
  of Cessford, 69, 87, 229
  of Fernihirst, 68, 69, 229
  of Graden, 78
  of Samuelton, George, 8
  Sir Andrew, 135
  Sir John, 132
  Sir Thomas, 130
Kershope Burn, 392
Kerss, Rob., 205
Killiecrankie, 137
"Kilmeny," 271
King Arthur, 244, 347
"King of the Woods," 125
Kingledores Burn, 357
Kingside, 286
Kinmont Willie, 144, 179, 392, 399
Kirk Andrews, 416
Kirk o' Field, 85
Kirkhope Linn, 278
  Tower, 278
Kirk Sessions, 62
Knight of Liddesdale, 246, 326, 383
Knox, John, 52, 214

L

Lacy, Richard de, 4
Lads of Wamphray, 89
Lady of Branksome, 194
"Lady of the Lake," 322
Ladykirk, 48
Laidlaw, Will, 213, 297
  of Peel, 324
Laiton, 170, 227
Lammermuirs, 7, 29, 144, 212, 216

Lanercost, 409
Langholm, 418, 424
   Castle, 424
Langshaw, 235
Langton Tower, 20
Lanton Village, 93
   Tower, 128
Larriston, 78, 115
Lauder, French Prisoners at, 270
   Bridge, 5
Lauderdale, Earl of, 45, 213, 216
Lawson, Rev. Dr., 263
"*Lay of the Last Minstrel*," 118, 192,
   281, 322
Leader Water, 41, 212
Leaderfoot, 222
Le Croc. M., 111
Leet Water, 57
Legerwood, 16, 41
Leithen, 328
Lennox, 53
Leslie, Bishop of Ross, 110, 151
   General, 38, 46, 56, 254
   Norman, 170
Lessudden, 26, 206
Lethem, 165
Lethington, 216
   Mr. Secretary, 107
Leyden, John, 179, 190, 247, 322
Liddel Castle, 357
   Moat, 415
   Valley, 152
   Water, 78, 116, 152, 380, 386, 393
Liddesdale, 115, 144, 150, 152, 178, 378, 380
Lilliardsedge, 169, 222
Limekilnedge, 381
Lincumdoddie, 356
Lindean, 246, 252
Lindisfarne, Bishop of, 97
Lindsay, Sir James, 158
Linglie, 249, 252
Lintalee, 92, 125, 128
Linthill House, 18
Linton, 84
   Tower, 85
Lion of Liddesdale, 78
Littledean, 206
"Little Jock Elliot," 106, 387
Loch of the Lowes, 292, 301
   Skene, 369
Lockhart, J. G., 206, 208, 232, 353, 380
Longtown, 152, 399
Lord Maxwell's Muster Roll, 401
Lost Pay Chest, 38
Lothian, Lord, 135, 138
   Marquess of, 103
Lumsden, Margaret, 45
Lyne Water, 347

M

Maccus Whele, 73
Mackay, 137

"Mad" Jack Hall, 162
Maid of Norway, 5
Maitland of Lethington, 214
Makerstoun, 204, 222
Malcolm II., 3, 48
   IV., 236
   The Maiden, 91
Mangerton Castle, 390
Manor Kirkyard, 344
   Valley, 343
   Water, 345
Manslaughter Law, 29
Marchmont, Earl of, 22, 41
   House, 42
"*Marmion*," 51, 55, 94, 322
Marquis of Annandale's Beef Stand, 375
Mary of Gueldres, 23, 81
   Guise, 214
Mary Queen of Scots, 23, 52, 74, 104, 169,
   194, 208, 214, 250, 330, 408
Mathieson, 322
Maxwell, 53
   Sir Herbert, 2, 30, 72, 84, 169, 176, 338
   Sir John, 158
Meg Dods, 339
Megget, 300
Melrose, 71, 166, 170, 225, 235
   Abbey, 165, 172, 224, 256
Melville of Halhill, Sir James, 112
Menzion, 357
Merlin, 351
Merse, 21, 48, 134, 144
Mertoun, 206
   Bridge, 220
Midlem Bridge, 172
Miles, Sir George Heron, 147
Millford, 51
Milnholm Cross, 390
Minchmuir, 2, 38
Minto, 180
   Crags, 144, 180
Moffat, 369, 373, 375
"*Monastery, The*," 227, 233, 235
Monk, General, 59
Monks' Ford, 220
Monklaw, 128
Monmouth, Duke of, 196
   Anne, Duchess of, 316
Mons Meg, 48, 80
Montague, Sir William, 68
Montgomery, Earl of, 158
Montrose, Marquis of, 2, 38, 76, 254
Moray, Earl of, 106, 110
   Countess of, 112
Morebattle, 86
Morton, Earl of, 147
   Regent, 367
Mossburnfoot, 126
Mossfennan, 356
Muckle Mouthed Meg, 327
Murray of Broughton, 355
   Sir David, 355
   Sir Gideon, 327
   of Philiphaugh, Sir John, 247
Musgrave, Sir William, 405

Muthag, Provost, 272
Mutiny Stones, 30

N

NAESMITHS, 346
Napier and Ettrick, Lord, 55, 287
Napoleon, 24, 262
Naworth, 409
Neidpath Hill, 322
  Castle, 337, 342
Netherby, 416
Nettley Burn, 249
Neville's Cross, 415
Newark Tower, 278, 315
Newcastle, 77, 141, 145, 159, 160, 203
Newcastleton, 387
Newstead, 142, 166, 212, 224
Newton Don, 64
Nine Cairn Edge, 216
Nine Stane Rig, 381
Norfolk, 74
Norham, 4, 47
North, Christopher, 301
Note o' the Gate, 115, 378
Notman Law, 346

O

OAKWOOD TOWER, 276
Ogle, Sir James, 147
  Sir Robert, 67, 69
Old Jedward, 128
  Mailros, 28
  Melrose, 212, 213, 222
"Old Mortality," 362
"Old Q," 341
Oliver, Auld Ringan, 136
Oliver Castle, 359
Ormistoun, 35, 86
Otterburne, 72, 149, 170
  Village, 162
  Hall, 164
Ottercops, 149
Outlaw Murray, 35, 313
Oxnam Water, 87, 126, 166

P

PARK, ARCHIBALD, 315
  Mungo, 314, 326
Pearlin, Jean, 8
"Peblis to the Play," 339
Peebles, 309, 330, 334, 336, 340, 349
Peel Burn, 152, 379
  Fell, 1, 143, 379
Penchrise, 1, 176, 280
Pennecuick, Dr., 342, 351, 353
Pennistone Knowe, 292
Penshiel, 30
Penton, 415
  Linn, 407, 415

Percy, 40
  Earl, 153, 161
  Henry, 92
  Ralph, 158, 161
Percy's Cross, 162
Philiphaugh, 2, 38, 77. 315
Picts' Work Dyke, 379
Pinkie, 56, 130
Piper's Pool, 254
"Pitcairn's Criminal Trials," 86
Pitscottie, 51, 81, 198, 282
Plague, The, 246
Plummer of Sunderland Hall, 257
Poachers, 173, 242, 254
Pollution of Rivers, 94, 95, 185, 237, 238, 252, 327
Polmood, 356
  Burn, 357
Polwarth, 42
  Lord, 192
Porteous of Hawkshaw, 371
Possessed Woman in Duns, 45
Posso, 345, 347
  Craigs, 346
Pot Loch, 259
Powsayl Burn, 351
"Pride and Poverty!" 83
Priesthaugh Burn, 107
Prince Charlie, 77, 78, 114, 115, 117, 126, 409
Prisoners' Bush, 260
  Theatre, 268
Proclamation of St. James's Fair, 82
Purdie, Tom, 322

Q

QUAIR BURN, 330
Queen Mary's House, 104
  Illness, 109
Queen's Mire, 108
"Queen's Wake," 121
Queensberry, Duke of, 118

R

RAECLEUCH, 35
Raid of the Reidswire, 144
Ramsay, Sir Alexander, 383
  Rev. Mr., 64
Randall's Wa's, 347
Randolph, 347
Rankleburn, 2, 286
Raven Burn, 152
  Craig, 31
Redbraes, 42
Redesdale, 13, 141, 145
R. de Valley, 88, 115, 141, 151, 161
"Redgauntlet," 375, 417
Redpath, 30
Reedman, Sir Matthew, 158
Regiment, 94th, 266
Renwick, 292

Richard, King, 4
II., 208
Richmond, Sir Thos., 125
Riddell, 174
Rink, 2, 245, 249
Riskinhope, 292
Rivalry between Kelso and Jedburgh, 82
Rob o' the Trows, 205
Robert II., 208
Rhymer's Glen, 219, 231
Roman Road, 88
Rory dhu Mohr, 137
Rothely Crags, 149
Rowchester, 142
Roxburgh, 23, 67, 80, 126
Castle, 78, 92, 149
Newtown, 85
Roxburghe, Duke of, 71
Ruberslaw, 144, 183, 212
Rule Water, 107, 177, 212
Rushy Rig, 115
Ruskin, John, 94, 230
Russell, Sir Francis, 147
Russell of Yarrow, Rev. Drs., 281, 298,
307, 313, 316
Rutherford, 206
Alison, 319
Rev. John, 308
"Rutherfurd Bauld," 146
Rutherfurd, Captain, 123
Rutherfurds, 141
Ruthven, Lord, 134
Rutland, Earl of, 129

S

St. Abb's Head, 25
St. Andrews, Bishops of, 49
St. Boswells, 78, 206
Green, 221
St. Cuthbert, 206, 216, 357
St. Gordian's Kirk, 344, 347
St. James's Fair, 81
St. Kentigern, 352
St. Mary of the Lowes, 177, 295
St. Mary's Chapel, 296
St. Mary's Loch, 287
St. Ronan's, 327
"St. Ronan's Well," 339
Salisbury, Earl of, 68
Salmon, 209
-fishing, 222
Sandyknowe, 211
Sark Bridge, 402
Tower, 401
Satchells, 176
"Savoury Mr. Peden," 183
Scabcleuch, 292
Scots Brigade, 266
Scots Dyke, 418
Scott, Adam of Tushielaw, 282, 299
Sir John, 287
Lady John, 87
Mary, "the Flower of Yarrow," 305

Scott, Michael, 256, 276
Sir Walter, 2, 25, 38, 51, 68, 78, 83, 118,
144, 174, 179, 180, 198, 206, 208, 227,
236, 257, 261, 297, 305, 322, 325, 339,
343, 347, 353, 355, 369, 380, 384, 399,
417, 419
"Scott, Sir Walter and the Border
Minstrelsy," 213
Scott of Gorrenberry, 117
of Tushielaw, 198, 213
Scotts of Buccleuch, 71, 102, 144, 170, 192,
195, 286, 384
of Harden, 276, 327
Scrope, 174, 222
Lord, 397, 398, 400, 416
Selkirk, 26, 172, 231, 247, 249, 252, 269,
273, 314, 388
Cauld, 253
Common Riding, 270
"Selkirk Craws," 84
Selkirk Flodden Traditions, 256
Prison, 123
Selkirkshire Yeomanry, 257
Shaftoes, 145
Shielhope Head, 346
Shrewsbury, Lord, 130
Sidney, Sir Philip, 149
Sinclair, Oliver, 404
Singlie, 280
Skelfhill, 1, 2, 176, 280, 382
Skene of Rubislaw, 369
Skirmish Field, 229
Skraysburgh, 101, 128
Slain Man's Lea, 315
Slitrig, 1, 107, 188, 280, 381
Smailcleuchfoot, 136
Smailholme Tower, 144, 209
Snow Storm of 1831, 373
Solway Moss, 403, 406, 418
Somerset, 22, 127, 130
"Soor Plums in Galashiels," 240
Soulis, Lord, 381
"Souters of Selkirk," 53, 257
Southdean, 33, 148, 150, 165, 167, 380
Soutra Hill, 236, 241
Spirit of Borderers, 25
Spottiswoode, 217
Springwood Park, 71, 72
Spy at Southdean, 151
Stanhope, 355
Burn, 357
Stanley, 53
Stephen, King, 69
Stewart of Stewartfield, Colonel, 119
Stobo, 16, 348
Stobs Camp, 381
Stoddart, 34, 57
Stow, 244
Stuart, Lady Louisa, 333
Sir Robert, 8
Sunderland Hall, 249, 257
Sunlaws, 126
"Superstitions of Teviotdale," 121
Surrey, Earl of, 51, 54, 68, 97, 129, 130
Sussex, Earl of, 23, 37, 66, 134, 186

"Sweet Leader Haughs," 217
"Sweet Milk" Robin, 177
Swinnie Moor, 107
Synton, 175, 285

T

TALLA, 352, 357, 363
   Linn, 360, 365
   Reservoir, 357
Tarth Water, 347
Telfer, James, 136
"Teribus and Teriodden," 186
Teviot, 1, 33, 78, 94, 126, 166, 169, 176, 179, 193, 203, 280
Teviotdale, 16, 134, 144, 178, 181, 388
"The Eve of St. John," 209
The Great Unknown, 261
"The Young Tamlane," 273
Three Brethren, 271, 320
"Three days' blood," 89
Thief's Road, 346
Thirlestane (Ettrick), 287
   Castle (Lauderdale), 45
Thomas of Ercildoune, 217
Thomas the Rhymer, 76, 209, 217, 353
Thomson, James, 33, 124, 172
Thornilee, 327
Tibbie Shiels, 291, 301
   Tamson, 271
Till, 48, 50
Timpendean, 169
Tinnies, 348, 350
Tinnis (Yarrow), 38
Torsonce, 244
Torwoodlee, 2, 41, 243
Turn Again, 178, 232
Turnbulls of Rule Water, 145, 177
Tushielaw, 2, 281, 289
Traquair, 305, 330
   Countess of, 333
   Earl of, 38, 254, 331
Trout-fishing, 220, 241
"True Thomas," 217, 219, 231, 319
Tweed, 2, 3, 48, 173, 204, 212, 222, 231, 237, 245, 249, 260, 271, 305, 319, 347, 357, 371, 375, 377, 426
Tweeddale, Lord, 341
Tweed Shaws, 372
Tweed's Cross, 372
   Well, 372
Tweedsmuir, 301, 340, 357, 371
   Church, 361
   Kirk Session Records, 362
   Post Office, 359
"Tweed" Trade, 239
Tweedys, 349
Twin Law Cairns, 29
Twizell Bridge, 51

U

UMPHRAVILLE, SIR ROBERT, 96

V

VEITCH, PROFESSOR, 167, 342, 347
Veitchs of Dawyck, 348
Vivien, 352

W

WADE, MARSHALL, 77
Waich Water, 29
Walkerburn, 327
Wallace, Sir William, 208, 354
Wamphray, 89
Wark Castle, 50, 57, 66, 134, 149
Water-Bull, 234
Wauchope, 425
   Castle, 424
Wedale, 244
Wedderlie, 35
"Weir of Hermiston," 355
Weirdlaw Hill, 235
Well of the Holy Water Cleuch, 216
Wheeling Head, 152
Whele Causeway, 115, 150, 379
   Chapel, 379
Whitadder, 7
White, Mr. Robert, 163
Whithaugh Mill, 116
Whitterhope Burn, 381
Will's Nick, 254
Will of Phaup, 280, 288
William the Lion, 4, 48, 91, 255, 330
   le Walleys, 348
Williamhope Ridge, 325
Willie of Westburnflat, 387
Windburgh Hill, 144, 188
Wind Fell, 287
Windy Law, 286
Winter, Jamie, 43
Witches, 119
Witch of Fauldshope, 277
"Witch of Fife," 121
Wolfstruther, 35
Wooler, 51, 78, 149
Wordsworth, 118, 341
Wormscleuch Burn, 379

Y

YAIR, 176, 250, 319
   Bridge, 249, 318
   Cauld, 249
Yarrow, 2, 38, 39, 94, 176, 273, 287, 292, 294, 303, 317
   Dowie Dens of, 72, 311
   Kirk, 306, 309
   Manse, 306
Yetholm, 149, 150
Young Hay of Talla, 364

Z

ZEDON, 115, 149